WILD TRAILS TO FAR HORIZONS

When I stand at the beginning of 100 miles of moor, mountain, valley and meadow, I am standing on the threshold of a dream.

To Mike Cudahy who has been one of the foremost ultra fell runners in the country and now something of a fitness legend, these words capture the essence of ultra hill running. In the course of decades of running he has covered distances from 70 to 270 miles, finding inspiration in challenges such as the West Highland Way, the Scottish 4,000 foot peaks and the Coast to Coast. In 1984 he achieved the ultra runner's equivalent of the four minute mile, the first under three day completion of the 270 mile Pennine Way. The semi-autobiographical account of his ultra career constitutes the first part of the book.

'The Kingfisher's Wing' both continues and develops the theme of endeavour and inspiration. Included in this set of essays are three episodes from Mike's record traverse of the Munros, his 500 mile, ten day run through the Scottish Highlands, a 120 mile winter walk and a solo winter traverse of the 4,000 foot peaks shortly before a hip transplant. These tales of endeavour are seeded with essays of a more whimsical nature.

Throughout, Mike describes the inspiration which motivates and supports his challenges, in particular, the power and beauty of nature, the love and support of friends and the almost self-destructive will to succeed; this latter never more strikingly presented than in the final essay by fellow ultra runner, Mike Hartley.

The book contains guidance and advice for those who may aspire to emulate the achievements described. Above all, however, is Mike's observation that, 'the human condition is an amalgam of beauty, joy, sorrow and striving. Human frailty is not so important as how that frailty is embraced. Only endeavour which fails to enrich the spirit truly fails.'

WILD TRAILS TO FAR HORIZONS
'An ultra-distance runner'

Mike Cudahy

HAYLOFT PUBLISHING LTD
KIRKBY STEPHEN

This book is for my children and for my friends

This revised and expanded edition
published by Hayloft 2009
First published by Unwin Hyman Limited, London, 1989

Hayloft Publishing Ltd, South Stainmore, Kirkby Stephen,
Cumbria, CA17 4DJ

tel: 017683 42300
email: books@hayloft.eu
web: www.hayloft.eu

ISBN 1 904524 70 2

CAP data for this title are available from the British Library

Designed, printed and bound in the EU

Papers used by Hayloft are natural, recyclable products made from wood grown in
sustainable forest. The manufacturing processes conform to the environmental
regulations of the country of origin.

contents

acknowledgements

I would like to thank Ted Courtenay, Ted Dance, Geoff Bell, Chris Bolshaw, Rob Fergusson and the *Stockport Express* who donated photographs and I would particularly like to thank Inken who burnt the midnight oil typing the manuscript for me. I am also grateful to John Beatty for the special efforts he has made to make the photographs so successful and Mike Hartley for permission to use his essay.

Grateful acknowledgement is made to Unwin Hyman Limited for permission to quote from *The Lord of the Rings* by J. R. R. Tolkien.

foreword by Jim Perrin

Jung wrote that: 'Every statement about the transcendental ought to be avoided because it is a laughable presumption on the part of the human mind, unconscious of its limitations.' Most people would probably feel some measure of assent in that, yet there are times – as when reading Mike Cudahy's extraordinary book – when its scepticism can safely be suspended. Cudahy's whole text is a statement upon the transcendental which virtually avoids the use of that word and gives us instead a precise, richly-textured description of the states through which he moves to the surpassing experience. In a sense, it is clinical observation, but from inside looking out. The immediacy with which he conveys the physical actuality of British hill country – its forms, play of light, gradations of colour, even its feel underfoot is a tangible marvel of evocation and elevates his book to that select library which includes Borthwick's *Always a Little Further*, Praeger's *The Way We Went*, and the Monkhouse *On Foot* titles. But don't judge it simply on grounds of literary worth. There are two other remarkable dimensions here. Its presentation of the unpretentious, unheroic, unpublicised outdoor community from which these journeyings derive and amongst which they take place remove it from the isolated sagas of fraught individual achievement. This is communal activity, involving friends, lovers, family, within which Cudahy acts as excelling focus, always ready, when his day or time is done, to hand on the torch. This grateful interdependence is hearteningly humane. Beyond it and through Cudahy's consciousness as he engages in extreme feats of physical endurance and quest, we come to terms more clearly perhaps than in any other book written 'about' the outdoors with another dangerous and maligned word – mysticism. When Cudahy describes how 'a swathe of early sunshine falls on a thick bank of bluebells; raindrop-glistening lustrous blue against the fresh spring green' and gives him strength to carry on to his Pennine Way record, his language begins to take on the characteristic mystical concepts – of joy, of oneness, of the timeless moment: 'Never have I felt such sheer and simple joy . . . Moments such as these not only provide the answer to why one does things but why we are alive at all.' Read his book at whatever level you like – as social document, testament of friendship, sporting chronicle, topographical companion or transcendental quest. It sustains all these approaches, satisfies each of them, and takes you beyond exhaustion to an excitement and refreshment of soul which is perhaps the best response to our rare and beautiful hill country.

chapter one

DREAMS OF DISTANCE

National Hill Walking Conference, Buxton, 1985. A stage, a screen, a microphone and, out there in the darkness, a waiting audience. Waiting for me to communicate the incommunicable, my dreams of distance. I felt I should not have been there. I knew just where I should be. Out on the surrounding moors running gently through the soft October sunshine into the soft October mists. No need there to force unwilling words, to search the soul for reasons that others might understand, or might not. Nothing but the natural rhythm of my body moving at peace in the natural environment. How I wished I was out there now.

Yet I knew why I was in this new environment. I was there because I had seen lights shine in the eyes of those few people to whom I had attempted to communicate the experience of my long journeys. Long journeys beyond time and distance to new dimensions. Days and nights of running over wild paths to far horizons. Esoteric experiences, the joy of which, to my astonishment, I could share with others. At least, when I could find those elusive words. I was not there to justify what I did. How could I or why should I? I was not there to counter the half-dismissive, half-joking comment that my running records were 'obscene'. I was not even there because Alfred Wainwright had said 'bloody fool' when he had heard of my three-day Pennine Way. How could he think otherwise, his soul firmly anchored to a pair of stout boots? Against the odds of being able to do it I was about to attempt to share the intangible and unlikely product of an apparently mundane but extremely arduous activity with a group of people I did not know and could not even see. I was there to share my personal joy of running, my kind of running.

I hoped that those present would feel some of the magic and the joy that my running has brought to me. However, I had uncertain faith that my words alone could evoke the rich imagery needed to convey the altered sense of time and distance provoked by unceasing travel over vast changing landscapes. To help instil my words with a more powerful imagery I was to project a set of slides, the inspiration of my friend John Beatty. I triggered the mechanism, stared at the screen and paused as John's beautiful pictures, transcending the image and breathing the very essence of Nature, began dissolving poignantly above me. Bathed in the light of John's muse, I began:

Imagine a world where all the mountains are flat, where all the paths are paved, where all the grass is trimmed low. Imagine being lifted out of your bed and into your car and out of your car and into your office – and back again. Imagine a world where no effort was necessary – or even permitted. Imagine having no horizons to stretch your gaze, no difficulties to surmount, no aspirations to capture your imagination.

When I stand at the beginning of 100 miles of moor, mountain, valley and meadow I am standing on the threshold of a dream.

The sensory experiences I can describe and even provide a visual representation. I can describe the beauty which lies in the endless panorama which will move before me as the day passes into night and the night gives way to dawn, and the landscape continues its almost imperceptible change as I move across it and through it. But I cannot so easily explain how it is, that at the pinnacle of my physical preparation with all my senses tuned into endless movement and my mind totally occupied with the simplicity of running and walking, that I become more certainly myself and yet also part of the earth through which I am moving.

There are changes in mental and physical states which are somehow related to the act of continuous movement allied to minimal rest and sleep. For instance, time loses its exactitude, hours pass like moments, but a moment may expand and hang suspended outside any time constraint.

The longer I run the greater becomes my identity with the natural elements which surround me. I feel such times are as close as I will ever get to becoming an element in nature – a small speck but absorbed and absorbing. The edges of reality become blurred as weariness and joy enter into a vast swinging cycle and time, distance, dimension and intellectual processing all slide out of their usual relationship, and I move instead towards a simpler and more natural reality – a reality based in sensory and emotional experience.

Without doubt, one of the strongest sources of emotional energy, from which I draw enormous strength, is the support of close friends on my ventures. The bonding which takes place at such times is, for me, incredibly strong, and when I am spent, drained of my own resources, I will run for the love of my friends because they will give me everything and I can do no less for them.

What I find remarkable too are the troughs and peaks through which I move with a powerful rhythm from which there is no escape. From a trough of weariness and even depression I will climb to the heights of joy and optimism. Finally, as I approach my goal there is a tremendous release of joy and energy, which will spur me to quite astonishing feats of physical power.

Of course it is hard, the physical demands are enormous, the concentration and commitment needed leave no place to hide, no reserves to harbour – but in that giving of everything I find a release into peace and a great joy.

Do not make the mistake of thinking I rush through the hills with no feeling for them. As I am drawn out fine and stretched I find I become more impressionable to all kinds of things which impact on my senses and create images, which I will carry for all time. To give just two small instances: above Byrness on the Pennine Way after 230 miles [370 km] of almost continuous movement I entered the dusk of my third and final night. The murmur of the voices of my two friends and their warm presence cocooned me in a web of comfort. Against the dark, peaty ground the cotton grass floated and swayed in an ethereal glow and I found myself floating with it – detached and free of the ground and, perhaps, of reality. Another six hours on, with only 20 miles [32 km] of the soggy Cheviots between me and my long-cherished dream, the thick grey dawn entered into a conspiracy with a cruel east wind to imprison my mind and defeat my body. We retreated to a bothy and, with the trust of a child, I rested my head in the lap of a friend and, in perfect peace and tranquillity, I slept for just seven timeless minutes. When I awoke the wild spirit was rekindled and our last charge through the 'slutch' and rain was delirious and desperate, excruciatingly hard, impervious to pain and crowned with an indescribable joy.

I do not know what happens at such times, perhaps the artificiality of a conventional and sophisticated society is stripped away and the simple, ingenuous nature of a creature of the earth is laid bare. Our intellect places the scope of an amazing technology within our grasp and I will not gainsay that. But what calls to our nature is the beat of the bird's wing, the rise and fall of the seasons, the power of a mountain and the continuing rhythm and pulse of the earth as night follows day and my feet and heart and mind are drawn after.

While I was speaking floods of memories, both bitter and sweet, came welling up. When I reached the part played by my friends it was as if all their love, laughter and support was once more flowing round me and, quite astonishingly, I felt my eyes wet with tears. When I finished I was trembling, not violently but beyond my power to control. I cannot remember what the audience *did*, perhaps they applauded. It did not matter, for a few short minutes I had shared my dream with a group of sympathetic people and I knew it had been a moving experience for all of us.

I no longer believe it is futile to attempt to communicate my rather esoteric experiences. I can describe what I do but it is still not easy to put abstract images and emotions into words. I believe, however, that there does exist a common bond between all of us who love the natural environment and who have not yet lost that impulse enshrined by Tennyson 'to strive, to seek, to find, and not to yield'.

In attempting to discover the origins of my deep attachment to long distance hill running I find, perhaps inevitably, that it is not something 'grafted on' or discovered by accident but part of a long process of a running evolution. And so I spiral back to my childhood.

Why walk if you can run?

I was fortunate enough to be brought up in a house with a garden that bordered on a large natural park, an old estate. The park, of several square miles, had everything a child could desire: trees, ponds, a river, cliffs, grassy expanses, muddy tracks, wildlife and irascible parkkeepers to annoy. I climbed, ran, swam, caught newts and sticklebacks and generally made the place an extension of my home. My friend and I at 10 or 11 years of age even paced out a mile course and timed ourselves using an old alarm clock (I think we seriously threatened the 6.5 minute mile). I grew to love simply being active in such surroundings, and as I look back from a distance of nearly 40 years I can clearly see from where my roots first drew their nourishment.

I also began to realise that I could outrun most of the other children I grew up with and while this was pleasant, what was more deeply satisfying was the sense of having a natural gift. It was the only gift I believed I possessed but it really was a special gift. It gave me an edge in the competitive world of a schoolboy and it earned me respect and status. But above all it was good for its own sake. As I grew older I naturally channelled my ability into organised sport. A catalyst was provided when a friend at school having been nominated to represent the school in the under-16 championships at 440 yards tried to persuade me to take his place. We agreed that I should be timed round a track and if I bettered his 62 seconds I would race. I remember turning up in a pair of old cycling shoes – leather uppers and stiff rubber soles. I thought they really looked the part. I managed 60 seconds dead so I was in. My first race was at the old White City Stadium in Manchester. I got through the heats then ran in the final in a pair of borrowed spikes. I came second in 56 seconds, which rather surprised me.

My athletic career was not illustrious but great fun and I had the good fortune to join Stockport Harriers when there was a small but gifted group of junior athletes. The group split when we approached university and college age. I had not improved overmuch, partly because the club at that time was almost moribund. I got down to 51 seconds for the quarter mile and just under two minutes for the half when I was 17 but the following year, when I got very fit during the winter, we had no meetings.

It may seem odd that someone who was once a runner-up in the 'Youth Sprint Championship of Stockport'(!) should become a devotee of runs over 100 miles. You may think that inside the sprinter was a distance runner biding his time. It did not seem like that. Although I could get close to 4.5 minutes for the mile, races of a mile or more were anathema to me. What finally overcame these barriers was the combination of my love for the countryside and my inherent love of running (not to be confused with racing). The way it came about was this.

My club had a very long 'Harrier' tradition, that is cross-country running. Through all its vicissitudes a small band of devotees, who must have had mud rather than blood in their veins, would emerge with the onset of the autumn monsoons and engage in 'pack' runs through Woodbank Park and surrounding countryside for hours on end. Like an innocent to the slaughter I was brought to join them. Various strong influences made themselves felt now. One was my uncle, Wilf Brown, a lifelong Harrier and rambler. He was a bricklayer by trade, but at heart a runner and a keen walker. As our local scout leader he introduced me to rambling and camping, from the age of eight. He embodied all that was wholesome and good in Baden-Powell's philosophy. The banner-waving element occasionally evident in scouting he gently ignored. He loved his running, or rather, he lived his running. Wilf was a typical Harrier. During the summer he trained and competed on the track and during the winter returned to his real love, cross-country running. He was past his prime when he fostered my interest in cross-country but he was an inspiration for me. Not because of his ability but because of the simple joy he found in his running. As an impetuous, unthinking youth I loved Wilf but it took me till manhood to fully appreciate the worth of this gentle, wise man. I deeply regret I could not tell him of my Pennine Way record before his untimely death. But Wilf is and will forever remain a part of my running.

Another considerable influence at this time was my friend and contemporary Dave (Horsey) Clayton. Dave was a promising middle-distance and cross-country runner. He was also a dedicated athlete and much of his training 'habit' rubbed off on me. I remember he once threw his shoes at me when I was timing him because the watch showed he was several seconds slower than he had hoped. He was normally quite mild and chirpy and this show of temperament impressed me greatly. Dave tried to persuade me of the virtues of running distances greater than a mile, in order to 'strengthen the organism'. I enjoyed trotting round the countryside, but one Saturday afternoon I turned up at Woodbank to find him persuading me to join in a cross-country race. It was two whole laps, four miles (7 km). I demurred, but he said to just go round one lap and I could drop out if I wanted to. After racing for one lap I had had enough. The course finished with a hill at the end of the lap and this was hard, so acting on his suggestion I dropped out. Five minutes later I felt deeply ashamed. I could easily have gone on. I had quit for no other reason than I had felt a bit uncomfortable. I there and then made a vow that I would *never* quit any run while I could still put one foot in front of the other. This promise held good for many, many years and while I *have* quit record attempts I have never transgressed the spirit of that promise.

I actually began to enjoy cross-country running and, to a lesser extent, racing. What I liked best was the Harrier pack runs, when we would run for miles through the winter countryside chatting, joking, swishing up the leaves and

Stockport Harriers at Woodbank Park, winter 1963. Extreme left, Len Fitzsimmons; Wilf Brown, second from right; Mike Cudahy, extreme right.

squelching through the mud. On our way back there would be some unseen signal and the pack would begin to pick up speed, finally going full belt for the last couple of miles. I really enjoyed this and found I could run much better after I had been running steadily for eight miles (13 km) or so. I was to develop this attribute in years to come.

When I was about 17 another event occurred which served to shape my future running career. One of our senior cross-country runners, Ian Watson, lived on a farm on the slopes of Kinder, at 2,000 ft (610 m) the highest moor in Derbyshire. Ian was a gifted runner and with Kinder as a training ground he could get very fit. In the year he finished second in the famous Yorkshire Three Peaks race he was training hard and invited the club along to join him on one of his runs. I went along as, inevitably, did Wilf Brown. The memory of that day is still very much alive. I had a marvellous feeling of euphoria as I ran high above the valleys. It was almost like flying, up there between the earth and the sky. We ran much further than I was used to but I felt no fatigue, only elation. I remember Wilf turning to me and saying 'You're running a blinder Mike!' I knew I was, I could feel it in my heart. I had found my medium, my environment. On the track I enjoyed my speed but high up on the moors I had found and expressed my nature and it was gloriously and joyfully at one with the hills all around me.

I did not immediately start running in the hills, however. Instead, I continued to be active on many fronts. My excursions to the hills were mainly confined to fairly modest trips on the local moors, either alone or leading small scout groups. The solo trips represented excitement and adventure as well as a curiously refreshing spiritual experience. Of course I did not articulate this at the time, I was only aware of a sense of wonder and a sense of peace together with a kind of muted thrum of excitement that I was where I should be. With a very rudimentary knowledge of navigation and a compass whose needle would never stand still, my destinations were always in doubt. But I particularly well remember the first time I navigated my way straight across the Kinder Plateau after spending the night in the old shooting cabin in Ashop Clough. After what seemed like hours glued to my compass I suddenly burst out on to the sharp plateau edge looking down from a craggy outcrop into the beautiful green vale of Edale, the village nestling snug below me. Nowadays, the traverse of Kinder has become commonplace and my mental map is the only navigational aid needed, but that first time has never been forgotten.

Despite these early excursions I did not become a proficient navigator until I was introduced to the sport of orienteering by my mate Len Fitzsimmons. It was Len who was primarily responsible for my taking up the sport of fell running which is perhaps the strongest link in the chain which has led to my development as an ultra-distance hill runner. Len was one of the hardy souls who emerged every winter ready for the cross-country season. Despite his slight frame and gentle, self-effacing disposition, he was a redoubtable performer and a man of many talents and much initiative. While I was still a callow youth, Len was a county-class runner at both cross-country and steeple-chase. Always at the mercy of a chronic knee and deteriorating back condition, he would take himself off to the hills at home and abroad, usually solo, and demonstrate a tremendous ability to survive with the minimum amount of gear. In the years to come, Len was to enliven many a weary journey with spirited renderings of airs from Gilbert and Sullivan. On the hill his keen photographer's eye frequently drew my attention to subtleties of texture, light and shade I might otherwise have missed. It is now many years since Len and I raced, trained and tramped the moors and mountains, his knees and back severely limit his endeavours nowadays. Nevertheless, I regularly run past an inscription on a stone just below Shutlingsloe out beyond the Cat and Fiddle moors. Len pointed it out to me one training day about 20 years ago. It is from Burns and it says 'We clamb'd the hill the gither' – we did indeed.

Along with Ian Watson, Len had completed the 22-mile (36 km) Three Peaks race in Yorkshire. At the time this seemed a staggering achievement and a hell of a long cross-country race, way beyond my abilities, something to dream about. In his own quiet way, Len encouraged that dream. He set about preparing himself for the race and I began to join him on his longer weekend runs. As I continued to build endurance my dreams became ambitions and I decided I must attempt the Three Peaks as soon as I reached the minimum age of 21 years. In the event I had to wait till I was 22, but on the last Sunday in April 1963 I departed from the Hill Inn on my first Three Peaks race. Although I had prepared with long runs over Kinder, I had never done anything like this before. I was terrified! I thought I had an outside chance of finishing if nothing at all went wrong. After the first peak, Ingleborough, we got lost in the mist near Sulber Nick. Fortunately, I was with Len and another Stockport runner, Tony Broster. The field in those days was small, around 50 to 60, so there was no line of plodding figures to follow, nor were the paths the broad tracks they are now. Full of gloom and despondency I knew with this extra distance I would never be able to finish. Len eventually got us sorted out and galloped off leaving Tony and me to trot gloomily along. I do not know when I began to entertain thoughts that we might actually complete the course, probably when only Whernside stood between us and the finish. In the last few miles I experienced for the first time a phenomenon which has since become a familiar and joyful accompaniment at the end of any very tough challenge where high ambition has been commensurate with uncertainty of outcome. I began to feel stronger and fitter than I had done even at the start, and I wanted to prance off leaving Tony to manage as best he could. To my credit I controlled the urge and we linked arms and finished together.

Responding therefore to the very hard but stimulating challenge of long hill running I started doing the Three Peaks every year and in addition Len simultaneously introduced me to the new sport of orienteering and the Lake District Mountain Trial. This latter remains one of my favourite events. It is run over a different course every year and combines navigation with the fast traverse of difficult mountain terrain. The distance is not great, between 16 and 25 miles (26 and 40 km), but it demands around five to seven hours of hard continuous effort. I first entered in 1965, when the Lake District was wonderfully unfamiliar to me, and have run every year since. It really is a magnificent event, quite unique with a special atmosphere of fun, striving, continuing friendships and camaraderie as well as goodwill between runners and officials. Tales of fortunes and misfortunes over a beer later, the chance to make fresh acquaintances, to put one over on your mates or to help out a newcomer with a bit of navigation are all part of this scene. Here you can rub shoulders with some of the all-time great fell runners, Joss Naylor, Alan Heaton, Billy Bland or the one time greats like George Brass and Ted Dance, past winners, still competing an incredible 35 years after winning the event in the 1950s. All share common ground with the average fell runners/mountaineers who make up the bulk of the 250-strong field.

Len and I gladly took up fell running which satisfied our love of the hills and our need for competition, while posing the fascinating challenge of fast, often intuitive navigation. We tended to enter the longer races, partly to make the three-hour drive to the Lakes worthwhile, but mainly because the idea of long traverses of the beautiful hills was immensely appealing. I was also discovering that the further the races went, the more I could compensate for a lack of running ability with a kind of natural strength and endurance. These were the days of small fields, often only around 30 to 40 runners. One quickly got to know other runners and friendships were formed easily. On the long courses the runners were soon spread out over the miles of fell, and there was no sense of being part of a pounding mass of bodies. Today, with fields numbering several hundreds, a good deal of the attraction of fell racing has for me disappeared. However, one other race in which I still compete and which I associate with these early beginnings is the Karrimor Two-Day Mountain Marathon. This is a

Mike and Len Fitzsimmons with Thor training for the first Karrimor Two-Day Mountain Marathon, 1968.

race for teams of two and involves navigating round a mountainous course which is only disclosed at the start. Each pair has to be self-sufficient for two days, that is, they must carry tents, sleeping bags, food and spare clothing around with them. Len and I entered the first Mountain Marathon back in 1968 and I have entered every year since, only once failing to complete the course after an official inadvertently removed a control point we were looking for. This record is only bettered by my friend and current partner John Richardson who has completed every Mountain Marathon – or The Karrimor as it is now known.

There were only 34 teams doing one 50-mile (80 km) course in 1968. Today there are over 1,000 teams competing over five or six courses which range from the 50 mile/80 km 'Elite' course to the 30 mile/50 km 'C' and 'Score' events. The smaller number of 'Elite' competitors spread over the longer course reduces 'bunching' and trailing. This is further helped if the course offers diverse route choices and tricky navigation (not to mention mountain mist). However, both John and I feel that when we can no longer complete the 'Elite' course we should retire from the event completely. I already have misgivings about our invasion of erstwhile solitary mountain areas.

In 1968 Len and I had visions of a not too brisk stroll through the hills around Muker in Yorkshire. We were wearing heavy boots and our rucksacks bulged with picnic treats. Our one weight-saving gesture was that Len had jettisoned his torch batteries, scoffing at the idea we would be out in the dark. In a typically cunning move he had packed the empty torch with matches and other odds and ends. I certainly had the ethical edge on him as we descended a steep hillside of bog and heather in utter darkness, to say nothing of the edge I had whenever I got to a really awkward bit.

Transition to ultra-distance

Up to competing in the Karrimor the longest distance I ran or walked was 25 miles (40 km). I must have had the urge to cover longer distances, however, because in the summer prior to the first Mountain Marathon, Len told me of a route called the Derwent Watersheds. This had been evolved by the legendary Eustace Thomas of the famous Manchester-based Rucksack Club. It was, in effect, a huge circuit of the Bleaklow and Kinder Moors nearly 40 miles (65 km) in length. Along with route details, Len told me that Thomas and his party of 'grough-hounds' had completed the round in 11 hours 39 minutes. I resolved to have a go myself.

Without informing anyone I set off on a sultry summer day with my faithful dog. After 20 or 25 miles (32 or 40 km) of the unusually dry and dusty Watersheds I veered off the route and plunged into a rock pool competing with the dog for the deepest part! Having reduced my temperature, I decided to carry on into a cooler late afternoon. Eventually I tottered to the point on the circuit where I had started. I stood there looking down to the valley and my waiting van. I realised I had just completed my hardest ever run/walk. My dog just looked at me reproachfully. I told him we had done nearly three hours better than Eustace, he was not impressed.

WILD TRAILS TO FAR HORIZONS

My skirmish with the Derwent Watersheds and my competing in the Karrimor brought me into contact with yet another powerful influence in my transition to an ultra-distance runner. It was Eustace Thomas, former holder of the Lake District 24 hour Fell Record (65.5 miles (105 km), 25,500 ft (7,800 m)) and member of the Rucksack Club, who inaugurated the Watersheds route, and it was Ted Dance and Bob Astles of the Rucksack Club who won the first and second Mountain Marathons. There were quite a few competitors from the Rucksack Club in that first Mountain Marathon and redoubtable men they were too. Don Talbot, Neil Mather, George Rhodes, Stan Bradshaw and my own future partner John Richardson. Between them, these men had climbed in the Himalaya, run and orienteered for England, put up new climbing routes on rock, completed the Lake District 24 hour Fell Record and, above all, they had walked the most prodigious distances – including the first continuous traverse of all the 2,500 ft (750 m) summits in the Lakes, over 100 miles (160 km) and around 42,000 ft (12,600 m) of ascent.

I was on friendly terms with most of them from competing in the same fell races but I was only vaguely aware that they belonged to the same club. One fateful evening the phone rang. It was Ted Dance inviting me to join a Rucksack Club team which he had entered in the first ever High Peak Marathon, which was to be held round the Derwent Watersheds route. I was not a club member but Denis Weir had had to drop out of the team of four and as I was a local lad and known to Ted he thought I might do. I was exceedingly flattered and when I heard the names of the rest of the team (Don Talbot, John Richardson) I at once hurried out to get myself truly fit! Had some spirit from the future appeared to describe the years of torment to which I was committing myself, the lashing rain, the knee-deep mud, the sweat freezing on one's back, the mean winds whipping across the gritstone edges, the boggy holes which lay in wait, the numbed feet, the whole bone-aching weariness of it all, I might just have paused a moment to consider – but probably not. The catalogue of suffering, triumph, despair and humour associated with this deliberately perverse event requires a separate chronicle. Originally organised by Sheffield University Orienteering Club it was scheduled for February but the local press got wind of it and having no other headlines proceeded to fall upon the luckless students and their scheme. They produced lurid headlines; 'Peakland Killer Route Marathon', 'Carbon Copy Death Trek', and so on. Participants were informed that 'blizzards could strike without warning', and a Peak Park warden was reported as saying there was 'a point of no return on Bleaklow'. Strange to say, we never reached this point, but the short way off a moorland watershed is down not back. One was also reassured to hear from the deputy head warden that if anyone got into difficulties he would be on hand to 'pull them out'. Let me tell you, he was never around to pull me out of any of the black bogs into which I frequently sank. Having taken part in 12 events I now think the scaremongers were all absolutely right.

The Rucksack Club team duly won the first race, and indeed, we won six times in succession. Eventually anno Domini made an impact as did the emergence of ever keener opposition from what had now become the fast-growing sport of fell running. But the event still exacts a heavy toll.

The Watersheds race not only extacts its toll during the actual event, training for it during the winter months can inflict damage too. On one occasion the Rucksack Club team of Ted Dance, John Richardson, Don Talbot and myself deemed it expedient to have a run over the loneliest section of the route during the night. Don Talbot was particularly anxious to do this, as he had had flu the week before and thought it as well to test his return to health before the race.

The night was of the particularly dark variety, and though raining but gently when we stepped from Ted's vehicle, it promised to become much heavier ere long. At this point Ted announced that having now done his bit for the team effort, he was returning home to bed. We were, in those days, too polite to tell him what we thought of that and stepped, with nothing approaching enthusiasm, onto the inky moor.

Don lasted out very well. In fact, he lasted out long enough to let us reach the lonely depth of the moor, the dreaded 'point of no return', I guess. Here he suggested a rest stop, so we all sat around on tussocks enjoying an al fresco if somewhat soggy Mars bar in the refreshing rain. It seemed to John and me that Don was taking this rest business rather seriously for, as we stood up to go, Don was observed to be prostrate on the tussocks, eyes closed and the rain bouncing off his unprotected face, which we now noted had turned a very pale shade of white.

It was obvious that, if Don were to be left in that attitude, he would be asleep for a very long time indeed. Grabbing an arm each we hauled him up and started to drag him in the direction of the Longdendale valley road, two miles to the north. Fortunately, being a tough old boot, he began to come round and saved us the problem of what to do on reaching the rather frothy River Etherow by ploughing through like a ship. At first no one would stop for us on the road until a van chanced to draw up to ask directions. Before the driver knew what was happening, Don was pointing out the way to Glossop from the passenger seat! After not too lengthy a consultation it was decided that Don should give the Watersheds a miss that year. But do you think we applauded Ted's undeniable wisdom in eschewing the soggy moors for a warm bed?

On another occasion, in early spring, I combined training for both the Watersheds and the Mountain Marathon in one run. The idea was that I would follow the route of the Derwent Watershed but carry lightweight camping gear and spend the night on the moor around the half-way point. Setting off in the afternoon, I enjoyed a most invigorating run in temperatures around freezing and many a snow shower driven in flurries by an icy wind. As evening drew nigh the showers increased, it was still at the invigorating stage, but I deemed it wise to make camp.

In those days you could either have sound but rather heavy equipment or ultra-lightweight but chancy gear. Naturally, I had opted for the latter, after all, who ever expects snow on the moors in March? My 'tent' was actually a flysheet, open at one end, but my *pièce de résistance* was my 'groundsheet'. It had been sold to my wife as a plastic tablecloth for 15 pence and I had gleefully commandeered it, it was amazingly light and thin!

I observed, during supper, that the snow was now falling in a thick, wet blanket and was deepening rapidly. Very little was finding its way past the open end of the tent, however, and I consoled myself it would keep the midges away. During the night I awoke with my hip feeling very cold. The blasted tablecloth had sneakily crept out under the sides of the flysheet and was catching snow, which it funnelled back in my direction. I was lying in a pool of wet snow. It was fortunate I was using a very thin and nearly useless sleeping-bag at the time, otherwise valuable gear might have been ruined. Craftily, I placed my map under my hip, took a firm grip on my dog – a large and hairy Alsatian – and passed the remainder of the night in, almost luxury.

Next morning, the snow was deep and even, but not crisp. My now warm feet revealed something previously hidden while they had been frozen. My shoes (in reality rubber-soled football boots) had sliced a thick lump of skin from my heel. As it was still snowing and I had obviously not reached the 'point of no return', I returned, but on an easier line. The snow eventually stopped and the sun cracked the clouds; soon everywhere sparkled. Just near my car I met a grizzled farmer rescuing his sheep. He asked me where I had spent the night. I told him (omitting the tablecloth – I thought he might not understand) and he stared at me awhile, then he said 'By heck! You must be a redoubtable character', actually, he was some distance away and he might just have said 'Bloody hell! You must be a right daft bugger' – I am really not too sure.

Apart from probably reducing my life expectancy, what the High Peak Marathon did for me was to bring me into such close and enjoyable company with the Rucksack Club men, that I willingly overcame my native reluctance to join clubs and became a member myself. And so the die was cast. Or very nearly, cruel fate made one evil attempt at nipping my ultra career in the bud, striking at me through another great love of mine – basketball. One dire Saturday in November 1973, just one week after competing in the High Peak Marathon I tried just a bit too hard in driving through for a lay-up shot and broke my leg. The break was a split of the tibial plateau, the weight-bearing surface of the knee joint. I was given to understand that this meant the end of serious sport participation, but, to be honest, I do not know exactly what was said because I knew that, as soon as the cast was off, I was going to run again.

A year later I had to have the cartilage removed, it had been smashed by the femur as it had crunched down on the tibial plateau. The muscle did not re-build and eventually I started special exercises, working up to leg flexion with a 35 lb (16 kg) lump of iron from a rail track strapped to my ankle. Slowly, with much blood, sweat and tears, the muscle was rebuilt, though I have permanently lost the first and last degrees of movement at the knee. I paid dearly for my commitment and love of basketball and, although pain became an inevitable accompaniment of my running, I learned yet another lesson about perseverance and dedication.

Although many people consider events such as the 40-mile High Peak Marathon, the Mountain Trial and Karrimor should be classed as 'ultra-endurance', none of these races occupied more than a dozen hours of continuous going. In 1976 all this changed. On the calendar of Club events that year was a walk called the Grassington–Langdale. I had heard of Grassington vaguely and, as I well knew that Langdale was in the Lake District, I assumed it was somewhere in the same area. I cheerfully agreed to go along. Just the week before the walk I discovered where Grassington was situated – and it was not in the Lake District, it was not even anywhere near it! It was 80 hilly miles (130 km) away. I thought there must be some mistake – I could not walk 80 miles as a continuous walk, could I? 'Nonsense!' said Ted Dance. 'You are a fit fell runner, Mountain Trial, High Peak Marathon and all that. There will be members along who never do that sort of thing, just ordinary walkers.' Well, actually acknowledging my physical limitations has never been something I am good at but I really thought this was a bit much. However, I drove into Grassington with another new member, my friend Geoff Bell, and was immediately initiated into typical Rucksack Club walk strategy. In this club a 9.00 a.m. start does not mean you meet at 9.00, it means that at that time precisely, you are enveloped (at least if you are actually there) in a cloud of dust as everyone endeavours to keep pace with and tabs on the leader who is often the only man who knows just where he is going. Geoff and I arrived at 9.05 to find the place deserted. 'Typical!' I said, 'these things always get going half an hour later than they are supposed to.' Just then someone leaned out of a car. 'You on the Grassington–Langdale walk?' 'Yes, when they arrive' I said. 'Arrive!' he replied, 'they left nearly 10 minutes ago, we are driving round to Mid Pasture to fix them some nosh.' 'But, but . . . where did they go?' 'Over there' he said waving his arm in the general direction of a large hill. 'John Richardson is leading the walk and he is going like the clappers!' 'But, but . . .' we stammered. 'Sorry, got to go' – and he was gone! 'Do you know where Mid Pasture is?' I asked Geoff. 'No' he muttered, 'I only know where Langdale is.' 'Same here', I answered, 'come on.'

We did eventually catch up with the Club walk and we did eventually get to Langdale. I arrived there tireder but wiser. Amongst other things, I had learnt what a delightfully comfortable bed a tarmac road can make when you have been walking all day and all night. I cannot say that the walk did much more than confirm my suspicion that I had no gift for ultra-endurance. However, the fact that I *had* actually completed the 80 miles (130 km) must have made a subjectively greater impression. This short-sighted view lined me up for a good dose of suffering the following year.

1977 was the Rucksack Club's jubilee year and Geoff Bell decided it would be a nice idea to link two of the Club's main centres of activity with a walk. Although he might well have chosen to link, say, the Snake Inn on one side of Kinder Scout with the Nag's Head on the other, he unfortunately decided he would walk from the Club hut in the Lake District to the village of Edale – the southern end of the Pennine Way – a distance of around 120 miles (195 km). We set off with great enthusiasm on a hot sunny day with the ground, for once, dry and firm. How miserable is the lot of the foot traveller. No sooner does he escape from the almost perpetual bog and mud than his tender feet are blistered and burnt by the unaccustomed heat. In my case I developed a singularly painful complaint, not exactly blisters, but a prickly tenderness on the pads of my feet.

This quickly reached the point where I began to examine my socks for the bits of broken glass I felt sure had found their way in. Perhaps paddling across Morecambe Bay in bare feet had not helped, but at 60 miles (100 km) I had had enough. Unfortunately, our support driver, by chance or design, failed to pick me up before the start of an excruciating road section and when I had done this bit, I decided to carry on for another few miles, then a few more, and then some more . . . Eventually I hobbled into Edale with my feet feeling like barbecued steaks but my complaint forever enshrined in the Club's glossary as 'Jubilee Foot'. The pain had been sufficient for me to be unable to remember whether the walk had been tiring or not – a very minor compensation.

Looking through my log-books I realise that 1977 was, perhaps more than any other year, the time of my truly becoming an ultra-distance performer. However, the transition was gradual. Less than two weeks after the Jubilee Walk I climbed Black Shadow, a rock climb graded 'Extreme', in the Llanberis Pass in the morning, then ran from the valley to Snowdon summit and back in 72 minutes in the afternoon. This combination of activities pleased me and it is with some regret that deeper involvement with hard running has restricted my development of other mountain skills. In the face of increasingly high standards it is commensurately more difficult to excel at more than one activity.

A few weeks after charging up Snowdon I attempted something rather longer. In 1932 Bob Graham, a Lake District landlord, improved Eustace Thomas's Fell Record. He traversed the tops of 42 major Lakeland peaks in under 24 hours, a distance of around 65 to 70 miles (105 to 115 km) and about 26,000 ft (7,800 m) of ascent and descent. Although this has been exceeded many times since, Graham's feat has become a 'standard' for other aspirant ultra fell runners. I knew sooner or later I would like to tackle the 'Bob Graham' round, and when Ted Dance invited me to join himself and two friends, I gladly agreed. I only had a fortnight to prepare specifically for the event, so I spent a couple of days in the Lakes, concentrating on steep ascents and descents. My training methods of those days appal me now, though I also applaud my nicely amateur and carefree approach – no doubt inherited from Ted, one of the world's great non-trainers. Just four days before the attempt I was charging round Kinder Scout with the aim of getting fitter, but the probable effect of getting tireder!

Our first attempt was washed out by heavy rain, but the following week I completed the Scottish Fourthousanders (1,200 m peaks) with John Richardson. The latter route is about 80 or 90 miles (130–145 km) in length and starts with the Ben Nevis group in the west and finishes over the Cairngorm 4,000 ft summits in the east. A truly magnificent walk, it was yet another walk pioneered by the legendary Eustace Thomas, who used his Rolls-Royce both as a support vehicle and as a means of covering some of the slightly tedious miles between the two groups of peaks. As neither John nor I possessed a Rolls we covered these miles on foot. We found them long, indeed, but not tedious.

Nine days after this, I again joined forces with Ted Dance to make another attempt on the Bob Graham round. In heat-wave conditions and with a certain residual tiredness from the Scottish Fourthousanders, I was forced to a very modest pace. Ted, by contrast, was in great form and I finally persuaded him to press ahead on the last sections. However, summoning a final flourish, I managed to finish within the allotted 24 hours.

Having now successfully completed a number of extended walks or walk/runs I began to take a keener interest in the Club's tradition of long walks. I had, of course, known about the 40-mile (65 km) Derwent Watersheds for some time, but now I learned of the 70-mile (115 km) Colne-Rowsley. This had for a long time been the Club's longest walk and a gruelling moorland test piece for its 'grough-hounds'. In 1953, however, one of these grough-hounds had hit upon the novel idea of linking England's two highest pubs, the Tan Hill Inn in Co. Durham and the Cat and Fiddle on the moors a few miles from Buxton in Derbyshire.

Extending the Club's longest walk by 50 hard miles (80 km) was an audacious concept. It was, however, undertaken by a group of audacious and determined men. The walk was, appropriately enough, first suggested by the then landlord of the Nag's Head, Edale, Fred Heardman, himself a Club member and keen walker. It was Ted Courtenay, however, who transformed the suggestion into an inspirational walk. Nor was Ted unaffected by the scope of the concept. After phoning his plans to fellow-walkers, he excitedly left the telephone booth with a set of directories clasped under his arm and his maps and schedules reclining on the shelf. The 120 miles (195 km) and nearly 20,000 ft (6,000 m) of ascent exacted retribution, of course. Ted completed his dream, along with stalwarts Vin Desmond and Frank Williamson. Both Neil Mather and even the Club's fleetest grough-hound, Phil Brockbank, were forced to retire, however. In typical fashion they were back the following year, this time with the young tiger, Ted Dance, for company. All were successful and the completion time of between 54 and 55 hours has become a 'standard' for the walk.

Phil Brockbank, apart from his walking talents was also noted for his keen wit and humour. He observed, mischievously, that the Tan–Cat refused to be

The start of the first Tan Hill to Cat and Fiddle, 1953. From left to right: Ted Courtenay, Vin Desmond, Neil Mather, Frank Williamson, Phil Brockbank.

downgraded in line with the usual Club tradition. According to Phil the degrading of classic walks was achieved by subjecting them to increasingly casual modes of attack. He claimed that the second stage of degradation was the traverse by an all-male party in winter, the first being completion by a lady in summer. He left open whether the third stage was a double traverse by a male party in summer or a single traverse by a lady in winter. But by the time a lady had achieved the double version in winter, the walk had reached the lowest classification and was best left to the attention of beginners.

The classifications, of course, refer to continuous effort – snatches of sleep are allowed but going to bed at night and continuing the next morning is definitely unethical. Despite a number of repetitions there have, to my knowledge, been only two winter traverses of the Tan–Cat (one of which I had the dubious pleasure of accompanying), no doubles and only one completion by a lady. The line is a particularly challenging one in foul winter conditions. Almost without exception it cleaves to the high ground, it does not eschew that which is trackless and its last 40 miles (65 km) traverse high, desolate and intimidating moorland: Blackstone Edge, Winter Hill, Black Hill, Bleaklow and Kinder Scout. My mate John Richardson was a veteran of this route and, furthermore, he had done the fastest ever traverse, supported but solo, in 37 hours.

I wondered, could I better this time?

chapter two

TAN HILL TO CAT AND FIDDLE

It is difficult to decide what constituted training for my proposed attempt on the Tan–Cat record. For ultra-distance hill running a general background of running fitness punctuated by long days out on the hills constitutes the general kind of preparation needed. My first attempts at the Tan–Cat produced two resounding disasters, but my preparation had been quite thorough. In fact, my estimation of my 'natural' ultra-endurance ability is so low and my desire to succeed so high that I am usually likely to be guilty of over- rather than under-preparation.

I emerged from the spring very fit having completed the Three Peaks race, the White Peak Marathon and a number of good solid 'mountain days' in Wales. The Welsh days were in part a preparation for a scheme I had hatched with Ted Dance and Geoff Bell to complete a double traverse of the 14 Welsh peaks over 3,000 ft (900 m). This was to be no record attempt, just a good hard day in the hills. What made it good was that the route would link a superb succession of summits in a satisfying logical line. We would see sunset and sunrise from some of the most beautiful hills in the country. What made it hard was that it entailed about 46 miles (75 km) of mountainous terrain and around 21,000 ft (6,300 m) of ascent by our line.

We started at lunchtime and, as I remember, Ted set off at a very smart pace which took us over the first two summits and onto Snowdon in one and a half hours. In just over two hours we were back in the valley enjoying a brew in our Club hut in the Llanberis Pass. From here the climb to Elidir Fawr is very long 2,700 ft (810 m) and Ted was obviously feeling in good form! Unfortunately, Ted is often the victim of his own enormous ability. His natural talent will carry him almost effortlessly and at great speed through a 'normal' hard day. Training is almost superfluous for him at this level. However, beyond the normal, even the greatest must needs be sustained by many, often boring hours of conditioning, a process which Ted assiduously avoids.

We jogged pleasantly over Y Garn and in the early evening we had Tryfan and the Glyders practically to ourselves. I love being on high ground in the evening, there is always such an air of peace about. The mornings can be special too, but then there is a more expectant air, a fragile stillness that is soon to dissolve into the bustle of a full day. The evening hills have the promise of a yet deeper peace.

At about 9.00 p.m. we reached our car in the Ogwen Valley. We ate a prepared meal, picked up supplies and torches and put on warmer clothes. Our ascent of the massive Penyrolewen was hampered by very full stomachs and it was dark by the summit. Quite magically, however, a full moon broke through sparse cloud and we had only occasional need of torches. Our pace had now slowed to 'very comfortable' which meant that as I had mentally prepared for a fast pace and donned appropriate clothes, I was rather chilly. The Carneddau are a big, rolling range of hills with a good deal of ground close to the 3,000 ft (900 m) mark. The very real sense of vastness is enhanced at night when the moonlit bulk of the mountains seems to occupy all space, one can imagine that under the sky's canopy there are nothing but endless mountain ridges over which one may journey for all eternity, would it were so.

On the col below the outlying summit of Yr Elen, Ted, abetted by Geoff, decided he would like a little snooze. I created such a fuss about already being frozen, they were forced to humour me, but I could see I might have some trouble getting them past the refuge hut at Foel-grach! Although our schedule was intended as a guide I had hoped to complete the whole journey inside 24 hours. However, we did not reach our terminus on Foel-fras until 2.30 a.m. which meant we had already taken 13 hours for the outward leg. It did not matter, the night was one to be savoured; a gossamer mist caressed the ground and overhead the stars glinted sharp around a moon bright enough to cast shadows. Unfortunately, by now Ted was too sleepy to enjoy this to the full. He made a bee-line for the Foel-grach refuge hut, where, to our surprise, we disturbed another walker. On finding a ready ear Ted immediately perked up while Geoff sneakily had a quick zizz. In the meantime Ted had invited this character to join us, which he did despite being hampered by a mass of clothes and hand-held carrier bags. He kept up amazingly well and I suspected he had little idea of where he was which consequently made him nervous of being left behind. At 6.00 a.m. we were dropping down to the Ogwen valley again. It was going to be a beautiful day. The valley was still sleeping in a pale grey dawn, but above us the crags had blushed pink and the sky was innocent and blue. At this priceless moment Ted decided he had had a surfeit of good things and would partake no more thereof. Morpheus beckoned him rather more imperatively than the golden hills. Geoff and I were thus left to complete the traverse alone.

Naturally, the tiredness entered our legs, but our spirits would not be denied. On Snowdon we survived a bombardment of stones from two little boys watched over by a fond father – that is until the normally imperturbable Geoff (having just headed a stone) drew daddy's attention to certain sub-sections of the Mountain Code. We brought our route to a fitting climax with a somewhat stiff-legged traverse of the narrow and airy Crib-Goch ridge. Ted was waiting for us at Pen-y-Pass and together we drove down to the hut for a wonderful shower and endless pots of tea. We had been out for 28 hours and in that time the hills had drawn our strength but nourished our spirits, we had shared the hills and we had shared friendship.

Less than a month after our memorable double Welsh 3,000s Geoff and I again teamed up to attempt a 'double Shap-Wasdale'. The route, from Shap on the eastern fringes of the Lake District to Wasdale at the very heart of the Lakes, is a traditional Rucksack Club walk of about 35 miles (56 km). Once more John Richardson was leading this classic and once more we were late (by 50 minutes).

A steady economical line brought us up to the Club, prostrate in midday heat, outside the Kirkstone Inn. Both Geoff and I had very fit 'hill legs' by now and found the hilly route to our liking. At the end of the day we dropped into Wasdale at a perfect moment – just as the setting sun was casting a marvellous and rare Alpenglow on Pikes Crag behind us. It was so beautiful we descended at least half the distance to Wasdale with our heads screwed round to gaze at the rocks behind us, not a recommended practice.

Now came the rather harder bit. While everyone else stretched around in a variety of luxurious attitudes and poured beer copiously down dry throats Geoff and I, pretending not to notice, didn't so much enjoy a meal as refuel our systems. With loins well girt and upper lips suitably stiffened we left at midnight on a balmy moonless night. Rarely do the hills fail to reward the patient traveller. As we meandered wearily past Stickle Tarn we were rendered immobile by a scene of immense beauty. At 2 a.m. on a still summer night, Nature was painting with a range of blacks and sombre blues. Before us stretched the waters of the Tarn, one would have said black had not the encircling arms of stony land clasping the Tarn been yet blacker. At the furthest and blackest extent of the Tarn and its rim was what had first drawn our gaze. Presage of a summer dawn was a band of the most delicate blue. We followed the pale blue ever up as it dissolved by imperceptible stages into always darker hues. At last with craning heads we stared into the immense void of the true night sky. We sat silent and motionless as the stones around us, then we got up and finished our walk. Pink Pikes Crag and cobalt eternity.

First Tan–Cat attempt

After all my solid preparation I might have been forgiven for feeling confident. Alas, I had yet much to learn! Geoff and I elected to start from the 'wrong' end, that is to go from the Cat and Fiddle to Tan Hill. For some reason this immediately felt wrong and my only other attempt to go this way also proved a disaster. Nothing seemed to go quite according to plan including Geoff and I getting separated. After waiting for some time I set off convinced he must be in front of me, I even picked up his stud marks! Despite my good pace I could not seem to overhaul him. I decided to press on alone to Todmorden, 50 miles (80 km) hence, and phone Geoff's home. As I was considering this I discerned very heavy breathing and turned round to discover a rather warm Geoff galloping up behind me. Being Geoff he was soon laughing about the incident as we enjoyed a large ice-cream and lemonade in Todmorden. We put the remains of the lemonade in a plastic bottle and jogged off. There was a subdued explosion from Geoff's sack and suddenly his nether regions were bathed in lemonade! We traversed the ensuing moors in gentle summer rain losing a little time, not much, just enough to ensure we would be tackling Jackson's Ridge in darkness.

Jackson's Ridge is Lancashire's answer to the Bermuda Triangle. It must be named after some long forgotten surveyor or insane navvy, for it is not a ridge at all, just an interminable ditch running along a parish boundary. It looks quite innocuous on the map and should give a direct line across the still private moor below Boulsworth Hill. At night it is a shifting malevolent place. The ditch disappears and attempts to find it using 'off-line' bearings lead to one becoming quite disoriented. Whole drainage systems displace themselves and the flat contours are blandly inscrutable. It is truly devious, in reasonable conditions it will drop its defences and allow untroubled passage. But return in mist or dark thus disarmed and it will trap you and spit you out hours later. You will be disillusioned, demoralised and you may be in Lancashire or Yorkshire for all you know or care.

I had reconnoitred Jackson's Ridge and had it well taped – with a slight doubt about a night crossing. But I was sure I could handle it, after all what moor can stand before the powerful magic of the Silva compass? We were soon to find out.

I am still unable to calculate in what way we managed to get off line. My suspicion is that the ground cunningly shifted or perhaps Jackson's ghost bewitched me for I remember abandoning my foolproof plan and trying something I had not rehearsed. We should have been going NE but when we did so the ground dropped away on our right so I corrected by moving back NW. Now the ground dropped away to our left so I swung back to the N – too late! We were now traversing awkward sloping ground but decided we must stay with this bearing. Wrong! We began to drop into and climb out of small valleys which split the hillside. As each valley was choked with wet head-high bracken we were soon soaked from head to foot. We tripped and fell down to each stream then fought our way up the impenetrable stuff on the other side. After some incalculable period of time we were brought to a halt by the unlikely prospect of a cluster of bright lights floating above the moor some distance away. We looked at each other – the bloody moor was haunted! Reason prevailed. Out came the map which revealed the only pub in the area, the Herders Arms high on a remote moorland road and well off our intended line.

Drawn as if by a magnet we approached the pub. Despite the midnight hour it was vibrating with noise, life and unthinkable pleasures of the flesh. Suppressing a sob we slunk past, bedraggled, outcast figures, out of blackness into blackness. Now we exchanged high bracken for a forest of tussocks. Tussocks are, perhaps, the walker's worst enemy. Now, I fell over one and banged my nose on another. It was the end, the final indignity – no, it was not!

At last, descending in now lashing rain into the haven of Cowling I skidded to a halt just in front of an electric fence and just in time to realise that Geoff was right behind me and closing fast, too fast. The fence was at a very unfortunate height and in splendid working order – unlike certain parts of me for some time after. Geoff's wife, Mary, was waiting to support us at Cowling. Before she could enquire of our needs Geoff was issuing home-bound instructions from the back seat of the car, and I was in such a hurry getting changed in the phone box I left several items of clothing behind! 'After all', I said to Geoff, 'if we quit now after 70 miles (115 km) we will still be fresh enough to have another go next weekend.' 'I'm sure you will' said Geoff, 'and, better still, next time *you* run and I'll support!'

I am at a loss to understand why some kind but strong friend had not the wit to tell me that a fairly rigorous 70 miles (115 km) one weekend is not ideal preparation for a further 120 miles (195 km) at record pace the following weekend. Perhaps I never asked.

Second Tan–Cat attempt

This time I started my attempt from Tan Hill and the most, in fact the only, enjoyable thing about the venture was the quart of Webster's fine beer I consumed the night before. I set off in humid conditions, which I detest. Soon it began to rain and did so for 10 hours non-stop. Despite a certain residual tiredness, which I found puzzling, I was making reasonable progress until Great Whernside, 30 miles (50 km) on. In the mist and surrounded by a maze of high stone walls I lost my bearings somewhat. When I reached the road a helpful motorist advised that Conistone, where Geoff was waiting, lay to my right. Three miles later I jogged into Kettlewell, reversed and jogged three and a quarter miles back to Conistone. This was a nasty psychological blow and, worse still, the road did something naughty to my right shin. Each succeeding bit of road or track wrought its own mischief and soon even soft, but rough, going began to send stabs of pain up the shin. I should have quit at the road before Jackson's Ridge, but I was determined to show the moor that I was equal to it. Although the light would soon fade, I deliberately refused to take a torch despite knowing that failure to keep to my scheduled speed across the moor would mean . . . well, do not think of the consequences, just get out and do it. It was the only satisfaction I got from the attempt, I just made the crossing in the last glim. Again, I should have quit at the support point, but stubborn pride would not let me. I reasoned that the slow night pace across the soft moors above Todmorden would allow my leg to recover. The pace was slow all right! The night was Stygian in its black impenetrability. Inexplicably, it did not seem to cure my shin.

Geoff was curled up, fast asleep in his cosy car, radio issuing soft music. If you ever do support, please at least attempt to give the impression it is hell for you too. Meanwhile, my demon was explaining to Geoff that it was necessary to test whether the air of Todmorden had miraculous shin-healing properties. Geoff nodded sagely and I limped off. In Todmorden the demon explained that one should never make a decision to quit in the small hours when low morale held sway and it was now 2.30 a.m. Geoff accepted this logic. But I knew that Todmorden was only 69 miles (114 km) on from Tan Hill and last week I had managed 70 miles (115 km) and the demon was thus not satisfied. I started on the five miles (8 km) to the White House. On the hard tracks by the Warland Reservoirs the pain made fresh investigations of my levels of tolerance. My limp reached very ungainly proportions, yet when I reached the car I said nothing but ate briefly and stared into the dirty grey dawn over the dirty grey moors. Geoff sat patiently waiting. At last I spat the words out 'Take me home, Geoff.' The demon started; 'But I'll get you next time !' he screeched petulantly. 'I'll try again next year, Geoff', I muttered.

I prepared very thoroughly, after receiving such a rebuff on the Tan–Cat. Along with other Club members, I did a walk of about 100 miles (160 km) in Wales, and the week after the Mountain Trial I decided to attempt the Colne–Rowsley. Logically, I should have tackled this route before taking on the Tan–Cat as it is similar in terrain but, at 70 miles (115 km), it is 50 miles (80 km) shorter. I knew John Richardson and Denis Weir had completed the route in a brisk 19 hours in semi-winter conditions – the fastest time, but not intended as a definitive record. In fact John now accompanied me for the first 30 miles (50 km), after which I continued alone. It was a lovely run, though tiring after the Mountain Trial. The moors were clean, empty and windswept. I can still recall the sound of the wind swishing through the rough moorland grass. I ran on into darkness picking my way along the gritstone edges above winking lights in the Derwent Valley, then finally descending to Rowsley where I arranged for Ted to pick me up. I was so weary on finishing that I donned all my spare clothes and curled up inside a horse-trough outside the rather posh portals of The Peacock – much to the chagrin of its clientele ('Oh, I say, do look at that old tramp asleep in the horse-trough!'). My time was a rather pedestrian 17 hours 20 minutes but the time was far less important than the sense of satisfaction I derived from the run as a whole.

The Colne–Rowsley rounded off my ultra exploits for 1978 and I then set to work on a more systematic programme of training than I had ever before attempted. I was careful this time to include road stretches in my training. The basis of my training was a long day each weekend – around four to six hours and several mid-week runs of eight to ten miles (13 to 16 km). Nor did I neglect to keep in touch with the long stuff. In March Geoff and I did a very tough 90-mile (144 km) Peakland circuit battling with the remnants of winter. At the end of May I put on a Club walk of 70 miles (115 km) in Wales. I found this relatively easy and relaxing and decided I must by now be ready to pit myself once more against the Tan–Cat.

Tan–Cat record 1979

We arrived at Tan Hill at 1.00 a.m. – regretfully far too late to sample the Websters. In any case I had to be up at 5.00, so perhaps it was as well. I set off alone at 5.30 with feelings of excitement and tension only just under control. I have always had a natural tendency towards slow, steady starts, but now I had to make conscious efforts not to run uphill. As I flowed over the first stretch of moor I became aware of tremendous concentration and a drive to succeed that was like a pure energy force. Tension is always greatest in the first stretches of an ultra attempt and because of this I generally prefer to be by myself. Alone, I can come to terms with myself and the course. In the first few miles I create a harmony in relation to the extreme demands I shall experience. I seek to establish a calm acceptance and a peaceful strength. If I cannot find these at the start, I will have nowhere to come back to when the going gets really tough.

I was to have plenty of company on this attempt, however. In order to give Geoff a break from driving I had enlisted Sue, a friend from the college where I lectured. Sue was a strong and committed walker who had taken to running, she could drive, rustle up a roadside brew in seconds and was as versatile as an egg! In short, a perfect member of a support crew. She was a good listener, too. When she joined me to stretch her legs after I had been running alone for several hours, I responded to the release of tension by talking non-stop for miles.

The day continued pleasantly with Geoff and Sue alternating running and driving round to meet me at road crossings with drinks, etc. I cruised gently over the rolling Yorkshire hills, Great Shunner, Buckden Pike and Great Whernside. I made sure of getting Great Whernside right by having John Richardson as my guide. This hill is very much on his patch, so there were no six-mile (10 km) detours this time. By lunchtime I felt hungry and ate a large helping of fish and chips. As each section of moor and meadow passed behind me I began to feel increasingly confident. By the time I ran into Todmorden at 70 miles (115 km) I was nearly two hours ahead of my schedule. Instead of halting for a substantial meal, I decided to press on to the White House. This meant that I could concentrate on running the flat reservoir tracks on an empty stomach. Perhaps the ghosts of last year's anguished hobble still lurked here because for the first time I began to experience a real weariness, and I tasted fear in the simple arithmetic of 120 miles (195 km) minus 70 (115) still leaves 50 miles (80 km). I put my trust in my training and a good feed.

I had quite a long stop at the White House as I was preparing for a solo night section of some hours. Up to now I had run in shorts but the night was turning chilly and a damp moorland mist was licking over the hills. I put on warm tights and a jersey and picked up a small rucksack of spare gear. Finally I confirmed my estimated time of arrival at the dawn checkpoint with Geoff and Sue and with their words of encouragement in my ears I stepped across the road and onto the empty midnight moors.

In my heart I knew that the next few hours would almost certainly decide the record for me. First, my mind quickly probed my body. After a few dozen stiff and painful steps I noted with relief that my legs became loose and comfortable. My next concern was with route finding. To my consternation I observed the mist thickening. I was not going to have the clear, transparent summer night I had counted on. Now the map and compass provided the structure within which I used my memory 'feel' of the route to maintain me on course over the featureless terrain. I became utterly engrossed in this game which, at its best, is like establishing an extra sense, a direction sense based on information from many sources. So engrossed was I that I hardly realised how slowly I was moving. Of my two hours in hand all but 30 minutes had slipped away with the night.

It was with a feeling of great relief that I came out straight and true at the support car just as a steely dawn fingered its way into the eastern sky before me. I was touched to discover that Sue had sensed my approach and was already waiting with a warm drink. Despite my protestations they both insisted on driving to the next road crossing only 90 minutes running time away. With support like this I knew I must not allow myself to fail. I set off with fresh determination into a clear, grey dawn, the wild, lonely call of a curlew floating above the moors.

As I began to run the night pace out of my legs I detected a sense of urgency replacing the patience of the night section. I had opted for a slightly novel approach to Black Hill, one of the three major high moors which lay between me and my goal. Black Hill is usually approached from either the Pennine Way route over Black and White Moss or up the Wessenden valley from Marsden. My plan was to start on the Pennine Way path but outflank the horrible bogs of Black and White Moss by descending to the top section of the Wessenden. Working without a map I left the Pennine Way path and headed for the valley track. Suddenly, everything looked wrong; I had missed my 'attack' point. If I went down in the wrong place I could easily be committed to a hopeless deviation. At last I opted for the more southern of two alternatives on the basis that I was heading south overall. After 10 minutes of descent I dropped onto the path I had been seeking. I breathed a sigh of relief but cursed my fallible memory.

Soon I was crossing Black Hill. A vast area of rough tussocky grass capped by a black, oozing bog, Black Hill is a place with few definite features, just huge empty spaces. Feeling very strong under the waxing power of the early sun I began to trade accuracy for speed and slipped off route twice. Fortunately, I quickly recognised my errors and regained my line safely.

At Crowden I had a short food stop trying not to notice the bulk of Bleaklow looming before me. Sue joined me for this tough leg to the Snake Inn and helped to take my mind off the endless climb. Crossing the top of the moor at 8.00 a.m. in beautiful sunshine we were startled to see Ted Dance suddenly pop out from behind a grough with his camera poised. Ted's unexpected appearance gave me a great boost and I picked up from my steady plod and swept up to the Snake Inn in fine style. I had now completed 99 miles (158 km) and as the 100th took me straight up the side of Kinder Scout it was arguably the toughest. I felt I was crawling and became despondent until Ted authoritatively told me it was a perfectly reasonable pace after 100 miles (160 km). Ted's authority cannot be gainsaid and, sure enough, I emerged strong at the top of the climb.

However, I was now certainly into the area of fatigue. The steady uphill walking sections were not bad, but running on the flat called for a very definite act of will to get started. I kept plugging away, reaching out with my mind for the end of my journey. I had been sure of breaking John's record for some time but seemed to lack inspiration to summon any final flourish. At last, as I topped the high point on Comb's Moss above Chapel-en-le-Frith I could make out a tiny bump on the yet higher moors above Buxton; the Cat and Fiddle. The end of my pub crawl was in sight. For no good reason it suddenly entered my head that I must get to the pub before afternoon closing so that my friends could celebrate with a drink. This thought quickly assumed obsessive qualities and I increased my efforts, driving my tired legs through the wiry, clutching heather. As I approached the last hill I asked Ted, who was pacing me, to go a little faster; he did so. A few seconds later I suggested I could go faster still; again he increased speed. When I repeated the request for the third time he stepped aside and told me to take it on myself. I began to pump my legs hard, I reached my maximum walking speed and broke into a run. I crested the hill and reached the final undulating mile of track to the pub. I was expecting to pay for such a

*Mike and
Geoff above
the Snake Inn
on Kinder
Scout – the
Tan–Cat.*

ridiculous waste of energy at every rise, but instead my body was suffused with a vibrant and unassailable energy and I simply ran faster and faster, leaving my support behind me and my brain to wonder what the hell was happening! Two hundred yards of tarmac separated me from the Cat and Fiddle, I sprinted up, gave the gable end a resounding smack with my hand, then immediately turned to go back to my friends. As I looked for them the glorious energy which had flowed into my legs, flowed into my heart and mind. It entered my eyes and emerged as tears. I hugged my friends and the energy became still, changed now into a deep and peaceful joy. A joy that remained a guard against the ravages of fatigue for many days after.

I had taken over five hours off the record, finishing in 32 hours 20 minutes, which meant we were able to celebrate in appropriate style after all.

With Geoff and Sue outside the Cat and Fiddle. Mike's first successful Tan–Cat.

chapter three

BEYOND LIMITS

It is difficult to describe the euphoria I felt after running the Tan–Cat. Running has always been a very important part of my life. If I am honest, I suppose I should say it is not only part of my lifestyle, it *is* my lifestyle. I am reluctant to admit that, however, as I believe other things, family, friends, books, music, are just as important. In any case, what for me elevates running to such a position of importance is the intimate connection I have made between running and the hills. It is not necessary for me to run over the hills to enjoy them, nor do I have to have hills to derive satisfaction from running, but the whole is frequently greater than the sum of the parts.

For nearly a year I had cherished my dream of running smoothly and swiftly down that long stretch of the Pennine Moors. I had been out in rain, hail, snow and occasional heat. In the long, dark days of winter, when I might have been cosy before a fire, I had ploughed my lonely furrow. As spring had blossomed, so had those dreams of distance, long summer miles to hazy horizons. And along with the dreams was the desire to expunge the bitterness of pain and defeat, the physical and spiritual suffering which this tough sport had exacted as a first payment for my audacity. Well, I had paid my respects over the long months of training and now I had bought back my pride and won a degree of satisfaction and fulfilment, which I contentedly let lap about me. I had no immediate plans for any other epic runs, though there were a number of long walks I had in mind. I had established I could run a fair way at a continuous steady pace, but I did not particularly regard myself as an ultra-distance runner.

I ran contentedly through the rest of the summer and into autumn. Then one day as I ran along a muddy towpath I turned to my mate and said 'I think I'll have just one go at the Pennine Way record, but only one go because I don't really think I'm capable of it.' What a fateful decision, and what an abysmal lack of self-knowledge.

History of the Pennine Way Record

In 1969 when a friend told me that Ted Dance and Denis Weir had completed the Pennine Way in under five days I was staggered. Though I knew Ted and Denis from fell running, I wasn't a member of the Rucksack Club and knew nothing of its tradition of long continuous walks. (Ted still describes the achievement as 'only like doing five club walks one after another'.) The previous

The Old Nag's Head

Ted Dance (left) and Denis Weir after their definitive Pennine Way record in 1969.

best time seems to have been some six and a half days by Arthur Puckrin. Denis was obviously confident of bettering this as when Ted arrived home to enjoy a long weekend he was told that Denis had arranged to start the Pennine Way next morning. 'But', protested Ted, 'I've only got three days holiday'. 'That's all right' replied Cath, 'Denis says that's enough!'

The idea of fast Pennine Way traverses began to catch on and in 1972 Alan Heaton and Mick Meath of Clayton-le-Moors Harriers did just over four days. Alan could undoubtedly have gone faster and had he been solo and fully supported the three-day issue might have been settled there and then. However, the big guns were assembling and in 1974 Joss Naylor stepped down from Mount Olympus (well, the Wasdale Fells anyway) and made an attempt that seems to have depended on gaining sufficient momentum to carry him through the three day 'barrier' as it had now become. Joss covered 108 miles (175 km) in a remarkable and, to my mind, ill-advised, 18 hours. Thereafter he proceeded to become painfully stiff and shortly before Kinder, with his goal almost within grasp, he was forced to stop and rest. He slashed the record but was still some three and a half hours adrift of the three-day target. (At the time one pundit proclaimed that this record would not be bettered in Joss's lifetime!)

In 1975 the modest and unassuming Pete Dawes of Kendal AC made an attempt that excites my admiration more than most. He seems to have taken a rather dim view of the prominence given to Joss's effort and made a heart-warming bid to get back to the light-hearted amateurism of the Dance/Weir approach. Ace ultra-distance man Boyd Millen tells of turning up in Kirk Yetholm and wondering where all the support was gathered. Pete's wife informed him that she would cover the road crossings and he was the only runner for the first 90 miles (145 km). After accompanying Pete for the 30 mile (50 km) Cheviot stretch Boyd stood down for a rest but was so stricken with remorse as the diminutive and lonely figure disappeared into the Byrness forests that he accompanied him thereafter. Pete's plan was simple: go steady for 20 or so miles (32 km), pick up and go strongly for the next 40 to 50 (65 to 80 km) then hang on for the last 20 to 30 (32 to 50 km), have a few hours sleep then repeat the process – twice. Despite eating problems and associated stomach disorders (always a problem), Pete succeeded in smashing Joss's record (his declared priority) and coming close to three days (3 days 1 hour 48 minutes).

With three days now an enticing target, Brian Harney and Roger Baumeister attempted the record in 1977. Sadly, Roger had to retire at 140 miles (224 km) with a stress fracture, while Brian gave up at 90 miles (145 km), his feet like raw steaks. As ultra-distance fell runners both these men were of the highest calibre – Roger went on to complete a unique double traverse of the Bob Graham round, 140 miles (224 km) and around 54,000 ft (16,200 m) of climbing inside 48 hours. Two years later I heard that Brian, as he had vowed, was going to have another go at the elusive three-day barrier. Like most of the other attempts, Brian elected to go from north to south but unlike them, he intended only to take sleep when forced to. He set himself a very tough schedule for the first day and a half, hoping to hang on later. Brian raced through the first 113 miles (180 km) in 24 hours taking no sleep. He continued to press on and passed the half-way point in under 30 hours. At 163 miles (260 km) and starting his second night I believe he made a crucial error. His support team had a bed ready for him at Hawes, but feeling good he decided to keep going at least to Horton 15 miles (24 km) away. After reaching high ground he became very weak and his support got him into a sleeping bag where he slept for 45 minutes. After this Brian was still very slow to Horton and took another hour's sleep there. He had only a further 30 minutes sleep in the remaining 92 miles (148 km) but as he'd started at 9.00 a.m. he had to suffer Black Hill and Bleaklow in the dark, difficult conditions in which to recoup time. He came mighty close to the three days however, just 42 minutes short, taking over an hour off Pete Dawe's record. He professed himself well pleased and not particularly disappointed to have missed the 'barrier'. His statistics were very impressive, not to say daunting: 113 miles (180 km) on day one; 81 miles (130 km) day two and 74 (118) plus two (three) to finish off. He had two and a half hours sleep, which was included in his total stopping time (for eating, changing, etc.) of around six hours.

Having myself just experienced the reality of runs extending through day and night I was astounded. I did not feel my own effort was degraded. It had been a tough run over more continuously rough ground than the Pennine Way. And, just as important, it had been my best effort. I do not think you should feel ashamed of your best effort and I did not, but I was certainly impressed by Brian's performance!

The Training

When I announced that I would have just one crack at the Pennine Way record I meant just that. I had thought through the concept and what it entailed quite thoroughly and my decision was based on a sound rationale. I found the concept of a three day Pennine Way an intensely challenging one. I knew I would love to be able to meet this challenge and the possibility of being the first ever person to complete the route within three days was a powerful additional incentive. There was little doubt in my mind that such an achievement would represent for me the pinnacle in my life of running. As far as my running was concerned, I had never before felt any need to express any ultimate, but now an ultimate beckoned with an astonishingly imperative finger. At the same time, no matter how imperatively the finger might beckon, it was unlikely to be able to propel me along 270 miles (435 km) of hilly terrain. It was not that I ever doubted I should have the necessary strength of purpose. Unfortunately, sheer determination cannot replace ability.

Did I have the ability? I knew I had the motivation to undertake a long and rigorous training regime, but I had no conviction that I was actually capable of succeeding from any training base whatever. My feeling, on the whole, was that I had not the ability to achieve the record, but I owed it to myself to try. I set my limit at one attempt in order to not 'waste' more than one season in special effort and in order not to subjugate everything else to a hopeless dream for too long.

I must reflect here that it is little wonder that we have problems in communicating with others when we (by which I really mean I!) cannot communicate accurately with ourselves. I actually said to myself (and others) just *one* attempt at the Pennine Way record. What it transpired I really meant was, just one attempt which establishes to my satisfaction that I am never going to be capable of running the Pennine Way in under three days. This never happened and in that sense I stayed true (despite my seven unsuccessful attempts!) to my original promise. In that I was finally successful I suppose I might claim my judgement was vindicated, though of course you might well claim it was a triumph of bloody-mindedness over good sense. I shall not argue that point.

During the winter of 1979/80 I maintained a schedule which included some very demanding routes, mainly walking, but sufficiently strenuous to develop a deep endurance. The most ambitious of these walks was a winter Tan–Cat with John Richardson and Geoff Bell. The walk took place in severe winter conditions and occupied us for over 60 hours with little sleep. On a rather more lighthearted note, Geoff and I set out to improve on my Colne–Rowsley record. We only had one support point, at 30 miles (50 km), and after we had eaten and set off again I discovered I had left all maps and route cards with times and bearings in the support car. I assured Geoff I could find my way just using our one navigational aid, his compass, providing it did not get misty. This was the signal for an impenetrable mist to descend, and though I did my best, we were eventually forced to take a food break while I pondered our position. I was just about to suggest we go in a straight line in the general direction of our destination when we were surprised to hear the drone of a car in the middle of the desolate moor. Further investigation revealed we were about half a mile (0.8 km) from the main road and only about 200 yards (180 m) from our correct line.

Recovering from this mishap gave us heart and we set out to cross Bleaklow and the Derwent Edges to Moscar and the Snake road. Eventually, with my more intense training regime I began to do better than Geoff on the gentle but long, grinding ascents. However, on reaching the fields just before Rowsley, he suddenly flew past me at an amazing speed. Astonished, I raced after him and just succeeded in catching him As soon as I did, he collapsed like a punctured balloon, it had been a last defiant effort, but Rowsley was still one and a half miles (2.5 km) away. It was a weary but triumphant Geoff who tottered with me into Rowsley just four minutes outside our scheduled 16 hours. This time Ted was prompt in arriving and I was unable to initiate Geoff in the delights of The Peacock's horse-trough. Instead, we drove to The Monsal Head, where before a blazing fire we demonstrated the potent effects of real ale on the exhausted human body. Memory is hazy, but I think Geoff fell over and I fell asleep – or perhaps it was the other way round.

Having established a good solid mileage base during winter I now began to get down to serious training encouraged by a beautiful early spring. Throughout April I averaged between 120 and 140 miles (195 and 224 km) per week swinging from extreme fatigue to smooth effortless running – and back again. Hardly easing down I did my best marathon time, 2 hours 42 minutes, in the White Peak Marathon along the old mineral rail lines in Derbyshire. Early in May I started to extend the length of individual runs. In one period of nine days I ran and walked 250 miles (420 km), then, after only four days active rest, I entered the 60-mile (100 km) Fellsman Hike. After such high mileage this proved a tough event, particularly as it took place in very high temperatures. I got caught up in the competitive spirit and, despite the heat, found myself 'eye-balls out', as the saying goes. I was satisfied to finish in third place and felt I must be developing some endurance. In retrospect, I think this was when I peaked and should have started looking for a couple of easy weeks. After three days rest I did an 'easy' 35-mile (56 km) run on towpaths and was displeased to find I felt very fatigued. I followed this a couple of days later with a training weekend on the Pennine Way which, with the benefit of hindsight, gives an accurate estimate of my level of motivation and the extremes to which I allowed it to drive me in my efforts to attain even higher fitness levels.

I drove 200 miles (320 km) north to run the Roman Wall section of the Pennine Way. My old car was as subject to breakdowns as I was and I did not get to bed until nearly 1.00 a.m. However, I rose at 5.00 a.m. and during the day covered 58 miles (93 km). I started by feeling totally exhausted but began to pick up under the influence of the beautiful scenery. My slow pace meant I did not finish running until 9.00 p.m. and by the time I had eaten and changed I did not get to bed until 11.15. I was up, bleary-eyed, at 4.15 a.m. to drive further north to reconnoitre the next section. I covered 22 miles (35 km) in very hot conditions and returning to the car for lunch decided to run with as little spare gear as possible for the afternoon session. As I reached my turning point 14 miles (22 km) on it began to rain furiously. I cowered in a barn waiting for a break that never came. Eventually I set off back in vest and shorts, not only unprotected from the rain, but also too weary to manage more than a plod, which did little to keep me warm. When I reached my car I was in a wretched state; exhausted, cold and hungry. Relief at being able to sit in relative comfort and warmth obscured all other problems and I counted my hard won statistics, 108 miles (173 km) and nine and a half hours sleep in two days and two nights. I drove home, a box of food next to me, finally collapsing into bed at 2.00 a.m. I could not help reflecting that if I did achieve the record I could say I had earned it. I even began to wonder whether I deserved it. My conclusion was that this was a nonsensical and probably pernicious notion, which shows some sense.

After this tough weekend I scheduled an easy three weeks of gentle running. In retrospect I had, perhaps, ravaged my resources, both mental and physical. At any rate, I seemed unable to generate any feeling of concentrated calm. Instead, I simply became more and more nervous. Having experienced the crushing fatigue of training for the record I was anxious of what the real thing might mean. But this was not my major fear. What I was frightened of most of all was . . . failure.

The First Attempts

I stepped out of the car at Edale and cowered into the shelter afforded by the Nag's Head. It was 3.00 a.m., and still dark. A powerful west wind flung sheets of rain across the sleeping village. Ted Dance shook my hand and without the least sign of irony wished me good luck. Before me lay storm lashed and soggy moors, precursors of the 270 hilly miles (435 km) I hoped to cross step by step. Where was the fire in the belly? Where was the unquenchable spirit of 'to strive and not to yield'? Where was the bloody demon even, he of the insatiable ego? All gone. Only the black empty moors and me a small speck on them, searching to find a little hope. At 3.30 a.m. on the Kinder Plateau where a midsummer dawn should have greeted me, the furious grip of the storm wrack was clamped across the land, a grim hand permitting neither hope nor light. I had no torch but I could just see the luminous dot on my compass. I rallied a little. These were my moors and if I knew where north lay I could find my way. Stumbling up and down the groughs I manufactured my line across the moor acknowledging recognisable features as they loomed up: Crowden Brook, Kinder Gates, Kinder Downfall. Old friends, old memories they were, but now I was alien, they had no part to play in this mad ambition.

Thank God Ted was going to meet me on the Snake Road before I crossed Bleaklow, my morale needed some attention. As I approached the car I was appalled to see it swaying in the wind, morale sank even lower. Inside the car the roar of the wind and the harsh tattoo of the rain made me feel even more dismal. I was not, however, anxious to get out. Ted drove to Glossop to pick up Geoff so after Bleaklow I had someone to run with. Taking it in turns they made the way a little more cheerful for me. Disregarding the energy I was burning I bent into the storm clouds. I was almost up to my scheduled times but this was misleading. The wind and rain continued unabated and the effort needed to drag myself through the bogs sometimes against the wind was enormous. I was pouring three days worth of energy into these first few hours. Unless the storm abated, and quickly, I was doomed. Already, by Widdop Reservoir at 50 miles (80 km), I had used up all my spare clothing. These were pre-Gore-Tex days and under a heavy cagoule I was as wet as if I had had no waterproof at all. The end came quite suddenly, I guess I had been preparing for it unconsciously since leaving Edale, nevertheless it took an unexpected form. I had been aware of a dull ache in the Achilles tendon since just after Bleaklow. On the way over from Widdop to Cowling it flared into a crippling pain. I knew injuries to the Achilles were not to be treated lightly. I limped painfully, but perhaps with some relief, into Cowling to announce my retirement. As Geoff and I entered the village a stricken looking Ted greeted us with the news that he had had a collision in Geoff's car. What a wretched and bitter conclusion to those recent dreams. I was exhausted, injured, demoralised and now I was the unwitting cause of my good friends suffering for nothing on my behalf. For nothing? No, 60 miserable miles (100 km) less than nothing. Even the bloody demon kept his mouth shut. I knew I could not do it.

After such an abysmal failure as I had just suffered it was necessary to rebuild morale as well as recover from the injury. The tendon quickly improved. As regards the rather more sensitive injury to my morale I had to assess how much was due to my weakness and how much to circumstances. It was obvious that the weather would sooner or later have drawn a curtain across my attempt anyway. There might have been people around who could have withstood such conditions and maintained schedule, I was not one of them.

The injury remained a mystery but I guessed it might have been psychosamatically induced. I had been psyched up to the point of being psyched out! Instead of focusing on positive aspects my mind had been occupied with negative thoughts – fear of failure. I had thought less about success than how dreadful a failure would be. It has taken me a number of years to evolve appropriate strategies to cope with the formidable pressures of ultra record attempts. These pressures arise from my tremendous drive to succeed in an activity where there are no cop-outs, you either break the record or you do not and failure is always the more likely outcome.

At the time of my failure, however, such coping strategies were all in the future. My immediate response was, characteristically, to emulate Don Quixote and fling myself at my windmill – with much the same results. Unlike the Don, I had a plan. In fact I have had several plans in my battle with the Pennine Way, most of them nicely unorthodox, too. Alas, the Pennine Way had the big battalions and it would not play by the rules. It just hauled up the big guns; storm, tempest, floods or, for a change, searing heat, and contemptuously flicked me off the battleground.

After a month licking my wounds and devising a plan I was ready to tackle the Pennine Way again. My plan was to start, not in the morning, but quite late in the evening. This was not an attempt to catch the Pennine Way slumbering, I should add. My rationale was based on two principles; first, an evening start would ensure that I would have at least one night when I was fresh and better able to cope with the difficulties that darkness brings; second, it brought the second night much closer. This was important because I had scheduled a short sleep stop on the second night. On my first attempt, a 3.00 a.m. start had placed the second night a massive 44 hours and about 170 miles (272 km) away. I had not been able to handle this psychologically, but a 9.00 p.m. start meant that after a short night I would only have to run through one day before I grasped that little island of rest. A period of 26 hours and about 110 miles (176 km) was something I was better able to cope with.

The week before the second attempt my spirits had been rising as a spell of perfect weather set in. Perfect for me means cool and dry with periods of sunshine to lighten the spirit. If I can also have a sky full of those billowing fair weather cumulus clouds sweeping like galleons before a summer breeze then I am transported.

The good weather lasted an hour. By Kinder Gates a light rain began to fall. On Featherbed Moss I mistimed a jump across a black, oozing grough. As both legs sank to the knee I toppled slowly but inexorably backwards into the ditch. With a gentle sigh I extricated myself and continued my solo way across the deserted moors. The rain, equally gentle but also insistent, wept through the moorland night. As a sparse dawn light brought a rank mist rolling over the boggy wastes, I became aware of two disturbing events: one was that the mist seeping over the moors was warm and sticky, settling suffocatingly on the flesh; the other was that my feet, particularly the heels, were feeling sore.

And so, off into a day which constitutes one of the most unpleasant running experiences of my life. The mist transmitted the heat of the invisible sun like a warm, wet blanket. The sweat lay on my skin like an oily film. Encouraged by the warmth and the total lack of air movement swarms of flies rose from the ground and formed a buzzing cloud around my head. And as I ran it felt as if progressive layers of skin were being stripped from my feet. Soon, I imagined, I would be running on the flesh alone. My mind harked back to the sight of Brian Harney's feet when he had quit the Pennine Way. They were red and raw and their texture was like the bark of a tree. It does not matter how tough you think you are, when the pain gets bad enough, you quit.

In the meantime, I kept going. Still running solo but supported by Geoff I passed through Cowling with mixed feelings and headed for the limestone country around Malham. I was more or less on schedule despite frequent stops for foot treatment. I hoped the day might freshen, but it did not. Instead, a light rain settled on the hilltops and below all was dead and still. I began to try harder after Malham and made a little time up over Fountains Fell and Penyghent. However, as soon as I hit the stony track leading to Horton my shoes felt as if they were full of broken glass and in my heart I accepted that I had had it.

At Horton I confronted a dilemma. Len, my friend from the early days, had driven out with Ted to support me on the night section. I could not face telling them I wanted to quit. In any case, I thought that for the sake of our old friendship I owed it to Len to let him stretch his legs on the 15-mile (24 km) section via Dodd Fell to Hawes. We set off in gathering gloom. At first, I found I could just tolerate the pain and so pressed on. This was a mistake. Once the green lane gave way to bouldery track, I was like a cat on hot bricks. The darkness ensured that I was unable to pick a tolerable course and then it began to rain stair-rods.

That handful of miles over to Hawes remains one of the blackest memories in my battle for the Pennine Way record. The agony in my feet confirmed I was finished. In turn this meant that I had lost my concentration and commitment. We went astray several times and, in addition, despite the rain I had to slump down for a 10-minute sleep. From Horton at 92 miles (148 km) to Hawes at 107 miles (171 km) I had scheduled a generous four hours, it took me over six hours on the clock, but there are things time cannot measure – my spirit wandered in a dark eternity. Where was the gentle, effortless running over the sweep and roll of the curling fells? This experience was enough to break my spirit. And it nearly did, but not quite.

The Battle for the Pennine Way

A few years ago I was invited by Denis Weir to give an after-dinner talk on the occasion of the jubilee of the athletic club Horwich RMI. 'What sort of thing shall I talk about, Denis?', I asked. 'Oh just talk about all the amusing things that must have happened to you in the course of your eight attempts on the Pennine Way record'. I thought carefully. 'Denis, there weren't any amusing events!' Given my somewhat manic sense of humour this was a disturbing revelation. With the exception of some rather black humour, like a support runner almost dying of exposure in a May blizzard on the Cheviots, it was nevertheless true.

I am always embarrassed at having to admit to so many attempts at the Pennine Way. It sounds as if I just bashed away at it until it gave in or I got lucky. It was not like that from my perspective. Each attempt was planned with careful attention to detail. My physical preparation during the winter and spring was thorough and always arduous. As the miles slipped by, road, muddy tow-path, boggy moor, snow-crisp fell, so my thoughts would be ever turning to that twisting path down the long Pennine spine. And each time I failed was a time of deep grief for me. It was as if some living cherished entity had just died. Silly perhaps, but I would limp home with my broken dream, nurse it to me for a while then lay it to rest – stillborn again.

There seemed only one way to assuage the sense of loss. That was to plan again, train harder, try harder and pray that next time I would be granted a slot in the weather and that little slice of good fortune so far denied me. I wrestled with the objective and subjective data. Subjectively, I knew from my successful Tan–Cat that I could run better than I ever had on the Pennine Way. Objectively, I could point to the vicious combination of rain, wind and heat which had accompanied all my attempts. What I have now come to realise is that the time spent in training for, planning and attempting the record constituted the most thorough of apprenticeships in ultra fell running. Of course one had to survive it in order to benefit, and I nearly did not.

One thing the Pennine Way was unable to do to me however, was to destroy my faith in myself as a runner. I did eventually get round to accepting that I might well never achieve the record, but I would not accept this until I had adequate grounds. In 1981, for instance, I had a further two attempts at the record. The first took place at the end of May and I 'peaked' my training three weeks earlier. Running and resting a couple of days at a time I had clocked the equivalent of a marathon a day for 14 days, 360 miles (575 km) in a fortnight. It did not make a jot of difference. I practically swam as far as Hawes. Fortunately, I had fallen over a sunken notice board on Black Hill and this caused a sufficiently incapacitating injury for me to retire, if not gracefully, at least justifiably. My next attempt, however, was a very significant one and marked a turning point.

In addition to starting at evening time I now had an additional 'plan'. This was to take a long, 40 to 60 minutes, rest every six or seven hours. The idea was to break into the fatigue spiral by resting and stoking up on food and drink. The snag was that I had to run faster between those rest periods. The attempt took place at the end of August and I realised that with nearly nine hours darkness I would be under pressure to run faster during the daylight hours. Prior to Brian Harney, most runners had taken a break at night, but both my style of running and the keen record demanded running through most of the night. My poor luck

Mike, on the Pennine Way, standing in the River Aire near Malham trying to cool his feet.

continued, the night hours were of an impenetrable blackness making navigation very tricky. To compensate, however, the days were roastingly hot. The
heat bouncing up from the ground began once more to play havoc with my feet,
and the sticky heat made me feel as if I was running through treacle. Climbing
up by Malham Cove I could hear and feel the blood pounding in my head. I
wondered if I was acting sensibly, decided I was not and carried on.

I eventually reached my rest point at Hawes after 28½ hours, 108 miles
(173 km) three hours down on schedule. My support insisted I had a proper rest
and I was too weak to argue. After three hours I was roused and then John
Richardson broke one of the cardinal rules of the game. Being now some five
hours adrift of my schedule I was ready to quit, both to stop wasting my support's
time and to put an end to my suffering. The decision to quit is by strong
tradition the sole prerogative of the gladiator. In a kindly but firm voice John
said that he and Ted had discussed my plight and noted that Hawes had become
something of a sticking point for me. They therefore suggested I go as far as I
could during that day and retire at night-time. They also stated that they were
willing to support me even though they realised I would not complete the route.

The ensuing day was fiercely hot. I trundled on in a daze, my mind fixed on
Dufton at 162 miles (260 km). I tried not to attend to the crowds of sunbathers
along the Tees, licking melting ice-creams or sipping beer – not too difficult
since I was nearly blinded by sweat.

It was as Don Talbot and I left the Tees behind and climbed towards High
Cup Nick in the early evening that the miracle occurred. A deliciously cool
breeze sprang up and almost immediately the layers of fatigue sloughed off. Like
a snake slipping out of its old skin or a phoenix rising from the embers of my
burnt feet I suddenly discovered myself running effortlessly – even up the
inclines. It was ridiculous. I felt fresher and more full of energy than at any time
during the previous 160 miles (256 km). Yet this energy was unfortunately
unable to either regain my lost time or repair my damaged feet and, as agreed
with John and Ted, I retired at Dufton. However, from that moment on I *knew*,
rather than just hoped, that I could break the Pennine Way record.

This knowledge was confirmed in a despairing sort of way on my attempt the
following summer. I was probably running better than at any time previously,
slicing chunks off my scheduled leg times almost effortlessly it seemed. But the
conditions were again too hot for my feet. I noted signs of deterioration almost
with disbelief as early as 50 miles (80 km). By 70 miles (115 km) they had
become extremely painful, but I was running so well I could not bear to think of
retiring. I tried Vaseline, chiropodist's felt, moleskin, even stuck needles in to
try to find blisters. But nothing worked. I endured the pain for a further 100
miles (160 km), then, when I could not endure the extra pressure of moving
from walking to running, I gave up. With the record beckoning and my reserves
quite untapped I had to quit. For the first time I shed tears, tears of despair,
nothing was worth this frustration and heartbreak.

Now, also for the first time, I came to terms with not being able to achieve the
Pennine Way record. I knew in my heart I was capable of covering the Pennine
Way in under three days and this was a tiny consolation. But it now seemed

unlikely my feet would last out long enough for me to actually do so. I made my peace with myself. There must be dreams we have and always cherish, which, despite our best efforts, we will never achieve. I could not see the point of even making another attempt. The pain and the grief, to say nothing of the vast calls on friendship, were such a heavy burden to be set against the chances of success. Such chances, always slim, were now apparently non-existent unless I could find a solution to my foot problems.

Still in the grip of despair I announced that I would not attempt the Pennine Way again. My friends smiled and shook their heads. I was adamant however, it was pointless. There now arose a somewhat paradoxical situation. My friends all thought I would go on attempting the Pennine Way, but I suspect they did not think I could succeed. Whereas I *knew* I could succeed, but believed I would make no more attempts. The resolution of this paradox came about as the result of three interesting factors: John Richardson stating an intention to have a go at the record himself; the discovery of Spenco Second-Skin as a foot treatment; and, later in the same year, a record Colne–Rowsley run.

Colne–Rowsley

Until Ted Courtenay evolved his Tan Hill to Cat and Fiddle walk in 1953, the Colne–Rowsley had been the Rucksack Club's longest walk at around 70 miles (115 km). Since its inception in 1926 it had gained a distinguished reputation as one of the Club's test pieces. The Club has a marvellous record of initiating long, arduous walks of great character. It has also been gifted with members possessing the literary ability to write entertaining accounts of them. I had steeped myself in the history of these walks and often, as I carried on the Club tradition of 'bog-trotting', I could sense the ghosts of those hardy men travelling at my shoulder, their indefatigable but wry humorous spirits sustaining my own. For instance, each time I pass by Marsden village, I recall Frank Kiernan's tale of arriving there in the early hours on his first Colne–Rowsley in 1936. After a large meal in Blake Lea Farm he sat dozing before the fire, praying his companion might have also succumbed to the weakness of the flesh. Alas, with a sigh his friend arose. They stumbled footsore and weary out onto Marsden's cobbled streets with Phil Brockbank's brisk words of advice echoing in Frank's ears 'It is essential to arrive at Marsden in such a condition that after a meal and a rest one feels perfectly fresh.' After sitting in a grough on Black Hill most of the night when their torches failed, they eventually completed the walk. They were exhausted, footsore, had been lost several times and chased over private moors by belligerent game-keepers. Nevertheless, Frank's sense of triumph over adversity comes rollicking down the years.

Like so many other walks evolved in the days of few cars but excellent rail links, the walk starts and finishes at a rail terminal. The one at Colne still survives, but Beeching's axe put paid to the other. It is also a matter of regret that the old cart tracks winding up onto the moors out of the Colne valley have been metalled, but if you are handy with a map, alternative footpaths may be found. Should you attempt this walk, and very few except Rucksackers do, you should aim to do it in one continuous go, or with just a brief pause to allow a couple of night hours to slip by. You should also choose a dry period. This is very much a moorland walk and after 50 miles (80 km) of oozing bog you may well be in no state to enjoy the last easy and picturesque miles. After leaving Colne you will have chance for second thoughts, because beyond the first set of moors (Black Hameldon) the necessity of crossing the Calder Valley will bring you into Todmorden. A great place is 'Yon Tod' and a brew and a bag of chips will set you up for the steady climb back up onto the moors. You should remember that unless you make the traditional detour into Marsden you will have little chance for further indulgence as the route commits itself to high lines from here onwards.

However, the moors are not so empty these days. For 20 miles (32 km) along Blackstone Edge, Windy Hill, Standedge, your route is shared by the more recent Pennine Way. The thought that the sometimes cheerful souls who greet you have 200 miles (320 km) further to travel than you may strengthen your resolve. If you are wise, you will turn aside down the old packhorse track to Marsden, for not only is it a homely village with welcoming pubs, it allows you to neatly avoid Black and White Moss. If you have a sadistic streak you may like to watch the antics of those with large packs trying to cross this vile piece of ground, but do not forget, it will be your turn soon . . .

The other great advantage in visiting Marsden is that you may then utilise the Wessenden valley to approach Black Hill. Furthermore, the summit of this soggy lump my be turned on its left (east) flank as you are now heading for Holme Moss and the lonely guts of the walk. Your route will take you past the transmitter mast near the summit of the Holmfirth road. Should you pass by on a windy, mist-shrouded day, or better still, at night, I defy you not to feel a tug of apprehension as the wind moans sadly through the mast's vaulting cables and invisible superstructure. Maybe it is only sound effects, but when all you see is dank mist wreathing to the murmurings and sighings all around and more particularly high above you, then, perhaps, like me you will hurry past.

Across the Holmfirth road, after a brief battle with the rather token resistance of a few minor bogs and peat hags you will win the relative ease of a winding path-cum-sheeptrod. Following an apparently erratic course this path strengthens its resolution and gains you access to the Swetland and Britland Edges with surprising efficiency. In fact, when I forgot my map and route card on the record attempt I made with Geoff, I discovered that there is only one overall bearing needed. Following this bearing using 'reck'o'th'ee' (reckon of the eye) will bring you just where you need to be. (I will not spoil your fun by disclosing this bearing!) Where you want to be is coming off the moors near the head of the Longdendale Valley road, Saltersbrook.

You are now, so to speak, at the backside of Bleaklow. Your task is to gain the Derwent Watershed line. To do this it is best to first visit the source of the River Etherow. This is not essential but it is a rather charming spot on an otherwise dreary section of moor. After imbibing of its waters (a very unsafe practice a dozen miles further on) a steady climb through foot-tripping heather will bring you to the broad moorland area whose only immediate feature is the faint track of the Watershed route, plus perhaps a few stakes. This is a good place to check your compass, and essential to do so in mist. In some ways this is the best part of the walk. It feels lonely and remote, and it is. The 'path', a fairly recent product of the High Peak Marathon, comes and goes and your reck'o'th'ee will be as much needed as your compass. Eventually, probably just as you are losing patience with the rough tussocky going, a boggy ascent leads you onto Outer Edge. At last a definite point which offers an unbeatable moorland prospect – at least on a good day.

The respite is brief. There follows rough going over to Margery Hill and as you make your way to Abbey Brook the path disappears entirely. You can take the easy option of descending to the Derwent valley and following the reservoir track. This is charming at first, but the flat going quickly becomes incredibly monotonous. I prefer to follow the trods to the west side of Margery Hill which keep the fine valley prospect in view and then enter the shallow valley of the Abbey Brook itself. The going is tricky but your mind is occupied in picking a line, hopping over tributaries or jumping across the stream.

At a sharp elbow in the valley the brook tires of the moor and goes rushing steeply down the hillside only to be swallowed by the Derwent Reservoir. Do not be tempted to follow the short but admittedly impressive clough carved by the brook but continue on your line. After just another couple of tough miles you will be rewarded by gaining Back Tor, one of the striking, elemental gritstone outcrops hereabouts. For me, Back Tor marks the true beginning of the Derwent Edges. From here on, you are very aware that your route lies along an escarpment edge. Notwithstanding a few obligatory bogs, there are now definite paths to carry you to your journey's end. However, before you gain the eastern edges proper you must follow the Derwent Edge to its end, swinging off to the east and crossing the Snake road below Moscar Edge. Since crossing the Longdendale road at Saltersbrook you will have covered 14 miles (23 km), it will seem longer.

But now you gain your reward, a dozen or more miles of superb gritstone edges redolent with a hundred years of climbing and walking history. Ignore Aunt Florrie and Uncle Jack out walking their dog. Forget the chrysalids harnessed to their hang-gliders. They are users of the moorland edges, and good luck to them. But after nearly 60 miles (100 km) of treading the peaty ground, breathing the air of the moors, enduring the mist, the night, the winds of the moors, you have stitched yourself into the fabric of the moors, you *are* the moors.

So tread firmly but go with awareness of the historic ground which you tread. Here is one of the cradles of northern climbing and walking. Mighty men have sported here, strode the edges, clasped the tough and rasping gritstone. Peer down Right and Left Unconquerable as you move onto Stanage; imagine Brown and Whillans, cloth caps and baggy pants, unsurpassed ability. The history makers are still here. As you move across onto Froggatt Edge, that lean figure emerging like a liquid spider from below a repulsive overhang could be Ron Fawcett, maybe completing another 100 Extremes within the span of a single day. Look into the eyes of the climbers sauntering back off the crags at the end of the day. There are those who will never belong, but in some you will get the flicker of recognition of a kindred spirit. Do not despise the Lycra-clad dandies, today's brilliant butterflies who may become tomorrow's Himalayan heroes. Should you be here in the dusk of early evening, with the awareness of the history of these places and with the weariness of the miles blurring the edges of reality you may well hear the calls and cries of long departed climbers. Hemp ropes, Norfolk jackets and the ethic that the leader never falls, for there were no runners in those days. I like to think that when everyone has left, the spirits of departed hill men return to the places they have loved and there sport again. Surely it cannot be that the spirits of those such as Stanley Jeffcoat, that affable giant and archetypal rucksacker who never came back from Flanders, do not return here to regain the peace of the moors, the sport of the crag and the love and laughter of long-ago friends? So tread firmly but with compassion and understanding, you may be treading on hallowed ground.

Although the Edges continue on, dwindling slowly as they follow the Derwent towards its rendezvous with the Trent, the route you follow leaves the Edges rather more swiftly than it gained them. An abrupt right turn beyond Baslow Edge brings you into Baslow itself. Nice houses, but not a place to linger, I think, unless you imitate Geoff and Eric. Towards the end of a hard 90-mile (145 km) moorland circuit and against my stern advice they gobbled down a large ice-cream apiece. Five minutes later Eric parted company with his in the local convenience (I must confess I had a little snigger). Leaving such doubtful pleasures behind, your way now leads across Chatsworth Park, ancient home of the Duke of Devonshire. It stands on your left, palatial or monstrous, impressive or ostentatious, depending on your view. It reminds me of the carcass of a dinosaur being picked over by hordes of day trippers. Perhaps I am unkind, but my eyes did so recently behold a greater glory. If you are tired, the open expanse of the estate will weary you, so follow close by the river. This is the river above whose gathering ground at Swains Greave you strode nearly 30 miles (50 km) ago. Then it was young and active, now it is broad and content, sliding past green banks and the well-tended meadowland. After a weir injects a little life into it you and the river leave Chatsworth, but before doing so look for the spring issuing from the stone wall on your right. In defiance of any drought these clear sparkling waters flood generous and cool into a small stone trough. Drink deeply, if these waters were good enough for the Duke's thoroughbreds, they will do wonders for you! Now Rowsley lies only a couple of miles away. When you get there visit the old (now dry) fountain outside The Peacock. If you are as weary as I was on my first Colne–Rowsley, settle down in the old trough, you will find it wonderfully comfortable. You could try The Peacock, of course, but you had better change your boots first! (It is a bit posh.)

A Record Run

As I mentioned earlier, I had done the Colne–Rowsley twice, one time at the end of summer by myself and the other time in semi-winter conditions with Geoff. Good do's they were, too. I thought it was a route that invited a fast traverse, nor too long, not too hilly, many sweeping vistas and an inviting finish. After our 16-hour traverse I said to Geoff and Ted 'I bet a good man, going well, in the right conditions, could get close to 12½ hours.' 'Pooh, pooh', they said (or words to that effect). Then, at the end of the dry summer of 1981, Denis Weir gave me a ring. Now Denis is a good man, very good. Formerly a top class fell runner, latterly a redoubtable performer at any distance from five (eight) to 100 miles (160 km), he had recently done nearly 130 miles (210 km) in 24 hours in a track race. And the conditions *were* good, in fact the moors were in part closed due to fire risk. Anyway as Denis chirpily explained, he had just done the Colne–Rowsley in 12 hours 35 minutes. I immediately felt vindicated, and perhaps just a little piqued. Well, 12½ hours was too fast for me, so I waved that ambition goodbye.

The following year I spent the two months after my despairing exit from the Pennine Way getting back into some steady fell walking and a little climbing. Then, for no good reason, at the end of July I felt I wanted to have a go at Denis's Colne–Rowsley record. I had a couple of weeks trying to get used to steady running again but my log-book reveals very lack-lustre performances. I decided to take a couple of days complete rest and trust to the superb condition I had been in for the Pennine Way attempt. For such a relatively short course as the Colne–Rowsley it is best to be in sharp condition, I was not, but somehow I really wanted to do this run, and do it well.

Sticking with his belief that 12½ hours was too fast to complete the Colne–Rowsley Geoff decided he would support me at road crossings rather than run with me. I left Colne railway station at 8.00 a.m. on a fine, sunny day with a cool wind holding temperatures safely in check. I entered immediately into a real cut and thrust battle with my schedule. Not being optimistic about bettering Denis's time my schedule gave only a 10-minute improvement on his record. I found I was coming into each support point a couple of minutes up but by the time I had had a drink I had lost them again. Although I only took a total of eight stops at an average of 3.5 minutes per stop, I could not seem to break through my schedule to gain some time in hand. Eventually, on the section over to Standedge I lost patience and throwing caution to the winds bought myself a 10-minute 'cushion.' Not only that, but when I had dug down I could feel there were reserves in hand.

This became the pattern of the day, whenever I ran as I felt I should, I maintained schedule. Whenever I wanted to gain a few precious minutes, I had to dip into those reserves. The reserves were there all right, but they had to be prised out of aching muscles and straining lungs. Then after Black and White Moss (mercifully dry) I found I had overestimated the severity of the rough leg over Black Hill to Holme Moss. Instead of 55 minutes it took just 43, another crop of minutes in the bag, and now I 'only' had to hang on for another 37 miles (60 km) and I would have the record. ('Hmm', I thought, 'that's more than half the distance still left!')

In my haste I lost the trods over the Britland Edges and went galumphing over the tussocks. Little time lost and feeling strong I homed in on Saltersbrook where Geoff was waiting to hand me over to Eric Mitchell for the rest of the journey. Eric had also brought a running friend, Pat Grundy. I did not particularly need company or a pacer but I did want someone to carry some water for me over this long, dry crux of the route. The watershed section over Outer Edge, Margery Hill, Back Tor and the Derwent Edges to Moscar is a rough and unbroken 14 miles (23 km). If I had miscalculated my schedule or if I had drained too many of my reserves then my ambitions would be in tatters by the time I had reached Moscar and the Snake road.

In fact, with the moors dry underfoot this was a lovely section to run. I soon finished the water, but it enabled me to reach the first good stream just above Cut-Throat Bridge. I sustained my effort across the Derwent Edges and down to the Snake road and cut five minutes off my scheduled time, but as I jogged woodenly up the road I felt shattered. I collapsed onto Eric's deck-chair and told him, very unhelpfully, that I did not know what I wanted. Wise and experienced, Eric thrust forward a bottle containing Complan, a composite 'complete' food in liquid form designed for invalids(!). 'Here', quoth Eric, 'double strength.' 'But, Eric, I can't manage that.' 'Gerrit down!', growled Eric. I gorrit down, all of it. It was great. I lurched athletically out of the deck-chair. 'See you at Fox House, Eric.' With a little smile Eric folded his deck-chair.

I was now in something of a dilemma. Not for the first time I found myself a victim of my ambition. With just 17 miles (27 km) remaining I had only to stick to my schedule to be a handsome 20 minutes inside the record. How nice to just cruise those last few miles, I thought. No good! An insistent voice was whispering 'Wimp, you're copping out' and 'You might be able to do 12 hours if you try.' I had been wondering when that bloody demon would stick his head up. In vain I pointed out that even my schedule times were optimistic. Nothing would satisfy him but I should continue to sweat blood. Tentatively, I tried an uphill jog, excruciating, but possible!

Chasing the minutes past the departing Stanage climbers; slowly up and stiff-legged down Carl Wark and Higger Tor, Stone Age hill forts; silly visions of woad-spattered figures defying the legions, did they too dodge among these boulders? A two-minute drink stop at Fox House and off with a lad called Alex, out for his trot along the Edges and interested in what I am doing. What he does not realise is my brain is scrambled and I have the greatest difficulty forming coherent sentences. My pride will not allow me to admit this, however, nor will it permit me to tell him he is running too bloody fast. Hey I have run 60 miles (100 km), slow down you bugger! No, just gasp nonchalantly along and try not to collapse at his feet. Thank God! He has disappeared over to Birchens and I can go at my own pace down to Baslow. Amazing! I have taken 10 minutes off the scheduled time for that leg – well done Alex!

Now only the flat meadows of Chatsworth Park before the run in to Rowsley. Pat is joining me for these last four miles (6 km) and I am glad because over the broad meadows one seems to be hardly moving. A chat will help the miles pass more quickly. The trouble is, Pat seems to think it appropriate to hold a conversation from five yards ahead of me. No sooner do I get to his shoulder than he is off again. Does the silly sod not realise the inherently difficult nature of carrying on an intelligent conversation across a five-yard gap when you are at the end of 70 miles (115 km) of eyeball-popping effort and your legs are like a pair of bent Woodbines? Obviously not. If only I can find the strength I will screw his wotsits off on the final run-in along the lane. Aha, got him! He thought he could stop when we reached the A6, he does not realise my penchant for The Peacock's horse-trough another 200 yards (180 m) on. What a finish! Zoom up in a lather of sweat and peer at my watch. Wow! Eleven hours, 44 minutes, 30 seconds, perhaps the demon got it right for once. 'Pat, there is something I need to say about accompanying a tired runner.' Pat grins 'It was Eric's idea. He said to keep just in front of you and never let you quite catch up.' Well, the crafty old bugger. But perhaps Eric got it right too. Now, where is Denis's phone number? I spent the drive home practising a modest nonchalance . . . 'Just had a spin down the old Colne–Rowsley. Lovely conditions, managed to pip your record, yes . . . a little under 12 hours, actually.' I picked up the telephone. Oh, sod it. 'Denis, I've had a great run. I don't know how, but I've done the Colne–Rowsley in under 12 hours!'

Pennine Way 1983: Final Tribulations

Some time after my frustrating defeats in 1982 John Richardson rather surprised me by announcing that as I had stated my intentions of retiring from this particular battle, he would have a go himself. At first I wondered whether he was serious, but John is not the sort of person who makes idle remarks. In many respects he shares the same attributes as Geoff, that is, a slow steady strength that seems to wax rather than wane with distance, a resistance to injury and enormous power uphill and over heavy ground. Naturally, I vowed my intention to assist John in every way possible. After all, few knew the route better than I and more than one aspirant has come to grief with faulty route-finding on night sections. Unfortunately, as I envisaged myself striving valiantly at John's side for mile after wearisome mile, the question of just how long I could run alongside occurred to me. In the twinkle of a demon's eye my concept of lengthy running support had changed to the concept of a two-man record attempt. My support I now envisaged as keeping John entertained with a stream of witticisms and possibly giving him a leg up over the stiles. In fact, had it been anyone other than John, with the possible exception of Geoff, I would never have entertained the thought of a two-man attempt. Two runners impose large extra burdens on the support crew. There is also the disparity in abilities. Quite a few attempts by pairs have under-achieved due to one member fading and the other being unwilling to press on and abandon his friend. However, John and I had shared many an epic walk and run in the most exiguous circumstances. I felt our close personal relationship would enhance our ability to meet the considerable psychological challenges of the undertaking. I also harboured the hope that my miserable luck with the weather would change with John as my talisman.

John was enamoured of the idea of 'running home', that is doing the Pennine Way north to south. We therefore drove to Coldstream on Thursday 27 May to enjoy the unaccustomed luxury of a bed and breakfast. It was a beautiful day, high fluffy clouds rolling round an otherwise blue sky, the most perfect of English spring days. As we strolled round the village on a mild and tranquil evening there was only one dark cloud anywhere. Invisible to everyone else, this cloud was floating gloomily above my head. In Albion nothing is more perfidious than the weather. The rest of the team chided me indulgently (and behind my back probably confided 'Poor sod, his nerve's gone!').

The next morning the sky was rather grey with a light drizzle that might stop . . . or might not. We set off on the undulating 10-mile (16 km) climb to Cheviot summit with Pat Grundy as our running support. The wind began to increase as we ascended and the drizzle made up its mind and became rain; heavy rain; then cold, heavy rain. Below the Schil we dived into the old railway cabin and crammed on all our spare gear. Stepping outside we observed with interest that the rain had stopped, it was now snowing; heavy and wet. Despite the wetness, the wind was sufficiently strong to plaster a layer of snow to our clothing.

At the corner of the border fence, in order to save Pat the worst excesses of the bogs around Cheviot summit, we advised him to follow the fence line while we visited the trig point. Going, at times, up to the thighs in icy water we 'collected' the summit and set off back to the fence and Pat. He had not gone far. Being unfamiliar with the route he had been concerned about getting off line without us. Consequently, when we caught him up he was rather chilly. Normally, we would all soon have warmed up, but despite going as hard as we could we were fighting a battle with possibly the worst conditions the British weather can impose, a wet blizzard, and we were losing the battle. At one stage I stepped into a bog which swallowed me up to the very vitals! Sinking into the ooze beneath the water I desperately grabbed a wobbly peat hag and dragged myself free of the sucking bog devils. For a time I was too shocked to continue the monologue of vile imprecations with which I had been warming myself. Of greater concern was the fact that Pat was having problems keeping up with us. Plucky man that he is, he kept on reassuring us he was OK and under the twin lash of schedule demands and the griping cold John and I pressed on.

Eventually the distance between us and Pat grew, so that for longer periods we lost sight of each other. The Cheviots are broad and featureless, Pat had never been over them before, he was cold, getting colder and slower. My mind flashed back to the runner who had died of exposure on Ingleborough during a Three Peaks race. After waiting for several minutes above the Roman Camps at Chew Green I told John he should press on while I went back to look for Pat. I did not have too far to go, he came slowly towards me still protesting he was OK, really! My hope now was that Dave Crutch, our support driver, had guessed our plight and had attempted to drive up the military road to below the Roman Camps. If he had he could look after Pat, but even if not, I told Pat he must follow the road back down to the valley and safety. Good old Dave had driven out. He had even walked half a mile from the road with flasks for us, but being unsure of our whereabouts and lashed by the storm had retired to the car again. Rather more far gone than I suspect he realised, Pat found Dave, who later unconsciously amused us with his account of the incident. Dave has a slight stammer and recalling the drama of the moment told us 'He got into the car and turned b'b'b'b'blue!!'

Tough and experienced, Pat made a swift recovery and was able to accompany us on further stretches. It was quite obvious, however, that unless the weather improved dramatically we might as well go home. Lower down, the snow ceased but the rain continued. In order to give it time to improve we decided not to run through the first night, but have a couple of hours sleep at Hadrian's Wall (70 miles/115 km). With John's usual, commendable efficiency he was stretched out in his sleeping bag, eyes peacefully closed within minutes. Unfortunately, this simply meant he had to endure my elbows, knees and feet as I performed my usual ritual of getting disorganised for sleep.

Next morning was better, but continuing wet. The support was having problems preparing nourishing food and we were getting by on large amounts of tea and biscuits. This was OK for me, but John has something of an aversion to tea administered ad lib. After a few hours the early morning quiet was disturbed by loud honkings as John was violently sick all over Wain Rigg. Ian Grant, accompanying us, was touchingly concerned at this performance. I had observed it many times before, notably during the High Peak Marathon races, and had a rather more callous response. Indeed, as I expected, John picked up very well after this episode.

The conditions continued to be abysmal. By now the ground was running with water, paths were like streams and the bogs were replete. At Alston (90 miles/145 km) we were informed that the forecast was for the bad weather to continue. We agreed it was senseless to carry on, but I suggested that we at least go over Cross Fell to obtain the scant satisfaction of completing 100 miles (160 km). This was not a soft undertaking. Water was pouring off the summit plateau in white frothing cascades and a biting wind out of the east mingled mist and rain. At Dufton there was no problem adhering to our decision to quit. For some reason, John has never expressed a further interest in running the Pennine Way.

I was reluctant to let the summer pass by without trying to cash in on the fitness so painfully acquired during the preceding winter and spring. I spent many happy and hard hours in the hills. It turned out to be a good summer after that unpropitious start and I became very hill-fit. Sense dictated that I should have a go at something with large amounts of up and down in it. I had long cherished an ambition to complete a continuous round of all the 2,500 ft (750 m) summits in the Lake District, something John, Geoff and Ted had achieved and which I had been promising to attempt with Don Talbot for years. Perhaps sense plays a relatively minor role in my life, for, instead of the Lakes 2,500 ft (750 m) summits, I flung myself back onto the Pennine Way.

The combined temptation of good conditions and what I imagined was my own level of preparation was too much. Furthermore, I had had a very generous offer of help from a friend and colleague, Inken Blunk. Already a lover of the hills, Inken had demonstrated a natural aptitude for endurance performance which I encouraged her to develop. I introduced her to tough club meets and after she had skipped her way through a few of these, I thought I noticed a few members blanching and muttering in their beards whenever she appeared. Inken had offered to do car support for me during the first night and most of the second day – the attempt was on.

Being holiday season, other support was a bit thin on the ground. However, for the first time, I had the help of my eldest son, Mark. When I first attempted the Pennine Way Mark was a spindly youth of 14, now, at 18, he was much more the part, a fine runner with natural endurance. As Mark could not drive, Eric had agreed to cover the first 50 miles (80 km) and Mark joined me on selected sections. At Hardraw my support would ring Ted to bring him out if the attempt was still on.

Conditions were very dry and I had problems with dust flurries in the stray winds. From the start I never went well. The heat and dust made conditions uncomfortable, but that was not the main problem. Perhaps there was something wrong with the body chemistry or perhaps my immediate preparation had been incorrect. The ground was so dry it was like running on concrete in places. Somehow, my legs would not seem to adapt and instead of settling into a comfortable rhythm they began to get stiffer and stiffer. We all have our strengths and weaknesses. While I never seem to lack for sheer strength, I have a tendency for stiffness and cramp. The further I went, the stiffer I got.

In contrast to the day, it was a balmy, sweet-scented night. Unfortunately, the slower pace did nothing to alleviate my stiffness and after any pause or walking section I found it difficult to start running again. The long section between Horton and Hawes was once more the place for unpleasant decision making. I deferred my decision until I began to descend Cam Fell. Here I observed that the stiffness had become so incapacitating I was barely able to overtake brisk walkers. I hobbled across the meadows to Hardraw and announced it was necessary to inform Ted he would not, after all, be required. Within an hour of stopping my knees became swollen and my legs locked solid. A deep depression entered my soul and a bitter sense of shame. The Pennine Way had at last given me a fair chance and I had completely failed, for the seventh time.

chapter four

THE WINNING OF THE PENNINE WAY

The wracking stiffness passed off within a couple of days, the bitterness burned on. I looked around for a scapegoat. What could I blame? I decided that it was either just one of those things, an off day perhaps; or I was not fit enough; or, though fit, had prepared wrongly. An 'off day' was possible but placed me in no position to remedy a future occurrence. I did not know what 'fit enough' was, but I was certainly hill fit. That left the last option. My log revealed plenty of good hill days, but the Pennine Way had been like concrete and I had done nothing on hard ground. That was it! With all my knowledge and experience I had prepared like a novice! The more I thought about it, the more disgusted I became with myself. It was not the hard ground that had stopped me, it was my failure to prepare for it.

After three days' rest I began to train with an anger and aggression I had never before experienced. I knew my body should be treated gently after just covering over 100 miles (160 km), but I had to expunge the feelings of humiliation and shame that followed my critique. For three weeks I lashed myself round my training routes, always pushing, always running at the 'hard limit'. After this time, inevitably, a great physical weariness began to engulf me. But by now, I had done penance for my sins. I had also reaffirmed my belief in myself, and I had made myself a promise that I would never quit my struggle for the Pennine Way until old age had blasted my vigour or arthritis had locked me into a wheelchair, and maybe not even then. At one and the same time I both avowed my implacable resolution never to quit trying, while I freely accepted I might still go to my grave with my dream unfulfilled.

I settled into a more sensible training pattern. I had begun to experience increasing stiffness in my knees. They had never been the same since I broke my leg playing basketball in 1973. Since then the thousands of miles in all kinds of weather conditions had encouraged the incursions of 'Old Arthur', as John, also a sufferer, terms arthritis. So I kept my road mileage to a maximum of 80 (130 km) per week but at weekends always had a long run or walk. I reserved one day, usually Saturday, for 'rest'. On this day I would take my younger children for a walk and my third son, Gerard, for a gentle run over the moors, introducing him to my favourite footpaths and haunts.

Despite my reservations about doing the Derwent Watersheds race every year,

Following in father's footsteps. Mike plus his children on the moors.

the start of March again saw me alongside John, Geoff and Denis for my eleventh successive event. Now competing as 'veterans' we finished second overall and won the Veterans Prize, a magnificent sculpture by John of a scene from the event. My training was paying off, I had gone well and recovery was swift. Two weeks later I did the 'Haworth Hobble' with John. This is a 33-mile (53 km) event over the bleak Brontë moors around Haworth. The next day I ran the local 'Otter Half Marathon' in 1 hour 21 minutes, starting tired but getting better. My satisfaction was mitigated by my son Mark (aged 19) finishing over a minute ahead of me. After a small mental adjustment, however, I decided the moral victory was mine!

By the end of March I was ready to commence the 'long' hard stuff. In retrospect this was one of the most satisfying and enjoyable periods of training in my career. It started with an unexpected treat in the form of a snowy out-and-back circuit of the Welsh 3,000 ft (900 m) peaks. This was largely thanks to Inken who being brought up in Germany, barely knew the Welsh hills. I thought the 3,000s would be a fair introduction. I was not expecting the layers of both old and new snow plastering the higher ground. Wearing fell running shoes and carrying ice-axes we set off at first light on a fine frosty morning. The traverse of the snow-encrusted ridges connecting Snowdon with Crib-Goch provided an enormously entertaining challenge. Descending the steep 'Italian' (north) ridge of Crib-Goch I tied onto Inken with a rope – much to her disgust. Even without snow and ice, however, Crib-Goch is notoriously unforgiving to the misplaced step. I was ready to effect the classic technique of arresting someone falling off one side of a ridge by jumping off the opposite side. Thankfully the technique remained theoretical.

The glare of the sun on new snow over the Glyders was almost unbearable and I began to have thoughts about snow-blindness. I need not have worried, approaching the Ogwen valley over humpbacked Tryfan we could see streamers of cloud sailing across the previously immaculate blue. Over the Carneddau the light was failing, temperatures had risen and the snow was around our knees in places. I thought I began to detect the slightest flagging of Inken's pace at times, but I was not sure. On the return leg back over the Devil's Kitchen to our base in Llanberis it was not just Inken who was flagging! Some time around midnight we got back to the car. What a fabulous, tiring and wonderful day, and what a way to achieve your first traverse of the Welsh 3,000 ft (900 m) peaks.

I caught a cold after this which actually worked in my favour. Instead of going out on exhausting 50 mile (80 km) runs I had four relatively easy days of about 30 miles (50 km), just moving steadily. In the past I had driven myself as hard as possible and usually suffered some muscular problem or other. Now, the gentler approach provided a more stable base from which to stretch myself further. After a couple of days rest I commenced a pattern of two days covering around 45 to 50 miles (72 to 80 km) each, two days rest, then two days again of 45 to 50 miles. For once spring was kind, and my runs carried me into all parts of the White and Dark Peak in Derbyshire. As I ran I observed the return of the birds to the high moors and I saw the fresh new greens begin to swell from the lower valleys and dells and wash up and out onto the hills. I watched my native moors bend to new forms as the curving sun shaped and sculpted them on its journey across the sky. I rose to the pale spring mists and guided my sleepy first steps over the wet grass. A day of miles later the sun threw its glow above the quiet moors and I ran through dusk to home and rest.

These were truly days filled with love: of nature, of health and of life. As I ran I could feel the ebb and flow of my own life force. In the long, alone hours absorbing the immense but subtle power of burgeoning Nature I could sense the shared pulse. Again and again, as my body tired my spirit was sustained. When I finished this phase of my training I experienced a deep contentment. I was now physically and spiritually ready to undertake the most difficult part of my programme. A regime which I had attempted before but which I had never quite been able to accomplish.

I had long thought that it would be necessary to sustain consecutive days of around 60 miles (100 km) if I hoped to run the Pennine Way in under three days. For no particular reason it had become a symbol, signifying both sufficient fitness and adequate ability. To cover 60 miles (100 km) of hilly terrain in around 12 or 14 hours one must be 'fit', but, more importantly, the ability to repeat the run the next day requires that one has the resilience to absorb the miles without breaking down. My plan was to do two days of 60 miles (100 km), have a day's rest and then complete another two days of 60 miles (100 km). I intended to implement this along the Pennine Way, both to familiarise myself with every twist and turn and because specific training is best. Having rarely had success in involving my friends in joining my Pennine Way training I was delighted when Inken offered to drive a car so that instead of going out and back I could just keep going till my mileage was covered. Not only this, but she would meet me every 15 or 20 miles (24 or 32 km) so I could get a decent feed. Her 'reward' was that she would see large stretches of countryside that were totally new to her and could indeed mount an expedition of her own on my rest day.

It went perfectly. Well, to be honest, it was physically as knackering as I thought it would be! However, the first day was the hardest, after this I slotted into an economical if tiring rhythm. At the end of the fifth day when Inken and I had finished an out and back traverse of the Cheviots, I stood in a stream washing off and contemplating the best week's training I had ever had. I was tired, certainly, but I felt I could have gone on with that regime indefinitely. In that, I now believe, I was in error.

My training plan was not yet complete. I had the background now, but for a continuous 270 miles (435 km) traverse I felt I needed to complete an effort occupying a full 24 hours. Running all day is one thing, but running on into and through the night poses additional hardships. I had tried 100 mile (160 km) training circuits in the past and found motivation a problem. I needed something to 'go' at. I decided my Tan Hill–Cat and Fiddle record of 32 hours 20 minutes looked rather pedestrian now. A run of 120 miles (195 km) on hard but familiar moorland would do very well, I thought.

Now there was just one problem. I would need about three weeks recuperation after a hard 100 mile (160 km) run, so that fixed my proposed Tan–Cat for the weekend of 6/7 May at the latest. The problem was that I should then have had

*Mike setting off
from Tan Hill.*

only one week's rest since my 240 miles (385 km) in five days on the Pennine Way. Ordinarily, this was nowhere near adequate, but I remembered how relaxed I had felt at the end of training. I decided to go ahead with my plan.

The Tan–Cat strikes back

The Tan–Cat is a tough route. I had no right to treat it in so cavalier a fashion. But I was a different runner from he who had set out with such trepidation six years ago. I had now been over the 100 mile (160 km) mark at least a dozen times and twice over 150 miles (240 km). Perhaps it was the memory of those hard miles that gave me a very serious air as I set off from Tan Hill supported by John Beatty and Rob Ferguson.

Initially, I moved effortlessly and freely. Unfortunately, this is not usually a good sign. Perhaps, paradoxically, a sluggish start often indicates the gradual retrieval of those reserves of strength which only result from a good rest. Going over Great Whernside at only 30 miles (50 km) the tendons behind my knees began to feel stiff and sore. At Grassington with only 36 miles (58 km) completed I knew my legs were 'running on empty'. There was no fuel in them, they felt like wooden planks. All my running body/mind knew beyond doubt that my legs were finished, I had simply not had sufficient recovery time. But now a dilemma; I needed a long run before the Pennine Way, if I did not take this chance there would be no other. Yet the thought of another 80 miles (130 km) on these empty legs filled me with dismay. Eventually, I decided to 'come off' the pace a little, but keep going and treat it as an exercise in will-power. Well, it certainly became that. I could remember no other run when each stride seemed to call for a separate act of will.

Early breakfast in Todmorden. Rob Ferguson on support duty on the Tan–Cat.

WILD TRAILS TO FAR HORIZONS

The miles dragged by, each one occupying an eternity of time and space. Only John and Rob's wonderful cheer kept me clear of despair. I could now no longer run for myself, I had lost all contact with the route, but somehow I began to attach my spirit to theirs. I ran through them and for them. John ran 50 miles (80 km) with me and Rob 40 (64 km). Earlier, John Richardson had guided me over Great Whernside and his home ground around Cowling. Without these friends I would truly have been a lost soul travelling in desolation. This image was heightened rather horribly as we moved onto the moors beyond Todmorden. After a very dry spell the moors had ignited and we began to run through rolling banks of choking smoke. At first I held my breath, but the fires became too extensive and we staggered along, half-blind and half-suffocated, while flames licked around our feet. The fires died out by Black Hill and I could focus my full attention on finishing the route. There comes a time when your destination is only a couple of dozen miles away but if you are desperately tired this can be a terrible time. You can think of nothing other than finishing but there are hours still to go, and you are weak. So it was now.

At last, Combs Moss, my 'home' moor and the Cat and Fiddle in sight. A final indignity: I climbed painfully to the top of a shaky drystone wall, it was high and my legs were so painful and stiff I just could not get down the other side. 'John,' I croaked 'I'm stuck!' An amused but sympathetic smile lit his face, then he came back and gently lifted me down. At the last road crossing two of my sons, Gerard and Mark, were waiting to run in with me. After 24 hours of pain and effort it was, for me, an emotional moment. We ran the last few miles together, and as the Cat and Fiddle appeared around the corner I picked up my tired legs once more for that final flourish.

No tears of triumph this time, just total relief at finishing. A new record certainly, and at 29 hours 11 minutes over three hours better than the old one. John and Rob were delighted and for their sakes I tried to look pleased, but I was not, I had hoped for better. I kept my mouth shut, however, and made a mental note to renew the battle at some later date.

Thanks probably to my good condition the hammering I had just given myself resulted in no injuries, only an exquisite stiffness. However, once I had recovered the sleep loss I began to realise that the tremendous effort which my mind had wrung from my body was going to have to be paid for, and it was to be paid in a coin I was not used to expending. The week following the record I experienced a weariness which was not only physically crushing, but one which invaded my mind and, worst of all, my spirit. Perhaps for the first time ever, I felt spiritually weak and impoverished. I could find relief and comfort in nothing. Neither my music, books nor writing. I did not want the company of my friends and I could make no plans for the future. I waited with more despair than hope for the shadow to pass. Then, a week later, I ran round the park for the first time since the record. I felt like one emerging from a dark tunnel, the grass was soft and green, the sun was warm, somewhere a bird sang and at last my spirit stirred to the sound. I was going to run again. I was going to run through days and nights. I was going to run the Pennine Way, all of it.

The Pennine Way Record

The Nag's Head, Edale. Time: five minutes before 11.00 a.m. Weather: fine and sunny, a breeze and some cloud. Pulse: 90. Why must they play sentimental music as I wait for the radio time signal? Tears are for the finish, win or lose. I feel like an emotional time bomb. So many times have I stood at the bottom of this 270 mile (435 km) ladder, nerves twanging, stomach churning. So many hard miles, so many defeats, so much anguish. Please let me run well this time.

There goes the time signal. Touch the pub and go! Along the lane, down the steps, over the bridge, hell! Here's a family struggling across it. 'Excuse me, but I've only got three days to get to Kirk Yetholm.' No, keep quiet, you can afford five seconds. The meadows; run a bit, walk a bit. Now, at last, the symbolic 'Boundary of Open Country' sign. I turn to Inken who has elected to cover this first mile with me, give her a kiss, wave goodbye to her and Edale, and embrace the moors.

These early miles are awful. The animal instinct is screaming for me to hurry but the running brain, developed and honed by 30 years of running and racing, begins to exert an iron control. There will be no rash steps, no wasted effort. Each drop of energy will be carefully measured and skilfully applied. Now, start by monitoring the body. Don't want to feel terrific at first, best a bit sluggish, give the strength time to come through. Not bad, all systems feel OK. Careful, economical foot placement up rocky Grindsbrook. Ah! The plateau. How I love Kinder, its warm familiarity soothes my still jangling nerves. So clearly I remember my first ever run over these moors from Ian Watson's farm. Gosh! Twenty-six years ago. Leave reminiscing. Get back to pace judgement, strictly no uphill running – yet. Just inside the hour at Kinder Gates – good. Across Featherbed Moss, dry until the end where there are endless wet ditches. Steady, just step across, don't jump. Hell! I'm going to be late at the Snake road. I am too, all of five seconds. Calm down you fool!

Over Bleaklow I continued on alone. I wanted these early miles by myself so that I could deal with the turmoil I knew was inevitable at the start. I did not want anyone trying to 'take my mind off' this challenge of early nerves. It was my show, I had to impose control from the start. No one could get inside my mind and do it for me, nor would I have let them had it been possible. It was all my responsibility; the navigation, the night hours, when and what to eat, the speed of each step, the pain when it should come, for all these things I had to have full responsibility. But at the end, if this time there is to be an end, then the joy will be shared, I have the greatest need to share that. Keep the pain, share the joy. Someone close recently said that was wrong; is it? Perhaps it is not even possible.

After recent spring showers, Bleaklow was unexpectedly wearing a mantle of fresh greens. Almost incongruous it was, like a grouchy old curmudgeon in holiday attire. Hern Stones and Wain Stones slipped by like old friends and, soon, the magnificently cleaving Torside Clough opened beneath my feet. I could sense in my positive response to the moors, a spiritual well-being. Slowly I began to come to terms with my nerves.

At the road crossing I meet my support team. Inken and Mark saw me off at Edale and then picked up Ted Dance. Mark is to be my main running support all next day so for today Inken and Ted will share the running and driving between them. Now I've completed 14 miles (22 km) I feel ready to talk. Unfortunately for Inken, it's all about pace and schedule but I must get it out of my system. Gradually the conversation becomes more relaxed and interesting; so relaxed that I lose six minutes over Black Hill to Standedge. Never mind, here's Ted eager to stretch his legs and indulge in one of his favourite pastimes; contentious debate. On this occasion he exasperates me with a presentation of his case for runners attempting the Pennine Way relay record needing rules aimed at protecting them from their possible follies. I secretly wish someone would protect me from mine! However, Ted's company is never less than stimulating and I still regard him with affection as my friend and mentor.

Alternating two such good conversationalists as Ted and Inken helps these early jittery miles to slip by enjoyably, even, at times, almost unnoticed. The apprehension and anxiety provoked by an undertaking as serious as this does not dissipate immediately the running begins. With an event of this length, it may take up to 100 miles (160 km) before the body begins to reveal its secrets. Will the muscles renege on their careful preparation? Will the feet decide to opt out of the endeavour? Sitting at the back of my mind has been the ominous memory of that physically and spiritually barren week after my Tan–Cat record, that could well turn out to be the most Pyrrhic of victories. Have the three and a half weeks since then been sufficient to restore my usually buoyant energy? Too late to withdraw now. With all the battle plans drawn up and a whole group of friends primed to slot into special support roles over the next three days I am utterly committed. And to what am I committed? I am committed to covering the 270 miles (435 km) to Kirk Yetholm in three days or less. To that end I am dedicating all the strength and determination I possess. And if I should be heading for failure I shall only quit when that strength and determination has carried me as far as I can endure. When the strength begins to fail, the spirit will sustain me, if the spirit can endure no longer I will quit, but only this attempt. Until the fire in the belly is extinguished I shall not willingly hand on this particular torch to any other hand. Yes, it is as well I have friends to lighten the miles, the intensity of concentration can swing too easily into oppressive introspection.

With Ted, convoluted disputation. With Inken, the delight of revealing the many charming and often unexpectedly beautiful places along the Way. Bleak moorland predominates over the first 60 miles (100 km) of the route but every so often one dips into a softer valley or wooded dell. A scattering of late primroses or bluebells will catch the eye, their carefree charm enhanced by the stern, almost industrially grim, moors and by my own hard resolution. When I am through with this I will return and wander timelessly through these dells and sit and stare for ever across the stretching hills. But for now, share the unobtrusive beauty of my life-blood moors; the ever-surging spring of purest water that spills through the stone trough below sombre Stoodley Pike; neat cottages clinging in precarious Alpine fashion to the steep Calder Valley; massive stone footbridge over Colden Water in its miniature verdant clough; High Withens, austere embodiment of Brontë's genius, mute and gaunt, staring sightlessly over these 'Wuthering Heights'.

By now I had covered over 50 miles (80 km) in around 10 hours. Running into a spring twilight with Ted I started to mentally prepare for the coming night section. The moors were assuming the quiet of the night as, in the gathering gloom, Ted and I dropped off Ickornshaw Moor and into the village of Cowling. Here, I was very cheered and touched to discover that John Richardson and Dave Crutch had driven from home with most of their respective families to wish me luck. I experienced a great uplift of the spirit and much good natured badinage was exchanged. At this point Ted was to return home, while Inken and Mark retired for a rest. Although I had some support arranged for the whole route, it would not be present in force until Dufton at 160 miles (256 km). I had therefore elected to go through the first night alone, relying on John to drive round and meet me at two road points.

Taking up a small rucksack containing extra food and clothing I set off through the village, words of encouragement from my friends still sounding in my ears. How fortunate I am, a perfect May night. There are stars overhead, soft grass beneath my feet, the evocative scents of spring, hedgerow rustlings of small, wild things. I am a solitary traveller and my journey will be long but it has truly begun. My earlier nerves have changed to muted excitement and I am at peace under the night sky.

My scheduled night pace is little more than brisk walking. However, the slight stiffness after my stop at Cowling soon eased and I began to jog suitable stretches. John was due to meet me at Gargrave over three hours beyond Cowling. Gargrave formed an important point on my mental checklist. Reaching it would mean that I had lopped off the odd 70 miles (115 km) and could begin nibbling away at the remaining 200 miles (320 km). As I started the pleasant field pasture approach to Gargrave I realised I would arrive there 20 minutes ahead of my schedule. I guessed if John had gone home for a rest he may well have judged his margins rather finely. At the old bus shelter I was not too surprised to find no sign of him. I resisted the temptation to stretch out on the wooden bench to await his arrival. Instead, I visited the very conveniently placed convenience and scratched a cryptic message on the flagstones. I had no qualms about pressing on to Malham another seven miles away. The happy confidence I had in my support team translated in John's case, to complete trust.

On then towards the Aire valley, munching some marzipan. It is a pity I cannot see the wild flowers I know are here but the smells are fresh and the grass long and cool beneath my grateful feet. At 3.15 a.m. the wink of John's torch flickers through the light which precedes dawn and I flash mine in reply. It is rather too early to enjoy much breakfast but shortly before 4.00 a.m. Dave Crutch delivers Mark and we set off on what will be a long, long day. This day is the crux of the whole enterprise. Starting in Malham at 77 miles (123 km) it will end 85 miles (136 km) later in Dufton at about 1.30 a.m. Far enough now to experience real fatigue but too soon to even begin to think of finishing. I try to draw some comfort from that phrase of Churchill's, 'This is not the end, it is not even the beginning of the end. But it *is* the end of the beginning.' Strangely, it provides no comfort whatever! Furthermore I feel rather apprehensive about the next three sections over to Horton. I've had some very bad times on them in the past and early morning is my time of lowest running ebb.

Concentrating very hard and feeling anxious, I manage to carve a few minutes from my schedule over Fountains Fell. Approaching Penyghent therefore, I feel most aggrieved when John and Dave ask what they should get ready for me. I tell them rudely that having just screwed myself to gain those few minutes I'm not prepared to hang around waiting for them to get organised. After this little outburst I pressed on, feeling a touch embarrassed. I realised however, that John knew me too well to take much notice of my tantrum.

Penyghent is hard and steep but it is my experience that the uphill does no real damage. Frequently, the change of pace acts as a rest and can be a welcome break from running. For once I ran into Horton with my feet in fair shape and, perhaps because of this, in good heart. I was now ready for that substantial breakfast which John provided so efficiently I was away again with a two-minute saving (surprise, surprise!). The next leg is a long one; 16 miles (26 km) across the side of Dodd Fell and through Hawes to Hardraw. I'm pleased to have Mark for company again and at 7.30 a.m. 30 minutes up on my schedule, we set off on the three-hour leg.

Near Kidhow Gate and 22¼ hours after leaving Edale we pass the 100 mile (160 km) point. I mention this to Mark and am relieved he doesn't say 'Good show, only 170 (275 km) to go!' My own mind touches briefly on this daunting statistic but I quickly switch to a positive thought; I am going well and will be able to leave Hardraw at 108 miles (172 km) precisely on the 24 hour mark. This proved correct but as I came into Hardraw my feet began to feel sore. In the past this would have been very disturbing but over the previous 12 months I had experimented with the use of Spenco Second Skin. I had found that when applied to burning feet it immediately cooled and soothed them. I taped a strip of jelly-like material across the pad of flesh just behind the toes. It soon went squelchy as I ran, but, as expected, seemed to eliminate totally any heat producing friction. It is difficult to describe what a sense of confidence the discovery of this material had given me. If only I had come across it sooner!

With blobs of Spenco squashing up between my toes I started to ascend one of the 'big lumps' on the Pennine Way. Great Shunner Fell climbs gently but does so for several miles. Rising to a height of 2,340 ft (702 m), it took me to my highest point so far. Assisting the effects of the Spenco a less welcome ally appeared on the scene; misty drizzle. The summit of Great Shunner is a lonely place in these conditions and I hurried down to the little hamlet of Thwaite. Real Yorkshire Dales country this, my own, more featureless moors, are now well behind me. The path over to Keld clings to the side of Kisdon Fell and affords the most magnificent views down into Swaledale. I have come to appreciate this area as one of the most beautiful along the Way.

By now a very familiar spot is approaching, none other than Tan Hill, the highest pub in England. Although the Pennine Way route to Tan Hill is five miles longer than the Rucksack Club's Tan Hill–Cat and Fiddle route, I have covered the distance an hour and a half quicker than when I set my record three weeks ago. This is an indication of the generally easier going along the Pennine Way but I also encourage myself by accepting that it must also mean I am going quite well. The ground over to Tan Hill becomes increasingly wet. The drizzle is changing to heavy rain and as I duck into John's car outside the pub, a real downpour ensues. I feel very reluctant to leave this haven but after 10 minutes John decides it is not going to stop anyway and kicks me out, alone. However, he does add that I'm going well. These words of encouragement from my close friend are sufficient for me to tackle boggy Sleightholme in arc optimistic mood. The heavy downpour eases and, back again with Mark, I start to hope for better conditions. Some 20 minutes later we are getting steadily wetter and belatedly retreat inside our cagoules. As the rain falls, so also do my spirits, only our arrival at the attractive old farm of High Birk Hat affords a quickening of interest. This is the half-way point, 135 miles (216 km) and, at 30½ hours, right on schedule.

The half-way mark on any very long event can be a blade which cuts both ways. A thirsty man will interpret a half-full glass as half-empty and a very tired runner may view the prospect of repeating all his previous miles very negatively indeed. I find it much better to tell myself that I'm now heading for home; Churchill's 'beginning of the end' in fact. Apart from this being a sensible strategy to adopt, it is also a notion based on my experience of changes which take place in the processing of time and the perception of distance on a long run. At the beginning of an ultra run I am frequently so alert and nervous each minute passes like an hour. After a day and night of travelling however, the hours start to pass like minutes. My mental faculties seem to adjust to the slow swinging rhythm of the run itself. Hence my perception of a long run is that the second half is much shorter than the first.

While this phenomenon continues to be reinforced, it did not, at the time, prevent me from feeling increasingly despondent. The rain had a nasty, insistent quality and I had begun to feel very tired indeed. Concern with the weather and my own, apparently, deteriorating form gnawed away at my self-confidence. A few miles outside Middleton-in-Teesdale a car shot past on the road ahead, screeched to a halt and rapidly reversed in my direction. It was Geoff Bell and Don Talbot coming out to help. It was a tonic to see such old friends and campaigners but somehow I could not match their good spirits, my response was lack-lustre. I departed alone for Middleton, still grousing to myself. When I actually reached the appointed place I indulged in a really good moan; they had parked the car off route. I had to go all of 100 yards to reach it. Isn't this journey long enough?

At this juncture I spotted Will McLewin of Dark Peak Fell Runners. Will had most generously offered to support me through the coming night and into the next morning. In doing so he filled an otherwise large hole in my running support. John and Mark retired here after supporting me for over 80 miles (130 km), nearly 50 (80) of which Mark had covered with me. Don and Geoff were nursing old injuries so had it not been for Will I would have had to continue the second night alone. It therefore behoved me to put on a less cantankerous face. I had never met Will before. He was thus the only member of my support team I did not know well but one glance at the determined jaw and the holes in his running tights convinced me I was in the hands of a real professional.

All through this long day I have been encouraging myself to get to Middleton on time. Getting to Middleton on time means I can negotiate the slippery boulders of the Falcon Clints in daylight. This in turn should ensure I will reach Dufton on schedule. Being on schedule at Dufton will mean I can have a short sleep. Dufton is where all my friends will be gathered, waiting and resting. From Dufton, with batteries re-charged, we can look forward with real hope to covering the last 108 miles (172 km) in 30 hours. And now there are just 20 miles (32 km) separating me from Dufton; just 20 miles (32 km) to rest and friendship.

The apparently easy miles along the Tees are in reality quite demanding. As they are predominantly flat, much prolonged running is required. By now, Will and I are chatting like old friends. There is still a strong camaraderie among fell runners. Will is a fell runner-mountaineer of the old school; highly individualistic, even idiosyncratic, determined and resolute. Despite the floating mist and steady drizzle we are able to admire the impressive river scenery. As I cast an eye over the brown froth of High and Low Force I can't help wishing it was less impressive; Maize Beck will be difficult to cross in the dark. On aching legs the alternating sections of wooden footways and wet boulders around High Force are awkward. If your feet and mind get out of synchronisation here you could snap your leg like the proverbial carrot!

At Langdon Beck we have a last support point before the 12 miles (19 km) to Dufton. Make this one quick; the shades of night are sliding through on the mist. I must get over the Falcon Clints while I can see where to put my feet. Hard away now across the pastures, deliberately taking the effort to where it hurts. A slight lifting of the cloud grants me at least half-light and I ask Will to go behind me so I can see far enough ahead to plan a line. As I totter along using hands and feet over the greasy rocks, I spot Will hopping nimbly over the boulders which are half-submerged along the river side. A slight miscalculation and Will hops nimbly into the river! He says some naughty words and hops nimbly out again. The slimy rocks seem never-ending; but apart from almost going headfirst into a massive block while being entertained by Will, I escape unscathed. By comparison, the rocky scramble beside the thundering cataract of Cauldron Spout is relaxed and enjoyable.

At the top of Cauldron Spout, a pleasant surprise; Geoff, after driving part of the way, has run down the private road with a flask and food. We sit munching chocolate while I carry out minor foot repairs. Now that the Clints are behind me and the rain has stopped I begin to feel my spirits rise; a little cautious optimism takes root. With a cheerful farewell Geoff gallops off to drive to Dufton where he will prepare for our arrival in some two and a half hours time. Will and I now step into a very black night. We step into other things as well. The moor over to Maize Beck is still very boggy and pocked with slimy holes. Will demonstrates an amazing aptitude for divining the deepest and slimiest of such holes. Putting his earlier boulder hopping performance to shame, he leaps with extraordinary vigour into holes I can't even see. By the simple ruse of staying several lengths behind Will I am able to steer a rather drier if less interesting course. I am nonetheless careful to remain in sufficiently close contact to profit from this opportunity to refine certain aspects of my vocabulary.

Maize Beck is only ankle deep, no need therefore to use the flood route. Across the other side is, I remember, generally good going. Only five miles (8 km) now separates me from my long anticipated arrival in Dufton. No sooner have we crossed the beck than a bank of mist rolls over us and we are alone, almost disembodied in two smoking pools of torchlight. There is nothing visible save the patch of ground beneath our feet. I am navigating by memory without even a compass. My knowledge of the topography of this area is good. High Cup is arguably my most favoured place along the Pennine Way; it has such a wonderful atmosphere of lofty spaciousness. Its rugged symmetry has a wild but architectural grandeur. Always, as I run along the craggy rim above steep walls sweeping gloriously down to the scooped valley, I experience an indefinable sense of excitement and mystery. Despite the mist I knew I was now heading for the rocky lip above the headwall of the valley. Intent on avoiding the least chance of falling over the unseen edge, I aimed off to one side. After some time, the feeling that the ground was not 'right' began to intrude on my consciousness. I expected that moving to my left would take me to the edge, rocky and unmistakable; all I found was a grassy slope. I tried again; same result. A feeling of shocked dismay swept over me and I began to curse my over-confidence and haste. Will produced a compass; at least we were heading in the correct direction. My mind now started to race with all manner of possibilities and their consequences. We must be coming down a wrong valley, parallel to High Cup. How far from and to what side of Dufton would we emerge? If I did not stop at Dufton could I regain time lost? Would everyone start looking for us if we failed to arrive on schedule?

After an indefinable period in this confused state my befuddled brain began to examine the coincidence of our being on a track remarkably similar to that leading from High Cup to Dufton. A more critical faculty rejected the coincidence, then my whole mind leapt at the sudden realisation that this *was* the track to Dufton. Though I did not realise until much later, I had merely examined a slope at the point where the rocks ended. Waves of relief washed away my despair but were immediately followed by a harsh self-criticism of my over-reliance on memory. It had, in fact, guided me correctly, but I should have reinforced it with the compass. Still, thoughts of the record, recently as insubstantial as the mist which had blighted them, took firm hold of my mind once more.

By now, the 45 minutes I had gained on my schedule had slipped away with the mist. The dark and murky nights are doubly treacherous; if you hurry on, trusting to instinct, knowledge and memory you will almost certainly make an error eventually, then, your very speed will be your ruination. If you opt for absolutely precise navigation, you will hardly realise until daylight returns just how slow your pace has become; it may then be too late. I had gambled and I just broke even, but my nerves were frayed; I needed a rest.

I still cannot properly account for what happened at Dufton. Since leaving Edale I had fixed Dufton in my mind as the most important sub-goal along the Way. I believed that if I could reach Dufton on schedule I would have time to sleep a little, eat a lot and regain strength enough to battle through the remaining miles. Not only that, I had arranged my support plan so that everyone would be at Dufton, ready to join forces on the final assault. This was not just good logistics, I had also been very conscious of the tremendous drawing power which would be generated by the thought of all my good friends gathered together, waiting to run with me over those last climactic miles.

But now in Dufton I feel so tired I can hardly eat. My mind seems to be moving through treacle and whichever way I sit, joints, muscles and feet produce pain. The plan is for Geoff to feed Will and me, allow us one and a half hours sleep, then get us up and off again. Everyone else, John, Mark, Inken and Don should, at 1.30 a.m., be sleeping, gathering their strength. I cannot understand therefore, what Inken's doing up and about. I ask her very bluntly and she seems a bit upset because she got up to help Geoff and because she was concerned. I didn't mean it like that, I simply cannot understand anything outside my plan and I cannot express myself clearly. No matter; I'm bundled into a tent, onto a mattress. I mutter something about my head and a kindly hand slips a pillow under me and gently pats me on the head, more eloquent than words this little gesture, reaching through the fogs around my brain, Inken again; thanks.

It might have been better not to have attempted this sleep. I cannot find rest for my legs and my knees are sources of shooting pain. I can remember no dream as such, but through the desolation which begins to sweep my mind as my conscious defences fall, there stalks a spectre whose name is haste. There is no rest in this; asleep, the spectre's lash drives abstract images of haste through my brain; half-awake, I hear the depressing, deadly tattoo of heavy rain on the tent. Locked into this grotesque state of consciousness I spiral into a black void. For an incalculable and horrible period of time I experience an almost complete negation of mind and spirit, is this to be the sole and bitter fruit of my high endeavour? I no longer care for I can no longer think.

Some time later Geoff appears in the tent doorway. He has a cup of tea ready, but the rain is still hammering its message of despair. I wait for him to say 'Hard luck Mike, you've done well but you can't go over Cross Fell in this weather.' To my surprise he just hands over the tea with a few cheery words. I don't understand this; it's quite obvious I can't go on, so why the charade? My own mind seems paralysed and numb and, quite mechanically, I begin to effect foot repairs. I'm not really interested, I know I've had it. I refuse all food, I'm not hungry and I don't need to eat if I'm quitting. I find myself outside, outside in the cold dawn rain. This is stupid and uncomfortable. Still I will not say the fatal words of quitting to Geoff, I leave it to him, he's experienced enough to know the score. Then I spot Will. Will looks almost as tired as I feel. The slow thought dawns that Will is ready to go over Cross Fell with me because that is what I came here to do and he came to help me do it. OK, so I'm not going to quit in camp, I haven't got the guts to turn to Geoff and Will and say what is in my heart. I'll make a token gesture out there on the hill, protect my pride a little, go through the motions. I set off walking slowly, no need to go faster, no call for haste now. I feel craven and defeated and what is worse I haven't even the strength to acknowledge it. The only flicker of spirit remaining is that manifest in the dull awareness of being in the midst of friends, friends who have endured alongside me over the miles, indeed, over the years, that I might accomplish this dream. For their sake, if not mine, I must go on until I can *truly* endure no longer. Such an end will be full of bitterness but I will have avoided the shame of not at least trying to crawl out of this pit.

Slowly then along the grey wet road, dragging down to defeat. The bulk of the fells is lost in darkness and mist. It is 4.00 a.m., was there ever such a grey and weeping dawn? At odds with the uniform drabness, a peculiar light attracts my attention. A tiny patch of what for a moment appeared to be blue sky, opened then closed to my view. I frankly disbelieve it, but then it shows again. I am very puzzled, this is quite anomalous to the scene in which I am acting. I dismiss the possibility and carry on. Automatically, my mind explores my body. Again, with disbelief, I register that my legs are no more than morning tired, no aches or strains, and my feet are fine, almost comfortable. I decide to suspend both disbelief and acts of faith for a time and start a conversation with Will. We both gain vigour as we stretch our legs into the miles once more. Then, around a bend in the track, a small miracle. Oblivious to my disbelief, a swathe of early sunshine falls full on a thick bank of bluebells; raindrop-glistening lustrous blue against the fresh spring green. The impact on my parched and weary spirit is almost tangible. It is all so innocent and generous, so heartbreakingly beautiful.

In the scant moments it took to absorb the scene my spirit was restored. I was emerging from the pit and carrion despair would not take hold of me again. One strange thing, I have passed that spot several times since, in spring too, but I have never again seen my bluebells on that bank. Furthermore, I would have thought that at 4.30 a.m. on the west side of the hill we would have been hidden from the sun in the east. Ah well, 'There are more things in heaven and earth Horatio, than are dreamt of in your philosophy.' Must either Nature or our spirits be circumscribed always by laws of matter?

The climb up Knock Fell to reach the high ground leading to Cross Fell was long and hard. I felt to be going very slowly but was content to take my cue from Will. He also seemed to be finding it tough so I reasoned the pace was adequate for the time being. The hard effort gradually restored us to full wakefulness and just as well. Above 2,000 ft (610 m) a thick wet mist was sweeping along on a biting easterly. Next, we traversed the two Dun Fells where I realised that in my despairing mood at Dufton I had left my map and route cards behind. However, I was full of confidence once more and with the compass a little west of north I brought us across the boggy gathering ground of the Tees watershed and at last onto the mighty summit plateau of Cross Fell itself. This flat and featureless plateau is often ravaged by fierce storms. At 2,930 ft (895 m) it is the highest point on the Pennine Way. It is also truly remote, being miles from any real sanctuary. In bad weather it can be an awesome place with a desolate, almost primeval atmosphere. Perhaps because of this, it is magnificent. It does not compromise. As mountains go, it is not even beautiful but it commands respect. I do not doubt it is the most committing place on the Pennine Way. While it has nearly always been kind to me, I fear it as much as love it.

Navigating again from my mental map, I aim for the top left-hand corner of the plateau. Sure enough, the trig point looms out of the mist and at last we can descend to softer climes. A fairly good descent, just a little astray from the path, but, with an eye to ethics, avoiding Wainwright's suggested shortcut which saves a mile on the official footpath. Our slight deviation produces a few green Sphagnum bogs for us to avoid or stumble into, but soon we are near the refuge of Gregg's Hut, damp, but a possible lifesaver in a storm.

As I looked back, grim Cross Fell was encircled by a string of old snowfields which it seemed to be wearing like a gigantic necklace. We turned our steps towards the South Tyne valley, Garrigill and breakfast. Truly, Cross Fell is magnificent but it is not trustworthy. I was not sorry to be leaving it. As we dropped lower on the interminable stony track leading directly to Garrigill, the mist disappeared entirely. The views were enormous. My tiny patch of blue now stretched across the horizons and in the rain-cleansed air we could see the brown hills rolling to impossible distances. Brown may seem monotonous but under the low sun every imaginable hue and shade was represented; curving, rolling, sweeping; a heaving brown sea in its vastness and, above, billowing cloud ships and the sweet blues of an early summer sky.

We rolled gently down the track, not speaking much, absorbing the peace, solitude and beauty around us. A wonderful healing was taking place, my life forces were being restored as I ran. I switched on to automatic pilot, letting my mind become empty of thought but open to the power around me. I was in a state somewhere between sleeping and waking, sensate but without cognition. After some time my mind re-surfaced, stretched itself and began to re-engage with reality. My crisis at Dufton which had almost paralysed mind and body had resulted in the loss of 45 minutes on my schedule. Better get moving! I increased pace, kicked a large stone with a tender toe and gave vent to a loud curse; 'normal service has been resumed'.

Garrigill is a charming little village on the banks of the South Tyne. Geoff had everything ready for me including a perfectly-angled deck-chair. Then, as an unexpected bonus, he switched on 'Nimrod' from The Enigma Variations. I had such a feeling of comfort, well-being and total relaxation there was considerable danger I would never leave the deck-chair. In Dufton I had experienced a black despair, but for my friends it would have engulfed me. In traversing Cross Fell I had crossed not only a topographical watershed but a truly significant psychological watershed. On the most important run of my life I had survived a terrible crisis and now I had reached further than I had ever reached before. At Garrigill, 180 miles (288 km) along the Way, I believed at last that I was going to reach my journey's end and achieve a record, not 'eventually' but now!

It could be that my unbounded optimism was not entirely appropriate. Whereas my support were beginning to feel a cautious optimism based on a review of the objective factors involved, I had no such concern with mere cautious possibility. I had emerged from a journey through dark and horrible caverns. I had given all, more than I thought I possessed. In return I seemed to have become imbued with an unassailable strength of body and spirit. For a while a powerful inspiration would enable me to transcend the limitations which restrict merely physical endeavour. I did not question the source or scope of this inspiration. Nor yet did I concern myself with the remaining brute statistics of this journey. Perhaps I should have done, they were not without interest.

At Garrigill, in order to finish within three days, I had to cover 90 miles (145 km) in 26 hours. At the time I felt nothing but confidence. The weather was superb and I was enjoying an almost unique sense of well-being. Of course, one long spell of bad weather, a bad route-finding error, an inability to survive the third night without sleep, all, or any of these things could easily blast my hopes, but I hardly considered them. Had I known what the Cheviots had in store for me I might not have been so blithe.

Perhaps in a euphoric state I looked no further ahead than sufficed to guide my footsteps along the river footpath beside the sparkling South Tyne. This is a delightful stretch of the Pennine Way and in the new summer sunshine my eyes drank in the verdant and glittering greens. It had been a long, dark night and even the beautiful moorland browns below Cross Fell had carried a sombre echo of it. Down here, soft sweet Nature bestowed gentler charms. There was joy in being here, joy in being alive, and there was joy too in my running.

Moving with a slow but easy rhythm, just beyond Alston there was a happy moment for me as the support car from Dufton drove by. I allowed my pace to surge a little and waved enthusiastically. I was slightly surprised to see anxious faces peering at me. Surely everyone could sense that the time for anxiety and fear was past?

Accompanying me from Garrigill to Slaggyford was the last hard toil for Will. He had joined me at 141 miles (226 km) and, with only that one short break in the night, had covered 48 miles (77 km) through the difficult hours. Now he insisted on sprinting ahead to open every gate so I could pass through without pausing. As these few miles were littered with gates he was engaged in some very arduous interval training indeed. At Slaggyford he at last stood down. I tried to thank him but just couldn't find the words. 'Never mind all that,' he said 'just go on and take the record.'

Now at last I was joined by my old friend and Karrimor partner, John Richardson. John and I have shared so many hard and humorous miles together, it was like slipping into a pair of comfortable old shoes. John had the ability, like no one else, to lift from my shoulders some of the burden of the heavy miles. His experience, his wisdom and his concern meant that I could safely transfer to him some of my weight of responsibility. He told me that I was going well enough and that he would only start to prod me along if it looked necessary. It was as well he took this stance because although I was indeed going strongly, I had perhaps become dangerously euphoric. I had begun to think that now nothing *could* go wrong.

And for a long time nothing did go wrong. I established a superb rhythm of

*Coming into
Alston with
Will McLewin
on the Pennine
Way.*

running and walking, each blending into the other without conscious thought as I followed the ebb and flow of the Way across moor and meadow. The day became very warm and as I am a lover of cold, dry conditions, I began to suffer a little. However, at 2.00 p.m. I received a great boost as the 200-mile (320 km) mark was passed. I had been going just two days and three hours. In fact I was an hour and a half down on my schedule but this was not critical. Over this last day I had allowed for both increasing weakness and a two-hour sleep. Not only did I reject thoughts of weakness, I believed I could, if necessary, dispense with the need to sleep.

Going north, 200 miles (320 km) marks the start of the Roman Wall. This is a fine stretch, endless vistas to the north and beneath one's feet history, both sensed and real. Hadrian's Wall once acted as a barrier to marauding Scots, now it serves much the same function for Wayfarers. Describing a vicious switchback of ups and downs, it precludes any rhythm but presents every chance of a stiff-legged trip to bring the whole affair to a fractured close. After 10 miles (16 km) of it I was pleased to slot through Rapishaw Gap and wave the Wall goodbye. Somewhat wobbly of leg I headed with John for the welcome shade of the Wark Forests. By now John was encouraging me to jog the gentle uphill stretches. I would have like to have walked but he either believed I could manage it or needed to do it. I trusted his judgement and reached yet deeper into the well of my reserves. Would they be sufficient? I had never before run so far or drawn so much from myself. But never before had I felt such glory spreading within me.

At Ladyhill a familiar enemy assailed me. Jubilee Foot with all its burning pain began to hamper my stride. I had been wearing a comfortable but sloppy pair of road shoes. Now I discarded them, stripped my feet of all dressings and applied layers of Vaseline. This done, I crammed my feet into my usual rough terrain shoes. I walked rather circumspectly out of the support point, with 53 miles (85 km) still to go, sore feet could easily slow me to failure. After just a few but painful moments, the burning eased and the shoes expanded. I fitted a pair of soft insoles to ensure my feet were well locked in place and there they stayed until the finish.

Relieved, I began to chat to Inken back on running support. At first she eyed me anxiously. She had caught a glimpse of my feet back at the stop and I don't think she had been too impressed. As ever my mouth was the barometer of my spirits and under the influence of my incessant, if perforce, inane chatter she began to relax and we talked pleasantly on into the mild still evening. Like Will, however, she was alert to any gates which might be opened in advance to facilitate my progress. At one such spot I observed her ahead of me wrestling with one of those dilapidated constructions held together with wire and string. This one had obviously relinquished its role as gate years ago and settled for a less demanding existence as a barrier. I called out to Inken not to bother but she ignored me and with a display of ferocity quite remarkable in one so slight and gentle, proceeded to utterly demolish the recalcitrant obstacle. I jogged through the gap and over the debris regarding Inken with a new respect. I fear her recent acquaintance with the genus 'fell runner' has marred her previous rather more

*'Embracing'
the mug of tea
above
Bellingham,
225 miles
(360 km) from
the start of the
Pennine Way.*

ladylike qualities. I had to endure some quite unnecessary remarks when I made a smart diversion to visit the loo in Bellingham.

As I approached the support point above the town, Don placed a mug of tea enticingly on a gatepost and I 'sprinted' forward to embrace it. I was in great spirits now. Often the evening hours are my best times and over the easy moorland which followed I ran almost effortlessly. I thought I was mentally very sharp too until I realised I was correcting a route error I had not made; perhaps too sharp!

At last I started on the final leg before Byrness. Byrness, the last major support point before I began the 30-mile (50 km) traverse which would take me through my third night over the Cheviots to journey's end at Kirk Yetholm. The early summer night had an atmosphere of immense stillness and calm. Don and Geoff led away and I followed the gentle murmur of their voices as they chatted with the easy comfort of old friends. The sky held the pale northern light but a soft dusk was cloaking the peaty ground. We ran through a bank of fluffy white cotton grass which floated ethereally in the darkness and I, suspended in time and space, floated with it.

The much despised pine forests above Byrness were, for me, perfumed avenues of easy progress. I knew the track through them ran for miles so I felt no impatience, I simply soaked up that wonderful sense of quiet peace. And as I jogged and walked, I prepared myself for the final test.

The plan was simple. John, Inken and Mark were all very strong and keen to accompany me the whole way to Kirk Yetholm. Don and Geoff would attempt to drive to Chew Green where the Way passes close to the road used for military purposes. This road is apt to be closed at times but we had hopes it would provide a chance for a final food stop and even, maybe, an opportunity for me to snatch a half-hour's sleep. Right now though I had to consume as much food as I could manage and change into warmer clothes. I thought I was very much in control of myself and the situation and could not understand why John kept peering through the car window asking if I had finished my plate of stew. I thought this hardly the best of manners, most unlike John. After all, I'd only just sat down hadn't I? No! I hadn't. Apparently I had been ladling stew into my mouth in slow motion for 20 minutes. My mind and body were working well but only at half-speed. My original plan had allowed for a sleep stop at Byrness but with night hours and the boggy Cheviots ahead John reckoned that with now less than 12 hours of the three days remaining, I should keep moving.

We set off just after midnight and, despite my tiredness, I could sense a muted thrum of excitement within me. The steep climb out of the valley passed comfortably and soon we were on uneven but level ground, heading for Chew Green. I began to experience some difficulty on stretches of going which were rougher or more stony. My torch threw shadows across the irregularities, and as I moved, so did the shadows. My speed of information processing continued to be slow and from time to time I stepped over shadows that were not bumps and stumbled over bumps that were not shadows. Down in the next valley we could hear the sounds of gunfire, the army playing at soldiers. There were amusing references to Geoff and Don being mistaken for the enemy but more seriously we were concerned about the car being prevented access to Chew Green.

My progress must have been even slower than I realised because John and Mark could not resist forging ahead, ostensibly to look for the car. I was grateful to Inken for staying with me. I felt fine physically and also in spirit but, staring into the torchlight, I found it difficult not to become disorientated and lose touch with reality. After a brief re-grouping John and Inken moved ahead leaving Mark to look after his dad! I observed that a cutting easterly had sprung up and asked Mark if he was cold. 'Not at all,' he replied. A few minutes later as the wind increased I made the same query and got the same response. After the third repetition I realised that hints were useless and ordered the callow youth to help me don a windproof. Only just in time, the wind was now penetrating to the bone. Then we saw returning torches, Geoff and Don had run the gauntlet, the car was close by.

In view of my tiredness I had been counting on having a short sleep in the car. Despite my fuddled thinking I quickly realised this was not a good idea. The car was small, and with Geoff and Don there would be six people plus a mass of gear to accommodate. I would not ask my friends to stand around in the cold wind while I snoozed inside. I climbed into the car, the heater going full blast and proceeded with the laborious task of getting more food down. I can vaguely remember a convoluted discussion about what clothes I should wear in view of the deteriorating conditions, then off we set on the last lap and into the final crisis.

It was 2.00 a.m. and the weather was most definitely on the change. A strong and bitter wind blew into our faces from somewhere north of east. There was no light in the sky and a pall of cloud held back the dawn. Although I did not feel physically weak I could not control my brain which was making efforts to close down in sleep. I continually stumbled over tussocks as sleep snatched my legs away. Those tussocks looked so inviting; if only I could curl up among them.

I realised my progress was becoming ever slower and despite exerting my will I could not force my brain to a normal level of consciousness. After about five miles of this, as we were approaching a refuge hut near the border fence, John asked me if I wanted to take a sleep. Hell! What a conundrum to wrestle with. Time lost sleeping versus time lost stumbling compounded by the unknown factors of would I be able to sleep (or wake up) and would it help anyway? I realised the importance of coming to the correct decision, and quickly. Although the mental effort actually aroused my brain a little, I elected to try a five-minute sleep. Inside the wooden refuge all was amazingly quiet and peaceful. The wind was a murmur and it seemed positively warm in comparison with the hostile elements outside. Reviewing the various muscular alternatives available, I quickly chose Inken's as by far the softest lap on offer and with my head thus pillowed stretched full-length on the hard bench. I allowed myself a moment to switch off all systems and then, with the trust of a child, I slipped into a wonderfully deep, calm and refreshing sleep.

'Come on Mike, you've had seven minutes!' I felt my heart give a bound of excitement. Swinging my feet to the floor I shot through the door like a startled hare. John was already steaming up the hill. I stuck my head inches from his rapidly retreating backside and followed his lead. This was the only time in the entire run that anyone set a pace for me and it was perfect. I knew John was going as hard as he possibly could and I knew he was right. There could be no further weakness now. I was finely poised between success and failure. A merely ordinary finish at a speed commensurate with having travelled 255 miles (408 km) would not be enough. I had to produce something special. That wonderful sleep had opened up the chance to do just that.

So nearly it was not enough. As we ploughed onwards the ground became wetter and the bogs deeper. Eventually we were too tired to steer round the swamps but charged desperately through them. The route over the Cheviots trends steadily uphill to Cheviot summit itself. Time was slipping by and still the summit seemed no nearer. From leaving Byrness with the three-day record apparently safely in my grasp, I began to see my dream sinking into the mire around me. By now my throat was inflamed, I could not swallow properly and when I tried it felt like tearing open glued paper. Sucking boiled sweets helped and I chewed these as if my life depended on it. I longed for a drink but did not want to cause upset to my loyal support by pointing out they had neglected to bring any water. I thus deprived myself of the liquid they had carried from Byrness as a matter of course.

At last, the bog-encircled summit of Cheviot itself. I examined my watch and was suddenly filled with a joyous astonishment. If I could cover the last 10 miles (16 km) in two hours I would finish a full two hours under three days. We swung away from Cheviot re-tracing our swampy footsteps in the direction of the Schil.

John and Mark were jogging ahead and this meant my supply of sweets kept disappearing. Eventually, I raised myself on a peat hag and screeched for Mark to come back to me. Like the dutiful son he is, he did. I then delivered a very stern rebuke indeed. Did he think that I was Superman that I should be able to keep sprinting after him in order to re-lubricate my poor throat!?! I thought I achieved a splendid note of righteous indignation; dignified and firm but reasonable and so on. However, while Mark seemed suitably impressed, I noticed Richardson smirking in the background. I made a mental note to give him a hard time on the run-in – if I could!

Cheviot summit now behind us and the wind no longer in our faces, I begin to pick up pace. I shout to John that if I can reach the summit of the Schil by 8.00 a.m. I will throw everything into an effort to finish by 9.00 a.m.; that two hour sub-three-day target. Gradually the bog gives way to better going and after painfully picking my way down the steep slopes of Auchope Cairn I get onto a gentle descent and start to stretch my legs. After over 260 miles (420 km) of carefully hoarding my reserves I joyfully abandon caution to the wind and let my energy flow as it will. Layers of clothing go flying off for the support to snatch up. Schil summit is looming some 500 ft (150 m) above us but a reckless charge carries me nearly half-way up before I consent to walk. I can tell from his breathing that John is having to hang on ever so slightly here and Inken has started walking quite early. I've no intention of blowing away all my energy here however and a brisk walk claims the top by 8.00 a.m. Again on the steep downhill it is my turn to suffer on legs which have strength but no elasticity. Yet I will not be denied. There seems to be an upsurge and swell of power and energy within me. The pure joy of running into my dream has flooded my entire being and there is no place for weariness and fatigue. After all the years, all the countless miles, the crushing disappointments, the pain of body and the lonely aches of the spirit, I am finally running into my dream – I am truly now running the record. It is glorious. There is no fatigue, no pain. There is a pulsating excitement, a joy in movement and a thrilling urgency to reach the finish. Yet, if I could, I would live these moments forever.

In my haste and excitement I lead us down the wrong hill! The only penalty is more rough going, the added frustration merely fuelling the fires within me. We reach the road rather early and I have to restrain myself from sprinting down it, my breathing informs me there are still limitations in the amount of oxygen I can consume.

The last hill on the Pennine Way is half a mile of road at a gradient of one in six. I attacked this with the resolve to yield not one step of walking. I had the satisfaction of seeing Don peering down in some amazement then Geoff, with camera, having to back-pedal furiously to keep us in shot. Like wild Border raiders the group of us swept through now lashing rain up to the Border Inn. I grabbed the gable end and tried to focus on my watch. Before I could do so John's voice rapped out 'Two days, twenty-one hours, fifty-four minutes, thirty seconds.' After only 30 years of steady training I had become the first person to run the Pennine Way in under three days.

Yards from the finish of the Pennine Way in Kirk Yetholm. Left to right: Mark, Mike, John, Don.

My memories of what followed are quite clear in some aspects and hopelessly vague in others. Immediately I heard the time announced I turned and jogged back up the road to meet Inken who, after 60 miles (100 km) of hard running and countless hours on support, day and night, had been unable to stay with our finishing speed. I gave her a kiss and then, at a rather more sedate pace, returned to the portals of the Border Inn. I remember by this time I was fairly saturated. The proprietor of the establishment had opened the door as he thought we should sign the Pennine Way book he kept. Without being particularly presumptuous I thought he might at least offer the use of his garage so that we could change out of the rain. No chance! After I'd signed the book and entered the time, he politely but firmly closed the door in our faces. What a miserable bugger, I thought. I was on such a high I could not feel the cold but felt very aggrieved on behalf of my friends. I need not have worried, they're as tough as they come and soon we were all changed and snug in the cars. First stop a transport café where my mouth would not stop working. I think I must have been almost delirious; I chattered incessantly while my friends looked on with indulgent amusement. It was several hours before I began to calm down and as I did so, sleep at last claimed me.

There are (thankfully) no medals for breaking these kinds of records, but when I arrived home I found something which I would not change for any olympic gold. It was a brown envelope and it was stuck on our front door. It was from my four youngest children and on it was written: 'Welcome home, Dad. And well done. Gerard, Liam, Sara, Michael.' I have it yet, and always will.

chapter five

LIFE AFTER THE PENNINE WAY

It had taken me five years of specific training and eight attempts before I was able to break the Pennine Way record. As gratifying as my achievement had been I felt much valuable time had been lost and other ventures had passed me by. Life is short and our fleeting dreams run faster than our failing strength. I had no plans for a prolonged period of recuperation. I was as keen to run as ever. I felt I could now enjoy my running without the burden of unfulfilled ambition to carry with me. Unfortunately, my joints decided to play a part in past and future dreams. Painful knees reminded me that the price of victory was a mortgage with a lifelong term and a high rate of interest.

That the Pennine Way had not destroyed my tendency to over-ambition was demonstrated three weeks later. I thought I would just 'tootle' round as much of the Bob Graham as possible (meaning all of it!). Starting at Threlkeld I set off in the evening to climb Blencathra, Great Calva and Skiddaw. The only reason I can find for relegating the prestigious Bob Graham to a relatively minor jaunt was that after the Pennine Way it appeared very much shorter and easier. I did however take the sensible precaution of packing an extremely thin and most unwaterproof cagoule. Should I experience a stiff-necked obstinacy to continue in the face of bad weather, this garment would not enable me to do so.

As I started up Halls Fell ridge in oppressive conditions, writhing tongues of mist licked down from unseen heights. The summit-springing ridge carried me to a rain-splattered, wind-blown top. However, with the wind on my back the rapid deterioration in the weather system was easily ignored. A fleet-footed ascent of Calva and Skiddaw followed by a raid on the 'chippie' in Keswick would, I blithely imagined, see me safely onto the Derwent Fells, easy ground for the dark. This attempt to bolster my morale was blasted as I turned headfirst into the weather on Great Calva.

Thrusting against a wet gale I desperately sought lower ground where I hastily unpacked a small torch and the thin cagoule. The latter exceeded all my expectations, I was soaked through in no time. Without, for once, the slightest hesitation I bolted back to my car at Threlkeld. Later, as I drove back with the huge wind bending the summer trees and squalls of rain being flung across the windscreen, I reflected that the weather had done me a favour. I had gone just far enough to establish that my legs (and probably my head) had not recovered to do even half a Bob Graham.

Gradually, I did recover my hill legs and at the end of July led a club walk round most of the summits above 2,500 ft (760 m) in North Wales. Unlike my ill-fated tilt at the Bob Graham, the major problem on this walk was tremendous heat. I remember we were refused pots of tea at a café on the Aber Glaslyn Bridge. As the Afon Glaslyn thundered past we were sternly told that we should realise there was a water shortage and lemonade was all we could have. Our subsequent ascent of Moel Hebog was accompanied by much popping, spluttering and minor explosions; no tea, just very large bottles of fizzy lemonade.

The North Wales 2,500s was a walk of great character, undertaken in the best of company. Although the route is a demanding one, there was nothing at stake other than that we should enjoy the hills and enjoy the camaraderie; not too difficult a task. After 22,000 ft (6,705 m) of ascent on this Welsh walk I felt my legs were sufficiently prepared for my next and final adventure for 1984. I hoped to simultaneously support and accompany Inken on a Bob Graham attempt. To an unfortunate minority of fell runners, the Bob Graham represents little more than the ultimate test of prowess in running the fells. There are those who lose sight of the fact that it is a superb route in any circumstances. The round sweeps over much of the best ground in the Lake District. It covers all the 3,000 ft (915 m) summits and nearly every other major peak.

The route stands on its own merit, the challenge to complete within 24 hours simply adds that extra spice of competition with oneself. With customary thoroughness, Inken reconnoitered the round by sections, building fitness, knowledge and that indefinable sense of being part of, or 'belonging to' the route. After coming through the final test piece of the Welsh walk so well, I thought she had a good chance of completing the round and a fair chance of completing within 24 hours, a target with about a 30 per cent success rate. After her sterling support of my Pennine Way record, I was determined to render Inken every assistance on her attempt. To this end I had to examine my conscience that I really was prepared to subjugate any personal ambition for hers, there must be no appearance by that bloody demon on this occasion!

Looking back on the round I think it epitomised much of what characterises ultra-distance fell running and the Bob Graham in particular. Initially, we were blessed with good weather and we had the joy of being in high places with so many of the Lakeland hills stretching ahead in the sun, beckoning us onwards. There are many runners attempting the round nowadays yet there never seems to be any shortage of friends to accompany them at all hours of the day and night. We too picked up that wonderful golden thread running ever through these endeavours; companionship, laughter and the strong sustaining love of friends. Completion of the round is a deeply satisfying experience. What I find even more remarkable, however, is the willingness of friends to assist in the endeavour, to lighten the burden of the miles with good cheer, to suffer fatigue and hardship so that faltering steps may yet carry the runner within reach of his dream.

By Dunmail Raise it was time to prepare ourselves for our night section over the Helvellyn range. It was also time for me to assume sole responsibility for navigating Inken safely through the night. With the exception of my eldest son, Mark, all our other friends had to return home. With farewells and good wishes exchanged on both sides we departed on our very different ways, they, on the hectic journey down the motorways, we, onto the high and by now empty fells.

We left Dunmail with time in hand on our schedule but as the night deepened, so it brought an opaque, soaking mist. As the mist continued to thicken I was forced to navigate ever more carefully. In turn, this meant that we were unable to jog over the easier stretches of ground. Beyond Helvellyn, there are paths which are perfectly satisfactory as lines along the grassy Dodds, but which frequently cut under the summits themselves. I agonised over the possibility of bypassing a summit. There are mountains in the Himalaya where respect for a summit-dwelling Deity does not permit the actual top to be violated; such an ethic would scarcely be entertained as an excuse for shortcutting a Bob Graham round!

Despite several minor miscalculations we 'collected' all the required tops. However, as we stood at last on Clough Head, I realised all our time in hand was gone. The weather too, was continuing its unhelpful ways. Associated with the mist were very heavy banks of cloud which smothered any chance of an early dawn. We lost more time on the rough descent with my temper mounting in direct proportion to the number of drainage ditches into which I fell.

At 3.45 a.m. in the village of Threlkeld, it was essential that Mark, waiting in my car, should have everything ready for immediate consumption. He was in fact so well organised that we were fed, watered and away with a two-minute saving. Mark shouldered the rucksack and led off up Blencathra, Halls Fell Ridge springing unseen into the still dark sky. The ridge, rocky and greasy, vaulted endlessly upwards. Speed was both impracticable and inadvisable, and the dawn stubbornly refused to come to our assistance.

It was 5.30 a.m. before we finally had the benefit of true light. I guided us down early to the track in the valley. My own legs were shaken and tired after the steep descent from Blencathra but with a good track to follow and only Calva and Skiddaw remaining I felt a surge of optimism. It was with a sense of shock therefore that I heard Inken say 'It's no good. I've lost it!' There was a note of despair in her voice and her face was drawn and pale. I had never seen her like this before and I felt a deep dismay. I tried to re-assure her but just when I felt I should have been of most help, I found she was not responding as would every other fell runner I had ever known. She interpreted my encouragement as an attempt to force from her the kind of effort of which she was no longer capable. Her feeling was that the round had been a wonderful experience so far and the kind of effort I was now demanding would destroy her appreciation of it. She felt she was no longer capable of finishing within 24 hours and that fact was far less important to her than that she should be allowed to finish the circuit in her own way. These were ethical points whose validity I could not very well deny. They did, however, place me in something of a dilemma. I knew she was right but I also knew that steady application might still achieve full success whereas anything less would certainly not. Totally exasperated, like Dr Doolittle, I thought 'Why can't a woman be more like a man?'! My best efforts at encouragement, being perversely interpreted, I was unfeeling enough to utter harsh words. Eventually, I noticed that despite avowals to the contrary, she was still trying harder and going faster.

Struggling to keep my disputative nature and hot temper in check, I focused my attention on both finding the very best lines across the hills and covering the ground at the optimum pace. The country Back O'Skiddaw is rough and a sore trial to weary legs. I now realised however, that Inken was going as well as she possibly could. I would have liked to have offered words of encouragement. How galling! With all my knowledge, experience and silver-tongued eloquence to place at Inken's disposal, I was condemned to impotent silence.

After crossing the fence below Skiddaw summit we reached the top with a suddenness that took me unawares. Surprisingly, we still had an hour and a quarter to cover the remaining five and a half miles (9 km) to Keswick, most of it downhill. I pointed out to my protégée that she now had both aspects of the round within her grasp and left it to her. Several miles of often steep downhill is not an easy way to finish a tough 70 miles (117 km) of mountainous terrain. Our progress was not fast but it had about it a steady determination. I could now address myself to the final problem. I was not absolutely sure of the last half mile of the route through Fitz Park to the official finish at the Moot Hall in Keswick. One wrong turn now and it would be I, not Inken who had blown the chance to finish inside 24 hours. My mind flashed back to my own Bob Graham. Entering the boundaries of Keswick, I had been just about to toddle off down the road to Carlisle, when Boyd Millen laconically called from his recumbent position on a bench 'Oy, Mike, over here!'

This time it was Mark who quested ahead and, despite a slightly erratic course across the park, found an improbable route through a car-park. We popped out of a narrow ginnel and saw the Moot Hall 50 yards away. 'Can you do 50 yards in seven and a half minutes?' I asked rhetorically. We did rather better. Inken became only the twelfth woman to achieve the Bob Graham as, with just seven minutes in hand, we arrived back at the spot from which we had started 42 summits ago. Unlike Inken, I don't think I had ever come to terms with leading her to a complete but out of time Bob Graham. My chief emotion on finishing was one of tremendous relief and thankfulness.

The rather nice ethical points raised towards the end of the Bob Graham provided scope for many a subsequent discussion. I think both our points of view are valid in theory. In practice it is essential that the individual sets his or her own levels of striving.

The Bob Graham had taken place in the middle of August and marked a satisfying conclusion to my long-distance running that year. To some extent it had marked an act of faith with myself that life would not end with the Pennine Way. Though I continued to train I began to feel as if I had asked as much as I could expect from my body for one year. After the Marsden-Edale race at the beginning of December I did not run again until Christmas. The tradition of running with friends over Christmas and alone on Boxing Day, which is my birthday, is a long and a strong one. I have never probed the significance of these runs, I just accept that they restore, heal and bless. Echoes of a happy childhood perhaps.

As the year drew to a close I ruminated on just how good a year it had been. I could not hold all the outstanding events in my memory and began to jot them down in my log-book. This is my list:

1984. Summary of a Good Year:

7/Jan.	Double Marsden Edale (Walk)	45
14/15 Jan	Lakes Passes (Walk)	45
3rd March	Derwent W'sheds Race (11th Consecutive) 2nd overall, won vets trophy.	40
17th March } 18th	Haworth Hobble with John. Otley V₂ Marathon 1.21 45/400	33 13
6th April	Welsh Threes Circuit in snow. with Luken.	25
10-13th April	4 × 30 mls round home	120
16-20th April	4 × 50 mls in 5 days round home, lovely weather.	200
24-28th April	4 × 60 as above - on the PW. More lovely weather	240
6/7th May	Tan/Cat record (29 hr 1hr) Very hard work!	120
31st May-3rd June	Pennine Way record (2.21.54) At last!	270
7/8th July	Saunders M.M. tough first day. heatwave!	40
21/22nd July	N. Wales 2,500's Wonderful club walk.	60
5/6th Aug	Bob Graham round with Luken (Just made it!)	70
1st Sept.	Bullock Smithy race. 2nd, equalled previous record. (5hrs 38m)	56
9th Sept	My 20th consec' Mtn Trial - pity I was knackered!	25
5th Oct 6th Oct.	The Cairngorm 4,000's in snow - real mountains! The Mamores ridge in clearing mist	
27/28th Oct.	The Karrimor - at home My 17th ('Ow', 9th with John	55
2nd Dec	Marsden-Edale race (full circle!) 3.08. 19/70	22

MILES 1,500

(Calculated running miles = 2,000)

chapter six

A LONG WAY FOR A PADDLE

Preparation for the Coast to Coast Record

It had been my ambition for several years to attempt the Coast to Coast record as soon as I had successfully completed the Pennine Way. The route was devised by Alfred Wainwright who, despite his marvellous and indispensable *Pennine Way Companion* seems to have been disenchanted with the Pennine Way itself. Wainwright set about planning his own line for a long-distance walk taking as his main theme the linking of points on the north-west and north-east coasts of England. Obviously not a lover of the Pennine Bog (who is?), Wainwright sought to steer a somewhat drier line while still including high, and often remote, areas.

The route is an easy one to conceptualise. It starts in the west by traversing the Lake District, its central section crosses Yorkshire Dales country and the final section takes one across the North York Moors to finish at the quaint and romantic Robin Hood's Bay. Wainwright gives the mileage as 190 (306 km) and the three sections are roughly equal in length.

When I reconnoitered the Coast to Coast in the spring of 1985 I found both pleasure and disappointment. I found places of great charm and beauty and the start and finish both offer wonderful cliff-top scenery. In particular, the traverse along the cliffs above Whitley Bay is inspirational. My other impression however was that this was a walk of good sections linked far too often by stretches of road and hard track.

The two miles of road into Bellingham is easily the longest continuous stretch of road on the Pennine Way, whereas the Coast to Coast has a number of road sections of several miles. For me, roads destroy the character of a walk. Disparate and illogical as the Pennine Way might appear to be, it has a sense of unity. 'Wild trails' do not belong to roads and each time one is used, the trail is lost. One of the delightful aspects of any continuous traverse of a long-distance route is the sense of completeness and cohesion that it brings. The slow exploration of a route is also rewarding of course but unfolding it continuously is an experience I find uniquely satisfying.

After training on the Coast to Coast I had some misgivings about the amount of road. Apart from the eight-mile (13 km) section beyond Richmond however, these were slight. Wainwright's later edition of his companion book to the walk stated that poor behaviour by walkers had resulted in permissive footpaths round

Orton being withdrawn. He stated that it was now necessary to follow some seven miles (11 km) of road through the village due to lack of rights of way. This is happily not correct. A little beyond Beacon Hill, a system of bridle ways and field paths (all on rights of way) skirt Orton and give an attractive approach to Sunbiggin Tarn. These paths are clearly marked on the Ordnance Survey maps and I was determined to use them as being more in keeping with the general ethos of the walk.

Part of my training plan was to again include extra long runs with something at stake to help me 'peak' my preparation. My success on the Pennine Way had not imparted any sense of invincibility. Indeed, although my training for the event had passed off with no real problems, I had never felt particularly good. A wet spring had not helped, but even allowing for this, I felt I had to prove to myself that I had not burned out in my struggle for the Pennine Way.

I set myself two subsidiary targets prior to attempting the Coast to Coast record; one was a hundred-mile (160 km) event, scheduled for the end of May and organised by the Long Distance Walkers' Association (LDWA). The route of the LDWA Dalesman Hundred followed an attractive course in Yorkshire Dales country. It contained a good proportion of hills, some remote country and scenery both beautiful and varied. I thought the odd road section annoying but not too intrusive. I subsequently discovered that many LDWA members complained that the course was too tough. It appears that the chief concern of many is simply to complete 100 miles (160 km). To these, the nature of the course seems to be unimportant excepting that it must not hamper that ambition. I feel that those who do hold this view are mistaken. Miles which do not feed the senses and nourish the spirit are just empty statistics. Distance is, in a sense, meaningless. It is the journey through time and nature that matters. This may be physically as hard as you wish to make it. It should always be spiritually satisfying.

When I had finished reconnaissance and training for the Coast to Coast it was the end of April. I decided I had time to fit in one other long event before the Dalesman Hundred at the end of May. I had no time to learn a new route so I turned to an old adversary to provide a challenge. The Tan–Cat would certainly not respect my new status. Its 120 moorland miles (193 km), still heavy with spring rains, would be as testing as ever.

It may be difficult to understand how I could entertain self-doubts after 'proving' myself on the Pennine Way. I did so partly because it is in the nature of an athlete never to accept that he is at his peak of fitness and strength, but apart from this, I did not know what last year might have cost me in terms of a real depletion in the energy reserves needed for me to continue to participate in my sport. Although I had enjoyed most of my training during spring, I had found the wet conditions very trying at times. My knees, in particular, were becoming increasingly stiff and sore. Continuous hours running through mud and rain can dull one's appreciation of even the best scenery. The necessity of always having to bulk my training in spring forces me out in conditions I would often prefer to avoid. I had noted a reluctance to face some of these miles. If I had indeed developed any mental or physical chinks in my armour, the Tan–Cat would surely discover them – and it would show little mercy!

Comfortingly, I had as ever a top class support team. My two eldest sons, Mark and Sean, were to act as runner and cook/driver respectively, while Inken would share the driving and accompany me on the night section. One other important aspect which gave me confidence was my mental preparation. On the drive up to Tan Hill I felt relaxed but alert. My mind seemed to slip away onto some remoter plane so that although I was aware of everything happening around me, I was also detached from it. I could sense the 'motor' was ready to go but mentally I enjoyed a feeling of peace and calm.

The run itself turned out to be almost a reverse of last year's effort. I ran only moderately well to begin with and the big sweeping hills in the north; Great Shunner, Buckden Pike, Great Whernside did not give me an easy passage. Coming off the last into Grassington at 36 miles (58 km) I felt distinctly tired. It was here that last year my legs had 'gone' and I feared the same kind of thing was about to happen. I need not have worried. I came in feeling tired and left feeling strong. The parts had bedded in after their two week lay-off and I was now ready to start running economically and purposefully.

The rest of the run was both tough and enjoyable. I felt I was being stretched but my rest had restored my reserves of strength. And strength was certainly needed. There was a scythe of a wind whistling out of the east. I ran dressed for a winter's day and my poor support looked frozen. Once again I probed the night-time evils of Jackson's Ridge. It was that treacherous hour before first light when body and brain are at a low ebb and anxiety for the dawn may lead to uncertainty and poor judgement. This time Jackson allowed me to pass almost unchallenged, just one grough system of finely reticulated drainage channels wandered across our path, unmarked on map or memory.

By Todmorden at 5.40 a.m. and now 70 miles (115 km) beyond Tan Hill, I was into the uncertain light of a pinched and bitter morning. 'Yon Tod' provided a brief but cheering respite from the searching wind and I gulped a hasty breakfast. The attractions of the bleak little town grew in my mind's eye as I ascended once more to the even bleaker moors. Here, the wind, with little to oppose its progress from origins in what appeared to be Spitzbergen, screamed over the walls of the huge Warland reservoirs. Despite this arctic blast, my head felt muzzy and my senses seemed out of focus. I departed from the White House over Blackstone Edge feeling anxious.

Under the stimulus of this anxiety I ran the next leg very quickly and, what was better, strongly and smoothly. From here on I slipped into a lovely running–walking rhythm, I even found strength for little extravagances such as having a boost up Rollick Stones ridge on Bleaklow. I suppose such surges represent a delight in gaining a temporary freedom from the carefully regulated shackles of a strict schedule.

From Bleaklow Head the route takes the line currently used by the Marsden to Edale Fell race. The Marsden–Edale is also one of the most venerable of the Rucksack Club's winter walks and long familiarity enabled me to follow the most economical lines to Edale. With only 12 miles (19 km) remaining, the sun belatedly remembered its spring duties. More out of bravado than warmth, I changed into shorts, enjoying a sense of liberation, fresh air on bare legs. After the windswept northern Pennines, the long cold night and the bitter desolation of the moorland morning, it was so good to be treading my home ground; a pale sun on my face and the wind on my back.

The top of Long Hill is but a mile from my Buxton home. Foregathered to see me safely to my destination were my three eldest sons, Mark, Sean and Gerard. My fifth and youngest son, Michael, was also there. At seven, he was too young to run with us but being in my mid-forties, I was too old to be doing this kind of thing much longer. Before I am reduced to reminiscing in front of those fires which warm from without when those that burn from within are extinguished, I want my children to have a memory of me as a strong and active man.

Dotage is still some way off thankfully, at least surrounded by my fleet sons I was inspired to dismiss any weariness. Together we made short work of my scenic Goyt valley extension of the original route and once again joined that exhilarating charge for the Cat and Fiddle. I can't outsprint the lads any more but I could at least make them blow a bit as the now familiar adrenalin surge picked me up and carried me powerfully to spot height 1,690 ft (508 m), home of the second highest pub in England.

My time was 26 hours 36 minutes, over two and a half hours faster than my painful record of last year, nearly six hours faster than the record I had been so proud of six years previously. The latter had represented a major achievement for me, an anxious yet exciting journey into physical and mental unknowns. Now the run had become a test piece, an opportunity to prove and hone my fitness. And yet I had lost no respect for the route and the challenge it imposed. It was like an old and very tough friend, always ready to give you a metaphorical box on the ears should you attempt to take too many liberties.

My new time made me reconsider something I had thought theoretically possible for years. In the mid-1970s, George Rhodes, a club member and former international cross-country runner, had set off with Denis Weir to attempt a 24 hour Tan–Cat. Their attempt foundered when their support failed to materialise with torches for the night. I'd heard however that they were on target at the time. It is not too difficult to be on target half-way through a run and it was intriguing that neither had seen fit to try again. When I inspected the breakdown of my schedule times I reached the conclusion that, for me, a 24-hour completion would require 'speed training', perfect underfoot conditions, good weather, a short summer night, a dash of inspiration and a slice of good luck; a fascinating combination of variables which *may*, some day, tempt me to rattle these old bones just one more time.

The LDWA Dalesman Hundred

I'm not sure I was ready to tackle the Dalesman Hundred. One really should have extra reserves for an event of this length and be looking forward to it with fresh anticipation. I felt rather too relaxed and a little jaded as I set off alongside John Richardson *en route* for Ingleborough and Penyghent, two of the famous Yorkshire Three Peaks. We were in a group designated 'runners' while in the group of 'walkers', set off four hours previously, was Inken on her first attempt at 100 miles (160 km). There was good company around us too, Brian Harney, whose record I had broken on the Pennine Way, was there, as also was Pete Simpson, whose record I hoped to break later on the Coast to Coast. I did not feel to be running very well and constantly re-assured myself that this run was simply a build-up to that record attempt. It is difficult however for an old war horse not to respond to the bray of the battle trumpet – and these guys around us certainly meant business! Either they were over-estimating their abilities or I had, up to now, over-estimated mine.

My schedule was a fairly trustworthy one however and produced a final time of 22 hours. Having covered the route in training, I thought this was a slightly over-ambitious estimate. The leading group were already well ahead of my leg times. I decided to let them get on with it and concentrated on keeping a tight rein on John who was in danger of being dragged along with them.

The light rain at the start had assumed stair-rod proportions on Ingleborough and by Penyghent I thought we were in a monsoon. Having endured this kind of weather throughout spring, I became totally disenchanted. I felt tired from my Tan–Cat, I was not up with the leaders and altogether, I just wanted an excuse to quit. To make things worse, John was suffering from painful ankle tendons and was unlikely to be able to keep me company for much longer. The only excuse I had to quit was severe lack of enjoyment! Good enough really, but as my demon readily pointed out, I still needed this one as preparation for the Coast to Coast. I splashed onwards.

The ground was astonishingly waterlogged. The valley paths, in particular the Dalesway, were sticky mud ribbons along which I slid, skidded and cursed. After about only 25 miles (40 km), I began to pass walkers, often well-clad figures in stout brogues, some with the traditional blackthorn stick. In comparison I felt like a drowned and ill-equipped rat. A bad-tempered rat who muttered rude things about their great feet, nearly 400 pairs of them, which had churned this mud up to a quagmire.

By now, John had dropped behind. I pottered on alone thinking jaundiced thoughts about the British climate, the futility of ultra-hill running and my own recalcitrant stubbornness. Following the Pennine Way across Dodd Fell and down to Hawes brought me to Hardraw, a major support point. Here, the demon belatedly emerged and flared his nostrils as he caught sight of Brain Harney and an impressive group of other hard men. They looked rather cold, wet and tired. This was exactly how I felt, in fact I'd been ready to have a good feed and change into drier clothes; until now. I grabbed a cup of tea and a bun and, with a cheery wave, galloped straight out again. It really is amazing what a stimulating effect the misery and suffering of rival runners can have on me. I suspect something quite nasty is lurking under my pleasant exterior (probably the demon).

Light was fading and I hurried to make use of what had not been trapped by the sullen grey clouds. After a few miles I came across a stricken figure who yet had the guise and gait of a classy performer. It was Pete Simpson and he was suffering from 'hunger bonk' (hypoglycemia – low blood sugar). As he had just applied the usual remedy of a chocolate bar, or several, I assured him he would soon recover. In fact as darkness fell, he re-joined me and together we dropped back to the road.

The next support point was one I had been looking forward to. It was almost at 50 miles (80 km) and in my terms meant I was ready to head for home. In the support tent was one of those characters who represent a, thankfully, rare infestation on this type of event. An erstwhile leader, he had obviously started to run out of steam here. The rules of the LDWA Hundred allow the organisers to require walkers to form groups of four or more during the night; those first in are given 'waiting time' until sufficient numbers arrive to form a safe group. When dawn comes the group may split and those with 'waiting time' carry this advantage with them. As this particular night was merely damp with a little mist, the grouping rule was not being applied. However, this character complained that he did not know his way over the next set of hills and he should therefore be granted 'waiting time' until he could attach himself to someone who did!

I resented both his dependence on us to do his navigating and on his gaining a half-hour rest without penalty. By the time Pete and I arrived he was sipping his umpteenth cup of tea and grooming his feathers. As the three of us set off up Wild Boar Fell I made some pointed and rude remarks in this man's direction, they slid neatly off his back of course. I was not sure what rules were being applied but I had every intention of leaving him in the lurch at the first opportunity.

Such opportunity was sadly not forthcoming. Pete was far too much of a gentleman to divine my intentions and I had no axe to grind with Pete. Soon I had to concentrate all my intention on good navigation as a thick swathe of mist rolled across the fells and obscured all but a few feet of ground ahead. After successfully visiting the control point on Wild Boar summit we headed across Scarth Fell for remote Grisedale. Once we dropped below the mist route finding was relatively easy and I'd lost my chance to slip away I thought. However, at the next control both Pete and the other man seemed slow to get organised. Seizing my chance I poured my scalding tea into a plastic bottle and crept surreptitiously out of the shelter. No one followed and after a few fairy footsteps I went scampering off down the road. I kept up the pressure for a mile or so then eased off. I felt pleased to be rid of the pest but sorry for Pete.

After crossing the moor below Aye Gill Pike I began the three-mile (5 km) road section to Dent. I was now running almost effortlessly and passing scores of mainly silent, shuffling figures, like some ghostly, vanquished army. I had also passed another runner who thought he was the leader but as a matter of caution, I disbelieved him. Approaching Dent I heard a cheerful hail; it was Inken. I had not expected to see her so soon but she had spent an unscheduled hour on a scenic tour of Swarth Fell. She was in remarkably good spirits, however, so I guessed she was not too perturbed, as I would have been.

Together we ran into the church hall at Dent where I quickly swallowed a jar of peaches I'd sent on here. At 3.00 a.m. I did not fancy the cooked breakfast on offer but got moving quickly again. I'd heard there was only one person ahead of me. He was 15 minutes up but with 37 miles (60 km) left to catch him I fancied my chances. After only a few miles I passed a small group and ascertained that the former leader was one of their number. He was lightly clad and carrying only a 'bum-bag' which could not possibly have held all the equipment demanded by the rules. I was not concerned, I could see by his gait and the look in his eyes that he was a spent force. As I ascended high on the shoulder of Whernside *en route* for Ribblehead, a long, cruel shower came splattering in on the chill dawn wind. I guessed it would demoralise my rival sufficiently for him to give up the ghost at the next checkpoint, which I believe it did. I was more concerned about the men of proven character like Brian Harney, Pete Simpson, Roger Baumeister and so on, they were behind me now but they would not fade so easily nor would a little rain deter them. I also thought about those 'walkers' who were still ahead. What if one of them was a dark horse who had joined the 10.00 a.m. start to disguise his intentions? I decided I would only be really sure of my position when I had passed all the early starters too and was first in the field.

Acting on this decision I set out to press home whatever advantage I had. At Nethergill I came upon my old friend Denis Weir out for an 'easy' day with the walking fraternity. After sharing a mile or so with him I set off with much lighter tread. Following the very muddy path of the Dalesway to Yockenthwaite I observed that instead of keeping to the official route on the Dalesway footpath, there were people on the other side of the river following the road which, in these conditions, was easier and faster.

Shortly after, I arrived at the village of Buckden and enjoyed a cup of tea with another old friend, Alan Heaton. Now in his late fifties, Alan is a former holder of the Lake District Fell Record; 65 peaks within 24 hours and of course, a former Pennine Way record holder. As usual, Alan sounded very pessimistic about his own form and fitness but imparted the useful information that only two walkers were now in front of me.

I set off with some trepidation on a climb I had been dreading, the long haul from Buckden over to Litton. I was now feeling leg weary and hoped that a glimpse of the two in front would spur me on. I was rather mystified when I crossed a large patch of smooth mud in front of a gate to discover no footprints whatever. I examined the mud; not even a hole to indicate someone had pole-vaulted across! Well, I must be in front now. I relaxed a little.

Coming down to Litton I glanced back casually and was horrified to see a figure in shorts less than five minutes behind. Sensing the cup of victory, which had begun to be very important, being dashed from my lips, I galloped along the road, covering over two miles (3 km) in 15 minutes. The steep ascent of Yew Cougar Scar slowed me down but looking back I could see no sign of pursuit. Still not convinced, I pressed on until I felt almost dizzy. I never found out who the figure was but he certainly got me moving again.

I was now only a handful of miles from the finish on good running country round Malham Tarn with the sun at last bursting through. At each checkpoint I received much encouragement from the cheery, selfless souls who manned them. Their friendly banter lifted my spirits out of my rather grim resolve. Suddenly, round a bend, I came upon a pair of figures, quite obviously the two incredible mud-gliders. I expected a cut and thrust battle over the last miles and hitched up me loin cloth! However they subsided with merely a polite 'Good morning'. After a last cruel knee-wracking descent I jogged somewhat stiffly back into the finish at Settle High School. My time was 21 hours 45 minutes, pleasing in the circumstances. Despite my alarm at Litton I had to wait an hour and a half before, fairly predictably, Brian Harney trotted serenely over the bridge and into the finish. What really delighted me however, was to see Inken running freely and easily along the road in nineteenth position. She was the first woman to finish and over four hours ahead of the ladies national 100-mile record holder.

Later, I met one of the incredible mud-gliders and asked him rather pointedly about the route he and his friend had followed from Buckden to Litton. He admitted they had not followed the official route but assured me their alternative was no easier, 'just less muddy'! I commented that this was strange, as when reconnoitering for the event, I had used the route they had taken to save time because it was half a mile shorter and 200 feet less climbing. This did not stop the same man going forward to accept his badge for having 'completed' his tenth 100 mile (160 km) event. I was, however, amused to read recently that several people had been disqualified during spot checks on the 1987 event. Guess who was one of them?

Such petty self-betrayal does more harm to the culprits than those they take advantage of. However, the ethics of ultra fell running are close to my heart notwithstanding their absence from tablets of stone. Occasionally I am asked, though never by fellow runners, how I 'prove' I have followed a route and not taken short-cuts (or even caught the bus!). My invariable answer is, 'Because I say so.' At times I have certainly 'lost' the route and this has always resulted in going further and taking longer. A successful run is nearly always marked by crisp, accurate route finding. On my longer runs I am usually accompanied but I reserve the right to cover sections solo when I choose. Some runners have taken to dropping notes on summits and getting passing walkers to sign route cards. Though laudable in itself and certainly having a safety value, I would not like to see this becoming obligatory. I would certainly refuse to follow any such scheme. I first of all run for myself and meeting my own standards I find exacting enough. By the same token, if the likes of Martin Stone, a prolific soloist and note placer, tells me he has run 26 Munroes in 24 hours (which he has), I only need his word, and so should everyone else. Our sport has a glorious freedom and individuality, but it is a hard one. To achieve success in it you must somehow reach a truth within yourself. To cheat is to truly embrace failure, you forfeit your integrity, you have lost.

The Coast to Coast

Having trained through a wet spring, endured bitter easterlies on the Tan–Cat and paddled round the Dalesman Hundred, I was looking forward to better conditions for my Coast to Coast attempt. I was making the bid on the midsummer weekend and surely after the tribulations I had suffered from the weather recently and over the years, I was due for a run in perfect conditions?

My support team consisted of my son Mark who would be a strong runner, while his brother, Sean would also run sections but be mainly responsible for the driving. He enjoyed this latter role, being something of a thwarted rally-driver at heart. Inken was to be 'anchorman' for the whole support strategy and John Beatty was to fulfil the role of 'official photographer' and runner. This team would take me as far as Keld, just about half-way, where John Richardson and Dave Crutch would take over. As usual, I was confident that I had planned well and was very happy with my support team.

We drove up to Cumbria in perfect conditions. My intention had been to start at 3.00 a.m. after a few hours sleep. By starting very early I hoped I could get away with only one full night out. A local forecast at 7.00 p.m., however, foretold of a strong front moving in from the west. My luck with the weather was not due to change after all. The front would reach the Lake District about the time I intended to set off. Although my schedule had been planned to have me at certain places at the right time, I guessed that if I were to waken to the sound of heavy rain being driven against the tent at 2.30 a.m. I might very easily not start at all!

Bravely or rashly therefore, on reaching St Bees shortly before 9.00 p.m. I grasped the bull by the nettles, leapt out of the car, tightened my laces and set off on my 190 mile (304 km) journey across England to the North Sea. By the time John Beatty joined me I had established a rhythm and accepted, quite without relish, that I would now be running through two nights. The record I had to beat was a relatively 'soft' one. It was a little over 51 hours and had been set by Pete Simpson and Frank Thomas of Dark Peak Fell Runners. When one became 'lame' the other had selflessly stayed alongside and so forfeited the chance to complete the run under two days. My own target was 46 hours but I had secretly thought that I might get down towards 42 hours if all went perfectly; that ambition subsided with the 9.00 p.m. start.

At Ennerdale Bridge the contents of the car boot filled a lay-by. Travelling with Mark alongside Ennerdale Water and through the ensuing pine plantations was an eerie experience. There was a mighty but restless wind soughing through the trees, sometimes on our backs, sometimes on our faces. No real force of wind could reach us through the high wall of pines but it threatened trouble when we finally emerged. The night was now very dark. Splats of rain began to dash at us. The atmosphere was oppressive and our mood very subdued. Suddenly I spotted a tiny incandescence to the side of the track. Stopping, I discovered a glow-warm, a tiny jewel in a black eternity. Its physical presence was as nothing, its power as symbol limited only by my own frail and mortal spirit. But if I had been neither frail nor mortal I would have no reason to quest or to strive. Lead kindly light indeed! My spirit *shall* strive to follow.

As I crossed from Ennerdale to Honister, the brain as well as the spirit had to rise to the challenge. Mark had obtained a set of compass bearings from John but was not sure what they referred to. After following one which threatened to lead us down into Buttermere, I got my mind into the navigating. We endured anxious moments in the mist and rain, moving over ground I had never intended covering at night. Gradually the paths re-appeared and the contours fell into a recognised pattern, all was well.

WILD TRAILS TO FAR HORIZONS

We arrived with the dawn at Rosthwaite, a misty dawn it is true but not particularly wet. Perhaps the forecast of bad weather was exaggerated? Alas! as Inken and I climbed towards Greenup Edge heading for Grasmere, the wind screamed down to meet us. On the ridge to Helm Crag, heavy rain was driven into our faces by a wind of unusual power.

The front had arrived as forecast. However, there were two aspects of the storm which were not as forecast. First, the wind was not blowing out of the south-west but out of the south-east; second, while unpleasant enough in the valleys, there was a kind of 'jet-stream' effect such that above about 1,500 ft (450 m), the wind speed seemed to double. The general trend of the Coast to Coast is, over much of the first half, towards the south-east. Once I was above 1,500 ft (450 m), conversation with my support became impossible. The wind constantly knocked me off balance and I was simply engaged in a battle for survival.

It was a relief to drop into the comparative shelter of the valleys which were merely very wet. Climbing out of Patterdale and into the screaming misery of wind and rain on the long haul over Kidsty Pike, was perhaps the crux of the whole route. At least I had the prospect of the sheltered run alongside Haweswater to look forward to. However, on the section over to Shap, the rain amply compensated for any abatement of wind strength. Here also, as I attempted to lift my pace, Inken, on her second support stint, began to fade. She had a recurrence of a knee problem but also, I think, the savage beating we had just taken from the elements, had sapped her spirit. There was, in truth, little pleasure in this. Our hopes for a fine and happy run were being blasted away. The support share the hardships but may not always be able to access the inspiration which can so powerfully assist the runner. I eased off the pace and together we walked into Shap. What was a paltry 10 minutes from a record I was now unlikely to achieve anyway against a friendship?

Shap; 62 miles (104 km); 16 hours; rain bouncing off the puddles; wind sweeping the desolate A6, but . . . a familiar and welcome smell, fish and chips! I suddenly realised I was hungry, very hungry. I had to wait quite a long time before the feast was produced and the longer I sat contemplating the weather outside, the less inclined I felt to continue. Still, John and the lads did a great job of drying my gear under the hand-dryer in the public toilets. So, although I felt I was only postponing the inevitable, I decided I most certainly would not quit yet. With Sean for company I headed off on cold, stiff legs but with a fortified feeling inside.

As we traversed the rather dreary countryside approaching Orton, the rain eased for a time and then continued as heavy and prolonged showers. The wind felt like a big hand holding me back. Any running into the wind was impossible and I had to be content with sneaking a little run now and again as I turned temporarily out of it or followed a sheltering wall. Sean is probably the most cheerful of my sons and his company brightened the grey and depressing day. An eternal, sometimes infernal optimist, Sean carries his own sunshine with him. He cast it round us now and so, when I reached the car at Sunbiggin Tarn, I was, like Sam Ogelthwaite, moist but determined!

The moments at Sunbiggin Tarn are etched into my memory as a series of crystal clear and poignant images. The area is, for me, strangely foreboding and mysterious. The Tarn itself, a large sink-hole, is rush-rimmed and houses large colonies of sea-birds. These were now wheeling and gliding in vast numbers, their forlorn cries adding to the pervading sense of desolation. In the back of the car John Beatty sat looking both drawn and animated. He spoke elatedly of photographing the birds but he also told me that his Achilles tendons were very sore. It was John's turn to accompany me on the next section and he wanted very much to again share my burden of miles and play his part in what he considered an epic venture. He had resolved to take a chance with his injury and come anyway. I looked carefully into his face and saw the anxiety behind his eyes. Another friend willing to endure hardship so that I might achieve my dream. But no! Much as I had looked forward to the company and fascinating conversation of this remarkable artist I could not accept that my joy should be his anguish.

My disappointment was as nothing compared to the great strength I drew from the simple fact that John had been prepared to come with me. As I set off once more, my mere stubborn resolve to struggle on began to be replaced by a more positive form of determination. John's response had been for me another inspirational gleam in the dark.

In a happier state of mind I entered Smardale valley, where Sunbiggin is foreboding, Smardale is light and cheerful. Perhaps happy, long-ago spirits still inhabit the ancient village settlements above the valley. Whatever the reason, I have always experienced a feeling of peace and a lightening of mood here. I dropped out of the incessant buffeting of the wind, all was quiet and the rain eased. By the time I ascended once more to the wind's rough embrace I had established a little haven of calm within myself. This haven would stand against the storm for some time yet.

I trotted and walked towards Kirkby Stephen, my mind encapsulated in this comfortable state. All systems on low output, the body performing economically and mechanically. So switched off had I become that I missed my turning in the town. Jogging contentedly along, leaving the support point in my wake, I suddenly became aware of Inken racing up behind me shouting uncomplimentary remarks. I returned feeling a little foolish.

The next leg was likely to be a crucial one. First however, I must consider whether I shall undertake it at all. I have been going for approaching 20 hours although I have covered only 82 miles (132 km). Most of the time I have been battered by the weather and this must have taken its toll of my strength. The next leg is a long one over a bleak moor, Nine Standards Rigg. Once embarked, I am committed to going on into the second night as John Richardson and Dave Crutch are due to meet me at Keld at the end of this section. If I want to stop them coming out, if I feel there is no realistic chance of success, I must contact them now. I cannot bring them out and then quit.

I am hanging on by a thread. If I lose any further touch with my schedule, I will lose my drive. Once that happens, this weather will force me into swift submission. On the other hand my legs seem to have escaped the paralyzing stiffness which was gripping them at Shap. The thread is tight stretched but it has been well spun. It will hold me through another night – I hope.

Off then and up into the mists wreathing Nine Standards Rigg. Mark is with me now and he seems quite unaffected by the weather, he too has matured with his running years. As we climb higher we move into heavy rain, heaving bogs and almost palpable mist. Apart from 80 plus miles (130 km) in my legs it's just like being at home on Bleaklow! Quite to my surprise, I begin to feel amazingly cheerful. Then we lose the narrow trod coming from the summit. Follows an age of stumbling over tussocks as none of my intelligent guesstimates bears fruit. Eventually, Mark spots a stake and we regain the path which we have been following on a parallel course only 100 yards away.

At last we leave the moor behind and the ground becomes more interesting as we descend to Raven Seat and approach Keld itself. Although it is not yet 9.00 p.m. the light is fading under the heavy cloud blanket. At this time of the year I had expected to have useful light until nearly 11.00 p.m. I must minimise my stop time at Keld in order to utilise whatever glims remain. The urge to dwell in the car, to savour the warmth and dryness, to enjoy the company of good friends, must be resisted.

And in Keld, the entire support team were gathered. John and Dave, not having supported through a day and night of depressing weather, were in good humour. Although my own mood was serious, even grim, I could not help but respond in kind to the cheerful banter. I managed to retain my concentration however and within 10 minutes I had changed shoes, donned dry clothes and eaten.

As I set off once more, I realised that John Beatty was missing. We soon ran into the flash of his camera and his words of encouragement echoed through my mind as we crossed the River Swale and headed for the delightfully named Crackpot Hall. The bridge across the river sees the convergence of the Tan–Cat route, the Pennine Way and the Coast to Coast. What a place to steer my wheelchair towards in future years! I was now with Inken and John Richardson. Inken should really have stepped down before this, she's been on the go now for 24 hours. She looked intense and preoccupied, almost as if it was she who was attempting this record. I hoped in asking her to coordinate the attempt I had not imposed too large a burden on her. John, fresh, fit, experienced and resourceful was, as ever, a symbol of strength and steady optimism. Flanked by my two friends I felt suddenly transformed, full of vitality and hope. All thoughts of quitting vanished and were replaced by a hunger to consume the miles. Keld was half-way and by the time I'd left it I had taken 24 hours. It is almost impossible to improve on one's time for the first half of an ultra route, the sleepless miles have an insidious but irresistible braking effect. If I am to even approach that 48-hour target, I must drive on.

While the daylight permitted, I enjoyed the Dales scenery and the interesting ground with its remains of the ancient lead mining industry. John is a great conversationalist and his wit and warmth eased the miles. Inken also, responded cheerfully to this lighter, more optimistic mood and we travelled through the gathering gloom enjoying each other's company. All too soon however, the gloom became night and with the night came a terrible attack of sleepiness. As we followed the interminable, stony track to Surrender Bridge, I became both very tired and desperately sleepy. I long for the uphill section just before Surrender Bridge, I can allow myself to walk that. How tired my mind must be. I've reached Surrender Bridge having run uphill without being able to perceive the gradient. A mistake, but a revealing one. When even the mind abdicates its power over the body and seeks temporary oblivion, an idea deeply embedded in an uncompromising will may impel the body ruthlessly onwards.

Black midnight at Surrender Bridge. A subdued glow of light from the two tents where the others were settled down. A bleak spot. Yet I yearned with all my heart, it seemed, to crawl into one of those tents and lay down my weary head. But this desire must have been less than that which compelled me to accomplish my journey. I paused only long enough to say farewell to Inken. For 27 hours she had been the dynamo driving the support machine. Not only had her running contribution been considerable but in these conditions the pressure on all other aspects of support had been enormous. At last she consented to rest and I was glad.

My slow pace thus far meant that I was now, more or less, where my original schedule had placed me. However, although I had reconnoitered this section twice, the Stygian blackness made route finding difficult indeed. At one time John and I stood with torches, looking for a track which was only 10 yards away. It was one of those spooky nights, of which I have known only a handful, which seem to draw in and smother all light sources. Our torch beams had no power to penetrate the black vortex. Following the shapes and images of my mind rather than the ground, we proceeded rather haltingly. The concentration needed at least helped focus my mind. I emerged from the well of sleepiness amazingly alert once more. Sufficiently aware, for instance, to discern what a masterly job Dave Crutch had done in converting a spacious and rather period bus shelter in Reeth to a well-appointed support point.

The route from Reeth is intricate but my homework paid off and at 3.30 a.m. in Richmond there were faint glimmers of returning light. Leaving the town, still with John, I made an error and we found ourselves on the wrong side of a sewage works. John decided we should short-cut across the works to regain our line. This involved clambering up two eight-foot-high fences which were capped with strands of barbed wire. Swaying precariously on top of these, legs akimbo, I felt rather vulnerable. I bet Ted Dance's *Rules to protect runners from their follies* would circumscribe such practices in order, I suppose, that the practices should not circumscribe the runners (as it were). Still, one can see the funny side of it, particularly as from this vantage point there was a perfectly good path visible just outside the fence.

After this excitement, the next sections were rather tedious. Wet fields, long tracks and the notorious eight miles (13 km) of road to Ingleby Cross and the freedom of the North York Moors. Near Catterick there was one moment of unexpected splendour. Low on the horizon, the grey uniformity of the dawn sky was irresistibly penetrated by a gash of light. As I stopped and stared, a chasm appeared in the clouds. Next moment the incandescent orange flare of the rising sun sprang through the gap. In awed wonder I regarded the huge glaring eye of energy, and he regarded me . . . 'Puny mortal, of course I still burn. Did you think otherwise?' Another gleam of light perhaps, but this one too awesome for comfort. The rift in the grey curtain snapped shut and I was left to run and muse in the watery dawn.

I had thought the long road section would allow me to pull back some time. Unfortunately it coincided with my usual morning low point. Despite Dave's bright chatter alongside me, I felt sleepy and could barely shuffle along. The only energy I possessed was manifest in a feeble urge to strangle Dave! My stupefied mind told me this would be ungrateful and a misuse of energy. Eventually I began to wake up and then I was genuinely grateful for his cheerful company and his gentle humour. Dave and I share a common ambition; he wants to complete the Bob Graham Round and I want to help him do it.

At 7.30 a.m. the morning had become milder and drier. As I completed the last few miles to Ingleby Cross alone I could feel a pulse of excitement beginning to swell within me. Ingleby Cross marks the start of the final section, about 50 miles (80 km) across the North York Moors. It is also where I expected to meet my good friend and colleague from work, Ian Cockerill. A native of this area, Ian was happy to combine a family visit with some support running. It was to Ian I turned a few years and many thousand miles ago on a muddy Birmingham tow-path and announced my intention to have 'Just one go at the Pennine Way'. We had shared many a boring Birmingham mile since then and now, at last, we had an opportunity to share some real running.

As I swept into the support point a wonderful feeling of strength and happiness had filled me. At that moment, I truly would not have changed places with anyone on earth. I was a little embarrassed at having kept Ian waiting so long. At least he had been able to return home for a second breakfast. It was good to see him and as usual he was impeccably attired in a splendidly matched running outfit. I feel Ian is very much a Beau Brummel among runners, particularly runners like me.

Feeling therefore a mite travel-stained and shabby, I set off with Ian and Inken. My own tension gone, I had hoped to see Inken rather more relaxed too but while the runner may well enter states of euphoria as he embarks on the last stages of a long run, the role of the support team is to exercise constant care and vigilance. Well, perhaps smiles would come later, I thought. Still in a happy frame of mind I left for Beacon Hill with the two of them. It was at this point that John Beatty appeared with his camera and captured a picture which is now very dear to me. That I look a little weary on it still surprises me but I know the peace and happiness that glowed within at that time. The picture has become precious to me, and to Ian and Inken, I hope.

Gradually my euphoria begins to fade as a physical fatigue seeps slowly back. Under the influence of heavy rain, the paths over the moors have assumed the consistency of porridge. The constant fight for purchase and balance is sapping my strength. After the mud, the flat cinder track of the old railway to the Lion Inn is a relief. Soon, of course, the tediousness of these rather empty miles begins to weigh heavily. I start to fancy that the inn is round the next bend

Ian, Inken and Mike leaving Ingleby Cross on the Coast to Coast.

several miles too soon. I realise I must be very tired to make such bad miscalculations. Eventually we begin to meet runners in various states of disrepair coming towards us. Although at first this introduces a little variety, I soon get tired of saying 'Howdo' and relapse into a state bordering apathy.

At last the Lion Inn hove into view and, as always, I experienced that surge of pleasure which accompanies these little reunions. And finally, a real smile from Inken. With only about 30 miles (50 km) remaining, she too must be anticipating the end of what has become a more demanding venture than we ever envisaged. But now I have plenty of good company on all sections as my entire support team switch in and out as it suits them. With their good cheer I keep picking up but despite these better moments I seem to be on a slow downward spiral. I am tired with both the bone-aching weariness of physical fatigue and the mind-numbing effects of sleep deprivation. On the road out of Grosmont I have a desperate fight to stay awake. A few minutes sleep might help but I will not yield any more of my precious time.

At Glaisdale, perhaps for the first time ever, the support point elicits no response. I feel very dejected. With so few miles to go I should be feeling elated not depressed. I can hardly face getting up and going on. Even my support team seem to have caught my mood, everyone is very subdued. Only one person looks after me at the stop, the others hover quietly around. I notice John with his camera but he won't intrude and contents himself with some long-range shots. This is like a wake – my own! Although my mind is observant and distantly receptive, my brain isn't functioning as it should. John Richardson has just calculated that at my present pace I might slip under 48 hours. I have the utmost confidence in John but as I shuffle along with Mark and Dave my repeated efforts at mental arithmetic keep producing the same result: I cannot possibly achieve 48 hours, in fact, I may be two hours adrift of this. Eventually after several miles of stumbling physical and mental effort I realise the error is mine. The Coast to Coast mileage is 190 (304 km) but mentally I had always geared myself up for 200 miles (320 km). Now I was approaching the end, I had forgotten to knock off those 'extra' miles.

With an indescribable feeling of joy and relief I reduced my miles remaining from 22 to 12. The tentacles of anxiety and self-doubt which have been dragging me irresistibly down into the black pit of despair are severed at a stroke. Thus released, the spirit soars and begins to pull my tired body after it.

The lovely silvan path from Little Beck past Falling Foss restores me entirely and it is with a start that I realise I have reached my final support point, there are only 10 miles (16 km) remaining. An excitement begins to seize me. This run had been so very hard. I might have quit at any time yet both route completion and record now lie within my grasp. With John Richardson, Dave, Mark and Sean all gathered around me I set off up the hill. It is essential to run if possible. A crazy joy spurs me to put in two hard bursts which I note with glee have John wheezing – the run-in has begun.

This finishing effort must start early. The final cliff-top miles are undulating and broken by stiles, I anticipate difficulty in actually getting over them. Covering stretches of rough grass and heather, my leg-weariness returns. On track and road I have an almost aching hunger to devour the miles. Approaching Hawkser, where Ian is waiting, I know I can't run up all the hills, then somehow do, and now everyone is breathing hard.

Ian has sussed out the rather intricate route through the caravan park which we take at speed. John, rather ill-advisedly, stops to relieve himself and has great difficulty re-establishing contact. As we run ever more frantically, my mind recedes and I become a running machine. At last, the dreaded cliff-top path. As we twist and turn down vicious little bends, my foot pivots on a larger blister which bursts with a flare of pain. Although I am brought back to reality I will not stop. Gradually, the agony subsides in the flow of adrenalin.

By now the pace is taking its toll. I glance back from a stile; Dave is well off the back and John is pulling horrible faces. Mark and Sean, still in possession of their youthful speed, are enjoying both the run and John's discomfiture. Ahead, Ian seems to be running like a pursued hare as I strive to catch him. The path is never ending, will my strength or adrenalin hold out? I don't think I can keep this up much longer.

Suddenly I recognised the final approach to Robin Hood's Bay. I had long prepared for this descent to the sea through the little village. The road plummets down at 1 in 3 and even my best scenario had me trotting cautiously down to the finish. The expected reality of pain-wracked legs as stiff as rusty hinges, I had deliberately not entertained.

The finish of the Coast to Coast. Entering Robin Hood's Bay with Mark and Sean.

Sympathy for Dave who got left behind in the rush for the finish of the Coast to Coast. From left to right: Sean, Dave, Mike, Inken, John Richardson.

Sharing a quiet moment with John at the end of the Coast to Coast.

Miraculously, it was not like that at all. The frantic rush along the cliffs did not cease at the top of the hill. In fact, I accelerated down it with only Mark and Sean in contact.

Shortly after I completed the run I wrote up the account in my log-book, partly because I wanted to capture the unique flavour of this remarkable finish. This is what I wrote:

The final mad, utterly ridiculous flight down the steep hill to the sea-front is like a crazy dream. If I meet with a car on this bend I know I shall simply put one foot on the bonnet, one on the roof and be over! Nothing can touch me. I'm at the pinnacle of all my mental and physical powers. I am not merely alive, I am a life force, elemental, joyful.

Perhaps that is why another elemental life force, the sea, creates such an impact on my spirit as I rush headlong into it, cooling my burning feet. It's crashing around like a living entity, so welcome! How marvellous that it has swept right up to the edge of the cobbles and is in such lively form. I persuade the others to come and join me and we all embrace with the waves laughing around us.

Never have I felt such sheer and simple joy at the end of a run. Moments such as these not only provide the answer to why one does things like this but why we are alive at all. One moment of such joy is worth more, far more than countless years of steady rational living. To have encountered hardship, discomfort, to have experienced one's physical, mental and spiritual limitations and weaknesses, to have found a path beyond them, not conquering them but accepting and yet transcending them, to have been supported, guarded and guided lovingly by friends represents, for me, a joy both sublime and supreme. I ask for no more.

Postscript

Whenever my thoughts go back to the finish of my Coast to Coast, the overwhelming memory of it is the feeling of joy I experienced. When that mad rush came to an abrupt end in the sea it was as if that sublime emotion burst from me with all the power of a sunrise. Perhaps it was as well that fatigue later set in or I might have been consumed by my own fires! However, two more pleasures awaited me before the day ended. First, having been borne off to our rest camp I sneaked out and ventured down that fearsome 1 in 3 again, this time tottering very authentically. I then surprised the support team ensconced in the pub. I didn't want to be left out, and anyway, I thought I'd earned a pint. I can't remember whether I had one or two but what I next remember is being gently laid down on someone's lilo in my tent. I can still recall the absolute luxury of my aching bones finally coming to rest and kindly hands tucking me in.

Once I realised I was going to get inside 48 hours for the route I lost interest in the time. However, I recorded 46 hours and 49 minutes, this meant I had completed the second half over an hour faster than the first, my last burst was not without effect. Still, the record must be considered as 'soft'; the experience of it however, was not.

My Pennine Way record had realised for me an almost sacred dream. Even on completion my mind could scarcely grasp the reality and my joy and happiness seemed to reach sublime, even ethereal heights. The Coast to Coast record was relatively unimportant, but the experience, so unexpectedly demanding, was everything. The joy I experienced on completion seemed so natural, so simple, a burst of delight at being alive, of being strong, of striving and succeeding, of being so blessed with the gift of life and the gift of friends. That wild, exuberant finish was nothing other than a cry of joy and my own personal thanksgiving.

chapter seven

PLUNDERING THE SPIRIT

The Southern Uplands Way: Preparation 1986

As 1985 gave way to 1986 I began to cast about for a suitable venture. I had enjoyed the shape of my previous year, two minor targets and one major, so I thought I would attempt something similar. Several friends suggested I should consider running the Southern Uplands Way which I had only vaguely heard of. Perhaps as a hint I received a set of maps and a guide as a present from Inken.

It transpired that the Southern Uplands Way was a sort of Scottish Coast to Coast. It starts on the west coast at Port Patrick near Stranraer and finishes at Cockburnspath south of Edinburgh. There did not seem to have been any record attempts for this quite recent innovation, but at 212 miles (340 km) it appeared to offer the kind of challenge I sought. I was keen to do a long run in Scotland, the areas are less populated and the hills seem never-ending. For some time I had nursed an ambition to devise an overland route north to south through Scotland but the temptation of a ready-made route was inviting. I mentally postponed my north-south route until the days when only distance and not time is important.

As usual, I began hard training in early spring. Returning from the rigours of my annual Scottish winter mountaineering course I was surprised to find that even in Derbyshire, winter dragons held spring in thrall. I found training unusually onerous and I never seemed to be running well. Although the deep endurance always lay beneath the surface I felt jaded. Either my successes had satisfied my appetite for really hard ultra running, or I was over the hill – in more ways than one! Certainly my knees were giving me increasing pain, particularly downhill, but I did not like to think the ageing process had begun to gnaw at my overall strength. As ever there was one sure way to find out, head first, full tilt into a windmill. Well, perhaps not full tilt; as usual I had a look at the windmill first. The Southern Uplands Way represented my 'training carrot' that spring, and I was keen to get the feel of what would be an entirely new piece of ground for me.

I was charmed by the start at Port Patrick. I had the good fortune to begin my training run on a fine sunny morning. At 6.30 a.m. the place was deserted, but very picturesque in the morning light, and I began to think I had made a very good choice of route. As the miles unwound, however, I started to entertain doubts. The Way was turning out to be a real Jekyll and Hyde; relatively short stretches of great charm and beauty were interspersed by either long stony tracks, or, what was worse, boring miles of metalled road. I began to look forward fervently to the section through the Galloway Hills, which I knew were very scenic.

The Galloway section was indeed scenic. Unfortunately, much, too much, of the Way followed stony forest tracks. Road and track may offer swift passage but I found the unchanging rhythm required monotonous and tiring. Furthermore, the hard surface tends to jar joints and muscles.

I spent another three days reconnoitring the Way and my initial impression was amply confirmed. The going underfoot seemed to alternate between extremely wet, boggy terrain and hard track, an unfortunate combination, designed to cause severe foot problems. The route itself either took my breath away or bored me to distraction. For instance, I traversed the Lowther Hills on a fine spring evening with not a soul around. The slanting sun sparkled on the fresh spring mantle and cast deep shadows in clefts and hollows. The hills radiated to all points of the compass and here and there a patch of old snow glinted faintly. Descending from these boldly rounded hills I was faced with a mile of metalled road followed by three miles of forest track. By the time I was coming to the end of such a tedious section all sense of inspiration had evaporated.

My third day of reconnaissance took me over perhaps the most pleasant section of the Way thus far. From Daer Reservoir the route negotiates some surprisingly rough ground. I discovered that whenever forest tracks were left one followed forest breaks which were paths mainly in the minds of the route planners. Perhaps increasing use will establish better going, but at present you may encounter tussocks that tickle your nose. Having battled through both the tedious and the rough I crossed under the A74 at Beattock and was rewarded with a very fine ascent to Ettrick Head. Even the forest track was enjoyable, offering a greater variety of gradient and scenery than usual. Just before the final climb to Ettrick Head, the track and everything around seemed to spiral downwards into a green tree-shrouded hole in the hills. I had an eerie feeling that I was going down for ever and was quite relieved when a path branched off and made uphill again.

I followed a vigorous stream coursing between green, tree-lined banks. With the sun now dappling through the trees, the stream leaping into small quiet pools and the whole area containing no hint of any other human presence, the memory of the metalled miles faded to temporary insignificance. Better was to come. At the crest of the climb I reached Craigmichan Scar, an impressively steep hillside, where the exposed rock and scree could easily pitch the unwary into a closer acquaintance with the valley floor. This is a key watershed with Moffat Water flowing into the Irish Sea via the Solway Firth and Ettrick Water joining the Tweed, which it accompanies to the North Sea. The area seems to be a haunt for various species of birds, and if I was less ignorant of such matters I might relate what they were. I enjoyed watching their busy spring-time activities – and I know feathered killers swoop hereabouts for I discovered gory remains.

It is at Craigmichan that those responsible for devising the route play their most dastardly trick on the poor walker. Having gained a height of 2,000 ft

(600 m) the obvious option is to continue NW and reach the line of hills which then undulate north-eastwards above Moffat Water. I know these hills from club walks and they give invigorating, mainly pathless walking with excellent views north and west to the hills around Hart Fell and down into the famous gorge containing the Grey Mares Tail waterfall. Instead of this an easy but quite soulless expedient is followed. The inevitable forest track is reached and the route plunges rapidly down as if fearing the heights. This is bad enough, but worse is to follow; five miles (8 km) of metalled road to Scabcleuch whence one ascends to rejoin the line from the hills which need never have been abandoned.

Whether such planning is the result of fearing to expose the walker to a (modestly) high level traverse or fear of crossing some sacred grouse moor, I know not. But I deplore such pusillanimity. If Tom Stephenson had adopted such an unimaginative and weak-kneed approach to the Pennine Way we might well be walking to Kirk Yetholm along the A6. With all the silk at their disposal the Scottish planners have produced a sow's ear.

At this point I should either have abandoned my plans for the Southern Uplands Way, or modified the route to my own tastes. Instead, I used a car on all the major road sections and lied to myself that I would not mind coping with the road too much when I was doing the route for real. Thus my ambition to set records on definitive long-distance footpaths blinded me to the frequent lapses in those virtues which a route must possess to sustain my spirit while making the attempt. Whereas I had regarded the Coast to Coast as a series of wonderful areas of hill and moor connected by annoyingly frequent stretches of road, I was rapidly coming to the conclusion that the Southern Uplands Way consisted of almost endless miles of road and track interspersed with short stretches of tantalisingly beautiful country.

This feeling was confirmed in the area around St Mary's Loch. Leaving the loch behind, the route climbs easily up into the hills heading for Blake Muir. I reached the high point on a day of sunshine and sparkling visibility. Turning through 360 degrees I could see no cultivated valleys, no walls, no habitation anywhere in sight. The hills rolled away to the blue and purple distance in every direction. Yet again, I was tempted to believe such free and open country would compensate for the route's obvious shortcomings.

Beyond Blake Muir the Way follows an old drove road high over Minch Moor and the 'Three Brethren'. Although I did not realise at the time, once I had descended to Yair Bridge from the Three Brethren I had little more to look forward to. The attractiveness of a long distance footpath does not lie in its hills alone. However, to compensate for a lack of hills the alternative ground must be charming indeed. After crossing the Tweed at Melrose the route certainly traverses a further set of hills. I cannot believe they are really as dreary as the line chosen by the Southern Uplands Way would suggest. In traversing them I found I was surrounded by countless acres of monotonous grouse moor having all the variety of a desert and none of the romance. Apart from the odd dell or wooded valley, there was no compensation to be found elsewhere on the remainder of the route.

Perhaps covering these last sections, tired and in the rain, on my last training day did not help. As I thrashed down the final road miles *en route* for the cliff top finish, memories of the cliffs above Robin Hood's Bay spurred me on. An excellent footpath across a gorse strewn hillside raised my hopes still further. Alas! The cliff top 'path' was a precarious animal-trod one either inches wide or quite invisible. It crept apologetically outside cultivated fields which threatened to push it, and any user, into the sea. A timid path this, it disappeared regularly and, come summer, would inevitably vanish beneath the long grass, nettles, brambles and other weeds awaiting the nudge of Nature. Any attempt at a finishing sprint here would precipitate a very premature dip in the sea.

In theory, I had been postponing a decision to attempt the route or not until I had finished my reconnaissance. In practice, I had expended too much time and effort to shelve the plan, in any case I had nothing else in mind. I tried to think of the very beautiful stretches of the Way, and in my mind's eye I fancied myself gliding swiftly along road and track and savouring the delights to be found between. In this respect I may award myself full marks for optimism, no marks for realism and minus marks for prediction.

The Southern Uplands Way not only brought me to my knees, it caused me to corrupt my painstakingly constructed and delicately balanced beliefs which constitute my personal ethos of ultra-distance running.

Indigestible Aperitifs

The miserable, west spring continued, but I crossed my fingers and hoped Dame Fortune might produce a sunny smile for my two warm-up runs. After an absence of some years I had decided to enter the Fellsman Hike along with Mark and Inken. I had previously competed in the Fellsman prior to my first Pennine Way attempt when I finished in third place. It seemed to me that with the relaxing of one or two rules in favour of the out and out runners the standard at the top end had improved, and I thought I would be doing well to finish much inside the first ten. At around 60 miles (100 km) the Fellsman was not really long enough to condition me for truly ultra performance, but it covers tough, hilly terrain, and would, I hoped, get my legs into shape for the hill sections on the Southern Uplands Way.

Whatever the Fellsman did for my hill legs, it did nothing for my morale. Not quite true, it gave it a severe beating. In retrospect, what the event did for my hill legs was probably to induce arthritis. Even today, I recall my performance with pangs of embarrassment. As usual, at the kit check I had had to undergo the ritual sarcasm and bumptious cheek from a pimply-faced youth who stared aghast at a small hole in my trainers. He implied that it was most likely that he, personally, would have to turn out and rescue me when I succumbed to the hazardous effects of wet feet. I resisted the very strong temptation to shake him warmly by the throat and instead thrust a stout pair of breeches forward for inspection. As I expected, he was duly impressed. Once outside, I threw the breeches into the back of the car and substituted two pairs of thermal tights. I did not want pimple features to suffer apoplexy but, with the weather turning foul, cavorting round in stout but soaked breeks was likely to reduce my nether regions to the state suffered by that proverbial bear with his proverbial botty.

In view of what followed, I made a great mistake in restraining my natural inclination regarding the spotty youth. The punishment for justifiable homicide is not as severe as that inflicted by this particular run, and I could certainly have lived with my conscience. We set off in atrocious conditions and I felt awful from the start. The only change as the run unfolded was that the weather progressed from abominable to indescribable, and my performance did the same.

At the high, exposed checkpoint before swampy Fleet Moss I was extending a palsied hand to accept a desperately needed cup of tea from an official when the wind blew the entire tent away. In the battle to rescue capsized soup tureens and priceless samovars, not to mention the tricky extrication of tea ladies, palsied runners were understandably neglected. I was beginning to suspect this was not one of my better days.

The only cheering aspects of the venture were the performances of Mark and Inken. Mark trotted round the whole way with me always giving the impression he could have gone faster. He seemed quite pleased that we had finished in eighth place, and I wondered where we might have finished had I been in even reasonable form. As for Inken, I thought she would retire, being a protagonist of that dangerous ethic that if you are not enjoying what you are doing you should try something else. Perhaps I am not the only one to reveal a discrepancy between sentiment and behaviour. She arrived only three hours later, first lady by a wide margin, and as unconcerned as if she had just trotted round the block. Some people can be really infuriating. Still, I must admit it, pimple face was right: my feet were soaked to the armpits.

Rather to my surprise I failed to develop any subsequent complaint which might have provided a handy excuse for my dismal form. It must be old age, I thought. My next scheme would decide the issue. My next scheme was yet another Tan–Cat. Unfortunately, as May drew to a waterlogged close there seemed little chance of a genuine attempt at my record. The most I could hope for was a lull in the rain long enough to enable a quick squelch between my two favourite pubs.

As it was, the weather seemed to save its worst for the weekends. I decided therefore to set off from the south end to minimise the amount of driving in the event of failure. I also only involved my three eldest sons in support; Sean to drive, Mark to run and Gerard, now 14, for the experience. A 10-minute drive from home saw me leaving the Cat and Fiddle in a heaving miasma of wet driving mist and drizzle. Running alone, I moved into the night and onto the moors. The clinging mist settled around me, every tiny droplet of water absorbing then reflecting the pale glow from my small torch. No torch, however powerful, could have penetrated Kinder's misty vapours that night. A head torch simply brought the reflected light closer to the eyes. I held the light down by my knees, as near to the ground as possible. Unable to see more than a yard or two in any direction I navigated almost kinaesthetically over the beloved moor, adjusting my position by the slope and sway of the ground and the changing texture of the surface beneath my feet. Alone but strong, unable to see but sure of my position, I knew that my run was doomed, yet I could draw satisfaction from this state, for a time at least. Mark joined me over Bleaklow, and as the cloying bogs sucked at my legs the corrosive intrusion of a weary disenchantment gnawed its way into my heart. Slithering and sliding down the tomb-like hollows of deep groughs, the moorland gutter system, I was no longer running for a record. I was on a training run, and it was going to be long and hard, with no other reward than a very tired body at the end. But it had to be.

If Bleaklow was bad, Black Hill and Black and White Moss were worse. The peaty ground had drunk of the spring rain to its full capacity, it had sucked and lapped in dribbling excess and now it lay in its own obscene liquefaction like any bloated glutton. I slopped through the filthy mire thinking back two years when John Beatty and I had run through fire and smoke on these selfsame moors.

At White House I discovered Sean beneath his car contemplating what seemed to be a serious axle problem, apparently it was making a bid to lead an independent existence. I ferreted around beneath the recalcitrant vehicle myself, but more out of politeness than interest. The problem seemed insoluble and common sense dictated we abandon the run. I ate some breakfast with a dreadfully hypocritical feigning of deep regret. I must have overdone it, Sean's face emerged from the dark recesses to announce a partial remedy. I would be able to continue. Yippee!

At least I was able to let Gerard stretch his legs. After traversing the tedious but firm reservoir tracks we descended into sleepy Todmorden, just beginning to yawn and stretch itself. No tea and cake shops, no fish and chips, just the rattle of bottles from the humming milk floats and the curious gaze of a bored policeman panda-ing past. I wondered idly whether there were any by-laws forbidding dawn perambulations through the town environs in a state likely to promote a breach of health and fits of laughter? I hoped so.

Apparently not. Leaving Todmorden still unroused we ascended the steep side of the Calder Valley and prepared for the next 20 miles (32 km) of moorland excess. That is, Mark and I did. Gerard I humanely spared from what was to follow. Black Hameldon, Jackson's Ridge and Ickornshaw, each moor seemed worse than the last and I was weary indeed when I eventually arrived in Cowling. Here, I perked up briefly when Dave Crutch, escaping family shopping, volunteered to run with me to Skipton. Mistaking this temporary lift for a genuine rejuvenation I ran strongly out of Skipton waving enthusiastically to the support. No sooner had my crew disappeared and I turned off the road for Rylestone Fell, than I suffered an attack of fatigue the like of which I had never before encountered. For the first time ever, I actually had to fight the urge to just stop and sit down. It took an age to reach Linton, where the boys were wondering where the hell I was. I would have gladly packed in here. Earlier, I had promised myself that a sufficient training effect would be provided by whichever came sooner, 100 miles (160 km) or 24 hours. Though still short of both, by 14 miles (23 km) and about an hour respectively, I was for once ready to lower my standards. Unfortunately, I had promised Gerard a run over Great Whernside. I explained how cold, wet and misty it would be up there, how the light would be failing and what a grim place it was. His eyes lit up and I had not the heart to disappoint him.

It turned out for the best. The hard driven rain had a cold, northern aspect and, with nightfall imminent, it served to concentrate the mind wonderfully. Some of the physical weariness was also scoured away and I ran off the hill with my shaken confidence partially restored. The car, however, was deserted. Mark and Sean had gone up the hill to meet us. When they appeared out of the darkness Sean was limping badly. Whernside in the dark is a bad place for ankles. We started to drive home rather subdued. Beyond Cowling we punctured. I then discovered Sean had no spare wheel. At five minutes to midnight, Sir Lancelot Crutch, adjusting his nightcap, was surprised to hear his phone ringing . . .

Southern Uplands Way – The Attempt

After two weeks of gentle running I began to look forward to what I felt would be a revealing test of my enthusiasm and ability to continue to embark on these super-hard runs in defiance of anno Domini and 'Old Arthur'. The weekend before the event, I rose early and wandered round the Goyt Valley. Although it was now mid-June, the late, wet spring had held back summer's flowering. The fresh green foliage had the shy delicacy of all newly-emerged beauty. The faintest of mists, visible only when backlit by the sun, had strewn rainbow jewels over the sheep-cropped green turf. An utter stillness was in the air and my heart and mind went out to embrace my coming journey.

The next day I awoke with an irritating sniffle. I was annoyed but not dismayed at the prospect of a light summer cold. The following day I awoke weak and dizzy with a severe headache, racking cough and no appetite. I was furious with frustration and hurt pride. I *never* caught viral infections like this, but I had just done so! My dilemma was the usual one in such cases. All my support had been carefully arranged for the coming weekend. If I postponed, not only would I have to totally re-plan, but my work commitments meant it would be four weeks before I had another free weekend. Having just peaked my training it would be difficult to do so again while I was spending long days instructing mountaineering. Not without justification, I have great confidence in my body's ability to resist infection and recover quickly from any debilitating event. Monday and Tuesday were my lowest days, but by Tuesday evening I was starting to eat again. On Wednesday I ran to work, feeling awful but getting there. I rang my support to tell them I was still going but had postponed the run by 24 hours from a Friday to a Saturday start. On Thursday I ran again, coughing and spluttering but feeling better than on Wednesday. On Friday I drove up to Scotland and had a very sound night's sleep, not a good sign, I thought. My body obviously still needed recovery time. Ah well, in three days' time it could sleep for as long as it needed.

Despite my illness I felt quite calm as I set off from Port Patrick at 10.00 a.m. on a warm sunny morning. My original aim had been to strive to complete the route in 48 hours. After my reconnaissance I had thought this would prove difficult. Whereas Wainwright seems to calculate miles as they are actually walked, this route appeared to operate on 'map miles'. The Southern Uplands

Way is reported as 212 miles (340 km) in length. It was my opinion, however, that these map miles might convert to 220 or 230 miles (352/368 km) on the ground, this would make two and a quarter days a more realistic target.

After training through prolonged periods of foul weather, I felt it churlish of me to view the beautiful conditions with other than delight. The sad fact was, however, that I had had no opportunity to acclimatise to the effects of heat or sunshine. All too soon I could feel the stretches of tarmac returning the sun's warm caress. After covering the first 14 miles (22 km) by myself, I ran into the beautiful grounds of Castle Kennedy and met my full support team. In addition to John Richardson, Mark, Inken and Dave Crutch there were two more Rucksack Club friends to help me. I had assisted Eddie Thurrell and Chris Bolshaw on their Bob Graham round the previous year. We had become better acquainted, and when they had volunteered assistance on my venture I had gratefully accepted. Not only have both men a wealth of hard-won experience in mountain walking and fell running, they are skilled raconteurs and Chris in particular is a born entertainer. It is difficult now to envisage a time when they were not part of that close group of friends within the Club involved in participating in and supporting each other's ventures. Despite the loving attentions of the dreaded Scottish midge it was difficult not to linger at this support point. I had several conversations and a tin of fruit on the go simultaneously. Eventually, I was pushed off with Mark in attendance, happy that if the weather was overwarm for me, it would at least make my friends' role pleasanter than usual.

At New Luce, Chris and Inken volunteered to run with me to Knowe, a typical section of rough and boggy ground, hard forest track and metalled road. Chris at once launched into his usual non-stop conversation which requires a very determined interrupter to prevent from becoming a monologue. I think I have never known anyone who can produce such an intelligent flow of animated conversation at any time of the day or night irrespective of any physical exigencies. Rain, storm, fire, pestilence, flood, the fastest pace up the steepest hill have but little effect on the Bolshaw rhetoric. If you cannot hear Chris, it is because he is not there!

At Knowe the group had established friendly contact with the local café proprietor. He bestowed tea on us in copious quantities and allowed us the use of his kitchen. Better still, he granted us access to his garden hose and I enjoyed an unscheduled cooling shower. Lang may his lumb reek! The cooling effects of the hose-down were unfortunately short-lived, and as the sun's strength waxed, so mine waned. I was also finding the route tedious at times. The scenic sections seemed to flash by in an instant while roads and tracks wound on interminably. I longed for the traverse of the Galloway Hills which would take me through shady trees and into the evening.

Around 6.00 p.m. I reached Cauldons campsite in the Galloway Forest. This had been the venue for the Karrimor Mountain Marathon of 1976, the first year of my partnership with John. A storm had hit the event, and we had been one of only four teams to finish the Elite course which had seen a hundred pairs set out. There are not many good paths through the rough Galloway Hills but the

At Knowe, on the Southern Uplands Way, the 'Bolshaw Mobile Shower'. Left to right: Chris, Mike, Inken, Mark, Dave.

Southern Uplands Way follows one until the inevitable forest track is reached. As some compensation, the views are very attractive, ranging over small but tough hills cloaked in coarse grasses with an unspoilt air about them. As I trotted along now with Eddie and Inken a rather disturbing pain began to manifest itself somewhere in the region of my right Achilles tendon. Stopping and massaging the area helped for a time, but the pain kept returning. I alternated bouts of walking, running and massaging, but the pain had a nagging, insistent quality I did not like. The track alongside Clatteringshaw Loch seemed endless. The passage of events through one's conscious experience sometimes bears little direct correspondence to the passage of those units known as hours and minutes. In which does reality reside? I ran relatively quickly over the roads and tracks of the Southern Uplands Way, but was the suffocating impact of these miles beginning to distort my perception of time, distance and the nature of the route, or did my perception constitute reality?

As evening approached the light breeze dropped and immediately I reached the support point I jumped into the car to escape the midges. Partaking of light refreshment I was entertained by the spectacle of Dave and John kindly ridding Eddie of those pests by the ruthless expedient of vigorously swatting the midges and, occasionally, Eddie with fire beaters. Representing a somewhat larger target, Eddie seemed to fare rather worse than the midges. Cheered by the buffoonery and feeling the benefit of the food, I left Clatteringshaw with Dave and Chris heading for St John's Dalry. The onset of darkness coincided with a considerable temperature drop and I had to stop and pile on all additional gear.

Midge swatting. Left to right: John (Richardson), Eddie (Thurrell), Dave (Crutch).

After the sweltering heat of the day it seemed anomalous to be resorting to hat, scarf, gloves and waterproofs.

St John's Dalry was at 64 miles (104 km) along the Way, and as I left somewhat before midnight I was roughly on schedule. The section to follow had some tricky twists and I was now wishing for some light to aid my memory. The wish happily coincided with the arrival of midnight and the moon. But the moonrise was a slightly disturbing phenomenon. The disc which now began to slide from behind the black hills bore a strange orange reek like, yet unlike, the rising sun. And it was enormous. For a while the orange sphere hung there, in appearance so alien it might have been an ancient dead planet swinging by on some timeless orbit. Its sterile glow was confined to itself, no kindly radiance crept forth for our benefit. I watched it rise but before it could shed its orange mantle a thick bank of cloud rolled across the void and the strange light was eclipsed.

With Chris's excellent navigation supplementing my route memory we made our way rather cautiously to Stroanfreggan. It was now far into the night, and I was disturbed to notice a deep reluctance, both mental and physical, creeping over me. It was imperative to get moving before reluctance became inertia. While the hills of Manquhar and Ben Brack are trackless and, as such, to be welcomed, they hold little interest when approached from this side, particularly at night. The lower slopes are muddy and the higher reaches soft, tussocky and much too steep! At least, they seemed too steep for my present condition, which was not good. I had a tendency to wander off-line, but Eddie who had taken over from Chris kept us bang on target. With Dave staying as my close companion, Eddie led ahead. Navigating at night, in poor visibility, over trackless, difficult and unfamiliar country, he did not put a foot wrong.

As we at last traversed the final gradients, a pale dawn light began its barely perceptible incursion into the darkness. No rosy-fingered dawn this. It was ushered in by a cold, buffeting wind which flung a soaking mist over us. Moving along a broad ridge where gaunt pines fought an unequal battle against the uncompromising elements, we paused to gaze at the sun's luminous sphere as it pulsed and throbbed, a white and blinding light shining through the mist. The mist, wind borne, flew through the black trees and was shredded into tattered ribbons. These were moments of rare power and beauty. I realised that on this journey, in particular, such moments must be treasured and stored. It was becoming a hard and uncompromising run.

Once again, it was the support who provided light relief as we reached Polskeach. John had driven the long, winding roads which lead to the head of the valley at some speed. Chris, determined no wrong turns should prejudice the chance of meeting me on time, had kept his eyes firmly fixed on the map. He was now lying, swathed in all his spare clothes, in a bivvy bag. As I pecked at a first breakfast I could hear heart-rending groans coming from the car-sick figure. He was not long content with mere groans. Soon, a pale face peered out of the bag and a stream of recrimination pursued John, busily preparing to accompany me on the next leg.

Leaving Chris still locked in his struggle with the grim reaper John and I departed for Sanquhar. We strayed off route and onto a switchback ridge which, though pleasant in itself, was very tough. Our time loss was not serious and we soon ran into Sanquhar on what promised to be another beautiful morning. I enjoyed the stop at Sanquhar. It was 7.30 a.m. on a fine summer morning and the support point had been pleasantly organised by the river. I ate a rather more substantial second breakfast and felt that if the day should not become too hot, I might yet do quite well. Although a little down on my schedule, I had covered 90 miles (144 km) in something under 22 hours.

I had been anticipating the next section over the Lowther Hills with both delight and dread. A cap of dense white cloud sat over the summits, but this was hospitably doffed as we ascended. In contrast to my evening reconnaissance, it was now the bright morning light which revealed the almost miniature beauty of these round and steep-sided hills. It is sometimes the smaller hills, where steep gradients quickly alternate between up and down, which test the legs most. As is common on very long runs, I found the vertiginous downslopes particularly trying. As I plunged down the final slopes to the road, I could feel fingers of pain probing the sensitive domain where muscle meets tendon. Although the fingers withdrew on reaching the flat road, they had evidently decided they could return to work mischief later. With nearly 120 miles (195 km) remaining they could afford to be patient. For the present they delegated their role to other powers.

With morning well advanced and a genuine summer sun climbing to a position of power, the road was already reflecting uncomfortable heat. I increased pace in order to get off it quickly. As I did so, the incipient ache near the Achilles tendon, triggered alongside Clatteringshaw and nurtured by constant ankle twisting over Ben Brack, flared into a sharp pain. I ignored it and sought the expected cool depths of the forest tracks. The sun was now too high to be denied, however. There was no shelter from the heat and, despite careful foot placement, no relief from the pain. The ordeal had begun.

At Daer I ate with my legs dangling in the stream. The cool water was wonderfully soothing and might have begun to heal the injury had I been able to stay long enough. It was certainly a tempting proposition. After 110 miles (176 km) of pleasuring myself I felt I had had a good day! I pushed the notion to the back of my mind, slightly surprised to find thoughts of retiring there in the first place. There were over 100 miles (160 km) remaining, and though uncomfortable in the heat, neither the heat nor the pain in the tendon had reached critical proportions – yet.

Sweetshaw Brae, a beautiful name indeed. On my reconnaissance in the mist it had seemed endless. Now, in full visibility, I could see why. Descending and climbing on forest tracks, pushing our way through overgrown forest breaks, the section was interesting but demanding. Downhill, my feet were becoming very sore. Uphill, in the heat of the day, I was definitely wilting. Even the succulent bar of Turkish Delight which Eddie produced did not noticeably facilitate my progress eastwards as promised on the wrapper.

While the forest section between Daer and Beattock was hard work, it held variety and interest. In contrast, the road to Beattock itself was only hard work. I can remember little of this leg except the heat beating up from the road. And, I remember at every stage of this journey the nagging questions; had the recent virus drawn my strength? Had my vitality seeped away into those many miles on the Pennine Hills? Was this weakness an artefact of the heat? Or was I finally just not up to it anymore?

After the road the river meadows by Moffat seemed incredibly beautiful. While my senses registered beauty, my body was sending signals of despair to my brain. Between beauty and despair my spirit wandered. Gradually, the crushing effort of keeping my body moving beat down and overcame subtle beauty. And yet I was still going through the motions, I would not believe my strength was exhausted. The heat could not last. When cool evening returned, it would surely carry back my strength. I had only to endure, just hang on, don't quit. Stop thinking, move one step at a time.

Lovely Moffat Water was perhaps my first crux of despair, there were more to come. Steady rationalisation reduced the effects of this early crisis. I had now gone through the heat of two of the hottest days of the year, probably the only two hot days, I added cynically. I had covered about 120 miles (195 km) and had thus to survive for just another 24 hours. Yes, the worst was behind me. I would soon be climbing to the cool heights of Ettrick Head. A sweet summer night and fresh morning would see me well on towards the Lammermuirs, and after that? Well, after that I would undoubtedly gather impetus for the finish.

I managed to find comfort in this plausible scheme of events, but then faced the second difficulty. Having started on Saturday, not Friday, meant that I was due to finish to Monday evening. It was now Sunday, late afternoon. In response to various calls of duty all my support with the exception of Mark and Inken had to return south. Not only would I miss their good cheer and skill when it looked as if I should need it more than usual, but as Mark did not drive I would spend a good deal of the next 90 miles (145 km) running alone. I made a virtue of necessity, the harder the challenge, the greater the incentive to succeed. If you say it quickly, you might believe it. I am sure there is some truth in it. After the goodbyes, genuinely cheerful on one side, rather gritty on the other, I left with Mark for Ettrick Head.

Until the track through the forest began to gain height the sun continued to suck my vital juices. Slowly, we rose above the energy sapping heat and eventually exchanged hard track for grassy path. The soft, green path straddling the stream was a balm to weary feet and an impoverished spirit. To walk by sweet flowing water is to share its pure life force. What an extraordinary gift of Nature is a joyful mountain stream. What magic there is in the upswell, surge and irresistible flow of this earthsblood element.

I drew comfort and strength from the stream, feeling my spirit searching for and finding at least a temporary refurge. At Craigmichan Scar, I deliberately chose to traverse the precarious and eroded paths scratched across the scree. The concentration focused my attention and served to eliminate the numbness which at times threatened to engulf my mind. We crossed the watershed and immediately moved into a different climate. On this side of the hills we encountered a bank of damp, chill air which had rolled out of the east. Plunging endlessly down on the forest track we rapidly approached the section I had long dreaded, the five miles (8 km) of road to Scabcleuch.

In the now cool air and with the impetus of our rapid descent, I went very well at first. Meeting Inken in the car, I asked her to postpone support to the end of the road and to give Mark a lift so as to save him the tedium. My good spell was very short-lived. No sooner had the car disappeared, than I began to struggle. Not only fatigue, the numb pain in the ankle tendon suddenly erupted into sharp pain. Even a steeper camber on the road caused me to cross to the other side. Despite the folly of doing so, I started to imagine the car would be waiting round the next bend. It was the old track to the Lion Inn all over again. This time, however, there was no cheery chatter of friends around me, no looking forward to the last few hours of effort.

I tried to estimate my progress from the position of the side valleys. The dark valley marking the end of the road stretch looked unreachably distant. For an incalculable period of time I made no progress towards the distant smudge on the hills. I had once again entered that vicious time dichotomy; whenever the hateful road scourged my spirit, time slipped out of joint and left me cruelly suspended in an aching void. I fought, struggled, clawed my way through stagnant time on that mocking backward escalator. I ran with despair swollen and triumphant on my shoulders. The nightmare, running, running, moving with limbs not mine through a landscape that was utterly still. I was getting nowhere.

At last, rounding a bend, the indentation of the side valley jerked towards me. Progress became discernible, the treadmill creaked forward once more. It would carry me to new experiences, to worlds I as yet knew little of. I would learn – if I did but endure. I sank into the car, concerned only with immediate relief, the future would wait well enough. Realising part of my problem was lack of food, I ate large slabs of fruit cake and drank cups of strong tea. The old remedies for weary runners would work, I told myself. I was just a little tired and hungry, going through a bad patch, steady walking over the next set of hills would restore me. But Despair had not yet abdicated his role, he was lurking in the wings, patiently waiting while I finished my tea.

To Inken I confessed that my ankle was not too good, adding that I was sure the uphill and change of surface would help it. She knew perfectly well that, whatever terrain was to follow, I would claim it to have therapeutic properties. But I refrained from revealing the truth about my ankle, after all, it might easily clear up. The truth nearly revealed itself when, getting out of the car, I almost fell over. Blaming stiff legs, I adjusted my balance and set off. With an anticipatory leer, Despair crept after me.

It has not been such a stupid act to carry on as it might appear. Although the pain had been quite intense along the road, it had not accompanied me for a complete section. If I did not try, I would not truly know whether it would ebb and flow or just get worse. Had I been granted a preview of the agony I was to experience over the next few miles, I would certainly have opted out. Once I left the car I was more than half-committed. I could not or would not believe the pain might continue with quite this intensity. By the time I started to suspect it might, the car had left. I was committed.

Far from improving with the change of terrain, the pain grew worse. Any ankle flexion tugged at the tendon and sent fiery spears stabbing along it. The ground was rough and uneven. It was quite impossible to place my foot flat and secure. My folly was suddenly revealed to me. With an acknowledging leer to Self-Deception, Despair flapped forward and pinioned me with carrion claws. I bowed down in an excuse to tighten a shoe-lace. I stayed down, huddled on a grass bank, clutching the pain. Everytime I stopped, so did the pain, almost. A bank of mist rolled slowly down the hill. Cheerless and cold, it too fumbled for my soul with moist, chill fingers. Inside, my spirit wept.

Despair played a good hand. But the ordure with which he attempted to gild his lily was just a trifle too stinking – its bitterness sharp enough to rouse, not stupefy. I was alone on the hills in thick, cold mist. Night was not far distant and, miles away, Inken and Mark would be waiting anxiously for me. I could not choose to surrender, even if I wished to. And I did not wish to. With all my heart I wanted to be rid of this terrible ordeal, but I did not want to quit.

The mist was now so thick that I had to rely totally on the compass. The general topographical features I was following were simple enough to ensure I could not go wrong. At least that was the theory. The absence of a definitive path and the dense mist, compounded I suppose by my poor mental state, meant I was constantly unsure of my position. The compass was my talisman, I began checking it compulsively. It was perhaps fortunate I had no map to complicate the issue. Each time I consulted the compass, it pointed in the expected direction, but each time, the ground felt wrong. All I had to do, basically, was to contour above a valley for a time and then descend it to an old ruin, Riskinhope. My 'fail-safe' was to descend early to ensure I would not overshoot. After much stopping and starting, I ceased dithering and descended awkwardly to the valley. Relief! The smoking ruins of Riskinhope looked almost homely. But of course, I could not possibly have been wrong.

Route problems eased now, and before long I was hobbling down the stony track to St Mary's Loch. I was disconcerted to notice the light was already on the ebb, dithering has been costly. The sailing club at the end of the loch was quite deserted. A mournful wind rattled halyards and piled lonely waves across the shingle. I hurried past, anxious to use the remaining daylight. Overestimation of my ability had caused me to imagine I would not need my torch. The easy path and the light reached their limits, withered, then expired. Through mud, bog and darkness I skidded and stumbled, occasionally picking out ill-remembered paths. When I at last emerged, the forest track was no longer so unwelcome. Plodding along it, my thoughts turned to Inken and Mark. I hoped they would not be too worried. Chastened and depressed, I felt I had failed badly on this leg. Mark came out to meet me and we jogged in together. Inken was very quiet but calmly efficient. In fact, they both seemed rather silent. I wondered what they were thinking of this madness. I was harbouring the hope that they could not possibly know my true state. It would have been hard to justify continuing if they had.

But continue I meant to. With Mark for company, I set off for a piece of ground I had been determined not to cross in the dark. Odd that whenever one gets behind the schedule, it is the most difficult ground that slips into the night slot. The hills round Blake Muir were not merely navigationally awkward, they were really too good to be crossing in the dark. A sunset viewed from these hills would have been a compensation sufficient to offset a good number of road miles.

Our first error was to miss the bridge over Dryhope Burn. On this moonless, misty night we could fathom neither the river's width nor depth, but it sounded impressive enough. After wandering apprehensively along its bank without gaining the least idea of the nature of our adversary, other than we would certainly get our feet wet, I plunged in. Quite wide, but embarrassingly shallow. I noticed Mark politely allowed me to go first.

On my reconnaissance I had enjoyed the soft, grassy track leading up to the open hill top. Since then some maniac in a heavy tractor had torn the track apart. It was now little more than a pair of drainage ditches. How often have I come across what were once delightful causeways, mature and at one with the landscape, which have been brutalised, even eradicated by soulless philistines in heavy tractors. In the name of expediency the land is raped. Disappointed and struggling through the debris of the track I became very sleepy and took a five-minute nap against the bank.

Somewhat refreshed and very aware of the navigational problems ahead, I approached the start of the rough, pathless section carefully. I had just got a satisfactory line, when I noticed a post to my left. Thinking this marked the exact position of the Way, I crossed to it. It defined nothing. I had now lost my original line and could not pick it up again. From this moment on, I was never sure of, nor satisfied with our position. The bearing I was following seemed to collect all the worst going. No matter which way I tried, I could get no better terrain, and now the general lie of the land was beginning to puzzle me. Eventually, and very reluctantly, I decided I must go for a fail-safe. To our right (east) was a valley carrying the road to Traquair where Inken was waiting. We must descend into the valley and follow the road towards Traquair which, I imagined, could not be far off.

I pointed the compass east and started to descend. All was well for a time, and then to my astonishment the ground began to rise again. This was impossible, I asked Mark his opinion, but he was as puzzled as I. My instinctive response to such situations is to shout and swear. It is really infuriating when one does everything correctly and the gremlin starts changing the landscape. Unfortunately, the situation was too serious for the shouting, swearing ploy to have any effect. But I tried it, anyway.

That having failed, I was reduced to rationalisation. After a lengthy perusal of the map, I decided to act on the Sherlock Holmes principle; when you have eliminated the probable and the improbable then whatever impossibility remains is the culprit. There was a subsidiary spur leading NW off the main line of high ground. I guessed we must have wandered onto this spur on one of my 'probes', so that when I began to descend to the east we simply went down the side of the spur and started to re-ascend the line of the main hills.

Acting on this theory, we regained the high ground and soon picked up a path. Delighted with this unexpected triumph of reason over petulance, I resolved to stick with the excellent path. Then, in the light which precedes dawn, I discovered a hill where none should be. This time I was swifter off the mental mark. A glance at the well-kept stone walls and the generally trim nature of the land around led to the hypothesis that we had ventured onto some laird's estate. The map revealed the distressing fact, that just such an estate and the support point were on opposite sides of the same hill. There was no alternative but to traverse the estate and follow the road round the base of the hill.

Strangely enough, I was not as distressed as I might have predicted. After my inconclusive navigating so far, I felt it had all been inevitable. I had done my best in difficult circumstances, it had just not been good enough. This was the point where it would have been natural to give up. My unthinking resolve to continue was a surprise even to myself. When we reached the car, Inken was not there, obviously she was involved in a vain attempt to meet us off the hill. Mark set about serving the food left ready, and I was on the point of leaving when she arrived. I half expected some verbal recrimination, both for my lack of skill and my surfeit of obstinacy. However, despite her fruitless search she seemed neither surprised nor annoyed at my losing the route or my intention to continue. Mark must have felt some concern, however, as he insisted on accompanying me over Minch Moor to Yair Bridge. Ever optimistic, I was looking forward to this section as it was both attractive and offered easy going on the old drove roads.

It was a hard business getting the body to follow the mind's resolve, however. Both Mark and I were affected by the early morning 'sleepies'. What was far more serious and dismaying, was my inability to pick up the pace once we had completed the climb to the high moor. By now the ankle was rather swollen but had settled down to a bearable ache. Unfortunately, my thighs, the 'engine room', had become terribly stiff. Expecting to be able to pick up some lost time in the daylight I could manage no better than an agonised shuffle. The lengthy descent from the Three Brethren will live for a long time in my memory. Every downward step required a separate act of will and earned a separate spasm of pain.

I remember 'running' into the beautiful woodland at the foot of the hill. Everywhere was alive with the sounds and smells of a summer morning. My eyes registered the wild woodland flowers, the darting flight of birds through the stirring leaves. But my soul was locked in a fierce struggle with the incessant pain which clamped both body and spirit. When pain cripples the senses so that beauty is perceived by the brain but cannot be felt by the heart, it causes double sorrow.

When I reached the car, I felt almost completely exhausted and dispirited. I was still determined to continue. I would not allow myself to seriously consider the possibility of quitting, it would prove too much. I could no longer entertain the notion that Inken and Mark were not aware what this effort was costing me, it was too obvious, I could barely manage to lower myself into the car – or get out again. Had either said what must have been on their minds, it would have caused me great distress for I would have had to disregard them. As it was, the gentleness and care with which they were tending me reached past all pain, all weariness, all despair, and it gave me strength.

I actually made up some time on the next leg to Melrose. Thus it was that I found my two loyal helpers lying peacefully asleep. It would have been good to let them rest, but a long section was coming up and I needed to eat. I did however insist I would continue solo. Mark had given much already and there was more to come. I felt I was at last becoming stronger in body and mind, and I wanted to get moving quickly. With around 40 miles (64 km) remaining it was the beginning of the end, an end I so desperately wanted to reach. Unfortunately, as the warm sun emerged after early showers, all that happened was that I felt very sleepy again.

Traversing easy ground I was more asleep than awake, barely aware of what was going on. I inadvertently discovered a remedy for this state. Coming to an electric fence next to a gate I managed in my stupor to receive its full benefits. It had a remarkably energising effect! In fact, there and then, I conceived a plan to patent an electrical energiser for tired fell runners, something along the lines of a cattle prod. I have decided, on later reflection, to suspend its final development until my own retirement.

Perhaps I should have tried the shock therapy earlier. Despite my rejuvenation I must have made poor time. I met Inken coming down the long boring section of Roman Road over Mosshouses Moor. I expected a pleased smile, but she looked concerned and explained that they thought I had cracked up somewhere. I am not sure what upsets me most, being treated as a superman who does not need any special consideration whatever the circumstances, or as a frail old gentleman needing care and protection. The first is good for the ego, but painful. The second is painful to the ego, but can be very nice! I have not resolved this one yet.

At any rate, Mark took me in charge on the short leg to Lauder, where I apprehensively prepared for the long dreaded section over the Lammermuirs to Longformacus. I had been psyching myself up for this leg for the past few hours, 14 miles (22 km) of stony track rising inexorably to high moorland and finishing, inevitably, with miles of road. By now the pain in my legs had eased, but my feet were so sore it was best to remain standing at support stops. I thought the stony track would not be pleasant. I applied myself to the task ahead with all my strength and will. This was the last major challenge. After this there would be only 14 miles (22 km) remaining. I undertook this leg with very few reserves of strength and even today still regard it as one of my best efforts. I did not imagine I would be able to run the uphill track, but I did. I ran half-asleep and in a numb stupor. The spark that drove me was small, but it seemed inextinguishable. On reaching the rough moor I tried to change into my fell shoes. Balanced on one leg with Mark holding me up I forced one shoe on, but the other foot was so swollen no amount of brutality would make it fit. Feeling like one of the Ugly Sisters I resumed my road shoes and skidded down to the road. The road achieved what the track could not. By the time I reached the support the spark had gone out and I was an automaton.

But now it was simply frustration and not despair that attacked my spirit. I seemed to have poured my life-blood into this run, I wanted to have done with it. Seemingly endless road and track was frustrating this desire, but with only 14 (22 km) of the 212 miles (340 km) remaining, Despair could win no more victories. Travelling alone on the penultimate leg to the village of St Bathans I began to experience the strange sensation that this was not the second, but the third time I had run over this ground. The impression was very vivid, and I seemed to remember small incidents from two previous runs. One set of memories certainly belonged to the time I had reconnoitred the route, but what of the memory of a 'second' run? I am familiar with the hallucinatory effects engendered by sleep deprivation, however, I was not seeing things, but remembering an event which had not taken place. I found the experience intriguing rather than alarming, and it helped more dreary miles to pass. Despite the crushing weariness I could sense in my body, a desperate desire to conclude this run enabled me to maintain a good speed. When I ran down to meet Inken at the last support point I was able, for the first time, to give her a genuine smile and received one in return.

It was now 9.00 p.m. and I had hopes of covering the last 10 miles (16 km) in two hours. The hope had its roots in necessity. It would be very dark by 10.30 and the prospect of traversing a large proportion of the cliff path in true darkness was appalling. With Mark, ever willing, beside me we departed on the final leg of my terrible Odyssey. Thick wet mist obscured our line across cultivated fields. High wet grass dragged at our legs.

Once on the road section I flung myself into a painful but effective canter. My confidence rose as we approached, then crossed the A1 to Pease Dean. But thick mist was causing an early fading of the light. Through the impending gloom, the flowering gorse which bordered the path across the hillside seemed to vibrate and glow. Mark said he, too, was experiencing the same effects. It was as if the darkness was enveloping my fading mind, but as the darkness grew in and around me, so the yellow bushes flared with greater intensity. I could no longer consciously guide my legs over uneven ground for I could no longer see it, and in any case, the links between my mind and my body were dissolving. I allowed my body to flow on as it would, and my mind floated free. Once again it explored that 'memory' that was not memory. I slipped into an almost complete state of *déjà vu*. Rationally, I knew it was only the second time I had traversed this ground. On the other hand, I not only felt very strongly that I had passed this way twice before, I could also predict what was going to happen next. For instance, well before I came to an awkward gate I 'remembered' how I had crossed it 'last time', seconds later I observed myself crossing it in the same fashion. I found floating outside myself like this a curious and fascinating experience. Even while this was happening I attempted an objective analysis of what was happening; I was not successful.

A nasty steep descent to the road marshalled all my faculties into something like a cohesive unit. Before they could follow their own inclinations again, I was grappling with the intricate challenge of the cliff-top path. I could not focus my eyes properly, and we went round three sides of a crop-grown field before returning to the opening I had already passed. So, in a fashion perfectly suited to the nature of this venture, we found ourselves on the narrow path in the dark.

The prediction I had made after my reconnaissance of the path proved a gross underestimation. We stumbled and slithered, were stung by nettles and fought savage brambles. After a time, the path disappeared entirely beneath the weeds. I clambered over barbed wire into the adjoining field and immediately disappeared beneath the oil-seed rape which was at times above my head. This, I thought, is definitely farcical. Adopting the tactics of the fabled Hellarwee tribe I identified the lights of Cockburnspath ahead. The chill sea-borne mist was beginning to eat into me, but refusing to stop I ploughed a grim furrow down and under the ranks of the oil-seed rape. Quite suddenly we emerged onto a curious piece of old track that I definitely did remember. Amazingly, we were still on course. Just as I was attempting to piece together other elusive bits of memory, Inken loomed like a phantom out of the darkness. For some reason this was so entirely unexpected I thought I was hallucinating. Thankfully, I followed the apparition along the few remaining twists and turns. Now, at last, we crossed the A1 again, very circumspectly in my case, and started on the final yards of road into the village. I could no longer distinguish between road and kerb, while lamp posts constituted a major hazard.

At 11.35 p.m. on a cold, misty night the village square was, naturally, deserted. If there were any observers behind those few windows which glowed like warm eyes around us, they would have witnessed a rather motley group of runners approaching the stone monument in the centre of the square. They would have seen one figure, that of an apparently very ancient and frail man, detach itself from the group and salute the monument in a curious sardonic way. With no further ceremony, the group would then have been seen climbing into an old car and driving off. Had the heart and mind of the ancient runner been open to inspection, the only remarkable aspect would have been the curious void which existed where emotion might have been expected to reside. What such observers might well have missed, was the very subtle, almost cynical sense of satisfaction that accompanied the fag-end of this terrible, yet epic run. It was strangely appropriate to bring my ordeal to a conclusion under the interested gaze of no one. No one, that is, but those two who had shared the ordeal with me. It was right that it should end privately. The experience had been bitter indeed, its one sweet fruit was that it had drawn me closer to each of them, and for that reason alone I will not regret it.

As no one seemed to have completed the route in any kind of continuous fashion, what I did probably constituted a record. My concern with the route as a respectable record attempt disappeared on the first day. The only valid accolade I feel able to claim is a record for obstinacy. My schedule was for 54 hours, my actual time of 61 hours 35 minutes was in this context but a feeble parody of a record. It shouldn't prove too difficult to better this, but I shall not be trying.

Epilogue

Now the dust has settled, I begin to wonder if there are any lessons to be learned from my experience on the Southern Uplands Way. I felt, and still feel, in something of a dilemma about what happened, or rather what I caused to happen. The difficulty in resolving the dilemma lies in the conflict which arose between two equally important concepts. The essential quality of ultra fell running, for me, is the challenge of doing something which is exceptionally demanding in an environment which engenders the kind of inspiration necessary to cope with these demands. Accepting the concept that the challenge must be supremely difficult, embodies the notion that *voluntary* escape is not part of the game, once embarked – no quitting. What makes this form of behaviour so unlike banging one's head against a wall (or running Land's End to John O'Groats on the road) is the enormously increased sense of communication with Nature both during and partly after the event. If the latter is missing, then one is indeed confined to a crude battle of strength between obstinacy and fitness on the one hand and brute physical force on the other.

My illness, slight though it was, and the injuries I sustained during the run certainly tipped the physical odds against me. I was able to draw increasingly less inspiration from the route, and eventually only my obstinacy and desire not to 'need' to attempt the Way again sustained my effort. Obstinacy in pursuit of some goal may be acceptable. Obstinacy for its own sake is less admirable.

And yet, who will gainsay an experience that demanded the utmost tenacity and voluntary acceptance of pain and hardship that had so little reward? It was a bitter cup and a full one. I drank it to the dregs, and I shall never lift it again.

However, Mike Hartley did in 1988. Mike was joint winner of the Fellsman Hike and is one of the few people I have met interested in attempting my records. He covered the Southern Uplands Way in 55 hours and 55 minutes.

chapter eight

1987 – THE FALLOW YEAR

Decisions to have an easy year are never more easily made than towards the end of a long, hard run. As that 200 mile (320 km) mark approaches, one is heard to voice platitudes such as 'I'm definitely too old for this sort of game', or 'Well, you won't catch me doing this again next year', or 'This demands too much time and effort, I'm going to take up serious photography/writing/gardening/knitting . . .', or 'I've reached my limits now, I should retire from ultras while I still have some strength for other things'. The last was my reaction to the Southern Uplands Way.

Like most good resolutions, this one weakened in proportion to its removal in time from the event which inspired it. I did not want the Southern Uplands Way to be my last memory of an ultra run. I should bow out with a swan-song that would be a bang, not a whimper. I began to toy with the notion that I should have one more attempt at the big one, my own Pennine Way record.

I had never dismissed the possibility of making an attempt on this record which I had been so long in winning. It had been just a matter of allowing a sufficiently long interval for my interest to rekindle. If I really was going for a swan-song, there was no doubt in my mind it must be the Pennine Way. What most appealed to me however, was the idea of attempting the record in the opposite direction, north to south. To achieve a sub-three-day traverse both from the north and the south was a notion I found irresistible. It was also the only acceptable way I could envisage of ending my ultra career. It would, of course, demand the very peak of physical fitness. The sincere resolutions to take things easy made on the Southern Uplands Way were forgotten. I started to lay plans.

Preparation and training

Once the swollen feet and ankles had subsided and the sleep deficit was made good, gentle days on the hill restored my spirits. The Southern Uplands Way was soon pushed to the back of my mind, but it was not forgotten. The autumn and winter which followed saw me as active as ever. There was however, at times, something about my performance that made me wonder whether I had left some part of my strength behind on the Southern Uplands Way. Beyond any doubt was the fact that my knees were certainly deteriorating. Comments such as 'knees very sore downhill' and 'perhaps not many miles left in them' occur with increasing regularity in my log-book at this time. Well, this was sad but fitted in with plans for my swan-song year. If I could not go on much longer, that was all the more incentive to achieve a final success.

In an effort to preserve my knees, I cut down on my weekly road mileage but increased the distance of my weekend ventures. I was not exactly in the invalid class yet, either. Despite the obligation to descend hills in stately rather than dashing fashion, I still managed to finish twenty-ninth out of 240 in the Marsden–Edale race, one and a half minutes behind but 24 years ahead of Mark.

The pleasurable business of selecting subsidiary targets *en route* to the 'big one' occupied my mind. Inken, as a member of the LDWA, informed me that their 100 mile (160 km) event was to be held in Snowdonia that year. With images of running across the mighty Carneddau springing into my mind, I too sent off an entry form. I then recalled having read an article by someone who had made a speedy traverse of the West Highland Way, what a name to conjure with! However, I quickly ascertained that the route was mainly on the hard tracks of the old military roads. On the other hand, at 95 miles (152 km) it was the right length for a relatively short spring day. It was also sure to pass through superb mountain scenery. I decided it would constitute a useful 'speed' session to counterbalance my penchant for slow, steady plodding.

My reconnaissance of the West Highland Way confirmed what the map indicated. Most of the route follows unmetalled military roads built during the eighteenth century to facilitate the passage of militia intent on quelling troublesome Highlanders. Although well graded, the surface is occasionally of loose stones large enough to make running quite difficult. What really took me unawares, however, was the path along the east bank of Loch Lomond. In complete contrast to what had gone before, it was a jumble of mud, rocks and tree roots. Far from being able to run it, I had the utmost difficulty in not breaking my neck along it. Still, I could not complain, I was supposed to enjoy rough and natural terrain. Trouble was, I had to stop to do so!

I realised that if I was principally training for the Pennine Way, which demanded very long, but slow days, I could not also adequately prepare for the West Highland Way. The latter would ideally require short, relatively fast days of about 30 miles (50 km), whereas I intended between 40 and 60-mile (65/100 km) days. Indeed, with a limited period for day-long training, I had to cover such distances to allow reconnaissance of my three targets. The West Highland Way, Snowdonia Hundred and Pennine Way gave 465 miles (744 km) to reconnoitre. Even allowing that I need not cover all the Pennine Way, I had many miles to compress into my already busy life. Ah well, 'the harder the challenge, the . . .', *ad nauseam*!

In a hectic 10-day period I covered all the West Highland Way, nearly 200 miles (320 km) of the Pennine Way and most of the Snowdonia Hundred. I am accustomed to bulking my training in this fashion and have noticed it has a tendency to induce fatigue. I could not tell whether I was more weary than usual, but there was no doubt my knees were in a poor way. This sport is hard enough, I did not think constant pain should be part of it. Despite my performance on the Southern Uplands Way, or perhaps because of it, I was

*Running past
the Kingshouse
Hotel, West
Highland Way
training.*

*At the top of
the Devil's
Staircase –
West Highland
Way training.*

reluctant to continue accepting that my dreams should be realised through a cruel disregard of the state of my body. My resolve to make this a final and successful year hardened.

West Highland Way – A sort of record

It is all very well to set a subsidiary target which is unimportant in an overall context. Unfortunately, when one is cursed with a fierce competitive spirit and high level of aspiration, the discrepancy between drive to achieve and ability to do so produces conflict. At the time, the fact that my training was not appropriate to the West Highland Way had seemed unimportant. Now I was faced with actually doing the run, I felt very dissatisfied. I had also just learned that the record for this run between Glasgow and Fort William stood at 17 hours 48 minutes. This seemed exceptionally fast and it was obvious to me that such a time would be beyond my reach. I then discovered that the run had been established as a 'race', taking place close to Midsummer Day each year. For 'reasons of safety' the official West Highland Way route was abandoned in three places. Where the footpath followed natural terrain, the race took to the road. One of these changes would probably not lead to a marked time difference between road and path; the other two, however, would. At the southern end of Loch Lomond, between Balmaha and Rowardennan, the official path follows a very picturesque but tortuous route through woods, alongside the loch and up and down steep little hills. At one stage the path performs a little switchback, just a couple of yards from the road. The other section constitutes quite a deviation. Between Fort William and Lundavra the official route goes very pleasantly through the Glen Nevis plantations, then rather awkwardly over a couple of miles of large boulders set in boggy ground. The difficulties underfoot and twists and turns make it impossible to run this section swiftly. The race simply follows a minor road between Lundavra and Fort William and appears to be about a mile shorter.

There was no question in my mind but that I should adhere to the official route. I run on roads only out of necessity. On the other hand, I knew of no record for the definitive footpath. I supposed sub-24 hours would constitute a 'record', but I felt I would only gain any satisfaction by approaching the time of the 'road record'.

Now living in Scotland, Inken had offered to drive, and I took Gerard, 15, and Liam, 13, along for the experience. After camping in Glen Nevis and listening to the rain beating down half the night, I rose at 3.30 a.m., delivered my familiar, bad-tempered speech entitled 'Why does it always rain on my record attempts?' and set off at 4.00 a.m. It was still dark in the forest and only half-light across the boulders. I could understand why the race used the road. The sounds of legs snapping like carrots would have been heard in Fort William had runners with 90 miles (145 km) under their kilts attempted these blocks in the dark.

I lost time on this leg, which was not surprising. I also lost time on the next section over to Kinlochleven. The only excuse I had was that I ran too slowly. It was, I realised despondently, as fast as I dared go. I took Gerard over the Devil's

Staircase which is the highest point on the route. We both enjoyed the sight of the still snow-plastered hills around us; the Mamores behind us to the north and, much closer the Buchaille Etive Mhor and the Munroes around Glencoe.

Picking up momentum I ran hard past the Kingshouse and on into a head wind and heavy rain. By Inveroran I had knocked 15 minutes off the scheduled leg time but was still down overall. I felt very tired and dispirited after this effort. My lack of speed and the state of the weather made me want to quit. However, I had promised to run with Liam over the next hill to the Bridge of Orchy. He was obviously looking forward to this and I did not have the heart to disappoint him, so off we set. It was a tonic for me to see him skipping along lightly in front of me. Very small, light and nimble on his feet, he flitted over the ground apparently without effort. By the time we were descending the hill I felt much better and watched with amusement and fatherly pride as he floated easily ahead to take my order for refreshments.

I still did not feel fully committed to the run however, and thought the long track to Tyndrum would see me blown to a standstill. Curiously enough, the weather took a turn for the better, the wind switched west and stopped blowing in my face. So, 42 miles (67 km) and seven and a quarter hours gone, 53 miles (85 km) remaining, might as well continue.

The run along the 15 miles (24 km) of steep, densely wooded and rocky shores of north Lomond-side proved the crux. At first I ran well, enjoying the early views down the loch and the lovely silvan setting, such a contrast to the tedious military roads. However, I was concentrating so hard to maintain speed and balance over the potentially disastrous ground that I failed to notice the development of a massive hunger bonk. By the time I did, it was too late. I ended up shuffling to the car and lost all the time I'd gained and more.

After eating, probably too much at once, my digestion became disorganised and I never really regained my strength and rhythm. At the southern end of the loch, the path continued to wend an intricate way over little crags, through woods and up and down short steep slopes. Creaking along on my stiffening old pins I watched enviously as Gerard and Liam skipped nimbly ahead.

It took the 1,000 ft (300 m) climb up Conic Hill to restore my systems to some kind of compatible relationship. I began to run relentlessly, without fire or sparkle, just a determined drive forward, a drive to beat the dark. Time slipped inexorably by and with it the daylight and my hopes. It was nearly 11.00 p.m. when Gerard and I ran into the uninspirational finish at Milngavie railway car-park. Sadly, Inken and Liam, who were to run in with us, missed us in the dark.

My time was 18 hours 40 minutes, and as I had hoped to get close to the other record of 17:48, I deemed it an embarrassing failure. On the other hand, I had to admit I had actually run at a faster pace than I thought possible. I was sure I could go still faster if I trained for it, there again, I was not convinced I was interested in repeating the route. The next day I took Gerard and Liam round Edinburgh Castle, every step (and it has hundreds) was a reminder of the need for specific training. I cannot remember my legs ever being stiffer after a run.

The Snowdonia Hundred was the second LDWA 100-mile (160 km) event I entered, and after it I realised that the nature of the Dalesman Hundred, in its

Coming into Edale at the end of 250 miles (400 km) training in seven days.

rough and wild character, had not been typical. It has since become apparent that for many entrants to the annual Hundred, the motivating force lies in the desire to cover 100 miles (160 km). The desire to enjoy a pleasant route is also obvious, but, unfortunately, should any of Nature's real challenges prejudice the primary goal, objections are raised. I am in sympathy with the ambition to test one's physical and mental capabilities, it is one I share, but I will not willingly build a treadmill in my heart. Challenge need not chain the soul to the dead weight of empty miles. Inspiration is best derived from the renewal of our relationship with Nature and its forces. And when we are inspired, what can we not then achieve! If we must fail, let us do so reaching beyond our grasp for a dream that is worth all our striving. Then, even in our failing, even through our tears, we have won.

In our populous land it is frequently difficult to avoid using tracks and even road to connect the various sections of wilder country. Nevertheless roads, in particular, destroy a route's character, they are gestures of defeat. After reconnoitring the Snowdonia Hundred I was appalled by the large proportion of the course occupied by these 'gestures of defeat'. However, I had paid my entry fee and invested time in learning the course. I hoped that running the route as a whole would bring it the cohesive sense of unity which road sections destroy.

The long stretches of road and track seemed designed to punish rather than inspire. Suffering the effects of the West Highland Way, last year's Southern Uplands Way and general decrepitude I was finding this a dull, hard run and longing for something to break the monotony. My wish was heard and, in due course, maliciously misinterpreted.

Normally, I prefer to run alone in these events, but from about 20 miles (32 km) had teamed up with Mike Hartley. He was very cheerful and pleasant company and our common interests gave us plenty of scope for conversation. We made our way slowly through the field. Again, everyone had started off at suicidal speed, and it was interesting to pass them in various attitudes of disrepair at the roadside or recumbent at support points. Even so, I was quite surprised to be approaching Porthmadog, just beyond the half-way point, with only two men ahead. We then passed No. 2, reclining very elegantly, but rather pale, on a grassy bank. He was a victim of the awful hunger bonk and was busy reloading. I thought he should have been doing it on the move, but, there you are, even among the ranks of Sparta can be found the odd Sybarite.

At Porthmadog, I was surprised to find it was ace orienteer and fell runner David Rosen who was the leader. There may be some vital ingredient missing out of today's chocolate for he had met with what must have been one of the great hunger bonks of this world just a couple of miles short of the support point. A connoisseur of the genus hunger bonk, I could only regret I had missed this particular manifestation. However, quick to take advantage of a weakness, I swallowed my jar of peaches and nipped out smartly with Mike. Chatting away the flat boring miles to Harlech we reached the imposing, flood-lit castle as darkness fell. Rather complacent by now we jogged alongside the black waters of Llyn Bychan. However, as we started up the pass known as the Roman Steps to cross the Rhinog Mountains, a figure lurched after us. It was a 24-hour track and road expert, probably anxious to have some company over these rugged hills. Unfortunately for him, it was at this point that my request for a little break in routine was being slyly considered.

Almost immediately we veered left of the correct path but I rectified this mistake so quickly, I never heard the warning bells. Soon we came to a gap in a wall which I exclaimed was 'wrong'. Both my companions immediately agreed, and in my customary bold manner, I plunged leftwards off the path and was immediately engulfed in that jungle of vertical heather and huge boulders which characterises the Rhinogs. We continued to lurch across the broken hillside. From time to time I stopped to peer intelligently into the quite impenetrable darkness. Not unnaturally, I could see nothing.

The unbelievably bad ground became worse, as it will in the Rhinogs. We found ourselves on a very steep, unstable boulder field under crags. Obviously unfamiliar with this type of terrain the road expert was constantly 'off the back'. He appeared to be concerned for his well-being and safety and I shouted back words of encouragement and comfort. Unfortunately his cries grew fainter until they were mercifully lost in the stony wastes. I hoped my advice to retreat downhill to a line of bobbing torches had been heeded.

A belated scrutiny of the map gave me an approximate idea of our position, but it was mainly guesswork. Well, the next control point lay on the other side of those mountains, so no place to go but up. There followed an age of swarming up wiry heather and practising intricate climbing techniques on the greasy rock of a repulsive gully. At last we emerged close to a summit – but which? I feared the descent would be worse than the ascent, it usually is. We were lucky, at least Mike nearly was not. He was on the point of hopping down a little rock step, when our torches revealed it was a crag about 50 ft (15 m) high.

Eventually we reached better ground lower down. I was sure I recognised a forest edge as having been a line I had followed in a Karrimor event 10 years previously. I was just beginning to doubt this when I discerned a glow ahead. The light proceeded from a kit check station on the edge of the forest where the route emerged. Controlling my wild impulse to kiss the officials, I produced the items to be checked, ascertained that we would not get bonus points for including an unscheduled summit and discovered that there were only two people in front of us. Despondency gave way to optimism and we galloped out of the tent in search of fresh adventures. We had spent an hour longer over the Rhinogs than we might have expected, but we had at least broken the monotony!

We were now going very strongly and soon passed one of the two in front. At the next control we were told we were in the lead. Seeing is believing however, and I thought we should not slacken pace just yet.

With dawn came a very cold wind and a chill wet mist. Rather on my mettle now, I made a good job of nagivating over to the Manod Quarry checkpoint. I suggested we should not stop for refreshments but press on. Along the old railway track I kept noticing what appeared to be fresh studmarks among the tangle of older footprints. Not very much to my surprise a mile later, we saw a small, sturdy figure trotting economically ahead, Dave Rosen! Very slowly we hauled him in, and soon we were all engaged in racing over rough, boggy ground with an assumed nonchalance ('Yes, nothing like an early morning burst over the tussocks to get nearly 90 miles (145 km) of stiffness out of one's legs, don't you think!').

Catching him was one thing, dropping him was another. He stayed with us easily until the forest track, where Mike and I set off up the initial gradients at a suicidal rate. Very knackering it was, but it seemed to send Dave off the back. We left the Pentre Bont checkpoint before he appeared, and then I thought we could relax a little. I had to, I was shattered.

It was a beautiful morning as we ran over the River Conwy to the finish at Llanwrst. I was wishing I was just starting off fresh into it (with new legs!). We finished in 21 hours 35 minutes, but should have got close to 20 hours; still, it was a small price to pay for our adventure. Eschewing such excursions on this occasion, Inken came in at 24.40, the twentieth finisher, not bad for a woman! (I suppose the 250 men behind her would have agreed.)

After finishing, our 24-hour track man cornered us. Now we're for it, I thought! But he was very nice about being deserted in the middle of the night in a place he obviously found rather hostile. He had not, to my relief, remained perched on a boulder till dawn, but had joined the torchlight procession below. I explained how noble it was of us to provide him with this option rather than drag him up that horrifying gully; but I do not think he believed me.

The quack of the swan

Having completed my build-up which, if rather punishing, had at least been successful, I was ready to turn my attention to the Pennine Way. I was still pursuing the notion that it was time to stop chasing ultra-records, a notion with which my knees readily concurred, but I was determined to go out on a high note. Unfortunately, the weather, as usual, had something to say about my plans. This time, unusually, it had the decency to indicate its likely response should I set foot on the Pennine Way.

My log-book reveals that June had the wettest start on record. The ground became impossibly waterlogged, and with the bad weather continuing, I decided to postpone my record attempt. In the first part of July, I was again instructing in hill activities in the Lake District. After raising my hopes with several days of fine weather, conditions again deteriorated. There ensued a most frustrating pattern, where heavy rain would be followed by what, in my optimism, I anticipated as an improving trend. One day the attempt would definitely go ahead, the next day it was called off. Then there would be periods of uncertainty which would be the most frustrating of all. Friends phoned and I would say 'I'll probably go anyway', then I would ring back and say 'It doesn't look as if it's even worth starting.' The uncertainty gnawed away at me and I could not settle. No sooner had I decided one way or the other than the weather would change, and so would my mind. I could not bear the thought that I should decide not to go, then have to sit through a beautiful weekend when I could have been running. Eventually, I hit on a compromise. The weather was unlikely to produce the three fine days needed for the Pennine Way, I was already in the Lakes, I would attempt my Coast to Coast record.

Objecting to my efforts to escape from its game of cat and mouse, the weather became even more variable. A fine clear morning, giving every impression of permanence, would change to torrential rain by the afternoon and continue unabated throughout the night. The timing of this pattern would vary, but little else. Preparing to run a couple of hundred miles (320 km) over the hills at record speed throws a considerable strain on the nerves at the best of times. I found the added uncertainty quite unbearable. I cancelled any attempt on any record. On the weekend I was to have run, the country was divided north/south into two quite dissimilar weather systems. In the north, there were clouds, but a fair amount of sunshine and equable temperatures. In the southern half, there was persistent rain fortified by torrential showers and strong winds. As if anticipating my fluctuating resolve, the interface of these systems was poised on a line approximately coincident with the Coast to Coast route.

chapter nine

1988 – THE ROAD GOES EVER ON

The Road goes ever on and on
    Out from the door where it began.
Now far ahead the Road has gone,
    Let others follow it who can!
Let them a journey new begin,
    But I at last with weary feet
Will turn towards the lighted inn,
    My evening-rest and sleep to meet.

J. R. R. TOLKEIN
The Lord of the Rings

Having in 1987 failed to complete, or even attempt, my 'big run' of the year, I felt at first as if something was missing from life. Then, retrospectively, I became aware, in a way I had not grasped before, of the drain on resources which a 'long' ultra imposes. I was now much more ready to pick up training again after the summer break in routine. Above all, I discovered a very keen edge to my appetite for a really good year in 1988. My anticipation was such, that I even questioned whether in 1987 I had actually possessed the driving motivation to power a Pennine Way attempt. I realised that I had been not only thinking in terms of a swan-song, but also feeling almost relieved that it was to be so.

The lean year just past had both stimulated my appetite and rekindled fires. Unfortunately, my sheer enjoyment of running, short or long distances, was increasingly threatened by painful knees. At this point I commenced acupuncture treatment. Acupuncture was something I had intended to try for years, but I rarely have the patience to go and seek medical advice, let alone submit myself to treatment. I am extremely sceptical of the ability and interest of most conventional practitioners where sports-related problems are concerned. I also take a very jaundiced view of the use of drugs to treat minor disorders. Perhaps I am fortunate, but I find if I listen to my body, it will usually direct me to a healthy pattern of eating, sleeping, resting, working, and so on. Of course, I do not always choose to listen, but almost invariably, when injured or unwell, I try to let my body 'guide' me back to health.

My body did not seem able to cope with what I suspected was an almost inevitable and irreversible deterioration of my knees. I had never really expected not to pay in both the short and long term for the kind of running I love. What love does not bring pain? A love which suffers to be constrained by pain is indeed a pale love. Contrary to what those who are afraid of pain might think, endurance athletes do not enjoy pain. We accept the necessity of intense effort, and pain may at times intervene sharply in this, but I, for one, hate it. It is not only unpleasant in itself, it obstructs my ability to enjoy the physical and also the spiritual aspects of my running. When pain began to rear its ugly head too high therefore, and acting on trusted recommendation, I sought acupuncture treatment. I was gratified to discover that my acupuncture specialist described healing with reference to concepts I already accepted; the body would be helped to heal itself.

In a surprisingly short time I noticed an improvement. There was no instantaneous miracle, and my knees still reacted very crossly to sudden changes in routine, as when playing basketball, my inherently competitive nature would get the better of me. But gradually the most annoying pain of all disappeared. This was the vice-like band which gripped across my kneecaps on even the gentlest of downhills. Until that began to fade, I did not appreciate quite how much the associated pain had been destroying the pleasure I found in running. Once more, the pure and simple joy of running, just running for its own sake, came back to me, a love deformed by pain had become whole again. Eventually, though cautiously, I was able to start descending even steep hillsides with that sense of freedom which had constituted such a powerful attraction to fell running nearly 30 years ago. One day in spring, I descended from the top of Conic Hill in plummeting swoops that felt like flight. I paid for it a wee bit at the bottom, but I still had more than enough change left from that exhilarating sense of freedom, that joyful, almost arrogant feeling of mastery. 'That!', thought I, preening my feathers, 'is how the eagle feels!'

The only problem now was whether I would actually be capable of relinquishing my interest in attempting ultra-distance records. Certainly, the alleviation of the pain had removed one of the factors instrumental in my decision to set less demanding targets. However, I had a genuine desire to turn to other, less competitive ventures in the hills. I could not, on the other hand, relinquish my career in the inconclusive state occasioned by the preceding year's fiasco of a summer. I felt with increasing conviction that if I could bow out, not just as the first man to run the Pennine Way in under three days, but the first to do so in each direction, I would be content.

I was warned that I was attempting to relive what was essentially a unique experience. Irrespective of any time I might achieve, such an attempt to recreate the past was doomed to failure. I did not, however, wish to relive that experience, realising, indeed, the impossibility of so doing. What I did want, was to create a new experience and a new record. My ultra-running, with all its joy and sadness, its pain and pleasure, its often love, its sometimes hate, had wrought changes in my spirit which, even now, I can only guess at. The Pennine Way had become a symbol of those changes. My sense of affinity with it was almost mysterious. As a route, it could hardly be described as faultless. True, it has charms, but its beauty lies beneath what may be pardonably mistaken for bleak tedium. Perhaps during the long travail of our relationship, I had left behind the stuff of my spirit. And now? Well, perhaps now I wanted to visit those reflections one last time. I was aware of any anomaly only in the minds of others. Despite any difficulty I might have had articulating them, I was quite at peace with my intentions, with my dreams.

Preparation and departure

Having dreams is one thing, achieving them another. Plans had to be laid and, if I wanted this to be the last, exceptional year, they had to be laid meticulously. My battle plan was to crash my training early in April and so approach May having had time to recoup strength. Strength was certainly going to be necessary. I had again planned two subsidiary targets en route to the Pennine Way, and neither of these would give an easy passage.

Both subsidiary targets were in Scotland, but very dissimilar in nature. Firstly, I was going to have another attempt at the West Highland Way. During the year following my stiff-legged and hollow 'record', I had become increasingly dissatisfied with my performance. I did not know whether, adhering strictly to the official footpath, I could approach the record for the alternative route, but I felt I should try to better my own time. The West Highland Way suited neither my physical attributes nor my spiritual aspirations. It would, however, give me a long, hard and very continuous running session. My other target was, in truth, little to do with the Pennine Way, it was an end in itself. As a route, in scope and grandeur, it by far surpassed any official footpath. The venture I intended was a natural outgrowth of the Scottish Fourthousanders. However, instead of hastening between the summits on the west side of Scotland and those in the east as economically as possible, I hoped to make a more truly high-level traverse. Furthermore, my ambition was to keep moving ever eastwards over the high ground until I had run out of mountains!

Eventually, the scope of my ambition made it clear that, if it were not limited, I might as well relinquish hopes of doing the Pennine Way three weeks later. Even with compromise, the high traverse across Scotland promised to provide a physical and psychological challenge not much less than that posed by the Pennine Way. Still, I philosophised from the depths of my winter armchair, what is life without challenge?

West Highland Way revisited

In keeping with the theme of reversing my routes, I decided to run from Glasgow to Fort William. This is the direction the race takes and might add some variety, I thought. Unlike the race which is held in June, it was still April when I set off, thus cold and darkness were to provide additional problems. My support team was almost identical to the previous year's excepting that my second eldest son, Sean, was to share the driving with Inken. Gerard, who had run 30 miles (50 km) with me last year, was keen to exceed this total, and I could see Liam, who says little, was quietly determined. I was determined, too, but I made it clear that, while I was optimistic about improving my own time, I thought it unlikely I could better the overall record. This was primarily a training run, my way of improving my basic speed over 100 miles (160 km), very useful for Pennine Way record-breaking.

What a superb pre-dawn greeted my first quiet footsteps! At 4.00 a.m. it was perhaps more night than morning, but the sky was of a soft, dark blue, and against it the trees and hills were revealed densely black. Everywhere was wonderfully still. I ran alone under a dark canopy of branches following my circle of white light as it slipped onwards before me. At Craigallian Loch, mist wraiths dared my gaze, inviolate, but transient above their gloomy sanctuary. By tiny Corbeth Loch, the pale light was sufficient to discern a cloud of vapour floating pensively above the water, while around the perimeter, the vegetation crouched, black and waiting . . .

Waiting for a sun that failed to penetrate an increasingly grey barrier. It was to be a day without colour, becoming colder and wetter as we journeyed north. But it was pleasant to run those early miles in my full strength while around me all was sleeping. Still sleeping were my three sons, who were camped alongside Loch Lomond, 26 miles (42 km) from the start. There was no need to involve them in a 4.00 a.m. start, they could have their sleep and I could have the early morning to myself. I was trying not to consciously hurry, but soon realised that my comfortable pace was a mite slower than that required by the schedule. Although I preferred it, the 'off track' ground was saturated, particularly the stretch over Conic Hill. Belatedly, I also discovered these few miles were officially closed in order to save pregnant sheep embarrassment and worry. Crooning softly and smiling sweetly, I tippy-toed past. They were not a whit disturbed, but quite obviously enchanted by my charming, gracious behaviour. Safely past, I applied the skill born of long practice and snipped just enough time off that section to enable me to visit the lavvy at Balmaha without dinting my schedule.

On the pleasant, but tortuous, section along the side of Loch Lomond to Rowardennan I was joined by Gerard. I had suffered badly over this stage last year, and it was nice to be able to enjoy both Gerard's company and the winding, twisting path, ever rising, ever falling, through the trees, beside the water. This is the section where the path lies a yard or two from the road. At times, the path is narrow with tree roots and little switchbacks to impede progress. I was tempted, not to follow the entire length of the road, but to cut out the odd few yards of awkward going here and there. It would have made little material difference, I had always, however, intended to cleave precisely to the official footpath. I told myself that, if I could not break the race route record using the official Way, I would just have to be content with what I could achieve. I was either following the course of the race or the official route, not what happened to suit me at the time.

In retrospect, I am glad that, on this occasion, I covered the Way from south to north. The effect was to place me on the difficult ground at the north end of Loch Lomond while I yet had the energy to both move purposefully and appreciate the intricate path as it wound through the natural woodland, sometimes close to the water, sometimes well above it. Of course, a truly adventurous line would traverse the summit of Ben Lomond itself, soaring unseen, mist capped and snow girdled, above us. Well, that kind of journey would come later.

At the end of the 14 miles (22 km) of awkward ground beside the loch I was quite pleased. Not only had I enjoyed the running, but I had gained a few minutes on the schedule. Of course, a schedule is not sacrosanct. It is merely an estimate of how long one might realistically spend traversing a piece of ground. Unfortunately, a schedule may also have to be driven by the record, if one is being attempted. Knowing myself well means that I can predict quite accurately how long it will take to cover a section. However, on occasion, I sum the times for individual sections and the total exceeds the record! I know then that I am in for a tough run. A poor schedule is worse than none at all. Fighting a losing battle with an unrealistic schedule can be heartbreaking. I knew the times I had just allotted to the different legs were consistent with the variable nature of the terrain, but I did not know whether they were consistent with my ability.

Over the ensuing ground, it was apparent that conditions were much wetter than last year. I lost both my time in hand and more besides. I was now approaching Crianlarich, which meant I was approximately half-way. I was also experiencing a bad patch. As I came into the support point at Kirkton, Sean very cheerfully and, to my mind, very deliberately said, 'Great! You're *almost* half-way'. I could have throttled him! Checking my schedule, I saw I was a shade over half-way but had taken nearly nine and a half hours. I therefore needed to complete the second half in eight and a quarter hours to beat the record.

I ran in a daze to Tyndrum, where I noted in amazement that I had picked up some time. I then departed on a hugely boring leg to Bridge of Orchy. Most of the route follows the old Military Road parallel to the A82. The speed of the cars flying past served as additional mockery to my plodding progress, but I was determined not to go down without a fight. Gradually, I ran through the bad patch and even began to feel strong again. Perhaps unwisely, I rode my strength and increased pace. I was moving superbly until, with less than a mile to the support, my fine head of steam gave out and I almost clanked to a halt.

This time, despite the company of Liam, my little talisman, I did not recover on the hilly spur leading over to Inveroran and Loch Tulla. I guessed that unless I could improve on the nine miles (14 km) of fast, stony track leading me over to Kingshouse on Rannoch Moor, I would never regain contact with the schedule. The effort was there, but never the reward and nine minutes drifted off the schedule. I ran towards Kingshouse feeling rather depressed and more than somewhat knackered. I could see Gerard, who was accompanying me, striding effortlessly ahead with my request for sustenance.

I would not yet settle for less than 100 per cent effort. I ate standing up and again set off faster than I thought I could manage. This time, I did tap some hidden reserve and covered the short leg to the Devil's Staircase so quickly the support, disorganised for once, was caught *in flagrante!* I clawed back 12 minutes and was now three minutes ahead of my schedule. For the next, quite exciting

*Top of the
Devil's
Staircase with
Liam and
Gerard. West
Highland Way
record.*

section over the Staircase and down to Kinlochleven, both Gerard and Liam were to join me. A pity then, that the weather was not better. A fierce, gusty wind was hauling dirty, grey rain clouds out of storage. They were now massed behind us and closing fast. We paused briefly at the top of the col, gazing north to the still snow-plastered Mamores, mist shrouded and inhospitable.

The Military Road stays high for a time, and not all the going is straight-forward. Slippery rocks, loose boulders and short, steep descents tested both my legs and my patience. The top of the col lies at 2,600 ft (780 m) and Kinlochleven, as I belatedly realised, is at sea-level. Pounding endlessly down the stony tracks was a harsh test of my newly restored knees. They stood up to it marvellously well, but, for all our haste, we lost the three minutes I had just gained and another three besides. Then, as we ran up to the van, a vicious shower swept after us. I thought I had a fighting chance, but I needed help, rain of this severity would be difficult to resist in my, by now very fatigued, state.

The sky was darkening, the wind was gusting rain in wet squalls, 14 miles (22 km) still remained, and those miles demanded what I had only managed for eight (13 km) of the previous 50 miles (80 km) – that I outrun my schedule. I needed to outrun the dark, too, if I was to avoid the real peril of those wet blocks which raised a last threatening barrier to my final, gasping sprint for home. I think Gerard caught the drama of the moment. He had run 30 miles (50 km) already but was adamant that he should come with me to the end.

We set off on the last fierce struggle. Steeply up, gaining so painfully a thousand of those feet we had so recently shed. What was worrying me more, was the necessity to pick up a fast running pace when the climbing was over. The rain squalled in again, but, suddenly, I realised that the wind had settled to south by east! It was now on our backs. For once the weather was helping me. Feeding on its mighty strength, I gave myself to the wind, allowing it to change my pace as it rushed and roared down the glen. Sometimes I ran up hills, sometimes I could not, but always I drove on with the wind.

From the start I had known that my scheduled time for the seven and a half miles to Lundavra was optimistic, but I had thought that by the time I had reached this stage, it would not matter either way. How wrong I was! Despite my efforts and those of the wind, I lost yet another two minutes on that leg. Another minute vanished as I gulped a last drink. I should have had something more solid, but time was against it. Just six and a half miles to go, and still I needed those six minutes to equal the record! Strangely enough, I now felt quite strong. The excitement was stifling fatigue, and I began to feel the adrenalin buzz. No amount of adrenalin, however, would take me safely over some of the subsequent ground in the twilight. If I ran quickly, I would just come to grief. I went as fast as conditions allowed, aiming to rush the easy ground and proceed carefully elsewhere. The night was closing in alarmingly, and darkness blotted out the crucial details of where best to place my feet. At last, I started the final climb to the forest above Glen Nevis. Would it ever end! I expected it to be unexpectedly long, but this exceeded even my unexpectations! Was that my heart pounding? And would these empty legs really be able to cover the last three miles (5 km) in less than 20 minutes? No words between us, both grim with intent. Ninety-five hard miles (152 km) and no reward at the end? (It's only a training run, isn't it? No! It's life and death!)

Down steeply now through black rooty trees. For God's sake, don't trip. Suddenly, we burst out on the broad forest track. A mile of sweet downhill, fly legs, fly. I am stretching as fast as I can, but I cannot go fast enough. My speed is failing me, legs cramping. A barely detectable weakness begins to grow in my stomach. I am going to get hunger knock! Less than two miles and I will not make it. Think! Send Gerard ahead to where the van will be waiting at the start of the road into Fort William. Rehearse carefully what you are going to tell him, now . . . 'Go in front, Gerard, take next right, tell them to have ready a cold sweet drink, not too cold, remember, a *cold, sweet drink.*' Like an arrow from a bow he is gone. Already feeling dizzy. Don't give in fight it.

The van. Reach for the drink. It is only cordial! No spoonfuls of glucose powder stirred in. Might as well be water. No time to prepare another. Can I, through force of mental effort, for once resist the effects of hypoglycemia and hang on for the last one and a half miles? I must try. The road will seem endless, be ready for this. There is a rise to surmount near the end, save strength for it, and then you can unleash whatever is left – if anything is. Now concentrate.

My head must have been ready for that last mile and a half for a long time. Without slackening pace, but with my brain now locked out of my body, I seemed to reach, then surmount the incline with no conscious elapse of time. With a start I saw the bridge which marked the finish only 200 yards (180 m) away. Sprint! Damn, I could have gone sooner! Instantly I stopped, my automatic pilot switched off, and in the second it took for my brain to assume control again, I staggered and almost fell over, then strong arms came round me and bore me up. I was three minutes inside the 17 hours, 38 minutes I had been aiming for. I felt a bit embarrassed, three minutes is nothing to break anyone's record by. There again, I had done it the hard way.

There is a sequel to this. Next morning, in chatting to Inken, I explained I did not feel too good about knocking only three minutes off the record. She looked a little surprised. After I repeated myself she then confessed she thought I had broken my own record only, and had told the others that it 'didn't matter, it was only a training run'! I thought they were a little subdued at the finish. I had actually taken an hour off my previous run. There is a sequel to the sequel, too. A month later, looking through my log-book, I noticed that 17:38 was the scheduled time I had set myself, the record I broke was 17:48.

(The 1987 summer edition of *Fell Runner* magazine gives a record for the West Highland Way of 14:56 – for a nine-man team!)

Scottish High Level Traverse

Just as Eustace Thomas had been satisfied to motor his way between the 4,000 ft (1,200 m) peaks in NW Scotland and the 4,000 ft summits in NE Scotland, so those Rucksackers who followed deemed it satisfactory to raise the order of difficulty by walking the entire route but taking to the road at times. Very properly, John Richardson elevated the walk to the status of a true classic both by devising a 'pure' (road-free) line and by executing the entire route in a continuous fashion. Until John, Ian Grant and I completed this 'pure' line as a Club walk in 1977 I believe it had never been done before.

Both John and I had frightened ourselves considerably by reading accounts of previous traverses in Club journals. Blizzards, deep snow, the hallucinatory effects of hard and sleepless hours all featured graphically in these accounts. I particularly shuddered at Phil Brockbank's description of the ascent to the bleak watershed of the Bealach Dubh, a 'screaming desolation' was his phrase.

In the event we enjoyed a marvellous walk. Demanding it was, but it gave so much more than it asked. Thereafter, this traverse gleamed gem bright among my collection of superb walks and runs. For some reason it became established as an ultra fell running classic with perhaps half a dozen attempts to complete within 24 hours. I had experienced no desire to tackle the route from this perspective. I had, however, always determined to repeat it some day, at the right time. The only, very slight, dissatisfaction I had felt after our completion was the memory of mountains we did not traverse. First, the majestic line of the Grey Corries sweeping irresistibly onwards as we descended all too soon from Aonach Beag. And later, as we topped the Bealach Dubh, the vast bulk of Ben Alder dominating our approach to Loch Ericht.

The notion that I might be able to reconcile the romance of the route with the harsher practicalities of a record attempt for a time threatened to seduce my whole aspirations concerning a 'purer' form of the Scottish Fourthousanders. The possibility of a record and the certainty of a magnificent journey beguiled me. I was saved, as many a gallant crusader in times past, by my noble unflinching resolve and the plea of a fair damsel.

Well, 'noble resolve' may be interpreted as a stab of conscience about avoiding the soaring challenge of those intervening mountains. The damsel's plea was a timely reminder from Inken that I had promised to invite her whenever the Scottish Fourthousanders were repeated. There was also a not too veiled hint about the difficulties she might experience in getting time off to support my Pennine Way attempt, if I should be so foolish as to essay a solo effort. In truth, what I had in mind was such a wonderful prospect, I welcomed the idea of sharing it with someone else who I knew would truly appreciate the venture. I was, however, genuinely concerned about the matching of our physical reserves to the total concept.

The total concept involved not only traversing extra peaks in the west, but also an extension of the route further eastwards. It seemed illogical to 'collect' just the 4,000 ft (1,200 m) summits in the Caingorms when there were endless peaks and high plateaux in all directions. Like a child loose in a sweet shop, I described sweeping lines all over the map. My route moved ever eastwards, claiming Lochnagar and finally Mount Keen, the most easterly Munro. But why finish there? We were starting on the west coast, why not finish on the east coast?

At this point, realism raised its unwelcome head. The line my pencil had drawn to the south and east of the Cairngorm 'high tops' covered far more ground than we could encompass on a continuous traverse. Furthermore, the continuation of the route from Mount Keen to the coast was not only an unnecessary attempt to gild a noble lily, it was likely to be utterly boring! With ambition in check therefore, I decided we could still execute a superb extension by continuing the traverse over Ben A'Bhuird and Ben Avon, both mountains are a mere handful of feet below the 4,000 ft (1,200 m) mark and share the unique character of the highest Cairngorm plateaux. I still hoped to finish over Lochnagar as I had good associations with this hill from running my winter mountaineering courses from a base in view of its beetling crags.

I was excited by the route. It was a magnificent and logical line. But I was also a little fearful. We planned to walk towards the end of May, the timing was, in part, a response to our dissatisfaction with what the LDWA were offering as their 100-mile (160 km) event at that time. May in the Scottish Highlands can still produce winter weather. Snow, even blizzards are not unusual. Our great venture could quite easily founder on the first hill. Severe weather towards the end of this testing enterprise might not only jeopardise the walk, it could well jeopardise us along with it! On a different level, I began to have doubts as to whether I could get my head round both the Scottish traverse and the Pennine Way just three weeks later. Had I bitten off more than I could chew?

When I arrived in Edinburgh to rendezous with Inken, I was almost relieved when she informed me that at the eleventh hour John Richardson, who was to have been our sole support for the first day and night, could not make it. He was rather poorly after heading a piece of road while he should have been riding his bicycle. Once I found John was not seriously hurt, I prepared to put my feet up for the weekend. Too soon! Quite extraordinarily, another friend and newcomer to the Rucksack Club, Chris Bauer, had stepped in with a very generous offer to help. What was more, Chris's friend Sheila Cormack of the Pinnacle Club was prepared to come along to ease Chris's support burden. The traverse was on. I did not know about Sheila's support expertise, but she could certainly drive. We were in Fort William in no time and, after a battle with early season midges, settled in for another of those excited, fitful sleeps.

We left at 5.30 a.m. after a meagre breakfast but as much as the stomach could take at such an unseemly hour. The tiny voice which had been whispering that I should not be tackling these mountains with so little specific hill training, began to shout very loudly down my ear. It was too late, we were off. Butting up the steep skirts of Ben Nevis, I very deliberately chose a steady pace, always a little less than my natural inclination. Just as well, Inken told me later she felt rather overstretched, probably I was more keyed up than I realised.

I can be a real wimp at the start of a long event. Slow to get going anyway, I frequently suspect my physical preparation and, whatever the weather, find fault with that, too. The best I can do is to disengage my mind and wait for a magic moment. The current fault in the weather was that a fine day had been forecast, and it had not come! It was very dull and overcast as we plodded ever upwards. I skidded on black ice, hmmm, cold too. I'll bet the snow patches are frozen and I decided to leave the ice-axes behind. We'll become horrible accident statistics, 'Found dead after slipping on ice, the coroner stated they were wearing running shoes.' How embarrassing! (At least I'm wearing clean underwear.)

There was plenty of snow on the summit of the Ben. The famous gullies skeltered giddily down through black rocks into smoking depths. It smelled high, cold and remote. What a great place to be early in the morning! Care is needed to locate and descend the line to the Carn Mor Dearg arête. After a time, a large snow bank presented itself as an alternative to awkward blocks. How I missed the insurance of an axe poised to come to my aid should the snow contain ice patches. I stepped cautiously on, and letting my weight drive my heels through the crust began to clip down. Relief! The snow, if anything, was a little too soft. I began to feel better about omitting the ice-axes and thumbed a mental nose at the coroner.

As we hopped and skipped over the blocks which comprise the fine arête leading to Carn Mor Dearg, the moment of magic arrived. A flick of wind parted the curtain of cloud, revealing a gleam of blue, a flash of gold. Then it was gone. A few hops and skips later, it was repeated, longer this time. I unpacked the camera. By the time we were atop this, the second of the 4,000 ft (1,200 m) peaks, we were bathed in warm and gentle sunlight. Making a virtue out of the necessity of Inken's hunger, we stopped and ate, gazing around us at this unsurpassable world we had entered.

Do the physical payments which one must make in order to first enter, then journey through such worlds constitute not only an inevitable, but also an essential part of the experience of their beauty? Cool logic might refute such a notion. But what role has logic to play in that glorious fusion of physical, sensory and emotional energy whose pulse will thrust the spirit into a sublime relationship with forces of Nature of which it is a tiny part? The exultant cry of the spirit which is wild, free and joyful arises not merely from the contemplation of Nature, but from the sometimes fierce struggle to cleave to it. Who ventures in the mountains cannot remain passive.

It is very easy to resent the 1,300 ft (390 m) of descent from the top of Carn Mor Dearg. After crossing about 160 ft (50 m) of col one has to gather it all in again. Not quite all, some pawky surveyor with a theodolite for a heart robbed Aonach Mor of 4,000 ft (1,200 m) status by one improbable foot. Its cairn is certainly more than a foot high, however, and thus having regained our 1,300 ft (390 m), we climbed our third Fourthousander. Running, now over sparse turf, now over old snow banks, we approached Aonach Beag. This is the last 4,000 ft (1,200 m) peak in the NW group. We would need to cover around 60 miles (100 km) before we surmounted another Fourthousander. But now, instead of immediately scuttling down to follow valley lines to the Cairngorms, we would remain high on peaks and ridges for many hours.

First, we had to cope with the steep descent off Aonach Beag in order to attain the col giving access to the Grey Corries. As I expected, the remains of a cornice menaced the approach to the descent slopes. The cornice had degraded into a steep head wall which gave a possible descent line. The snow was quite stable, but steep. Fortunately, it was soft enough for me to kick steps and jab handholds firm enough to carry my weight. As the angle eased, I signalled to Inken that it was safe to follow. I also noticed another walker, rather more suitably equipped, delaying his own attempt while he watched mine – a canny

*Inken
approaching
the summit of
Aonach Mor,
behind is Carn
Mor Dearg.*

Scot, nae doot! From this point, I realised the snow was a great bonus. It was at just the right angle and consistency to facilitate a swooping descent. In no time we had whooped our way to the col. The penalty we paid, however, was frozen, wet feet, and these were to cause problems later.

After the insatiable Blunk had again tested my patience by burying her head in her nosebag, we launched upwards towards Sgurr Choinnich Mor. By now the sun was waxing warm. Having just compressed 7,500 ft (2,250 m) of climbing into very few miles, we found the steep grassy ascent quite a stern pull. Once on the summit, however, the ridge sweeps steadily north by east with relatively minor variations in height gained and lost. Gradually we approached Stob Choire Claurigh, at 3,858 ft (1,160 m) the highest summit on the ridge. After freezing in the wet snow, the stony going across the highest ground was hard on the feet. Such a combination is likely to produce bruising of the bones. We had also finished our liquid and were beginning to look forward to seeing Sheila and Chris down in the valley. We savoured our last peak, however. This was the end of the first section of the route. Only little more than 15 miles (24 km) in length, it had included seven major summits over 3,500 ft (1,050 m), and we had been blessed with glorious conditions in which to traverse them.

It began to look as if we might have longer to savour the views than expected. Our projected route off the summit lay NE. The steep slopes held snow fields on which the sun had bestowed only a fleeting glance. I tried kicking steps, but quickly approached the point of hazard. One slightly harder patch, and I could begin a descent to the glen likely to produce both the speed and effect of truly terminal velocity. While Inken has an abhorrence of sliding down slopes in the best of circumstances she can usually pick a safe and subtle line through aggressive ground (probably a feminine trait!), and she did so now. Soon we were guzzling our fill from delicious snow-fed rills and springs. Below the snow, the whole mountain was alive with water, leaping, dashing pausing to swell the green sphagnum bogs, clattering noisily down stony channels. Fast as we descended, with yet greater impetuosity rushed the water, eager to join its parent burn still far beneath. Had I been born on these slopes, I would not so hurry to chance the inevitable sea.

At the bothy in Lairig Leacach we savoured the luxuries of a splendid settee. Normally wary of adopting too comfortable a stance at support points, I could not resist this. There was, anyway, not the slightest temptation to remain overlong. The weather was holding fine, and we had just completed as inspirational an introduction to a long route as any I had known. Waving thanks and goodbyes we set off on the next stage.

It was now mid-afternoon and our plan was to reach Dalwhinnie a little before midnight. To accomplish this, we would have to be sure of traversing Ben Alder while it was still light. We began to swing into the steady jogging rhythm we hoped would cover the easier going swiftly and economically. Our route took us past the southern end of Loch Treig and then over to Loch Ossian. At first, along the tracks, it felt good to be eating the miles so much more quickly than over the ridges. Ere long, of course, the going became tedious. The sense of space was enormous and impressive, naturally enough it was precisely these features which gave us the impression we were barely moving.

Gradually, we wound in the miles, and the path became narrower and more interesting as we approached the 'screaming desolation' of the Bealach Dubh. It was hardly screaming now, though the sun had retreated behind a screen of cloud and a brisk breeze invited goose-pimples out to play.

Although the summit of Ben Alder stands at over 3,700 ft (1,110 m), we were already at more than 2,000 ft (600 m) and the summit plateau was not long coming up. Neither of us had ever been over Ben Alder before, the map showed it to have a fairly extensive plateau however, and I was looking forward to this. Perhaps as a child of the moors, my heart rejoices always in the great upland areas. Despite the map, I was totally unprepared for what met our gaze as we emerged on the plateau of Ben Alder. It was vast. It was so vast, I could not believe it. The so-called plateaux of the high Cairngorms are more extensive, but they fall from high summits, they are sloping plateaux. Stretched before us was a flat immensity. It seemed a tundra region of coarse grasses and wet snowfields, and it rolled out of sight. I thought it must be an illusion, a trick of the light. We set off jogging across it on a bearing for the summit cairn. It was no illusion. We were running but did not seem to be making any impression on the distance. I did not care. At that moment in time there was no better place to be in all the world.

Somewhere in the middle of the plateau I looked back. The sky was assuming the pale grey mantle of evening. But even as I gazed, the suble greys became suffused with the most delicate shades of pastels. It was like looking into a huge

Inken crossing Ben Alder summit plateau. Ben Nevis is in the far distance.

sea shell, steely greys and pale pinks. As the invisible sun lowered obliquely towards the western horizon, it slipped swathes of diffuse and misty light beneath the clouds. Low though the sun had dipped, it was high enough to bestow another gift. On the edge of our westering gaze there tipped a serrated line of peaks. Highest and whitest of them all was the Ben. The thrill of our journey leapt from that far distant summit. We locked it into our gaze, into our hearts, into our forever memories.

If we are fortunate, we can review our life in the hills and select treasured memories which have become focal and focusing points for the love we bear them. Occasionally, we can recognise an experience as vital even while it is unfolding. If we are very lucky indeed, there occur supreme moments which are so imperative they pierce us to our innermost spirit, they transcend words, engage not reason. They communicate directly with the stuff of our nature, our spirit leaps and grasps truth for a moment. That moment is sufficient.

Our journey across the plateau reached its conclusion with our gaining its highest point. We had made the most cursory investigation of the resources of this great mountain. I shall be back. An aspect of the exploratory nature of our journey now presented itself, we did not know the way off! We wanted to continue the line of our walk either north or east. To the east, there appeared to be a long continuous rampart of cliffs guarding the summit. To the north, the map indicated a likely looking ridge jutting towards the glen we wished to attain. We sped north over wonderfully easy running ground but with some trepidation, we were rapidly approaching what was obviously another line of cliffs.

The map did not lie. There was a ridge leading out away from the plateau edge, it did not look too promising, however. As best we could, we inspected the ridge from either side. It certainly was steep, plunging down in a series of steps which, if they were sheer, were high enough to bar our line of descent. There was no possibility of escaping down the craggy sides. If there was a way down, it would have to follow the crest of the plummenting ridge. The only feasible alternative was to retrace our steps, and neither of us was yet prepared to do that. 'Let's give it a try, eh?'

The ridge was magnificent. Resembling a huge flake of vegetated rock, its serrated edge tumbled down into the darkening glen. Each time we came to one of its steep steps I was sure we would be forced to retreat, each time a comparatively simple line would reveal itself, and down we would go to the next level. The sweet inevitability with which this happened bred a confidence which banished our anxiety. We began to glory in our situation. It was obvious from the tumbled chaotic slopes and crags around us that we had found the magic staircase by which mortals may traverse glen and summit. Too soon we reached the foot of our fairy tower and swished into the bush-like heather. Perhaps in winter I will return and clamber, steel shod gleaming, on the crisp white tower; spiral up to a cleaner, colder, purer world, once more, once alone, gaze westward into my dream.

The path ribboned down the glen parallel to the burn which chattered along beside us. With true dark still over an hour away, we had sufficient light left to enjoy our surroundings. It was a beautiful evening, calm and still. There is that about vast, unchanging panoramas which quietens the soul and lends it gravity and peace. We settled into a pace which flowed with the rhythm of the path. A little further on we saw columns of blue smoke pluming into the still air. Beside the now broad waters of the burn there were tents and dark clumps of figures gathered round various fires, anti-midge fires perhaps, or the ancient glen prompting some primordial instinct. The smoke was scented and lovely. We raised our hands in greeting. They would soon be lying down to rest beside the ever-flowing waters, their world would darken as the mountains locked them in night shades. Tomorrow, their lives would resume. As they slept, we would be following our journey ever eastwards, going onwards to reach dawn breaking, sun rising. Our first night was almost upon us, our second was waiting our arrival in the eastern highlands.

Spring can be a fickle season, as befits its youthfulness. The wings of darkness beat a thin wave of air against us. Imperceptibly the rolling wave increased in strength and our effortless rhythm changed into a strenuous battle against a power insistent and chill. In the dubious shelter of some dark pines we ate and donned our spare gear. Shivering by now, we launched ourselves on the broad and tedious track beside Loch Ericht. The lights of Dalwhinnie at the end of the loch seemed reluctant to let us approach, but our Scout's Pace of jogging and walking soon had heating systems going efficiently. At last, round a final bend there was a glow of light from a van parked by the track. A whiff of escaping steam carried the essence of ambrosia – hot stew!

The interior of the little van was a haven of comfort and warmth. Chris and Sheila kept a constant supply of hot drinks and food coming in our direction until I Billy Buntered my way out of the van and back onto the track. Having changed from contact lenses into my glasses, I stood blinking like a short-sighted owl, trying to penetrate the gloom. I do not rate my night vision very highly and was making very sure I was not on the point of marching firmly back in the direction of Fort William. Satisfied with my orientation, I was content to let Inken concern herself with the fiddling trivia of negotiating an accurate route through the few streets and across the A9. She is far more meticulous than I. I am inclined to paint my navigation with a broad brush. The creative results can be most striking, like finding oneself on an unexpected set of mountains.

Leaving behind the comforts of a support point at the midnight hour after a satisfying but tiring day can be something of a wrench. I remembered having to prise Ted Dance out of this very spot when he and Geoff Bell were traversing the Fourthousanders. Ted's reluctance to depart became manifest when, as the moment became imminent, he emptied his carefully prepared rucksack in an attempt to discover the half a Mars bar he felt economy dictated should replace the whole one he had just packed. For once, no such reluctance gripped us. The magical skein of this enchanted journey had bound us in its spell. The night would not be easy, we realised that, but by morning all the Cairngorms would be spread before us. For Inken the primary object of this journey, the 4,000 ft (1,200 m) peaks of Scotland, would be within her grasp, and for me the lure and excitement of a new and fabulous route. I wanted to surmount the barrier of the

Cairngorm 'High Tops', and from that height I wanted to roam on and on.

It was not an easy night. We endured it as a passage to better things, but we did not enjoy it. First, I was unusually sleepy and the track tediously following a leat winding up to Loch Cuaich did not help. If it had not been for the fence by the leat, I am sure I would have fallen into it. I remembered not enjoying the rough and boggy ground which led to Glen Tromie when John and I had come this way 10 years ago. Despite the early advent of a grey dawn it seemed to have become even rougher. Our progress was slow, weary, and, at times, very frustrating.

Close by the confluence of the Allt Bhran and the River Tromie we burrowed into a bank of thick heather and after a very early breakfast had a few minutes sleep. Although it was bitterly cold in the wind, the light was full and the sky promised a fine morning. I considered we had the worst over. Soon we would be in Glen Feshie for a second breakfast. How wrong I was. I should have read my old log-book which made comment on the very rough going from here on. Our progress through wroughty heather was a constant battle. The only bit I enjoyed was when I succumbed to the morning sun and stretched out on the springy bed, no sound but the tinkling burn and the sighing breeze.

Perseverance brought us at last to the very fine little valley which snicked up onto our moor from Glen Feshie itself. The morning was crisp and blue, and I was now impatient to get onto the real mountains while it lasted. A good track wound down the valley inviting a swift descent to the flat green glen. Clamping the bit between my teeth, I set off at a fair gallop. Frustratingly, I began to boil up in too many clothes. Stopping to remove a layer I glanced back and saw Inken quite a way behind. Well! This would never do. Just when we could get going and claw back some lost time, she had apparently decided on a go-slow. As she approached, however, I could see she was having trouble running and was obviously in some pain.

Sore feet, the walker's bane; and nothing simple either. Being a sufferer myself, I am a good 'foots-man', but this was beyond simple remedy. Frozen feet 50 miles (80 km) back, which had subsequently been pounded over rocks in thin fell shoes, re-frozen on Ben Alder and pounded again, had, naturally enough, responded in painful bruising. When the bones in the feet become bruised, the only real cure is rest. Cushioning and soft ground might mitigate the pain somewhat, but we were hoping to cover another 50 to 60 miles (80 to 100 km) of mountainous terrain. While Inken is ever ready to complain about the painful grind of tedious running, she has an extraordinary capacity to ignore discomfort on a route which she regards as inspirational. And I knew full well how the prospect and the current execution of this route had inspired her. Consequently, I realised immediately that the pain must be a savage one.

With the appreciation of the cause, nature and severity of the pain came a keen awareness of what lay ahead. In my heart I knew she could not make it, nor did I want her to try. There were an awful number of footsteps between us and Royal Deeside, an uncountable number of stones. With each step, pain, and each stone prepared to lend that pain an extra refinement; I could not bear to witness that, I knew it too well.

Inken insisted that she could follow if I would not mind moving a little slower. We sat off again with me looking for the grassy patches and seeing only stones. But despite the trauma, the beauty of Glen Feshie in the morning could not be denied. Owing to a slack bit of thinking, we had rather longer to admire the glen than intended. We could have started our ascent to the Cairngorm Massif just before Feshie Lodge. Unfortunately, we had indicated a spot three miles (5 km) further down where we were to be met. With the hills soaring above, we sweated away precious time and energy, and our progress became very slow.

Perhaps it was only that I perceived it to be slow. As we jogged to the bridge where our support mustered, Sheila made some flattering remarks about our pace. This was nice, but I still felt restless and would do so until I could actually set foot on the climb to the Cairngorms. I had been mentally gearing myself to go solo from this point. I knew how much Inken wanted to at least complete the Fourthousanders, but I did not see how she could do so. If she left this spot with me, and not Sheila and Chris, she would be committed to reaching Deeside. This would mean she would have to traverse about 30 miles (50 km) of very hard terrain, even omitting the summits. I said nothing, but waited and observed.

It soon became apparent that Inken was not going to retire. I hoped she knew what she was doing and trusted that she did. We prepared to depart. Preparations made were partly decided by the weather. It was now very warm and, with the hottest part of the day to come, it was tempting to take little more than shorts, vest and spare woolly. A degree of common sense prevailed, and we packed some warmer and windproof clothing. Had we not done so, we might not have survived what was to follow.

After ascending more than 1,000 ft (300 m) in shorts and vest, we suddenly crossed an altitude band above which a powerful wind instantly created a new climate. Although the sun still smiled serenely from a clear sky, it no longer warmed us. As soon as we had completed the most strenuous part of the climbing onto the rounded flanks of Carn Ban Mor, we hurriedly put on our spare clothing. Shorts were out of the question, no chance of an early season sun-tan after all. Rather more comfortable now, we made the slight detour to take in the summit of Carn Ban Mor, which, at 3,443 ft (1,075 m) was our first Munro since Ben Alder. I had a rose-tinted memory of the Cairngorm giants being but a cock-stride away once we had cracked the steep pull out of Glen Feshie. I was therefore puzzled to see no peaks around at all. There followed a few minutes serious reconciliation of map, ground and memory. The first condemned the last as a gross optimist. Cairn Toul and Braeriach were there all right, but even had we been crows, they were still five or six miles (8 or 9.6 km) away.

Not only did our peaks appear distant, they were separated from us by considerable snow fields. Obviously, late snow had visited the Cairngorms and, outstaying its welcome, lay in ever broadening wet swathes between us and the high ground. Navigation was thus not merely a matter of the most direct line, but rather the line which kept us out of the main snow fields and followed ridges in preference to crossing basins. It was a long and muscular struggle to gain the col beneath Cairn Toul, nor was the summit quite such a little way above it as I remembered. However, we enjoyed clambering up the snow-free boulders which jumbled up to the top of the peak. Unfortunately, I realised that unless the snow was swept clear of the high ground or was in better condition, we were in for a real battle.

Apart from the snow, the wind was also causing increasing problems. Although the sun was still shining, indeed the glare was very painful, the wind at this height was tearing through our clothing. Furthermore, I was determined not just to traverse Cairn Toul and Braeriach, but collect all the bumps over 4,000 ft (1,200 m) between these two. After all, we had come to do the Fourthousanders, had we not? Nice ethics but cold comfort.

The traverse of the minor tops on the way over to Braeriach could appropriately be described as taking place in a 'screaming desolation', at least, that is how it felt. Had one merely observed the scene from behind some sheltered partition, it would have looked innocent enough. But the Cairngorm wind is a deadly enemy. It has a primitive strength which is heedless of life for it was spawned in an age before life. It belongs to a primeval world of gaunt rock, empty seas and merciless cold. Refusing to yield its power to the passing ages, it snarls forever round the deep corries and craggy recesses of the Cairngorms. But when it gathers its forces and leaps like a ferocious beast across the high, smooth wastes, then beware, for it kills without pity.

Certainly, a primitive fear was gnawing at me as we battled towards Braeriach. There was no real danger yet, but our position was finely balanced, the wind could tip the scales with contemptuous ease. I have, and always have had, a robust delight in the vigour of a strong wind. There is in it that sense of affinity, a life force shared, even the feeling of a scouring purification. While we remain mortal, however, our physical and spiritual strength may soon be exhausted by its exuberant power. I was also aware that Inken did not share to anything like the same extent my love of the wind's rough embrace. The raptures were rapidly becoming more than even I could bear, and I knew they must be wasting her strength and wasting her will to persevere.

On the summit at last; a curious lull. The wind was screaming up the sheer headwall of the Garbhe Choire with such force, it must have been rearing into a vertical wave high above the summit which stands at the very edge of the precipice. Relief for a few minutes, but the realisation of how cold we had become and the urge and necessity to lose height without delay. Now came a problem. I could not remember the descent I had followed in times previous to reach the top of the pass, the Lairig Ghru, most safely and economically. I scouted round in the soft snow, aware that we were getting colder, but also aware that a wrong descent line would result in, at best, time loss and at worst, disaster. Peering cautiously over convex slopes, I eventually chose a line and started down. The wind had not polished the snow to ice, and, though awkward at times, our route proved safe and parsimonious. The uncertainty was somewhat trying to the nerves, however, I did not relish the prospect of any more doubtful decisions like that.

The ascent from the Lairig Ghru to the Cairngorm–Ben Macdui plateau is extraordinarily steep. It is only 1,000 ft (312 m), but feels a good deal more. Weaving a careful line under small outcrops and over ice-loosened blocks, we emerged wearily onto the plateau at last; weary, but with the knowledge that the final two Fourthousanders were at either end of this great piece of high ground. The major objective of our journey lay within our grasp. And once we had achieved this, what more could we not achieve?

But first the job in hand. We had emerged in the middle of the plateau, equidistant from the two summits. The usual route visits Macdui first, then goes north to Cairngorm itself. From here it is a wonderfully easy descent off the mountain to Glenmore and rest. The peaks over which I had planned to extend the walk lay to the east of Macdui. We therefore needed to visit Cairngorm first, then retrace our steps towards Macdui. Outside the winter months it is a pleasant and easy task to sweep across the plateau, the dearth of vegetation and the fine gravelly surface make for fast travel. Now, of course, almost the entire area was snow covered. We sat to work with a will, but progress was slow and laborious. And the wind, though generally behind us on this leg, had ushered in large banks of high cloud. We were in a grey, desolate and empty world.

As we traversed the long snow fields, I recounted to Inken the first time I had visited the Cairngorms with Len, nearly 20 years previously. A murderous blizzard had sought to trap us in the great basin of Loch Avon, and we had escaped across these very slopes, hauling our sacks on Len's home-made skis. In white-out conditions and ignorant of true reality, we had fortuitously donned crampons and shouldered the sacks just as the wind glazed sides of the Lairig Ghru were about to invite us to perdition. Now, the wind was neither so fierce nor cold, but we were barely sufficiently clothed to withstand it and the miles lay heavy upon us. In pursuing this fine act of balance between peril and ambition, I was relying on my experience, skill and strength to keep us safe. It behoved me not to indulge in any form of overestimation of those abilities.

The summit of Cairngorm was a turning point, both literally and symbolically. Onward now, first to Ben Macdui, second in stature only to Ben Nevis, then, into the furthest dream. Something Jeff Lowe, the mountaineer, said, echoed in my mind. First, he said, you have the image. Then the magic comes when you transform that image into reality. I was now at the very pivotal point of that dream reality. The very severity involved in reaching this point underlay my desire and determination to transform dream into reality. It was at this precise moment Inken told me that, beyond Ben Macdui, she did not wish to continue.

As strong as she was in body, and stronger still in spirit, yet the cold, ruthless wind and the constant bruising pain had exhausted her. She had drained her resources, and now her furthest peaks lay as distant images; magic, unattainable chimera. My immediate response was to commiserate with her, then I realised that not only did she feel she could not go beyond Ben Macdui, she hoped I would also finish my journey there. Such was the absolute and overpowering commitment that had grown within me as the journey had progressed, I could in no way comprehend what she was saying. Soaring on my renewed strength, flooded with optimism, stiffened with an implacable determination, I was on quite another plane. It took a long and painful period of time to leave that plane and attempt another. How perverse is my nature, while I avow to struggle for wisdom, I reject opportunities presented should they conflict with my own will.

It really was quite simple. Having shared our identical dream, having given everything she could possibly give to accomplish that dream, having quietly endured the pain to the bitter occlusion of the final part of our dream, she was spent. If I were to carry on without her, continue alone that fabulous dream we had shared, it would cause her pain beyond the endurable. With an effort I imagined myself in the valley, weary in body and spirit, while my companion with whom I had shared the journey for nearly 100 miles (160 km) was pursuing it still. What we had planned together, endured together and were now about to achieve together would be a complete and satisfying whole, if I were to make it so by concluding it together. A simple but subtle notion, whose paradox might yet evade my stubborn pragmatism. Where targets are concerned, I am frequently neither subtle nor sensitive. I struggled through the snow and the dilemma, then a softer, gentler, wiser part of my nature saw more clearly and acquiesced.

With our spirits once more at peace, we locked our bodies into the fight for Ben Macdui. As we climbed higher, so the wind almost imperceptibly, but implacably, increased in strength. First, we had to visit the outlying top of Carn Sputan Dearg, ancient Rucksack Club traditions demanded this. Before we could mount the inconsequential summit, the cloud base lowered and mist was flying around us like 1,000 demented phantoms. The cold became polar, it cut into me and through me, seeking, I knew, my warm heart's blood. It would not have it. I increased my pace, traversed Sputan Dearg without pausing and, body and will bent into the flying wrack, followed my compass into the white miasma. Kindled by fear, my concentration and determination were such that I barely realised Inken was being increasingly swallowed by the mist. A stricken cry recalled me to my duties, but I urged her to further and harder effort. We must get off this mountain before it killed us, but first, we would have its summit!

The second highest point in these islands, 4,296 ft (1,342 m). No time for ceremony, just turn and go. Run if possible, but keep moving. Fortunately, we had calculated the bearing we must follow from the top well before reaching it. We hurled ourselves down until we had crept from under the fiercest grasp of that colossal hand which gripped the summit. We paused to check our memory against the map and the visible ground. We had to go east, then descend a long valley which would lead us to Loch Etchachan, from where we would drop yet further to the remote bothy known as the Hutchison Hut. Inken had the map and I formed a mental image of the ground we must cover. We reached the head of a broad snow-packed valley and I started to follow Inken down it. It was good to be losing height and dropping to safety, but were we? I thought I remembered a shallow ridge between us and the valley we were to descend. I asked Inken if she was sure we were following the correct valley. Not given to over-confidence, on this occasion she was insistent we were in the right place. I was impressed by this, but not convinced. We *had* to get this one right. I insisted we should cross the ridge in front and then descend. Immediately we did so, everything slotted neatly into place. The valley we had started to follow lay only half a mile from this one and perfectly parallel to it. It would, however, eventually have committed us to descending into the great defile of Loch Avon where Len and I had so nearly been entombed all those years ago.

The light was slowly fading as we crunched endlessly down the valley towards Loch Etchachan. Having blasted us off the heights, the wind was content to stay there and made no attempts to follow us down. The air was suddenly preternaturally still. Away to our left, behind the beetling black crags rising sheer from the loch, clouds were parting, and the sky gave hints of a distant sunset. Pale, eggshell blues and a curious green cast combined with greys and blacks to impart a sense of arctic cold and arctic tranquillity.

I was anxious to reach the bothy as soon as we could. Sheila and Chris had departed for home from Glen Feshie (another world ago, it seemed!), but my friend Neil Spinks from Aberdeen had kindly agreed to make the long journey to the Hutchison Hut to bring us much needed provisions. Neil and I had in previous years combined forces to run my winter mountaineering courses and, though a Derbyshire lad, there are few who know these hills better than he. After Inken's declaration on the summit of Cairngorm, it seemed as if Neil had come out simply to escort us off the hill. However, as we descended to less hostile conditions, she appeared to recoup some of her strength. I therefore suggested that, as the walk-out from Hutchison to Deeside was long and tedious, she might consider finishing over Beinn A'Bhuird, which is a bit longer, but certainly not tedious! As this mountain stands but 75 ft (23 m) below the 4,000 ft (1,200 m) contour, she might have resented the suggestion, but she did not. She knew how much I wanted to continue the walk beyond the Fourthousanders, and I knew how much she wanted to come with me. With soft going between here and Beinn A'Bhuird, and with Ben Avon rising only 1,000 ft (320 m) across the intervening col, we might yet achieve a magnificent conclusion to our journey.

We were some three hours behind schedule by now, and I went ahead to reassure Neil that all was well. He was wrapped up in most of the spare gear he had brought out for us, but he still looked chilly. His welcome, however, was typically warm and enthusiastic, it did me good just to see him. When Inken appeared, hobbling once more on the stony ground, he embraced her in such a bear hug that the sun broke out all over her face.

Neil had used a mountain bike to transport himself and a rucksack full of food and clothes swiftly up the miles of Glen Derry track. He was rightly enthusiastic about this method of overcoming the notorious tedium of the typical Cairngorm 'walk-in'. There again, enthusiam is Neil's hallmark. His good cheer was infectious, and I soon began to feel as if I was about to start the walk rather than face our second night out. His optimism, too, complemented my own. We had soon reduced Beinn A'Bhuird and Ben Avon to minor excrescences on a rolling tableland, a pleasant stroll on a fine evening.

Packed to the brim with calories and rather more suitably clad, we hurried to make ground in the last of the light. Neil bounded cheerfully off down the path, keen to locate his hidden bike and make last orders in Braemar. I hoped he would not break his neck in his exuberance, but reflected he would probably just stick a plaster on it and declare it 'right'.

I had crossed the ground between Beinn A'Bhuird and the Hutchison Hut on a bothying expedition the previous winter. I remembered it as a laborious slog with much terrain awkward to read navigationally. In the event, it proved not unenjoyable. At this northern latitude, the light hung in the sky to provide an extended twilight. There was altogether less snow on this side of the Cairngorms, and none at all at our present altitude – around 3,000 ft (937 m). The ground was reminiscent of my Derbyshire moors, and I felt at home slotting a line through peat hags. It was very mild, too, and windless. Perhaps we were going to have a good night and a serene passage over these lovely mountains which waited so patiently in the night.

Optimism is fine, so long as you can bear disappointment with stoicism. I have had much practice, so I was able to remain reasonably cheerful as the wind began to slam into us once more. The 'jet stream' effect seemed to switch on at a little over 3,000 ft (937 m). As soon as we started our climb towards North Top, occasional gusts of wind thundered across the hillside and attempted to unbalance us as we clambered over large blocks and boulders. The higher we climbed, the more frequently came the gusts. Eventually, we were back in the constant gale we hoped we had left in possession of Ben Macdui. At least there was now less chance of being unbalanced, but the cold was returning, and, with the cold, mist.

North Top is simply a cairn on a very extensive and almost completely flat top. As a matter of navigational pride I wanted to find it. Using both technique and senses tuned to the feel of the ground, I led us almost directly to the cairn. Unable to decide whether satisfaction or surprise was the most appropriate reaction, I embarked on the easier task of guiding us down to the col before Ben Avon. An hour later I was still struggling to locate it!

To this day I cannot calculate what went wrong. I set bearings and timed us along them in textbook fashion, to no avail. The north edge of the col is the head of a huge corrie which bites deep into the mountain and forms a magnificent headwall of steep crags. The area is a superb and remote climbing ground, the famous Mitre Ridge being part of it. I had no wish to get too close to this edge, yet time and again my bearing left us poised above some unfathomable black recess which might be merely a gap in the minor rock outcrops or the headwall itself. Tantalisingly, the mist would part, then close in again before a decision could be made. I tried all kinds of tricks, but nothing worked. I would not risk descending unknown slopes without being sure they were safe and could gain us access to the col. It was looking as if I would at last have to resort to returning to the summit (if I could find it) and start anew. I made one last effort. It bore no fruit but placed us on particularly steep ground. I forced myself to think logically. According to the map, there was only one slope which rose on our left when we were walking north. There was a large granite tor marked at the head of the slope, Cnap A'Chleirich. I took us up, and there it was! I now had us precisely fixed and moved with confidence down slopes I could not in my earlier ignorance dare. None too soon, while my intense concentration, to say nothing of my hot-tempered frustration, had kept me warm, Inken was very strained and

Looking towards Beinn A'Bhuird from the col. Reconnaisance trip.

Training for the Pennine Way – lunch break on the Wain Stones.

chilled through and through.

After wandering across the mist-shrouded, wind-blasted slopes in anxious uncertainty, the col seemed a haven of familiar assurance. As is the way with high cols, the wind was roaring through, compressed by the enormous bulk of the mountains on either side. But I was once more in control, and I wanted to exorcise my mistake by crossing the col and ascending Ben Avon. Almost without discussion we reached the decision that Inken should go straight down from the col while I attempted a quick climb to Ben Avon's nearest and highest summit, returning to the col and meeting Inken further down the valley. It was important to me not only that I should reach the summit of Ben Avon, but that I prove myself capable of doing so in conditions of poor visibility on my second night out. Pride at stake, if you will, but more than this, the honing of technical skills and psychological strengths which in ultra hill running are as important as physical fitness and, perhaps more pertinently, capable of infinite development.

My solo excursion was a strangely satisfying and oddly spiritual experience. I felt as if I was alone in a mighty cathedral from which everyone had departed. Everyone except me and the entity which inhabited this place, this cathedral. And the entity was not evil, nor was it benign. It was, however, powerful and jealous of this abode. I was out of place at this hour, I should have departed with the crowd. I had no actual sense of danger, I was tolerated. Quietly, treading softly, I found my summit, made obeisance and turned. My journey was over.

Into a dawn-lit mist I turned. Grey wind-flung shadows brushed by and were swallowed in the vast black fastness of the Garbhe Choire. As the shadows ebbed and flowed, so did the light, throbbing to the rhythm of wind and cloud. Gentle, white slopes to my right tempted me down, too soon. In their seeming innocence they swept over the crag rimmed corrie edge, they would lead me to a world for which I was not yet ready. Dimly down now, sure, but not quite, until the slope eased and the col with its castellated lip of granite tors was revealed. Suddenly, on the periphery of my vision, a huge menacing figure lunged towards me. Stark still, hairs prickling in a response more ancient than *Homo sapiens*, I transfixed the gloom around the tors. A pulse of light, parting shadows, and there it was again. No longer caught unawares, I perceived the 'figure' for what it was – a huge regular column of granite some 10 ft (3 m) high. This 'man' guards the top of the col and I had met him before. Nonetheless, as I gazed towards him, I could not entirely overcome my first, primitive response. Even as I gazed, the light and streaming mist caused the 'man' to advance, then retreat. As he did so, he pulsated, expanding to an awesome strength, then contracting to a gaunt spectre. And he seemed to radiate menace, not as directly evil, but as one possessed of an ancient power both alien to and out of joint with these times. I am not superstitious and I knew I had been two nights awake. I held my position and regarded the granite column for long moments. 'I know ye for what you are', I said. 'You are inanimate rock, mist-shrouded, and I am sleep deceived.' The figure did not cease pulsing, nor did it abate its menace. I thought I had better go.

In the brown heather valley I found Inken again. Together, with grouse breaking cover, we wound across the huge gathering basin of Quoich Water seeing the grey clouds separate and early blues wash across the Highland sky. It was beautiful, but it was sad. Desolate, lonely, a precious environment, wild, yet vulnerable. We were walking to a close, an ending too soon. The mountains went ever on, why could not we?

Yet even my restless spirit found a large measure of peace in our journey. I knew beyond doubt it was a journey I would travel to the end of my days, and perhaps total satisfaction would have been a signal of that end. There was no doubt that Inken had achieved all that her brave spirit could encompass. Our long walk into Royal Deeside became ever slower. The nearest to complaint she came was to ask at intervals 'Is it much further?' Each time I glanced back, I got a little smile. A spirit fulfilled may bear much pain. And when we at last reached Neil, it was our contented and happy spirits which enabled us to gaze calmly across the Dee to where brown, tree-clad foothills began to swell upwards to mighty Lochnagar. Another journey? Another time? Perhaps, but sometimes I feel as if it is a journey I will never make again.

chapter ten

THE PENNINE WAY REVISITED

I had scheduled my Pennine Way attempt for the middle of June. Recovery from the epic Scottish Fourthousanders had been very good. Much of the route had been walking, albeit tough walking, but as such it was far less draining of the body's reserves than a run of similar length would have been. I had now achieved success on two very different types of terrain; flat and fast on the West Highland Way, rugged and steep across the Fourthousanders. The 95 miles (150 km) of the West Highland Way had occupied but 17½ hours, while 100 miles (160 km) on the latter had demanded two days and nights. I deemed my performance on the 'Fours' to be the more significant. I had finished hungry for more hills and had been more alert on the second of our two sleepless nights. This was important. I intended to go through three nights on the Pennine Way with no time for sleep scheduled.

When I had first decided to tackle the 'Three-day Pennine Way' years before, the problem of how to remain awake had bothered me considerably. Quite casually, with no thought of the implications, I had wondered if there was anything I might take to combat sleepiness. Ted Dance had remarked that someone had given him some amphetamine tablets, perhaps left over from the War, which he had carried but not used on his Tan–Cat in 1954. As I pondered the possibility of getting some myself and what their effects might be, I gradually awoke to the deeper implications. It did not take me long to abandon the idea. I did so on three grounds: first, there appeared to be a risk of injuring one's health; second, I believed no one in the past had used them; third, they clearly represented the intrusion of artificial forces as a means of replacing what should rightly be supplied only be physical preparedness and will-power, elements to which all have access. At the same time, I experienced the urge not to consciously *cheat*, but to simply enhance my performance. While acknowledging the essential innocence of this desire in theory, in practice there is no doubt that the taking of such drugs *is* a form of cheating, either oneself or others, probably both. Thankfully, but perhaps not surprisingly, my subsequent experiences showed that the desire to achieve my dreams was sufficient inspiration. So it should be for all. Gold medals are dross beside a spirit clear and true.

I was frequently asked if I thought I could improve on my sub-three-day record set in 1984. My reply was that I would not be attempting the run unless I thought I had a chance of doing so, but even if not, I hoped to get under three days by some margin. I could not claim I was confident of total success, but I

Training for the Pennin

:low Head with Jasper.

Training for the Pennine Way – below South Head, Kinder.

knew if I could survive three nights without sleep, I had a very good chance. Whereas on my early attempts the placing of the sleep point had been critical to my state of mind, I was now able to look forward to the prospect of three sleepless nights with more interest than fear. Physically, I doubted that I was capable of being fitter than in the early 1980s. 'Old Arthur', too, could hardly bide his time to penetrate my overworked joints. No, anno Domini was proving a patient and implacable enemy. Psychologically, however, I would yield not an inch. It was not that I found pain, fatigue or discomfort easier to bear, they were enemies as deadly and as hated as ever; but somehow I had distanced my essential spirit from them. My body might be wearing out, but in my spirit I sensed change and refinement. Above all, I sensed a move towards a calmness and gentleness which is the mark of true strength; a stirring only, but one I hope will continue to guide me.

My attempt in June was a disaster; embarrassing, but no fault of mine. My meal before setting off was fish and chips, frequently my 'last hearty meal'. Sharing an extra bag of chips with Inken I noted they tasted peculiar, rather bitter in fact. I thought no more of it, but suffered quite bad indigestion on the drive over to Kirk Yetholm. I put this down to waiting too long before eating and 'nerves'. I did not actually feel very nervous, only rather tense. Setting off at midnight to traverse the 30 miles (50 km) over the Cheviots, I felt strangely disinterested. Physically, I felt lethargic, but this often masks tension, so I waited for the motors to warm up. I was very confident of my physical condition and was content to bide my time.

The Cheviots were in excellent condition. As we turned on Cheviot Summit to begin the easy 20 miles (32 m) to Byrness I still felt heavy, but expected the power to start flowing. Nothing happened. I gave my body a mental push, still nothing, only effort. I then asked my inner body what it wanted. Quite unequivocally came the reply 'stop, rest, sleep'. I refused to believe it, while at the same time I knew I had heard the truth. My stomach began to churn and a lump of lead seemed to develop there. Forcing myself to keep to the scheduled pace for the next 15 miles (24 km), I eventually asked Inken how she felt. She said she was struggling to stay with me; I thought she had been rather silent!

We compared notes. We had identical symptoms: upset stomachs, tired legs, overall fatigue. For the first time in my life I had eaten a bag of chips that had disagreed with me, but why, oh why, now? I then made a very wrong, but very understandable decision. The 'food poisoning', if that is what it was, was obviously relatively mild. Under ordinary circumstances it might have passed unnoticed. I thought that if I were to run on quietly, my stomach would probably settle and I could recover any time lost later. Damned optimism! What a two-edged sword it can be. Realistically, it was not just optimism. When one sets up an event as major as this, it generates an impetus which is difficult to resist. Had I taken the time to reflect, I might well have walked to Byrness, postponed the attempt for 24 hours and started afresh.

I did not do this, I carried on. As forecast, my stomach settled down after a few more hours had elapsed. Unfortunately, the fatigue continued, my whole body was weary and there was lead in my legs. My will drove me on, waiting for a recovery that only rest could bring. Towards the end of the day, my tenacious grip on the schedule started to loosen, minutes, then hours began to escape. As night drew in, I was seized by the most appalling sleepiness. This time, the five-minute naps did no good. My body demanded rest; after 108 miles (180 km), I bowed to its need.

The attempt was to have been my last one. Having selected the prime weekend in June for it, I had accepted that subsequent work and family commitments permitted no other attempt. I moped around, filled with bitter frustration. Then John Richardson voiced what was obviously in my heart. He said he thought it right that I should try again. Perhaps more importantly, he said that he was willing to support me and he was sure that the rest of the 'team' would also be prepared to turn out. It is hard for me to describe the wonderful effect his words had. An oppressive pall of misery instantly rolled away. I had been given another chance to achieve the final consummation of my ultra career.

There was only one weekend available for the attempt and that was not without its problems. A week after the abortive run I started my three-week outdoor pursuits course, within four days of that finishing I was due to take my children on a walking trip in the Alps. I had always considered that the outdoor pursuits course never allowed me enough 'quiet time' to prepare psychologically for a big event. It had also hitherto seemed essential to plan an easy week after days of sleepless running. It was a measure of both my single-mindedness and my increased mental strength that I was able to accept these problems as soluble.

They were not unimportant, but I felt the degree of their impact on my mental preparation was within my power to control.

Ten days after my weary 108 miles (180 km) I completed a hilly circuit of the Lake District 3,000 ft (915 m) summits from my base at Coniston. The distance was about 60 miles (100 km), and I had the satisfaction of starting with an early breakfast and finishing in time for a late dinner. It was just about hard enough. I had not quite recouped everything, but in another ten days, I felt, I would be ready to go. Again, being at the absolute peak of physical fitness was less important to me than the fire in the belly should be well kindled; it was.

A *déjà vu* midnight in Kirk Yetholm. Once more setting off with Inken to Byrness. Not the easiest time to start such a venture, but, if needed, it would grant me nearly 20 hours of daylight on the last day; 20 hours, in which I could see to fight for that target of three days . . . The *déjà vu* experience ended very quickly. The route was the same, but the ground was quite different. In just three weeks the gross summer rains had first penetrated, then swollen and finally overflowed the peaty surface. It was difficult to conceive that such a deterioration was possible. Then I remembered the days of continuous rain. For the past three weeks heavy and prolonged showers had been judiciously visiting all parts of Britain, paying particular attention to northern England. The results were impressive.

Well, if this is how it was, then this is how it had to be. I had no other option than to accept it. The higher ground would be a morass, perhaps the lower

Tense moments at Kirk Yetholm. 1988 Pennine Way attempt moments before the start.

ground would not impede progress too much? I refused to fight the ground, but tried to go with it, taking what was offered, moving always purposefully but economically. At Byrness I was nearly 45 minutes slower than when I had run the section suffering from food poisoning.

At Byrness waited Chris Bauer and my sons Mark and Gerard. Mark had, of course, covered many miles with me on my successful Pennine Way in 1984. Gerard had been 12 then, at the beginning of his discovery of the joys of running in wild places. I suppose he had, most directly of all my children, grown into his running under the aura of my status as holder of the Pennine Way record. I think this has had the effect of lending a keener edge to his already strong natural inclination to run; to run far, to run fast. It was the most natural thing in the world that he should be with me on this record attempt. After his 45 apparently effortless miles (75 km) on the West Highland Way, he had certainly demonstrated his right to be considered a true support runner, although this had not been a necessary criterion for bringing him along. After my failure in June, he had said little, but he knows enough about the game to understand that even total determination cannot guarantee success. When I told him I was going to try again, he simply said, 'I didn't know whether you would, but I'm glad you are.'

I hoped very much that as I drew nearer home, it would be possible to bring all my family out and that they might cover at least a few miles with me. I had asked them to be prepared, and even though 250 miles (415 km) still separated us, this was another and powerful motive driving me on. For the next few miles, though, I went alone. I wanted some time to be with my thoughts, after that I would enjoy all the company I was likely to have.

It seemed strange to be running these miles again. Despite the boggy ground, which both slowed and tired me, I felt happier. I was in perfect health, and the temperature, too, was kinder, over-warm for me, but less humid than in June. Having accepted that I could not possibly maintain my pace over the softer ground, I did not waste energy in a futile battle. I walked much and injected more speed on better going. It was hard work, but I find the first 100 miles (160 km) difficult anyway.

Running with Chris along the Roman Wall, we discovered a mutual interest in classical music. Our animated conversation spread comfortably over the miles and even took some of the sting out of the steep switchbacks. It transpired, also, that we were both members of a clandestine music society, the 'Boring Bloody Beethoven Society'. We concluded he was the Sacred Cow of the great composers. In nominating the 'World's and Beethoven's most boring composition', Chris put forward the tuneless dirge from the Choral Symphony. However, I trumped this with the 'Grosse Fuge', and after I had treated Chris to a few dozen bars, he visibly wilted and conceded the point. When Inken suddenly appeared with the camera, therefore, we were cackling like imbeciles. It really does one good to meet a sensible person who shares one's prejudices.

As the miles grew harder and pulled me into an ever fiercer battle with fatigue and time, a small corner remained inviolate. The theme and some of Bach's Goldberg Variations echoed through my mind. Fragile notes of timeless

*With Gerard in
Wark Forests
on the 1988
Pennine Way
attempt.*

*1988 Pennine
Way attempt.
Leaving
Ladyhill with
Mark.*

1988 Pennine Way attempt. On the Roman Wall with Gerard.

*1988 Pennine
Way attempt.
Taking liquids.*

perfection and beauty, their totality transcending their individuality. Bach's genius penetrating some aspect of a universal truth. A small fragment of it lodged in my heart, helping me through these miles.

Gerard, Mark and Chris all switched in and out of support using a system I could not fathom! Each gave some aspect of his own uniqueness, each had his own conversation and style, each of them was special and reached my spirit, and they gave it strength. I tried to repay them in the only way I could, by physical striving and by emulating their cheerful spirits. Despite my efforts I had lost time inexorably throughout the day. The sun was settling into a bed of clouds as I ran the river paths along the South Tyne between Alston and Garrigill. After a day of undistinguished weather, there came a sudden blaze of colour as I crossed the footbridge. For once I paused without need and looked up the valley. Trees were silhouetted in rich blacks against deep orange. Beneath me, reflecting no light, the river slid effortlessly, creating no image of movement. For a moment the world was locked in a simple and stunning beauty. Then, almost carelessly, clouds eclipsed the sun's glory and all was flat and grey.

My schedule during the first day had been a particularly demanding one. Its aim had been to bring me to Garrigill with sufficient daylight remaining to traverse the key section of Cross Fell while vision could still aid navigation. On the previous attempt I had no managed this, and Inken and I had made serious

173

Checking the schedule with Inken – 1988 Pennine Way attempt.

errors descending Knock Fell. Now I was again arriving at Garrigill with no chance of covering anything other than the straightforward track before dark.

I left Garrigill in a sombre mood. I might have been slow reaching here, but my legs testified to the effort it had cost to stay even this close to the schedule. A feeling of lethargy was reinforced by a large supper. I had no inclination to run even the flatter stretches of the track and by the time I had, the stony darkness made it inadvisable. Though now this was, in effect, my second night out, I felt reasonably alert and was not tempted to sample the damp delights of Greg's Hut. I was anxious to get Cross Fell behind me before it brewed something wild and nasty.

All that it brewed was swirling mist, but of the impenetrable variety. With no obvious features to serve as handrails, we had to place all our trust in the compass and our ability to set and follow bearings accurately. Sometimes employing bearings 'blind' like this works like a charm. At other times, the gremlins seem to get in on the act and nothing falls into place. It looked like we were going to have the gremlins for company. First of all, we could not precisely locate the summit with the cairn, then the bearing Inken had set across the flat top appeared to be bringing us down not plumb in the centre, but to one side or other of the Tees watershed. This puzzle yielded to intuition aided by a sudden break in the mist. Thus heartened and back on course, Inken took us faultlessly across Little Dun Fell. I then took over for Great Dun Fell, doing what I am best at, that is using memory for the ground, guesstimation and a bearing to make sure I walk in a straight line, or, in this case, two straight lines. The chasm of Dun Fell Hush opened before us like the Grand Canyon, but moving a few yards right, we called its misty bluff and were soon on the ski road.

I did another nifty bit of intuitive navigation on Knock Fell, bringing Inken back from a line, the continuation of which would have led us to High Cup Nick. This, of course, would have saved several miles, but was a touch unethical. I was now feeling quite pleased with myself, this was certainly a vindication of the 'feel for the country' method of navigation. Beware of over-reliance on this method and, particularly, the overweaning swell of conceit that usually precedes it. Both should carry Government Health Warnings.

To be fair to myself, both Inken and I had very precise map-derived bearings which we now followed on the critical descent from Knock Fell. Unfortunately, the path failed to materialise and the instant Inken appeared a little irresolute, I pushed to the fore and allowed my 'feel for the country' to take over. Which is why we arrived half-way up the ski road, having carefully avoided the mistake made on the previous attempt by making precisely the opposite one. In retrospect, and perhaps another time, it would have been amusing. But there is nothing more bitterly frustrating than when, as a victim of your own ineptitude, you nudge your target even further beyond your grasp. The time lost in uncertain pondering, the gnawing anxiety and, now, the four miles (7 km) of road into Dufton might have spelled the end of earlier attempts. I was dismayed, but not demoralised. I had made the mistake and the consequences would have to be borne. Flinging all surplus food and clothing in Inken's direction, I galloped off for Dufton.

I must have been in a strong frame of mind. Even through the frustration I could savour the calm stillness of an early velvet morning. And off the rough, I was moving well. I might be four hours down, but the night was now behind me, I would soon emerge strong into a new day; I had to.

It was relatively easy to remain cheerful when I reached the van in Dufton. Geoff Bell, John Crummett, Rob Ferguson and Andy Llewellyn are themselves veterans of many an epic. They know the scene from both sides and their spirits are not easily dampened. Rob and Andy do a marvellous line in producing 'the goods' from a scene of apparent chaos. Almost before Inken arrived I was ready to go. Almost, but not quite. Inken had shared support since the run began 28 hours ago. She had covered nearly 50 miles (80 km) alongside me. More than that, she had insisted on sharing the exacting night miles. My two nights had taken me over some of the highest and most challenging ground on the entire route. I knew well that she had come to be my guard against those shades which may, under cover of darkness, assail both body and spirit. Using her own sweet spirit as a shield, she had sought to place herself between me and powerful adversaries. My own fell running toughness is not usually doubted. She had ignored it. With the innocence of a child she had stretched out her hand to take mine safely in trust. Now she was about to relinquish her care to other friends, because later this same day she was due to spend several hard hours competing in the Capricorn Orienteering event. How could I find expression in words? Even now I have not the power or skill. I promised to do the best I could and to think of her throughout the remainder of my journey. She probably guessed that anyway. I thought I must stop fumbling for words I could not find and get moving again.

We left Dufton shortly after 4.00 a.m. on a perfect morning. Cool and still it was with twilight pools lingering in hollows and under trees. Overhead, however, the sky was swelling to colour and I wondered if what I suspected would indeed happen as we crested the rim of High Cup Nick. Our timing was perfect. Although the Pennine Way trends north-south, it explores other points of the compass, too. From Dufton over High Cup the trend is easterly. As we gained the level ground alongside the deep scoop of this astonishing feature, the first irridescent sliver of the rising sun flashed like a blade directly before and precisely in line with our eyes. Swiftly the dazzling blade curved to a molten orb. In his 'chariot of fire' rose the sun, streaming glory to blind and command us. Stumbling over the fiery grass, the scale of my puny ambition mocked me, but if it were not for that tiny spark, should I have ever been here to witness its mirrored apotheosis?

Crossing Maize Beck, we soon lurched into more bog, which became black and smelly slime as we negotiated the area known as 'Moss Shop'. I had a wild, incongruous image of a pin-striped representative of Moss Bros. sinking unresistingly into the ooze and tried to plot a course by seeing which of Geoff or John was floundering deepest. It was no good, sooner or later the bog made its claim. The longer one prevaricated, the more miry one's eventual fate seemed to be.

By Langdon Beck I was beginning to feel a little concerned about the weather. Though not yet 8.00 a.m., I was down to just shorts and feeling the sun's low-angled power. Wisest, perhaps, to accept what is good while it lasts. Now running with Rob and Andy, I discovered neither had visited Teesdale before. They could hardly have had a more perfect initiation. At that early hour, there was no one else about and we had the thundering cataract of High Force to ourselves. The river was in powerful, brown spate, creaming like a well pulled beer over the rocky river bed. On that sun-sprung morning, the river and its environs were truly a celebration of Nature's life-giving elemental forces. It was not difficult to relegate fatigue to a subsidiary role in the scheme of things. My journey along the Tees with Rob and Andy was truly one of the highlights of my many journeys along the Pennine Way, and not least because their delight became mine too.

Middleton-in-Teesdale is a significant point along the route going south. Standing at 129 miles (215 km), it is the last support point before the 135-mile (225 km) watershed at High Birk Hat. The longer a route is, the more awesome is the feeling one experiences approaching the half-way point. Two nights out, 35 hours of continuous effort spread now over 135 miles (225 km). The immediate and inevitable emotion is something between fear and despair. My strategy is to try to convert the power embodied in the 'half-way concept' from negative to positive energy; it was about to be given its most severe test. I was already four hours down on a schedule whose demands, given the state of the ground, were beyond my capabilities. At this cruel half-way point, therefore, methodically, almost without conviction, I reviewed my strategy, re-affirming its efficacy and inculcating a sense of going homewards, downwards. Mentally I attacked the remaining miles; identifying, then dismissing them; at the end of this leg, less than 130 miles (215 km); then familiar Tan Hill; just over 120 miles (200 km) remaining; a couple of longer sections would leave less than 100 miles (160 km) to cover; and after that there would be no more psychological problems, I would be truly on home ground.

Almost beyond belief, it worked. There was no physical rejuvenation, but more important than that was the feeling of inner strength and optimism that ensued. I had embarked on this most special of journeys with a sense of mission. My last journey was to be a testament to the wild and painful beauty wrought from an act of striving which had no significance outside the fleeting breath of my own spirit. Against the weakness of a tired body I would keep faith with my last dream. My spirit would carry my fatigue; would it not?

Onwards then. On over the three stretches of moorland separating me from Sleightholme. Each moor was wet and heavy. The ground invited a test of strength which even fresh legs would have ultimately failed. I tried to conserve energy and use it where it would do most good. Occasions for swifter running were very limited, however. Time was slipping inexorably away. The 12 miles (20 km) between Middleton and Sleightholme should have been covered at 4.8 mph (77 kph) giving an elapsed time of two and a half hours. I could not quite manage 4 mph (6.4 kph) and spent 3 hours 6 minutes reaching Sleightholme. This was the pattern, the repetition of which might easily have led to frustration, despair and, eventually, surrender. In this case, it would not. I would keep faith not only with my dream, but also with my spirit and its power to transcend what was merely physically possible. As on no other journey there seemed to be growing within me a small refuge of light and hope. No matter what was happening outside, within this haven there was an untroubled peace, a happiness, a quiet contentment.

The voyage up Sleightholme Moor, 'a penance for sins' is how Wainwright describes it, was a curious combination of physical disgust and spiritual joy. I could establish no rhythm of movement over this troubled ground, but with Rob and Andy I once more shared a feeling of great friendship. And always ahead on the horizon the outline of Tan Hill, centre point of so many memories. Eventually, to my great delight, the stick figures on the skyline suddenly jumbled and re-emerged as the figures of more friends coming to greet me. Among them, as they came closer, I could see John Richardson and Chris Bolshaw, out for the first time, and my son Gerard. I had not seen Gerard since Garrigill, nearly 60 miles (100 km) and 17 hours ago. I reached out to clasp him briefly and reassure him of how well I was feeling. It was perhaps fortunate for my self-control at that point that I was so instantly surrounded and borne up by such laughter and good cheer.

I departed from Tan Hill in the irrepressible company of Chris Bolshaw and was at once engaged in non-stop dialogue. Time now adds its obscuring veil to the mists which then encircled my brain, I can remember no details of our discourse. Of our verbal communication there remains just one tale of Chris's whose significance, real or imagined, has lodged in my heart. I do remember deriving great joy from his company, finding myself once more astonished and amused by his wit and humour. Even fatigue could not withstand the continuing

*Changing
shoes at Tan
Hill – 1988
Pennine Way
attempt.*

impact of the kind of spiritual strength which was increasingly flowing around and through me from my friends and from the environment. I was slowly creeping nearer my scheduled times.

Beyond Keld, however, my optimism that I would at last outrun my schedule was dispelled as the intermittent periods of dampness coalesced into steady rain. Immediately, the limestone areas of path became slippery and awkward; pace was once more reduced. It seemed disloyal to even question Chris's declaration that this was nothing but a passing shower. I had, however, keenly watched the weather since that unbelievably blue morning. I had observed with mixed feelings the sheet of extraordinarily high cloud which had slowly, but surely soaked into the blue. At first welcome shade, but even by Sleightholme we had felt the isolated spots of rain which presaged a change of weather. I drew comfort from Chris's optimism, but I doubted his prediction. As if confirming my pessimism, the 'shower' intensified and we dived for our cagoules.

By Thwaite it was obvious that it behoved us to get into our heavy duty waterproofs for the traverse of Great Shunner. Perhaps the rain was of an intensity which betokened a swift passage to better conditions, but somehow I thought not. Despite its best attempts, however, if failed to either dampen my spirits or quench Chris's flow of anecdote and humour. We ploughed our way steadily up the swirling hill, to those regions where air and water seemed mixed in equal parts. Chris has the lovely notion that such 'damp' conditions produce an atmosphere super-saturated in oxygen. I trustingly inhaled great lungfuls, wondering whether in this case the conditions were more suitable for gills than nostrils.

As we eventually emerged below the heaviest cloud layers which hung like a grey shroud over the head and shoulders of the hill, Chris began to relate the story which has remained with me since. While he was still in his teens and immersed in ultra-distance cycling, he had gone out to help a friend who was attempting to break the Land's End to John o' Groats record riding a tricycle. Waiting on his own bike on one of the great sweeping inclines near Shap Fell, he had spied a tiny figure, quite alone, in the distance. As he watched, the figure grew larger and detail became visible. It was the friend he had come to help. These were not glamorous times and, anyway, this man had no pretensions. He was wearing an old flannel shirt and a pair of voluminous ex-army khaki shorts which flapped and cracked in the breeze as his legs pumped furiously and unremittingly on the pedals. Watching this brave and unlikely figure on his brave and unlikely journey, Chris had become so moved, for once he could find no words. He had no need to, as the figure swept up, he simply grinned at Chris, patted him on the back and said 'Aye up, Chris! You all right then?' It was obvious to me at once, even in my befuddled state, that this friend and this moment had become a symbol for Chris. Later, when my own journey was over and I sat with Chris's arm around me in the van, I wondered if I had shared that symbol, but I have never dared to ask and I do not want to know.

I did, however, draw a quiet inspiration from the story, and as insistent as was the rain, more insistent was I that my journey was good and would continue. After historic Hawes, the next leg would take me over Dodd Fell, firstly to Kidhow Gate, which marked the start of the last 100 miles (160 km), and then to Horton. I had lost only five minutes to the schedule over Shunner. If the rain ceased by nightfall I would still have a chance, albeit a very slim one, of completing within three days.

As I expected, my old and trusty friend John Richardson was to accompany me on the 15-mile (25 km) leg to Hawes. What was unexpected but very pleasing, however, was that John Beatty would join us for part of the journey. I quite frequently run with John, but not since the Coast to Coast had we shared miles on an actual attempt. I often find that John's words and pictures both articulate and enhance my own inspiration. His perception as runner, mountaineer and artist illuminate my attempts to discover the rationale for what I do.

He did not intend to go far, but he certainly had no easy passage. The rain did not relent, and as we breasted the level ground above the valley, a blustery wind threw squalls into our faces. At the junction of tracks at Kidhow Gate the mist obscured the van until it was almost within touching distance. In fact, I had not realised we were to be met here, but apparently it had been decided I should have a hot drink before the 10-mile (16 km) stretch into Horton. I remember leaning against the van on the sheltered side. Mark told me later that Geoff had insisted it was best I should not be allowed inside! He need not have worried, I may have looked a little weary, but I had no intention of losing time. Within three minutes I was away again.

PART II
THE KINGFISHER'S WING

Introduction

The following essays have been written over a span of around 30 years. I trust they reflect my abiding love affair with the hills, so much of my life has been among them. They are part of the warp and weft of what I have become on life's journey, perhaps the best part. Not all or even most of my experience on the hills has been about high endeavour, a modicum of humour has intruded now and then.

Much of what follows was written for my club journal. *'An amazing bunch of eccentric Brits'* was how the late Chris Brasher described club members. You will be able to judge the truth of that remark for yourself. Before you do, I would like to record my respect, admiration and affection for the friends who feature within and the club they cherish.

I have not included detailed descriptions of the routes I have traversed but, where relevant, there is probably enough information should you wish to repeat a route. Do please remember however, that over-indulgence may damage your health and sanity (as will soon become apparent).

chapter eleven

ZEN AND THE ATTAINMENT OF ECCENTRICITY

'All the world is queer save thee and me
And even thou art a little queer' (Robert Owen)

'Eccentric: odd; whimsical' says the *Oxford English Dictionary*. I like whimsical, but it is rather too delicate a notion to be applied to many of the decidedly odd beggars in this club. I may indulge in a little endearing whimsicality myself from time to time, but I am not odd. And if I am not odd, I therefore cannot be eccentric; *qed*. You might be odd but I am not.

Yes, I did recently do a four day bicycle tour of the Lake District on one leg (well, on a bike actually, but you know what I mean). Some of my friends were amused. They might all have been amused but a few are also polite. Anyway, I did not do it to amuse them. I did it because I wanted to do the tour and had only one leg of the pair normally considered important for cycling. I did actually possess two legs but one, like the Python Parrot was pining for the fjords. It spent the tour warmly wrapped against the winter chill and stylishly perched on a specially designed foot-rest viewing the scenery and enjoying the fresh air. The other leg did a lot of grunting and heaving and assumed such a height of moral ascendancy as to become quite dizzy and very boring.

During the course of my brief uni-pedalling career I was careful to hide the non-moving leg behind a pannier. Thus, from astern I appeared normal (a challenge from any angle). When approached from ahead I would simply stop pedalling and free-wheel with what I considered to be a fine air of insouciance (that's a posh form of nonchalance). Sober, sensible stuff you see and only on two occasions did I come to grief. Early on, when needing a little more uphill oomph, I stood on the single pedal which caused the opposite foot-rest to collapse and deposit me in the ditch. On the second occasion I allowed my competitive instinct to overmaster me. There was a flock of sheep showing no respect for my disability who were determined to dash across the road in front of me. Galloping on the flank, the thunder of their hooves increased by the second. They were numerous and aiming for a gap in the other side of the road (my road!) Naturally, I could not resist the challenge. With a slick downshift I upped the revs and surged triumphantly forwards – skidding straight onto a wet and greasy cattle grid lying at an angle across my path. Fortunately, my momentum allowed me to fly over the ironwork and I was able to break my fall on the tarmac beyond. Although the peg leg had fainted with shock, the other one was hardly damaged and, after a bit of hopping round and cussing, I hopped insouciantly back on the bike and rode off before anyone appeared. As I said, not only am I not odd, I wish not to appear odd or eccentric in any way.

If one aims to cycle tour and one has only one serviceable leg, one pedals with that one leg; *qed* again. And despite sly nods and furtive chuckles from 'friends' that is my simple philosophy. No accusation of eccentricity need apply. Where, you may wonder, is this leading?

Recently, two references to eccentricity collided in the otherwise vacant space occupied periodically by my mind. One was from the late Chris Brasher's foreword to *This Mountain Life* – 'An amazing bunch of eccentric Brits' was how he described Club members; the other was the invitation to join the Igloo Meet by its leader, one James H. Seeking to lure the unsuspecting he described it as another 'less than sensible venture to foster the kind of eccentricity to be increasingly valued in this age of compliance with the vicarious norms embraced by a virtual reality society.' I recognised the hyperbole as distinctly mine (it is a fine thing to be quoted) and you would therefore expect me to endorse the overall notion. You might, if you were unaware of my capacity to disagree with any statement irrespective of its provenance. (A capacity developed in the stimulating if provocative presence of that high priest of contradiction, EWD; though even Ted rarely disagreed with himself.)

Now here is the central thesis of my take on eccentricity: 'Some are born eccentric, some acquire eccentricity but no-one can thrust themselves into eccentricity.' Take, for instance, the aforesaid igloo meet (and you can, for I shall not be on it). Lured by Jim's hyperbole by proxy you spend hours driving up to darkest Scotland. You pack a sac that would kill a mule with specialised equipment. You bend to tie a boot lace, straining your back and smacking a fellow iglooer on the bonce with the haft of your snow shovel. He pivots away and rips your new goretex breeks with his protruding ice saw. You both apologise like fools. You set off. At 3,000ft the wind is gusting 40 knots. Your pack is a spinnaker, the shovel blade now a royal top gallant. You would like to put on crampons but they are deep in the sac and the others are disappearing into a white-out. You would like your map and compass but ditto crampons. You stagger onwards and at this point, if your name is Gordon, you fall through a cornice. If you do not, then, after further staggering, you rather wish you had. However: *Courage, mon brave!* this is the kind of non-vicarious eccentricity you joined the club for. You alternate staggering with floundering and the wind gusts 50 knots. You are losing touch with reality. Good! you will soon be enjoying some of those famous hallucinations as recounted by the club's hard men. You catch up with a pair of boots in front of you. But, puzzlingly, instead of seeing heels you are looking at toe-caps. Through frozen lips you mutter, 'Why are you wearing your boots back to front?' 'Because I'm facing you. I say, are you all right, old chap?'[1]

You have at last come to a stop on a completely exposed wind-blasted summit. (Cue strains of Mussorgsky's *Night on a Bare Mountain*.)

Well, this is the bloody Igloo Meet, so get on with it. Several frozen-fingered hours later you have constructed a lop-sided dog kennel. A passing group of walkers stop for a quick sneer and some amusing (not very) remarks. At the last blink of winter daylight, they will be ensconced in a warm pub and cold beer. However, they are not an amazing bunch of eccentric Brits. They are dead normal. At the last blink of winter daylight your dog kennel falls over. How delightfully whimsical! With speed born of fear you shovel your hovel together again. *Esprit de corps* seems to be failing. Morale has disintegrated with the dog kennel. There are several nasty encounters with sharp tools, blunt instruments and pointed remarks. But at last your haven is ready, darkness having drawn a veil over the hysterical

*Zen Master
EWD attains
Nirvana.*

---

[1] True incident from a winter club walk.

monstrosity into which you drag your exhausted body.

It is sadly inevitable that driven by circumstances and long tradition you proceed to restore jollity with copious libations of 'the creature'. You enjoy a transformation; you become cheerful, expansive, then hilarious. The various stages of intoxication follow inexorably; you are ecstatic, pallatic, erratic and finally static as you swap Bacchus for Morpheus and slip into a blissful coma.

You awake in Hades. The devil has his pitchfork in your bum and a demon is squirting icy water into your face. You are lying on your crampons and the igloo is melting. You look on the bright side. Actually, you look through a large hole at the moon flying in the storm wrack overhead. At least the hole is releasing those mephitic odours which have been horribly informing your troubled dreams. Well, bear up; a dream is but a virtual experience and you have opted for the full eccentric Monty.

Talking of virtual experience I can't help remembering that the same Jim H enjoyed his previous igloo meet from the confines of a sick-bed (his own, I hope), while the only team to survive the disappointment igloo'ed on the wrong mountain. I suppose one might say in the first case eccentricity in absentia and in the second eccentricity by dementia.

If you have followed me so far, you will realise that only this latter serendipitously bungled effort can be considered in the slightest degree eccentric. So you can pack that enormous sac and clear off this mountain – and take that bloody Mussorgsky with you. Oh, and don't be tempted to draw attention to yourself by falling through the cornice, except by accident.

If you wish to tread the true path of enlightenment to pure states of Zen eccentricity you must study the thoughts and deeds of the great eccentrics. I have recently researched the very subject. Modesty forbids me astonishing you with the details of my statistical prowess, nonetheless I will try. I tackled the problem through an analysis of co-variance. Taking all the important personal variables: age, height, sex (if and when), length of nose hair, star sign, IQ (where applicable), B&Q, status (Mr, Sir, Lord, Duke, Earl, HRH, club officer), how long a member (don't be silly, please), etc., etc. I subjected them all to a mathematical third degree: nesting, crossing, standard error, human error, logs, branches, algorithms, boogie rhythms, not to mention adding ups, taking aways and g'zinters.

After short-circuiting our local on-line link and wrecking my abacus I enlisted the services of the Enigma machine at Bletchley Park. There was significant hawking, spluttering and spitting before it finally coughed up a great big factor. I have identified it as the 'Mad as a Hatter' Factor. Study your eccentrics; separated by any number of personality disorders, physical defects and mental aberrations they are all united in just two things: they are all as mad as Hatters and all quite unaware of it.

Take for instance the sensible wheeze employed by one Peter B to descend safely from Dinas Cromlech in the dark with a large, heavy bag of climbing gear. You may know this descent, it lies below *Cenotaph Corner*, *Right* and *Left Walls*, *Cemetery Gates*, etc. Even in daylight it is potentially more hazardous than any of these climbs. But Peter, a creative thinker like all eccentrics, had devised a crafty plan to harness that great cosmic force gravity. He carefully packed his several stone of climbing gear into a large kitbag and slung it down the mountainside. Obviously he took the precaution of first tying himself onto the bag.

You remember that Hoffnung story? The one where the builder (on the ground) lowers a barrel of bricks from the top of the scaffolding via a pulley and the barrel is heavier than he is? *'As I was going up, I met the barrel coming down...'* and that is just the start of a rapid sequence of misfortunes for the builder, as it was for Peter. The Cromlech being 500ft above the road and as steep as a scaffold, the remainder of Peter's descent unfolded with considerable velocity. Not a smooth sequence however, as it was punctuated by brief but bruising pauses on ledges, where Peter and the bag engaged in furious hand-to-hand combat. When he finally came to a halt Peter was sufficiently disoriented as to en-cork himself almost inextricably in the Cromlech boulders. He used the time to muse over the minor flaws in his plan and, for all I know, is even now scheming a return match.

It is the nature of this creative or lateral thinking which I deem to be the mainspring of eccentric behaviour. To put it simply, the brain of the eccentric does not work the way normal brains work. (Naturally, and on legal advice, I imply no disrespect.) I hypothesize an eccentricity gene, perhaps mutant or recessive, the absence of which condemns you to mediocrity no matter how many bloody igloos you build.

Let us examine the thought processes of the eccentric (trust me, I am a psychologist). In the interest of verisimilitude and defiance of the libel laws all nouns are proper, as in Charlie. The eccentricity gene may manifest itself at an early age. I well remember years ago having lunch with a large club party near Alport Castles Farm and being somewhat embarrassed as my son Gerard drew from his very large coffee flask a very large woolly sock. There was some (to him) very logical explanation but it escapes me now. And CB, these many years later, will still, metaphorically speaking, resurrect the sock. Who is he to talk, though? Many of you will remember the ubiquitous pantaloons (sawn-off overtrousers, very – ahem! – fetching). The influence of the aberrant gene is, naturally, persistent. Not long after, during a mid-winter bike tour, I came round a bend to see the same son leaping almost naked into Crummock Water (it was his birthday), wrapped around his neck was a long scarf. One understands the skinny dip, but 'why the scarf?' I asked. 'To keep my neck warm.' Well, yes, of course.

The logic of the eccentric, if not impeccable, is usually unanswerable. Decades ago, just after he had failed to dip under three hours for the White Peak Marathon yet again, I suggested to EWD that he might do better if he did not set off like a bat out of hell. With a touch of exasperation he snapped, 'Mike, if I don't get my running in while I'm still fresh I certainly won't be able to do it later.' The same man, it is reported, complaining of sore feet at the end of a hard Alpine day discovered he had that morning put his boots on the wrong feet. Bridling at the unseemly sniggering Ted strongly asserted that (despite the growing agony) it was something simply anyone might do.

The incomparable Taffy was one who definitely might have. Returning with one very sore foot from a walk up Gable, he remembered where he had been keeping his small change, nearly two quids worth of it. Incidentally, I completed fourteen High Peak Marathons (you know, that race over 40 miles of peat bog, at night, in winter) and my shoes were always on the wrong feet, they ought to have been on someone else's. It was during one of these races that I discovered that two of my team mates were wearing three hats. No, that is not one and a half hats per person, three <u>each</u>. Don't ask! I did and got some gibberish about what percentage of body heat evaporates from the head of a bald naked man if he is eccentric enough to trot round the High Peak Marathon at night – it's a lot. But to Don and Dennis the only eccentricity would be in not wearing three hats at the time.

As you will agree, the behavioural manifestations of eccentricity are painfully obvious to the unafflicted. But only recently has the underlying psycho-pathology begun to yield to research. In particular Prof. Ivor Screwloose posits malfunctioning in sub-cortical thalamic nuclei with concomitant mitochondrial irregularity across selective synaptic junctions in basal ganglia. In other words, they're nuts.

Usually just a menace to themselves, conflict, indeed mayhem, can arise when two nutters, sorry, eccentrics, coincide. As happened when Geoff B, manic eccentric, was pursuing his notion of the utterly definitive watersheds walk, the all-England's Watersheds forsooth! We had been treading deep mire for several hours with Stoodley Pike, the day's objective, appearing, disappearing, reappearing as in one of the less hopeful circles of Dante's vision of hell. Suddenly, Ted (*eccentricus logicus*) stopped. Fixing Geoff with a gimlet gaze which managed to combine contempt with admiration he said, 'You know, Geoff, this is a cretinous walk.' What an incendiary remark to deliver to one in only the infantile stages of eccentricity. Talk about dousing a fire with petrol! I deem it responsible for a good deal of Geoff's later behaviour.

Like the time recently when we were enjoying a post-prandial stroll by the river during a biking holiday abroad. Geoff, a yard or two ahead, suddenly lurched to starboard and plunged six feet into the river. Surviving unscathed as the insane or intoxicated usually do (a double advantage in this case) he explained in the measured, reasonable tones of the eccentric fundamentalist how he had simply been practising his night-walking technique. He had just reached his 43rd step when the ground fell away. 'But Geoff,' we said, 'it isn't dark.' 'Not for you, perhaps, but I had my eyes shut.' In normal society such behaviour could leave one badly isolated. However, as a member of that amazing bunch of eccentric Brits he is part of a protected species.

It is not axiomatic that colliding eccentrics cause spontaneous explosion. Mutual reciprocity between kindred spirits explains why it is that some of the club's greatest screwballs have not been slaughtered where they stood. Take for instance the forbearance demonstrated by Dennis and John (both a couple of synaptic junctions short of a full circuit) on a winter Todmorden – Hayfield. On a Bible-black night Taffy led a 'short-cut' towards the lights of the Grouse Inn. Tripping over Turk's heads[2] – and bashing bones into boulders and ruined walls they politely enquired if it was all like this. 'Dunno,' said Taff, 'it's always looked too bad by daylight to try it.' Note once again the unanswerable logic. And allow me to remind you to shun short-cuts in general and, most particularly, never, ever accept a short-cut from the afore-mentioned pantalooned lunatic.

I can remember similar forbearance during a tea break on a long run. Perhaps we were simply mesmerized as we sat at the brogued feet and pin-striped legs of the one and only EWD. (Brogues because he had mis-remembered his trainers and pinstripes because a deceased uncle had left him a couple of very decent pairs and how else could he get the wear out of them?) We were listening with rapt attention to Ted's 'Rules for Debate'. In other words, how to avoid acrimonious squabbles with the Master while trying to penetrate Tedwardian logic. The first rule was borrowed from an earlier eccentric: *'When I use a word,' said Humpty Dumpty in rather a scornful tone, 'it means just what I choose it to mean – neither more nor less.'* The second rule was a whimsical mix of humility and cheek: 'Everyone shall have a limit of two minutes talk time; except me. I shall have twice as long, as I need more time to develop my argument.' No, of course we did not contradict him; well, not until he wasn't there. You see, dear reader, it is essential to recognise when one is in the presence of a true Zen Master.

[2] Maybe not PC – try 'Scotsman's heads' = very large tussocks.

Above all, do not insult by imitation. One either has that elusive gene or one does not.

One who definitely did have it was 'Mac'. According to record, when he was not 'scratching around underground' or trundling boulders with a Sisyphussian energy, he might be found jumping heartily into 'bogs, swamps and quagmires.' An early effort involved the Crumlyn bog ('said to have engulfed the ancient city of Swansea'). Mac attacked the bog (three miles by half mile wide) one February, wearing town clothes (those pin-stripes again!) and alone. As he proceeded the percentage of water encountered rose proportionately. Soon the only dry land was the tops of the Scotsman's heads onto which he hopped in a haphazard manner. With signs of a submerged canal somewhere across his route making drowning more likely than a crossing, Mac retreated. It is difficult and dangerous to thwart an eccentric. Provoked by the failure of the Crumlyn bog to swallow him, he chose Derbyshire quagmires for his next quest. Probably to egg him on, a friend bet him a quart of bitter that there were sphagnum bogs of unplumbed depths that could swallow a man whole. One has to give Mac credit. Not for him the tentative step into an oozy puddle. He was in full possession of the Mad as a Hatter gene (possibly even two). Having selected the largest and most ominous swamp Mac solemnly shook the hand of his friend then, with a firm peat hag providing a runway, achieved maximum velocity and elevation before plunging bogwards. His body has never been recovered! No, I lie; in fact he made a similarly unsuccessful attempt on another succulent candidate before liquidating his bet. He did, however, moot some interesting hypotheses and left many bogs unplumbed so should you feel that gene beginning to twitch (I think that is what they do), start measuring your run up.

Yes, funny Johnny is the gene. Ivor Screwloose (*ibid.*) likens them to a finger in the pie of the brain (as it were). He made a most telling observation: 'Despite genetic up-cocks in the cross-wiring of the cranial circuitry some faculties remain unaffected and the victim may appear almost normal.' What immediately springs to mind is the example of our recently joined member (by which I do not imply he recently broke apart; a trifle unhinged perhaps), Brian Slybacon.[3]

This man possesses outstanding technical attributes. You should see him standing in the mist on Bleaklow Head barking out coordinates from his GPS gizmo while others merely follow their compasses. His brain is a veritable computer; no up-cocks in his circuitry, just perfect techno-mathematical precision; well, almost. He recently came with us on a bike tour. I suggested it might be a good idea to fit a pannier to carry his gear. 'Pooh,

---

[3] This conundrum will require a clever porker to solve it.

pooh!' he poohed in scoffing tones. 'Far too outdated and cumbersome. I have the techno-answer: torpedo-tubes – elegant and aerodynamic.'

Unfortunately, this turned out to be techno-babble. The 'torpedo-tubes' were three small stuff-bags containing the kind of minimalist gear that denotes one paranoid about being left behind. But in his technological equivalent of a *coup de theatre* Brian really did impress us. The whole assemblage was secured to his rack with a length of Hairy Ned. Kindness prevented unseemly hilarity, but after we had wiped our eyes and blown our noses we proceeded to rattle down the Lake District braes. Imagine our collective gratification when at the first encounter with serious potholes the whole caboodle flew into the air before re-assembling on the floor. We paused in interested silence and elevated *schadenfreude*. How would the silicon chipped brain of the super-computer solve this one? Lights flashed, bells rang, circuits buzzed. 'Eureka!' came the cry, 'More Hairy Ned.' (Strangely enough, it worked.)

The same silver tongued teccentric somehow smooth talked a top designer from the world of Formula 1 to knock up a device known as a 'Kite Buggy' (a sledge pulled by a kite). This super toy designed to glide *legato con moto* from the South Pole across Antarctica never had its engineering tested as, once at the South Pole, 'someone' forgot to design the wind to go with it. Perhaps just as well or teccentric might have gizmo-babbled his way onto one of the Formula 1 teams. I can just imagine him leaning across Michael Schuhmacher in his cockpit whispering: 'Not too sure about the diagonal steam trap, could get a bit flaky around 180mph, but here, this ball of binder twine and wodge of chewing gum should fix it; *vorsprung durch teknik*!'

I think you have all got the idea by now. I've probably blighted the Igloo Meet forever but I always thought it was a daft idea anyway. Of course, if you really do happen to think what a sensible, fun experience an igloo on a bare mountain might be, by all means go ahead – don't forget the Mussorgsky though.

'A knight errant who turns mad for a reason deserves neither merit nor thanks. The thing is to do it without cause.' (Cervantes)

chapter twelve

A VISIT TO THE SHELTER STONE

The pure malt whisky traced a line of warmth down my gullet and spread an affectionate glow round my insides. I snuggled deeper inside the thick sleeping bag and settled comfortably on my 'Thermarest'. Outside, the world creaked in the iron grip of deep-frozen night. A darting wind rattled a handful of spindrift against my Goretex shell. Hard stars burned gem-bright in the winter sky. A pale light showed the hole through which we had entered this ancient sanctuary; sanctuary or tomb?

We lay under the Shelter Stone of Loch Avon, seeking sleep within a mountain legend. Perhaps 10,000 years ago this huge boulder calving from its eponymous crag had marked a final relaxing of the grasp of the last ice-age. Resting massive weight on lesser acolytes it created a natural cave or 'howf'. Descriptions of this wild bivouac set deep in an area of savage beauty had drawn Len and I to our first Cairngorm visit over 30 years ago. Intervening decades have confirmed my love of these elemental mountains and this special place. But the echos of that first, deadly encounter drift across all subsequent images. Before sleep could take me they resonated once again, harsh memories between thought and dream.

'A Cairngorm blizzard can be the last word in natural savagery.' There are those who will understand the irresistible lure implicit in W. H. Murray's statement. Blizzards killed people I well knew. I didn't want any-thing to do with that, but the cataclysmic power of Nature compels all mountaineers. I was ignorant of what a mountain blizzard was like. Perhaps I might view one from a safe distance, or follow the tail end of one, or have a little one, just to get the feel of things?

The Trek in

The air was moist and heavy as Len and I shouldered weighty packs below Cairngorm. Wet flakes of snow wandered aimlessly out of a leaden sky. Tongues of mist licked around us and soon we vanished into a world of cotton wool. The Cairngorms are rarely without wind. As we began a belated compass search for the summit, blasts of air assailed us from several directions. I was secretly pleased that these famous mountains were not quite as tame as they had first appeared.

From the summit we took a bearing down to Coire Raibeirt. The snow became deeper as we approached the trough of Loch Avon. Without becoming brighter the mist shredded and, directly across from us, was revealed the implacable face of Stacan Dubha. It was a dull, ominous black. Snow piled thick on every ledge and rough facet. It looked incredibly ancient, impersonally hostile and it spoke of northern wastes. It struck a chill into my heart and drove the last remnants of desire for a blizzard from my mind. This committing descent into a deep, remote desolation was enough. And perhaps more than enough. Even so, we still failed to realise the soft treachery of the day. The lure of this place was one of romance and wild beauty, it drew us on.

Wading thigh deep we cascaded down the steepening slopes. Soon we stood in the deep glacial trench and stepped out of time into the past. The loch was frozen and invisible under a layer of snow. Carn Etchachan towered above us and now we could see the massive cliffs of the Shelter Stone Crag. We were surrounded by vaulting white walls which swept into the obscuring mist. Shadowy outlines of rock protruded in gaunt menace and defied our guess. Perhaps it was 10,000 years ago that the loch had been a snarling, rasping glacier. And perhaps it was that long since the howl of the wolf had echoed across these desolate slopes. In stepping into this place we were, in essence, locked into a landscape outside time. And though we did not know it, we perhaps sensed it was a landscape that would seek to trap us inside its warp.

Our progress across the valley bottom was toilsome. Even the loch surface had a soft, cloying depth of snow. The snow enveloped everything. The cliffs were silent. The sound of our breathing and occasional conversation was local and muted. Still the fascination of this magical white kingdom compelled us.

The Shelter Stone was our objective. It was a little higher than the map suggested but unmistakable even at a distance. Its pink, snow capped bulk beckoned us and, discarding packs, we clambered towards it. We were rather disappointed. Maybe our expectations were unrealistic. No chink or cranny is proof against the insistence of spindrift. The Shelter Stone has an open entrance and we found snow had packed out most of the space. The surface was icy and the place smelt unpleasantly of previous occupation. We decided to use the tent we had brought but pitch close enough to the stone to enjoy its ambience.

While Len brewed up I employed my energies hacking a suitable platform. Soon we were comfortably ensconced, sipping tea and contemplating that wonderful sensation of being remote and alone with a new world to explore. It was March and the day still had light to spare. Len had spent many illicit hours at work manufacturing a pair of skis. We both yearned to ski but the genuine article was well beyond the reach of our pockets. The skis, like us, were yet untested, however we would soon change that.

The skis were long, also very wide, had no edges and only rudimentary bindings. They certainly took us downhill quickly enough but displayed a mulish resistance to any course other than the fall line of the slope. The bindings ensured the skis stayed attached in the event of a fall but were inclined to clatter one about the head and ears. I dispensed with them and took to ejecting prior to destruction. I then decided two skis were an unnecessary complication and experimented with surfing downhill, feet fore and aft, on one ski. This gave maximum freedom with minimum (i.e. nil) control. I retired, somewhat bruised, to join Len, previously bruised, in the tent. We had a technical discussion on the theory, principles and mechanics of skiing. I concluded that there was more to the business than met the eye and my opinion was that Len's skis would make good toboggans.

A Change of Weather

As I settled down to sleep I could hear the wind snuffling around among the boulders. It sounded like a large animal searching for something. An unknown time later I awoke to the slam and crack of a violent gust. We had anchored our tent with our rope tied to axes driven deep. Each time I awoke to another and more violent gust I thanked our foresight. These probing blasts seemed designed to tear us from our perch. At some stage I was conscious that the erratic gusts had coalesced into an all enveloping roar. Like a thundering sea the wind was pouring along the defile of Loch Avon. It surged across the surrounding rocks. In compressed fury it pounded into the headwall behind us and, undiminished in its awesome power, leapt with wild energy across the plateau 1,500ft above us. The trap was sprung, we were in a Cairngorm blizzard.

In the morning the snow was pressing down the top of the tent and constricting the sides. In full foul weather gear I went out and cleared it. Using Len's skis I cut blocks and built a protective wall four feet high to windward. I returned to eat a large and leisurely breakfast. There was no question of action that day. We ate, snoozed and watched the spindrift penetrating the zip and mesh ventilator patches. About 3:00pm I determined to venture out. This is what I'd made the stuff of my dreams, now to taste the reality. Walking with backs to the wind we could tolerate. But it was as if a giant hand was pressing us deep into the snow. The wind seemed to be drawing off all the air and we snatched at our breathing. After less than half a mile we turned to reverse our steps. We encountered another dimension. It was as if the storm had miscalculated our intentions and felt cheated. It fought against our return and lashed us with an ice-toothed whip. We held gloved hands against our faces, peering through occasional slits. Less than half a mile and nearly half a mile too far. I could scarcely believe it but I could now grasp the truth of Murray's words.

Next morning the snow was only inches from the top of the tent. It was as if it was trying to engulf and obliterate us. There was that feeling of dead space as in a snow hole. Outside the wind unabated, tireless as the ocean never ceased pounding. Another long, but rather more tense breakfast. We debated our situation. Briefly, we could stay or we could attempt to escape. In favour of staying was our experience of yesterday and the fact that we had rations for a further three days. Against, the knowledge that we were in a trap that was hourly closing around us. If we guessed wrong and the blizzard out-lasted our food I didn't doubt that hunger, cold and the enormous depth of snow would combine to snuff us out like so many before us. Better, I argued, to make our fight now, on our terms, while we were strong. Len agreed, waiting is the hardest part of any battle. But, 'which way to safety?' We seemed to have but two choices: back over the top of Cairngorm, the way we had come, or, keep low and follow Loch Avon until we could make a short ascent north to the head of Strath Nethy.

Neither option gave any confidence for its ultimate success. I just did not see how we could re-ascend by Coire Raibeirt given the depth of snow on the way in. The risk of avalanche must also be high. However, following

The Shelter Stone beneath its parent crag.

193

Loch Avon would mean meeting the wind head on and floundering in waist deep snow for many miles.

The abiding necessity to make independent decisions which impel us towards a direct confrontation with hazard is the cutting edge of that over-used word 'adventure'. It marks the division between games and 'risk activities'. Its elimination, either through loss of independence or removal of hazard, emasculates adventure. This, undoubtedly, is why such artefacts as way marks, pre-placed bolts, etc. raise violent opposition. Mountain-eering with hazard removed is a flaccid parody of that exquisite dance of the spirit around the quintessential fire of life. Sometimes the dancer is enthralled and the fire burns with a purer energy. It is only those who shuf-fle slowly in the dark and never suffer the light who, because they will not hazard the dance, truly impair life.

In the moments of decision-making in that storm-bound tent by the Shelter Stone I had yet to recognise, let alone resolve, the paradox between love of life and the chancing of it. I was conscious only of the need to make the right decision. Perhaps our immortal spirits responded to this duel with hazard, but just then my heart yearned, as Murray's had done, for '... a hot bath, an old arm-chair before a fire, ...urns of steaming tea.' Yet, un-deniably, there was a thrill in roving the map which must hold the key to the rhythm of our dance. We elected to perform a high and unlikely tango.

If we could follow the surge of wind over the plateau behind us we could descend to the pass of the Làirig Ghru and reach the Sinclair Hut. I might not make the same decision now. The head of Loch Avon and the slopes above the Làirig Ghru are steep, they are prone to both ice and avalanche. The plateau hovers close to 4,000ft and holds extensive snow bowls.[1] These perils seemed better defined than the greater uncertainties of other alternatives.

And now the master plan! Len's skis were to emulate the Eskimo pulk. I had an 'Orienteer' pack frame which could be lashed to the skis with Len's sack on top of that. Striking camp and constructing the sledge was a har-rowing experience. The rope was like wire, the cold was intense and the wind flayed us with bitter intent. We were close to our limits when the final knot was tied and we could find release in movement.

The old one inch OS Cairngorm Tourist Map is mercifully simple. The modern 1:25000 'High Tops' version would have been intimidatingly com-plex. We headed for the weak link, the line indicated by the Garbh Uisge Beag. After good early progress the slope steepened and we began to floun-der hopelessly. Eventually we arrived at an effective ploy. Len would climb

---

[1] The following year a party of six children and their leader were caught here in a blizzard and sadly perished.

some 30-40 feet tied to the sledge and take a stance. I could not see him, but when the rope went tight I pushed from below while he pulled from above. After 1,000ft of this grim effort the gradient eased. We were approaching the plateau. The map showed a spot height of 3,881ft, part of a subsidiary plateau lying above Lochan Buidhe and below the final slopes of Ben Macdui. This piece of high ground throws out a blunt spur westward. Our hope was to traverse the spur to the break of slope and descend 1,200ft towards the Pools of Dee in the Làirig Ghru. Following the latter northwards past the Pools would take us in less than three miles to the Sinclair Hut and safety. We were blissfully unaware that any overshoot northwards on our descent would send us over crags.

On the plateau we were now fully exposed. The wind had stripped and sculpted the snow to horizontal ribs and flutings. We could only stumble across the ground which was hidden by a total white-out. There was a strange and terrible beauty in our situation of which we were dimly aware. In this facet of Nature there was no compromise, no possibility of mitigation, there was nothing hidden or false, no allowance for human weakness. We were of no concern to the forces about us. By chance we might witness essential natural power and by chance we might survive the privilege. But there was no doubting we were overmatched.

We were never confident of our position – we acted on the premise that we were where we thought we were. Len pointed his compass forward as if it were a talisman, getting frostbite in the process. Occasionally the 'sledge' overturned. Each time I stopped to right it I could feel the wind scything through my clothing as if I were naked. The ground began to slope downwards and we allowed the sledge to run in front, pulling us by the waist. Then, curiously, it refused to run, infuriatingly, it tipped constantly. We decided to resume sack carrying. After five minutes of trying to unravel the rope I could feel my body heat being sucked away. I truly understood the peril of being warm-blooded in this element. There came a rising shriek of panic as the animal instinct recoiled at the inquisitive probe of a deathly chill. I thought briefly of the sweetness and warmth of life, focussed a desperate intent on the knots and, hoiking the sack, sprang up in an appalling burst of frantic energy.

We should have put on crampons. There was no time, we must descend. The slope steepened sharply. Had not the sledge tipped it would have yanked us helplessly down to the valley floor. An ice-axe in one hand, ski-stick in the other, we could just snick a boot edge into the wind-polished snow. A burst of air would explode on the bulky sack with its ski hoisted like a wind vane. We would cling to our axes and wait till it passed. We had become disoriented and moved in free space and time. Could we see the slopes across the valley, or was it the palpable mist? Had we descended 100 or 1,000 feet? Then, unmistakeably, we glimpsed the valley bottom. It was sickeningly distant. We moved down another 50 feet and found ourselves, senses reeling, standing in the Làirig Ghru.

It was only when I found myself staring at a frozen, raised footprint that disbelief passed. Senses once again engaged their perceptual counterparts and normal focus returned. For me, the footprint was a symbol of safety. I knew we had escaped. Had I been aware of the number of lives lost in the Làirig Ghru I might have been less sanguine. But the Fates had been kind to us. We had bisected the plateau on a 'best guess' bearing and missed the perils of a rocky edge which we didn't know existed. Even the sledge had behaved like a faithful hound.

We plodded to the head of the pass at 2,700ft. It seemed like a different world here, how relative are our perceptions! With immediate danger past the enormous cost of our flight became apparent. Our strength ebbed to weakness. The deep snow flounder to the Sinclair Hut reduced us to stumbling automatons. Only the anxious nag that we might not locate it kept us alert. But find it we did. It was sheltering two other lost souls who had been traversing the Làirig Ghru when the blizzard struck. The refuge was little more than a dripping concrete box but it was a haven for us. The other two had prior rights and one chose to sleep on the table, the other under it. Len, slightly sybaritic (he would argue arthritic) curled up on his three-quarter length air-bed. I was left with 'the bed' – well, it had been a bed. It was now a frame with a few bent wires and four legs. But if ingenuity could fashion a sledge from skis it could also weave a rope hammock round a frame. I slept in blissful exhaustion.

Next morning the skies were clear, the valley still. Above us the spin drift was pluming in graceful feathers. It would have been beautiful on the plateau, an Arctic dream. Our way lay down and out. There was nothing left but a brutal, dragging slog through snow waist deep in places. It was but a handful of miles down to Rothiemurchus Forest and out to the road. Exhaustion dogged our heels and numbed any joy of relief. Fate still smiled on us however. The van engine was engulfed in spin drift and the battery was flat. But, miraculously, a good push and it purred into life. The weather was obviously set to be fine for a few days. We didn't care, we just wanted three things: a hot bath, an old arm-chair before a fire and urns of steaming tea.

chapter thirteen

THE NORTH WALES HORSESHOE

Years ago, when I was in short pants, my friend and mentor EWD was in his prime and pomp: a practised and competent mountaineer, a sublime ultra-endurance athlete and blithely unimpressed by brute statistics. For Ted, concept and inspiration would subdue difficulty. Casting an eagle's eye over the map of Wales his original mind linked chains of hills in a new and challenging line. An expert interpreter of contour and symbol he quickly realised he had hit on something quite provoking. Running a nonchalant but well practised thumb over the sinuously beguiling outline he proceeded to verify its practicality. His thumb gave him around 70 miles of hilly going: a weekend's worth of pleasure.

He modestly broached the project to a group of his hard-bitten peers. After he outlined the sweep of his route there was a thoughtful silence, a rustling of maps and the careful tread of thumbs and little fingers over cloth-backed paper. Eventually, after a murmured conference a sympathetic but firm voice announced, 'Ted, great idea, but you've reckoned the route on a Bartholemew's half inch to the mile map; your walk is 140 miles long.'

At that time there were few (none!) takers for 140 miles of continuous walking, coupled as it was with 40,000ft of climbing. But, taking the hint, Ted snipped his route in the middle and led a party from Barmouth to Aber on the North Wales coast, finishing in style over the 3000ft summits. This is now a classic in its own right and gives around 70 miles with about 20,000ft of ascent and is usually done in 30-35 hours of continuous walking.

Nearly 25 years later Ted noted that *anno domini* was beginning to outpace him and he suggested that Geoff B and I might like to attempt his original plan. After a couple of false starts, which nevertheless saw us complete both the Barmouth-Aber and the 'other half', Barmouth-Bodfari, we assembled at Aber for the 'big one'. Ted's earlier thoughts had been to finish with the Welsh Three-thousanders, but after vainly trying to tempt my party over the fourteen highest Welsh summits at the end of the Barmouth-Aber I'd concluded that 'if it 'twere to be done, 'twere best done early.' So, it was not to be Ted's cherished long walk into the big hills, but a big walk into the little hills.

FIRST DAY SECTION: *The Fourteen 3000 Footers*

Our attempt began at 8:25am on 28 July 1979. We set off from Aber on a morning which 'gave promise of a glorious day.' Before the summit of Foel Fras we were enveloped in wet mist and it was fortunate that we did not then realise that we would have 50 hours of walking before enjoying a summit view. Apart from the gradually deteriorating weather the walking was uneventful, though as we sat sipping tea outside the cabin at Ogwen with the rain beating about our ears, we seemed to have an awful long way to go. Early enthusiasm is a fickle thing, but the prospect of a good meal at Beudy in the Llanberis Pass was a more substantial spur. Geoff's wife, Mary, plus two daughters were providing support and we ate long and hard before attempting to clear Snowdon before dark. We reached the silent summit at 9:30pm having taken 11½ hours to traverse the 'Threes'. Torches came out on the descent as the night assumed a wet and impenetrable blackness which was to become all too familiar over the next three nights.

FIRST NIGHT SECTION: *The Moelwyns*

Our first night section was to take us over the Moelwyns and bring us to Maentwrog for first light around 4:30am. As we crept out into the thick mist and heavy rain after a brief supper at Jack Henson's in Nantgwynant, we realised simply reaching Maentwrog would be sufficient, irrespective of time. Though we must have stuck to a fairly accurate line we were never sure of our path and we confirmed the Llyns by wading out far enough to ensure it was not merely more wet ground.

The rain eased with the coming of first light on Moelwyn Bach and as we descended towards Maentwrog the air was filled with the sweet, damp scent of mountain thyme. As we walked sleepily along a quiet lane I picked a piece, which slowly disintegrated in my pocket for the rest of the walk, but never quite lost its fragrance. We were a bedraggled and rather dispirited bunch entering Maentwrog some four hours behind schedule. Ted and I fell asleep on a parapet while Geoff availed himself of the local convenience.

SECOND DAY SECTION: *The Rhinogs*

After arranging breakfast for ourselves from Geoff's parked car we set off through dripping vegetation but under clearing skies for the Rhinogs. In some ways the Rhinogs are the crux of this walk. No succeeding section is longer or tougher and it is probably wise to tackle it in daylight. These rough, heather-clad mountains are about the same distance from the fresh enthusiasm of the start as they are from the commitment and euphoria of the finish. At first however, it was delightful to walk in the pleasant sunshine below Clip and enjoy some views.

The reasonable going gave way to rough heather as we headed for Cwm Bychan. Here a very tortuous descent through bracken brought us to the Roman Steps, where various repairs were made to various feet. The weather turned damp and misty as we strained up the final steep slopes of Rhinog Fawr and the equally steep and almost pathless traverse of Rhinog Fach. The anticipated easy downhill section to Barmouth over Y Llethr was more myth than reality, it seemed an age as we slogged along through cold, damp mist. We were all feeling tired and Ted was troubled with sore feet. Just as we should have been onto the final paths into Barmouth, Geoff and I went wrong. Rather naively we followed signs announcing 'Panorama Walk to Barmouth' and came out two miles down the road. Ted had a better line but limped in fifteen minutes behind us with badly blistered feet. He stated his intention of retiring and, though disappointed for him, we recognised the inevitability of his decision. The 25 year old dream will have to wait upon more thorough preparation, or perhaps Eustace Thomas[1] was being more than merely fastidious when he bastinadoed his feet and lovingly wrapped each toe in oiled silk. Notwithstanding the amazing achievements of Thomas, it is my opinion that it is the steady absorption of the right kind of training miles which guarantees success; idiosyncratic concern with diet, breathing, biorhythms, sexual rhythms, etc., has as its chief function the beguiling of weary miles with impassioned debate.

SECOND NIGHT SECTION: *Cader Idris*

Taking advantage of our situation we ate fish and chips till we nearly burst but resisted the candy floss and attacked Mary's home baking instead. Geoff settled down peacefully for a 30 minute kip, but I felt too restless to do more than relax. When we stood up to resume the walk, we were pleased to find that, after a few steps, we were moving comfortably without sore feet or stiffness. Thus the half-way point had been reached without real deterioration and now the 'easy' half awaited us.

We left the bright lights of Barmouth at 10:45pm and made an eerie crossing of the estuary by the unmanned toll bridge. The night was mild but overcast. We were a little slow in mind and body and began to make mistakes. An

---

[1] Previous holder of the Fell Record.

over-reliance on memory low down on the approach to Cader led to us becoming entangled with some unknown country. In recompense however, this detour brought us across a beautiful glow worm – the first I had ever seen. Eventually we reached familiar tracks and passed 'the last homely house' – a remote farm with cosy lights and a beckoning barn. We steeled ourselves to press on into the romance of the misty night and refreshing drizzle.

Before long we were in the diabolical double plough of a forestry scheme. Calling passionately upon the appropriate gods to deliver those who thus desecrate rights of way to an eternity of leaping over putrescent drains on suppurating feet, I bounded athletically forwards over the offending ditches until, suddenly, I collapsed into one, pulse madly pounding and eyes quite glazed. Geoff, like the gentleman he is, said he was agreeable to a break while my body resolved the question of whether to give up the ghost or resume battle. A ten minute nap righted matters and we proceeded more sedately on a strict bearing. We were heading in the direction of Craig-y-Llyn and, though we were about right, I wasn't quite satisfied with our precise position. With the 'ease born of long practice' (MLTB Handbook) I made a few adjustments and soon we were completely lost. A fortuitous break in the mist revealed that we must be either on Craig Cwm Llwyd or a quite different mountain. Acting on the former assumption we retraced our path to Craig-y-Llyn where, overcome with relief at confirming that fortune favours the incompetent, we sank to sleep at the side of the path – 'just a quick five minutes, OK?'

Forty-five minutes later I awoke with a start but couldn't remember who I was with. 'Hey! Err, thingy!' I called, 'Wake up.' This startled Geoff, who awoke with a screech of 'where am I?' in the approved fashion. Regaining our aplomb we pushed on again with a chuckle. It was disconcertingly close to dawn and we were still well below Cader summit. This was the sleepiest part of the whole walk, we stumbled against each other and across the path as sleep snatched our legs away.

Eventually, in full light and with clearing senses, we stood on the rocky summit, it had been long in the winning. Despite careful navigation we became committed to a terrible descent route, steep heather which was quite dangerous in places and dreadfully slow. After much frustration and anxiety we finally reached Bwlch-Llyn-Bach at 8:45am. This short section had taken ten hours, two and a half times longer than on the Barmouth-Bodfari. I could hardly believe it. It was such a dismal thought we decided to entertain it no longer. Anyway, we were hungry and after a mound of bacon butties the sun began to shine and we suddenly found ourselves feeling fresh and fit. With renewed optimism we strode off towards Waun Oer and the Arans.

John R. leading the second successful North Wales Horseshoe on Crib-goch with Glyders behind.

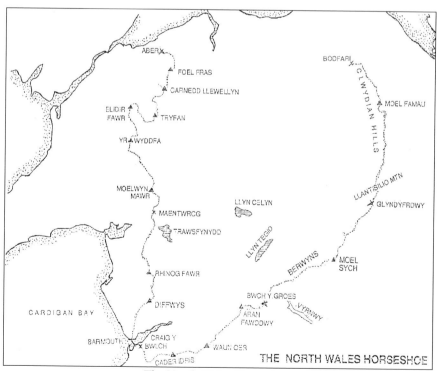

The North Wales Horseshoe.

THIRD DAY SECTION: *The Arans*

It was Waun Oer, one of the 'lesser' summits, that gave us our first summit views. The fine spell held long enough to encourage a ten minute snooze on the long approach to the Arans, but it didn't last and as we neared the summit of Aran Fawddwy the rain began in earnest with driving winds and a sharp drop in temperature. It was one of those situations where you know you should pause to put on more clothing but are reluctant to further expose yourself to do so. Just about fending off the cold we made our way along the ridge of Aran Benllyn resisting the temptation to head for lower ground too soon. We were rewarded with a long easy descent to Talardd, where another enormous meal awaited us. After eating our fill we set off with some trepidation on our third night section.

THIRD NIGHT SECTION: *Talardd to Millter Gerrig*

We left Talardd at 6:30pm under a threatening sky and hurrying to make the most of the daylight. Despite our previous reasonable line on the Barmouth-Bodfari, we opted for a different approach to the deep heathery slopes of Cyrniau Nod. It was a gamble to take the forestry track which initially led us away from our desired direction, but it placed us in an excellent position to attack the rough ground ahead. We hurried on, anxious to make the most of the fading light. I just had time to set the crucial bearing from Bwlch Cam over Cyrniau Nod when the light blinked out. I was well satisfied, the bearing would take us over the flat summit and eventually place us in the valley which we should follow east to the road at Millter Gerrig. At last we were going to have a straightforward night section, maybe reaching Geoff's parked car soon after midnight for a short sleep and the Berwyns before dawn! It is truly said: *whom the gods destroy, they first send mad.*

The night brought a wet mist and we plunged blindly through deep heather. As we crossed the high ground, we seemed to be away from the line we had last used to good effect. The mist, darkness and our sleep-deprived minds combined to create fantastic effects among the groughs which loomed around us like ruined castles. We stuck to our bearing grimly as the inevitable rains came stair-rodding down. In retrospect I think we must have been too high and 'headed' our valley or failed to 'read' the shallow depression we crossed as the start of the valley. Anyway, we were unsuccessful and ploughed on too far north. Eventually, Geoff thought he detected the gleam of car headlights away in the distance before us. As we headed in their direction we came across a stout fence apparently running along the boundary line shown on the map. This line (ENE) was 'spot on' for our original destination of Millter Gerrig, so I persuaded my reluctant partner to cease his wasteful (though safe) northward trend and follow the fence, which would undoubtedly lead us like a handrail to the road. After 30 minutes of brisk walking we discovered we were facing south and going uphill where the map showed no climbing.

The rain was now hammering down and we realised we didn't know where the hell we were. We turned north by east and began immediately to descend. Soon we were on vertical heather and greasy rock, Geoff in some kind of euphoric trance and me worried to death as I remembered there was indeed some dangerous vertical ground in the area and convinced we were on it. With the usually height-stricken Geoff warbling on about the spectre-like appearance of a nearby outcrop and the 'glowing colours' of the ghastly sopping heather we slipped and slithered downwards to my mental intonation of our joint obituary (*JR has a literary bent, wonder if he'd write it? Find it hard to reconcile the necessary piety with his rude sense of humour, I bet... etc.*). A totally unexpected safe arrival on the valley bottom put an end to my morbid musings.

Navigational alternatives being confined to north or south we chose north and were shortly astonished to find an, as yet, undefined structure. Aware of the insidious nature of illusions we glared at the shapes which eventually shrank from the vaulted arches of a huge cathedral to a pleasant farmhouse. Still making creative guesses as to our location we picked up a track and followed it with little conviction. Up and up it climbed, quite endlessly – we were losing our sense of time. We nearly trampled on an illusion that was actually a tent; it appeared, complete with startled occupant, incongruously quite blocking the track. Shortly after this Geoff thought that a manifestation of evil from beyond the pit was approaching us, as an inexplicable pool of suds and bubbles came creeping menacingly down the track. We couldn't furnish a satisfactory solution for this latest phenomenon until Geoff decided it must be 'Mary washing up'! Pacified by this calm, sensible interpretation we gained the road with great relief and walked along it seeking the quarry track where the car was to be parked.

On our third sweep of the road we were approaching exposure and despair. Then Geoff decided to walk to the back of a small lay-by we had already passed three times. It opened like Aladdin's cave revealing Geoff's car. However, I noticed he was staring at it, mystified. He explained later that he thought he was approaching a New Orleans chateau, complete with verandas (and red lights, no doubt), but he was not too disappointed when it turned into his car. After further complications with the key we finally climbed into the haven of the back seats. We seemed to be moving in slow motion, but eventually we stripped off wet clothing and settled down for an hour's sleep with the rain drumming on the roof.

FOURTH DAY SECTION: *Berwyns; Llantisilios; Clwydians*

At 4:50am the alarm chattered its infernal song and literally opening one eyelid at a time we began the mental and physical preparations necessary for the day ahead. The demands of sleep were almost overwhelming and it was only by reminding myself of what now lay behind us that I managed to get moving at all. Surprisingly, feet and legs were functioning well and at 6am Geoff went striding off looking disgustingly fresh. Unfortunately, I needed a five minute kip in a grough before finally banishing the lingering hallucinations of the previous night.

After a dull, wet start the day burgeoned into flashing sunshine and flying clouds. The walking in the Berwyns is generally akin to that in the Peak District but much drier. We seemed to be moving effortlessly and reached our 'breakfast' stop at Glyndyfrdwy ahead of schedule, surprising Mary and the girls into a flurry of activity. Soon the laneside was strewn with pots and pans as we got stuck into mounds of cereal and sausage. We managed to eat, change (shorts at last!), doctor our feet and be away inside the hour.

We were in great spirits and going well, though uphill was proving toilsome. The Llantisilios were fine and bracing, clean cut browns and greens under a fresh blue sky. On reaching the road beyond them we couldn't see the car. We sat down patiently and were thus discovered by Mary as she walked the dog. We hadn't the initiative to suspect she might have parked around the corner – so much for our impression of mental alertness!

After a brief stop we set off on the field section which leads to Offa's Dyke Path over the Clwydians. Crossing the road a young rabbit was knocked over in front of us and maimed. Sick at heart, I picked it up and dispatched it as swiftly as possible. The incident was so alien to the spirit of the day that it put a blight on the conversation for several miles. The other incident of note was far happier. Three months earlier, on the Barmouth-Bodfari, we had perched high above Clwyd Gates while Ted stretched our eyes and imaginations as he identified almost the entire sweep of the North Wales Horseshoe. I remembered now the awe I had felt then. We allowed our gaze to wander over the blue, lumpy horizon wishing Ted was again with us, then we turned and jogged quietly down the road.

At Clwyd Gates the mood of quiet contemplation was dispelled as we savaged a couple of pork pies. Before they were semi-digested we were up the first hill. Now we were astride the ancient and well trodden boundaries of Offa's Dyke, racing to the tops of the hill forts and swashing-a-buckle down the other side. Geoff was suffering with sore feet, but showing true British grit he gritted his toes and crashed on. At our next road crossing we were an hour up on schedule and realised that, with luck and effort, we could avoid another night out. Memories of the previous three lent wings to our feet and we almost flew off feeling like gods (of the minor variety) as we trampled the remaining tops under our feet – euphoria induced by sleeplessness can aid as well as hinder.

The land unfolded below us, lit slantwise by the declining sun and darkened here and there by local showers. Beneath our feet the grass was short and springy, sweet with the evening dew, a blessed balm to our weary feet. At 9:40pm, we stood together in the failing light on our last summit, Moel-y-Parc. We paused to lock the moment into our memory banks against the probable ravages of an arthritic old age, then wandered quietly downhill. As we began to unwind, the illusions once again loomed mockingly out of the shadows, thinking was an effort and muddled, it no longer mattered. We thought a pint would be a fine conclusion, but when Geoff tried to order, an incomprehensible string of words came out. Looking puzzled, he tried again with different sounds but equally mystifying results. The landlord looked startled, then wary, an Englishman disrespecting the Welsh, perhaps. Swiftly Mary interjected with a perfect translation and soon we were sunk in the amber depths of warm reminiscence. Sadly, Ted was not with us, but I couldn't help reflecting that this most satisfying of routes owed its existence to his blithe spirit and a little difficulty with map scales.

FOOTNOTE: To my knowledge, the North Wales Horseshoe has had only one repeat. It was done in fine style (and more clement conditions) by a strong Rucksack team, who inexplicably omitted both Moelwyn Bach and Aran Benllyn. They may have been trying to save me a third night out again – I was doing support.

chapter fourteen

WARPED BY THE WATERSHEDS

PROLOGUE *(For the unitiated)*
The Derwent Watershed is a 40 mile bog-trot devised by the late Eustace Thomas, one of the most celebrated of all 'grough-hounds'. Eustace, an engineer by profession, applied rather precise scientific methods of preparation to his feats of endurance, including 'Nostril Expanders'. The point of these was to allow the nostrils to suck in the exact amount of air required to maintain a given pace – providing you kept your gob shut and providing your nostrils weren't as wide as your gob. The High Peak Marathon is a race organised around Thomas's route. I took part in the first thirteen of these events including the six won by the (Manchester) Rucksack Club. Exact team composition changed, but the nucleus remained the same. None of us will ever forget our nights on the Watersheds – try as we will. With one exception, all the incidents which follow derive from fact. But memory is a funny thing...

In front of me, the dog for once mistimed his jump and landed plop! in the black porridge. 'Takes more than brute strength, you mutt,' I murmured. 'Skill, which is derived from years of experience, is what it takes.'

With the ease born of long practice I sprang with micrometric precision onto my take-off tussock and leapt in a graceful arc across the oozing grough. I hit my landing pad with nonchalant accuracy and, as the dog turned with a wolfish grin, sank to the very vitals. He then very wisely discovered something interesting several groughs away while, cursing, I peered round to make sure no-one had witnessed this dinting of my 'street-cred', as I believe it is known. Of course no-one had because, well on into a grey February afternoon, no-one else was daft enough to be slopping around in the mire of Swain's Head.

Yes, I was deep in Derbyshire Watersheds country. In fact, at the very 'point of no return' as one pundit had described this area seventeen years ago, when some idiots had decided to organise an 'event' round Eustace

Thomas's brainchild. The 'High Peak Marathon' they'd called it, for teams of four, at night, in winter. Point of no return! Can you imagine turning, defeated in your tracks to plod twenty miles back to your start, when in half an hour you could be down in the valley? 'Should be under the control of a senior mountaineer of Alpine Club status,' decreed one worthy, who assured readers of the *Sheffield Argus* he had, 'in his day,' climbed 40 peaks and passes in the Alps. (Did he mean within 24 hours, I wonder?)

'We'll be there to pull them out,' promised a Park Ranger. When poor old non-swimmer Eric M departed from Hern Bend en route for Grains-in-the-Water, completely submerged in the swollen torrents of Hern Clough, he was eventually trawled by members of his own team. Over many competitions I witnessed and partook of a goodly number of complete and partial immersions and sinkings in the mire, but never once did I see the hand of a Ranger extended to pull anyone out of anything.

As I plodded on, the shouts and cries, gaspings and cursings of the many Watersheds races began to invade my mind with soundless clamour. The keening threnody reached a pitch as desolate as the empty moors around me. Looming through the throbbing mist, I thought I could discern the small haven of Bleaklow Stones. Then, to my horror, wings of darkness fanned around me. The wings swept, folded, engulfed. I could not see. Stumbling blindly, I stepped into space from the top of a peat hag and felt myself spinning endlessly down into the black grough...

When I came to my senses, I was not at all surprised to hear a crisp voice saying, 'Right! 23:20 hours. Team 24 – Rucksack Elite. Off you go, lads. Good luck!' Steering an unerring line through Edale car park and pumped full of adrenalin, I lead the team out in the direction of Hollins Cross. Must get a good start, early demoralization of the team behind, blast past the team in front. The lads are gasping a trifle, good! That will cut down on the distracting chatter and badinage. Now, up the hill full bore. THUNK!!

'Ow!' Hello, what was that? Ah, I see. John's very carelessly steamed head first into an erosion control barrier. I do hope he's not gone and incapacitated himself. 'Let's have a look at you. Yes, you're perfectly all right. It's only your nose. Mop up the blood and try to be a bit more careful. Glance up occasionally.' (Hmm, his eyes had a funny sort of glaze when I shone my torch into them.)

What a wonderful beam has my torch, my secret weapon. No more fiddling with wonky switches, poor connections and fading batteries. I have wired a massive lantern battery to a large chromium-plated head torch. The battery is carried snugly in my rucksack with a long cable taped securely to the strap and connected to the torch via a sturdy two-pin household plug. All water vulnerable points are sealed with tape – fool proof! I leap over the first stile after Hollins Cross and, lassoing a post with a loop of cable, rip every connection asunder. Well, perhaps not *quite* fool proof.

Darkly then to Lose Hill, tobogganing down the slimy slopes in a worn out pair of Walsh boots, courtesy of Geoff and demanded by the rules: 'Boots must be worn or carried.' Figures come careering out of the night, arms windmill whirling, backsides smacking into the greasy clay. With the adrenalin still pumping its fierce and fiery course I lead the assault on Win Hill. We become entangled with another team. Gruntfuttock Ferklers or some such. I'll give them a ferkle to make their futtocks grunt! Feed in the uphill power, now a little more. Ha! The swine's still with me. Ring the engine rooms for full steam. I'll make your pips squeak, you audacious Ferkle. He's falling astern, but still he clings to my heels with gasping tenacity. But now the slope steepens and it's onto the toes, springing. How do you like that, you upstart? A strangled cry 'For God's sake slow down Mike, you're killing me!' Puzzlement. 'Is that you, John?' 'Of course it is, you idiot. What did you think?'

Crossing the moor beneath Moscar Edge a message is relayed from the rear of the team. 'Tell Mike that...' 'Tell Mike that...'

'Mike, Geoff says that he's just got to stop for a crap.'

'A what?!!! We've only been going two hours. Ask him why he didn't go before we started.'

'Why didn't he go...?' 'Why didn't he go...?'

'I did!'

'He did.'

'Says he did.' Now Geoff, while a rapid walker, is notoriously slow in other matters. We could have a serious problem here. My directions are precise. *'We will walk slowly on, make sure you catch us by the third mill-stone, or else!'* Amazingly, he is back with us in minutes and I congratulate myself; a little firmness is all one needs.

Swoop into Moscar Lodge control. Having forbidden anyone to sample the tea (it takes time to drink hot tea), we choke down half a pint of freezing, sickly orange. Out at the double, head swivelling to note with satisfaction that Gruntferkle Bogwappers are struggling in disarray a good five minutes back into the inky moor. But more lights are closing and, before us, the ascent to Derwent Edge is pinpricked with blips of light. Onwards then, ye Rucksack stalwarts, ye leather-lunged grough-hounds. Cry, 'Eustace Thomas for Rucksack, England and Barratt's Nostril Expanders!'

'Err, Mike?'

'Now what?'

'Geoff's got a problem.'

'Oh has he? Hard luck.' (Run, run, stagger, gasp, squelch.)

'Err, Mike?'

'What is it this time?'

'Geoff says he's got an urgent problem.'

'We've all got a blankety problem. It's called the blankety Derwent blankety Watersheds problem and we're trying to race round the blankety thing! Ask him what's wrong.' (Run, run, stagger, gasp, squelch.) Then: run, snigger; stagger, chuckle; gasp, giggle; squelch, guffaw.

'Mike, Geoff says he needs another crap.' A tremendous oath ends all merriment.

'He's only just had one and he's not having another without a full explanation and a note from his mother – preferably after the event. Tell him that!'

Run, mutter; stagger, mutter; gasp, fading mutter. Pause; then: squelch, returning mutter. 'He says you made him nervous last time and he had to hurry and he didn't finish and he's going to stop anyway.' Another foul oath.

'Well, tell him to do it properly this time and not to go looking for a quiet place and admiring the view like he usually does.'

'OK, Mike, Geoff's back with us again.'

'How delightful. Perhaps we may continue the race now. And watch the boggy bits, they're really sticky tonight.' No answer. Where the hell are they? Go back 50 yards to three figures peering vaguely into a black quagmire. Dennis W muttering, 'hubble bubble, toil and trouble...'

They give a guilty start as I snap, 'What's going on here?' (A rhetorical question this, as even in my adrenalin pooped, tunnel visioned race mode I can manage the obvious.) Possibly motivated by the ominous tone of my voice, Geoff imitates the action of the Bleaklow Bald Heron and plunges mudwards to emerge triumphant with one dripping shoe. 'We shan't wait, Geoff. Catch us up as soon as possible.'

Five minutes later, still no sign of Geoff. Conscious of the rules forbidding team splitting, I order a halt. As the moments tick by, I am to be observed hopping from foot to foot, stamping the ground and occasionally kicking clods into the air. (Not John and Dennis, I should add. Not yet, anyway.) A noise of a runaway steam engine and Geoff explains that, to forestall mishaps, he had double-knotted his laces at the start, then his shoe came off and then this knot, you see... For once, words fail me.

But now, as the wind begins to scream over the edges, we are joined in battle by an old adversary, Dark Peak Contemptibles. It's cut and thrust, lunge and parry, around the tors, among the boulders, through the swelling bog. Suddenly, J R whose low cunning, lack of sportsmanship and flair for taking unfair advantage are perhaps his most endearing features, murmurs to me that one of the Contemptibles is 'off the back.' While the other three

The mysterious moors.

are intent on staying with us, a quick glance in the rear view mirror reveals a dwindling flicker some way behind. As the three DPC torches disappear on the blind side of an outcrop, John and I whisper to our team mates, 'Keep up the pressure. Three of them have just gone the wrong side of that tor and the other one is off the back and suffering.' A faraway squawk confirms this diagnosis. Geoff, honest fellow that he is, compensates for any lack of subtlety by a surfeit of vocal power. 'Whats that?' he bellows, 'ONE OF THEM OFF The BACK?' The three torches reappear on our line.

'What did you say?' they ask suspiciously. 'Geoff's just complaining about his bad back,' I smoothly interject. 'I haven't got a bad aaagh...!!' 'You will have very shortly!' I hiss through the neck lock.

A good ten minutes later their team leader, possibly literate but certainly not numerate, makes the calculation that two times four should equal eight, not seven. 'Hey, anyone seen Alan?' he asks. With gleeful nonchalance we inform him that we last saw Alan disappearing in the mist in the approximate direction of Sheffield and making funny noises. DPC team leader becomes temporarily inarticulate and changes colour. We tut-tut sympathetically before waving a fond farewell. Well, serve him right. Team leader should be a caring sort of chap, like what I am.

With DPC in confusion and other torches at the point of break of contact, I turn the screws even harder. 'Death (gasp), or glory (gasp),' I gasp. Back Tor bulges out of the mist. If we drop down the other side quickly, we'll be out of sight for a long time and, with a bit of luck, Darkgruntock Ferwarblers will enjoy the scenic diversion to the aptly named 'Lost Lad.' As I move precisely right to tread the secret trod, J R casually remarks, 'I feel a bit peckish, this seems like a good place for a bite.' As he reaches for his laced napkin my steely claw grasps him warmly by the throat and through clenched teeth I chide him gently, 'You may have forgotten, but we're in a blankety race and I've just screwed me blankety wotsits off to get in front of that lot and now you want to stop for a blankety picnic so they can all catch up again. What do you think this is, some kind of blankety game!?!' Acknowledging the elegant logic and intellectual thrust of my argument, he shamefacedly crams the napkins out of sight and slinks after me. 'Here,' I say in kindlier tones, 'you can have this three-year-old piece of Kendal mint cake I've been carrying in my pocket for emergencies. Stuff it in your gob and mind you don't choke on the fluff.'

Deeply draws the night around our little band. Mist shrouds weave wet embraces. Ted seems to have joined us and like a guiding angel flows ahead marrying instinct and science in immaculate navigation. But at Cut Gate control a scene of high drama is enacted. Straining figures brace against the bending poles of a slab-sided tent. Another figure hurls itself onto flaps of cracking canvas as the tent, possessed by the wind demons, seeks flight in the storm wracked night. Hunched over a fitfully roaring primus a furtive figure stirs a mess of potage.

'You can't come in here,' screeches the crone over the stove, 'competitors tent is next door.' We look out to see a flattened handkerchief of wet nylon. John utters a single but coarse expletive and begins to strip off his wet garments. The crone peers up in sudden interest, cackles and drops a frog's leg into her broth. 'Come to order, John!' I bark. 'Only getting into my hand-crocheted liberty bodice,' comes the surly response. (So that's how he passes his winter months.) Meanwhile, Geoff and Ted recline at their ease, sipping the crone's evil brew from hand-carved plastic cups and nibbling raspberry foie-de-gras butties. Detecting early signs of deterioration in morale, with a deft flick of the left foot and a harder swing of the right, I manage to simultaneously scatter the brew and eject the team from this hell's parlour of pleasure.

Outer Edge, Swains Head, on into the very womb of Bleaklow. As I look behind I see no lights beyond those of my trusty team and, as I gaze, in some ghastly fashion their intermingled spirits fuse into one entity. I am left alone with a spectre whose essence radiates with the alter ego of all past and present team mates. Shuddering, I try to move faster, endeavouring not to look behind, but horribly aware of the flickering luminescence licking at my heels.

Swains Head control: a black unlit pyramid from which snores tremble forth. 'Wake up in there, you idle layabouts.' (Authoritatively and stentoriously.) 'Rucksack Elite here. When did Clayton-le-Moors Swivel Hoppers go through?'

'They haven't, only Dark Peak International Crumple Tights ahead of you.'

'Splendid! Now douse those lights and go back to sleep while we drag your tent behind that comfortable peat hag over there. And do try to keep the snores down.'

(Meanwhile, unknown to the rest of the world, Clayton-le-Moors Swivel Hoppers are hopping down one of the Black Cloughs looking for a point on their map where four years ago this control was sited. Two hours of swivel hopping stimulates the onset of dawn and the re-engagement of brains. Their leader, quite rightly, performs hara-kiri.)

The faintest of steely glims begins to infuse the eiderdowns of dank mist and, as I rise briskly from gulping a swift drink, the team corporate have once more particularized. They are individually sprawled in grough bottoms and scrabbling in their nose bags for tasty morsels. I glare at them, but they just stare sullenly back. I sense rebellion in the air and decide to let this one ride, but I shan't forget...

Bleaklow Stones rise like tombs before us. Are those carrion crows sitting atop them and regarding us with rapacious curiosity? 'Avaunt. Thou black servants of death!' I brandish my Silva compass aloft and two grouse fly off cackling. A drear spot this, but it marks the turning for home. Only Bleaklow Ridge, Featherbed, Kinder and Brown Knoll to traverse, yet still a team in front and one pressing from behind.

On grey race dawns Bleaklow Hill is a desolate wilderness. Gliding, stealthily secretive, a ground mist licks black peat hillocks which float to gentle invisibility. My solitary musings are invaded by a sense of contact which has no physical dimension. I turn to behold a figure half enveloped in the dank miasma yet faintly haloed with a glowing radiance. The figure is little over medium height but appears taller. He is carrying an old canvas rucksack, wearing heel laces on his pumps and sporting a fine pair of nostril expanders, which he slips into his pocket as he approaches. His face is gaunt. His eyes have peered through a thousand sleepless nights yet they possess an unquenchable fire. Trembling, I step forward towards him. 'Is that you, Ted?' How tired but indomitable he looks, my old friend, spent in pursuit of glory for the club. I take another step forwards, then stop. Imperceptibly the figure is changing – but to what and whom? A portrait in an old club journal springs to mind. It can't be! Impossible! But it is.

I kneel reverently, head bowed, before the figure. His hand resting gently on my head, he blesses me with these words: 'Take strides precisely 33.78 inches in length at the rate of 95.5 to the minute. At the next stop lie prone at an angle of exactly 13 degrees for 2.35 minutes and have your feet lightly bastinadoed and each toe individually wrapped in oiled silk. Consume six ounces of bread and honey and ten ounces of raw eggs in milk. These measures will adequately renovate the corporeal functions and victory will be yours. But especially,' he paused, 'show no mercy to anyone, least of all your own team. And, by the way, you might like to have these.' So saying, he thrust his very own nostril expanders into my pocket.

'St Eustace,' I breathe, 'guide thou my footsteps.' I raise my head slowly but the figure is gone.

What you doing down there, Mike, lost your contact lens?' JR's rude voice shatters the profound moment of vision. 'Never you mind, twazzock features!' I snap. 'Just get your finger out and follow me.'

The voyage along Bleaklow Ridge is not easy. Somewhere deep inside me, however, I can feel the thrill of inspiration. Leading by peerless example I throw myself into the fray and, quite frequently, the bog. 'Remember, chaps,' I cry, 'when the going gets tough, the tough get going! And also,' I added, sensing the deep impression I was making, 'through suffering shall the spirit be released.' An even greater hush descends and somewhere, out beyond Kinder Edge, I can hear the sonorous swell of a mighty choir. The holy silence is now complete and, a tear in either eye, I turn to embrace my team, my boys, my brethren... there's not a bugger in sight! I stop, gobsmacked. I wait; one minute, two... then, grimly, I begin to retrace my stud marks.

The mist parts and from behind a large peat hag three figures shuffle forwards. 'Well!' I thunder, 'what the black enamelled blue blazes have you lot been up to?' They continue to shuffle their feet, studying the ground very carefully. Then John is elbowed forward. 'Er, um, well, Dennis wanted to stop for the toilet and so we both thought we might as well have one at the same time, er, sorry.' While Dennis hides a snigger, Geoff hides behind Dennis. 'The... the... toilet!!!' I start to roar, but indignation over-masters my vocabulary.

Approaching the Snake Road control, key to the closing sections of the race, I outline my battle plan: 'We know the Crumple Tights are just in front of us and I estimate that Clayton Tussock Trotters are just behind. When we get to the control tent I will punch the card and you may grab a jam buttie as you gallop past the refreshment tent. Keep in close order and try to give the impression we are in tip-top form and going like the clappers. Above all, there must be no collapsing into deck-chairs or attempting cups of scalding tea. Got that?'

'Things in a boat for holding oars,' an unidentifiable voice abbreviated. 'When I get to the control,' said Ted, rather truculently, 'I am going to have a nice sit down, two cups of tea, a jam sandwich and, very possibly, a bun.' I finger the knuckle-duster I've been keeping in my sac. But it is too late, we are already in full view of the control tent. OK then, ploy number two –

the laid-back approach.

'Certainly chaps, time for a leisurely bite and a chat here, don't wish to embarrass the opposition too much, what? Oh, hello Crumple Tights! Splendid morning, what?'

'Crotch rub,' replied a Crumple Tights.

'I beg your pardon,' I bristled, taking a step forwards.

'No, no!' he whimpered, 'I've got it, crotch rub that is. Forgot the Vaseline and these tights went all wet and crumply under my...'

'Yes, yes,' I hurriedly interrupted a more precise anatomical description of his plight. 'What a dreadful shame, how jolly painful, what a pity you can't go on.' (Wimp! I thought. A dab of 'Fiery Jack' in the appropriate place, point you in the right direction and you'd probably break the world land speed record to Edale!) My condolences were interrupted by a cry of 'Looks like Clayton Tussock Trotters coming into view!' from the control tent. In one flowing movement I kick Ted's chair from under him, stamp on his bun and elbow Geoff's scalding tea all over John's feet. Which is why, as the Tussock Trotters limp in, they are dismayed to see Rucksack Elite go flying out, myself at the front hotly pursued by my three high stepping team mates. 'Cor!' says Jim to Alan, 'Didn't know the Rucksack had a battle cry. Sounds fierce, doesn't it?'

At the farthest end of Kinder North Edge a mighty dawn thunders into the unwilling sky. Tongues of orange light leap from out the east, licking swollen grey underbellies of cloud and picking out a diabolical 'danse macabre' across Featherbed Moss. By the Rushup Edge control I hold a five minute advantage over my team mates. Apparently, they have paused in their chase to celebrate the traditional J R early morning honking ritual.

'Fancy a drink?' offers the marshall.

'Thanks, that's very kind. I'm spitting feathers.'

'Do you think your friends would like to stop for a drink too?' asks the sweet youth.

'Of course they would, you cretin!' I snarl. 'So just you keep that flask out of sight!'

I was still chuckling nastily as I reached out to accept the weighty mill-stone trophy at Edale village hall. I was, however, rather surprised when the presenting officer also presented two wet kisses on my cheeks. 'Here, ger-roff!' I cried. Instead, taking advantage of my arms being filled with the large millstone, he pursued me into a corner of the room and began planting more smackers on my blushing cheeks. 'Bugger off, you silly swine!' I screech. But his big brown eyes were moist with affection and his cold black nose nuzzled my earhole... cold black nose?? I opened my eyes to find the dog slobbering delightedly over me.

'Jasper,' I gasped, 'I've had the weirdest experience. I wonder what the devil happened?' I was in no way astonished when he replied 'Well, actually, master, you appear to have tripped and fallen right into a Bleaklow time-warp grough, a somewhat rare but by no means entirely unknown phenomenon, I gather.'

'Get off, you daft bugger, and STOP licking me!' I snapped aiming a ferocious back-hander at his chops, which, being perfectly anticipated, he adroitly avoided.

Later that evening, I sat soaking my feet in front of a large fire. All that lying around in groughs, I was sure I had a cold developing. I mused distractedly over the day's events. Too many damn Watersheds, must be getting soft in the head, and yet, and yet... Suddenly I felt a sneeze coming on. I snatched for my handkerchief and as I did so, something rolled tinnily onto the floor. Stooping stiffly over my bucket of water I retrieved a small wire and brass object, highly polished. It looked familiar. It couldn't possibly be... could it? Very gently I eased the appliance onto my nose and felt the delicately tensioned spring lift and flare the nostril flaps. With a feeling of astonished joy I braced my newly burgeoned nostrils and inhaled a mighty draft of air. The answering resonance was imperative and catastrophic. From subterranean alveolar depths the sneeze recruited its forces; it flew along the bronchials, united at the larynx and exploded out of my nose like a miniature hurricane. Ping! The nostril expanders flew off my nose and embedded themselves in the depth of the fire. Aghast, I watched as they turned cherry red, then white and, before I could say 'fire tongs', melted into oblivion.

Stunned with grief I collapsed into my chair. Now, I fear, I can never tell my story, for no-one will ever believe me!

chapter fifteen

A WINTER'S TALE: TAN HILL TO THE CAT & FIDDLE

INTRODUCTION

As recounted earlier in this book, the Tan-Cat was my first real ultra-run. It had taken three attempts to complete the tough 120 miles. However, it was now behind me and I could look ahead to other challenges. The soggy, boggy interstices of this particular monster would not be figuring me on its menu ever again!

PART 1 – *The Devil Rides Out*

As gaunt November dragged to December's short-lived days I curtailed my training exploits in favour of the homely hearth. Then one evening the phone rang, it was Geoff. His message was short and pointed. In a nutshell, the club was getting soft. It behoved 'someone' to do 'something' about it. Now, let me explain that to most people who know him Geoff is an agreeable, easy-going and sensible fellow. Only a few intimate friends ever realise that within the broad, genial spread of his personality there lurks a rarely glimpsed phantom, a demon charged with the most obsessive, unrealistic and, ultimately, painful notions. Rarely does this devil manifest himself and when he does he is cunning. He speaks with Geoff's voice, he states his ideas with the same modest self-effacement as Geoff, he smiles with the same humorous reassurance as Geoff. But, he is a right nutter! As I heard Geoff's first words my Christmas greeting froze on my lips.

I listened to Geoff's genial tones and knew them for those of the demon. He was actually proposing that we take the club's longest walk, which a bare handful had ever managed in summer (and I had recently twice failed) and do it in mid-winter! But as my brain raced I saw a get-out. I remembered that the route <u>had</u> been completed in winter. It had been done by two giants of walking prowess who furthermore had been blessed with amazingly mild conditions. Despite the latter they had suffered pretty badly and in the memory of one of them at least, the journey stood out as an epic of almost unendurable darkness, mounting fatigue and strenuous route finding. I knew this because that particular giant was my close friend John Richardson. Now it is almost axiomatic that having suffered a real epic you have neither motive nor reason to repeat it, nor does anyone expect it of you. Chuckling inwardly, I therefore brazenly told Geoff I didn't think much of his idea but would certainly accompany him – provided John would go also! Congratulating myself both on knowledge of human nature and quick thinking I put the phone down and my head into a noose.

What I had failed to take account of was John's tendency to guilt. While, as he claims, this may be the reverberation of a strict Catholic upbringing, it has transferred itself to the real or supposed ethics of walking. When completing his winter Tan-Cat with the legendary Lancashire black-pudding-purveyor and ultra-distance athlete Stan Bradshaw, John had transgressed. Not a moral weakness, of course, but an ethical one. In repeating an arduous route it is permissible to make minor changes on unimportant sections. It is permissible, laudatory even, to upgrade the difficulty by including higher, longer or rougher sections. It is absolutely not the done thing to dodge the challenging bits by taking easy options. Poor John had confused these two issues. He had made some changes, not to avoid challenge, but to ease the problem of support on the route and to give a novel and attractive approach to the finish. All perfectly acceptable in principle but, unfortunately, in practice this entailed the exclusion of Bleaklow and Kinder. These two high moors, Bleaklow in particular, may be considered the last great barriers to the route's completion.

John and Stan's alternative lines were hardly 'soft' options. Indeed, John's inner voice might have eventually subsided had not a bony finger been applied unerringly to the sensitive area. That finger belonged to the late Phil Brockbank. 'Brock' had been a notable 'grough hound' and had made the second completion of the Tan-Cat. In him resided an encyclopaedic knowledge of the club's traditions. Always intelligent and amusing, his comments often had the cutting edge of a most rigorous ethic. He praised the epic walk of John and Stan, but his objectivity forced him to add, '... It was a pity that the strain of two long winter nights and the relapse of the weather forced them to by-pass Bleaklow and Kinder, ...such temptations should be resisted.' This remark burned like bile in the pit of John's conscience for over a decade. Then came the chance of expiation through: the admission of guilt, the scourge of penance, the forgiveness of sin and the promise of eternal bliss. Like a good Catholic, John heard the heavenly choir and prepared to join it. In the resounding beat of his *mea culpa* I heard the echo of my fate.

Prophesying doom for foolhardy others and watching them go to it engenders a certain morbid pleasure. The anticipation of one's own doom replaces that dubious emotion with the foreknowledge of suffering, a distinctly dismal state of mind. As I drove north with the other victims of Geoff's manic scheme I knew that the rain washing greedily over the car's wipers would soon be creeping down my neck. The fact that Geoff had contracted a bad cold and subsequently developed a most astonishing cough allowed me a few moments unfounded optimism. I had spent the journey musing on whether the more likely outcome to a well acted cry of, 'Heavens Geoff, you can't possibly go out with a cough like that!' would be, escape from the inevitable misery, or, having to face it alone on Geoff's brave insistence we must enjoy ourselves without him. I need not have bothered. Geoff's demon was quite adamant that we would all enjoy the nice walk, the fresh air was just what he needed.

It was two days after Christmas, a slightly clouded affair this year, but no-one could accuse us of selecting a soft slot in the season. With the advent of electricity I wonder how many people realise that around this time there are sixteen to seventeen hours of darkness in the day? It was a fact we were soon to become completely aware of. As we approached Tan Hill defence, or perhaps denial, mechanisms came into play. 'Rain as heavy as this can't possibly last long, can it?' 'No, of course not!' came the lying chant. John, weather-wise, predicted a front passing through to give us a clear moonlit night, an odd puff of wind to keep us from overheating and a sprinkling of frost to keep us brisk.

The reality was somewhat different. Forcing open the car doors against a wind wiser than ourselves, we huddled momentarily in the lee of the pub. There were four of us. In addition to Geoff and John, Eric had been invited to share our woes. The latter had so enjoyed a summer traverse of the route with John, that he had readily succumbed to John's blandishments. More importantly to us, Eric had produced a friend with a van who had volunteered to support us at selected road crossings throughout the venture. Waterproofs flapping in the wind we raised mock-cheerful hands to our support and stepped onto the moor.

It was fortunate that frost still bound the ground beneath the sheets of water which covered it. Had it been otherwise, we might have sunk without trace. Instead, we only occasionally found a frost-free bog which would however, swallow anything from an ankle to a complete leg. Our first section was twelve miles long and took us over Great Shunner Fell. Although only 2,200ft high this upraised moor is a sprawling, spreading mass with sponge-like qualities. In the failing light and driving rain and mist we seemed to be going nowhere. Having departed Tan Hill torchless at 1:30pm we had left ourselves fine margins by which to reach Hawes before dark. With John setting a steamy pace we just made it.

At Hawes we were a little surprised to discover that Eric's friend had made no arrangements to ease our burden. I grabbed my flask out of his van and stamped off to change in a nearby bus shelter. These were the days of non-breathable waterproofs, and quick-drying thermal underlayers were only just starting to contribute to comfort. Our rapid ascent of Great Shunner had left us saturated beneath our cagoules and osmosis sent moisture soaking inexorably up our legs.

Along the lanes leading to Stalling Busk the blackness of the night was unbelievable. Hoping to conserve torch batteries we walked without light. Within yards we were ricocheting off each other and, more painfully, the walls on either side. As we ascended the wind increased and the unceasing implacable rain came at us sideways. On the moor leading to Mid Pasture we took advantage of that fact, taking shelter behind a wall we consumed inevitable left-over bits of turkey and festive mince pies in a macabre parody of a Christmas feast. The prospect of a more substantial meal spurred us on. By 8:30pm we had crossed Stake Moss and reached the road above the little hamlet of Cray. As we descended the steep hairpins John was intrigued to note that the water flowing down with us was surging over the top of his light fell boots. The conditions were momentarily forgotten as we pushed into an open barn where our support was warming the massive pot of stew I had pre-cooked for the occasion. This time he'd done us proud. We ate and changed in relative comfort and set off for Buckden Pike in quite high spirits.

It was a stiff climb straight up the side of Buckden Pike but this was John's 'back yard' and he led an impeccable line. A flurry of snow flakes greeted us near the top and, ever optimistic, we began to predict colder, clearer weather. It failed to materialise as we slopped along the crest of the Pike and Tor Mere Top. Nor was there anything other than a sodden snowflake hidden in the driving rain as we crouched momentarily in a windbreak on the summit of Great Whernside. It was now midnight, about half-way through our first long night. In celebration I produced a flask of whisky whose warm virtues a little restored sagging morale.

Leaning heavily on John's local knowledge we followed an intricate line towards Grassington. Had he been suddenly swallowed up I'm sure we would have ended our days circling that maze of stone walls sprouting beneath the featureless acres of fellside. I remembered how Brockbank had described getting off line here. After clambering over an infinity of high, wobbly limestone walls he had ground to an exhausted halt beating his fists feebly against a last great rampart. No such problems beset us and by

4:30am we were plodding the deserted streets of Grassington, not a tourist to be seen! As we left the village a roaring of distant thunder began to fill our senses. Suddenly, I realised we were approaching the footbridge across the River Wharfe. I had to overcome an instinctive fear before stepping onto it. Only the faintest creaming of the water could be seen but the increasing roll and thunder of its passage was the more terrifying for that. Swollen to an astonishing power it seemed to be contemplating savagery as it snarled past the unsuspecting, sleeping village.

With the threatening rumble fading behind us we squelched across sodden fields heading for Thorpe. On an earlier reconnaissance John had spotted a barn half full of bales of hay. The master plan was that another friend, Alan, would drive to this barn with dry gear and, after a short sleep, he would cook us a good breakfast. On this wet and evil night the barn was a real haven. We climbed into our remaining set of dry clothes and then the others climbed into sleeping bags. It was now 5:30am and we reckoned on having about an hour's sleep. I had imagined the hay would provide sufficient warmth for a short stop. I was quite mistaken. It was with teeth-chattering relief that I heard Alan call 'time'. While the others enthused about the warmth and splendours of the barn I cursed my stupidity. At least I was keen to get moving again.

Alan did us proud with a scrambled egg and sausage breakfast, but now the rigours of the previous 38 miles began to show. There was incredible faffing and fumbling as fuddled brains attempted to come to terms with the demands of the next 20 hours walking to our Todmorden support point. Rucksacks were packed and unpacked, footwear was scrutinised and, as ever, the question which never ceases to irritate me was asked: 'What are you going to wear/eat/etc?' John, quite rightly, began to get agitated with our slackness. Our intended 7:00am start evaporated and we had foolishly started eating into our precious daylight before we dribbled out, individually, across the fields towards Rylstone Fell. When we foregathered on the last steep climb we discovered Eric was missing. In fact it was spring before I saw him again.

It was at Skipton, some ten miles on, that we finally realised Eric's friend was a broken reed. He had parked the van at the side of the road as arranged. It seemed not, however, to have occurred to him that we might appreciate a warm drink or a moment's respite from the clattering rain inside the vehicle. Having fallen behind our schedule it was imperative that we make up some of that lost time. Ahead of us was some very rough moorland, we must be across that before darkness came again.

It was now 10:30am, John told our support to expect us in Cowling before 1:00pm and to try to gain news of Eric. For some reason the man insisted we would not be there for one o'clock. With great self-control John drew a deep breath and repeated his statement very firmly. Muttering to ourselves we marched off up the road. After half a mile we encountered a section flooded to a considerable depth. We had paddled about halfway across when we observed a large flash car bearing down at speed from the opposite direction. Naturally enough it was preceded by an impressive bow wave which we were soon able to confirm was around head height. If our solemn curses have been effective there exists in the Skipton area a gentleman with a condition which will be of great interest to medical science.

We did reach Cowling before 1pm but our support did not. Neither, when he arrived, had he enquired about Eric. We spent time phoning around and discovered that Eric had followed our footsteps over the fell, had reached Skipton shortly after us but, unaware of our rendezvous point, had wisely returned home. This, plus having once more to organise our own brews etc., delayed our departure for Ickornshaw Moor until 2pm.

Our loss of time with its inevitable consequences, the total inability of our support to realise our needs and the relentless rain began to spread a weight of despondency in our hearts. Geoff's cough was getting worse and even John seemed to have become disheartened by the recent annoying events. For my part I had never much changed my opinion that a winter Tan-Cat was a preposterous notion. I was, however, with two of the staunchest friends and strongest walkers imaginable. In their company I was prepared to dare whatever else might be in store.

It soon became apparent what was in store. As we gained height, the pelting fury never abated but began to include large blobs of sleet in the barrage. By the summit of the moor the sleet turned to snow, wet and heavy. The snow was not sticking, indeed it seemed impossible it could do so as the ground was largely covered with water. We maintained momentum and reached the road before the next moor at 3:30pm. This moor, a private one, lies to the east of Boulsworth Hill and is known as Jackson's Ridge. It is a featureless area of heather, tussocks and ditches. It should be possible to navigate a simple line straight across, but it isn't. There are two reasons for this. Firstly, the moor is drained by three shallow basins which spread a spidery network of ditches across it. Becoming cross-grained in these is an exhausting and frustrating business. Secondly, there is a shifting malevolence in this moor which raises its own unpredictable barriers to simple navigation. Having had recent experience, I had been confident in volunteering to lead this section. But then I had imagined there would still be daylight.

The daylight, never strong, faded before we had finished the climb from the road. Now the snow returned with surprising vehemence. It seemed impossible that snow could settle in this saturated wilderness but settle it did. A strengthening wind flung a wet white curtain dizzying against us and beneath our feet the snow thickened. The combination of wet snow on slimy ground made good foot placement both imperative and impossible. Slithering off or stumbling over the densely packed tussocks we were either fighting for balance or dragging ourselves off the ground. My mind was almost completely occupied with maintaining our line but on the fringe of my consciousness I could hear Geoff's continuous hacking cough. Worse still, I began to realise that John was falling over with increasing frequency and that, each time he fell, he became increasingly reluctant to rise. It is a mark of his condition that, from that day to this, he does not remember me calling a brief halt and giving us all a good slug of the whisky I had been saving 'just in case'.

At last we reached the rough track for which I had been aiming. The five miles from the last road crossing had taken over two and a half hours. Strangely enough, the epic conditions through which we had been battling were beginning to fire my imagination. By now I was in the grip of a divine madness. Geoff's manic idea assumed the status of a noble challenge. We were due to be met at the end of the track. A quick feed and we would be ready for another stern moorland battle over Black Hameldon. Once this was behind us, a few miles would see us into Todmorden. Here, I had arranged support in a school house. We could eat, change, grab an hour's sleep and be away before first light. Then on to glory and a winter traverse that would reverberate for ever in the club's history!

At the track our long silence was broken. Geoff, coming to the end of a peal of coughing, apologetically ventured the opinion that he had better retire from the contest when we reached the van. John, impressed by his flirtation with the ghastly tussocks, considered it wise to join him. I began to calculate the factors involved in continuing solo. We were in a wet blizzard and the moor ahead, though not malevolent, was at least as rough as the one behind. On the other hand, Todmorden was a safe haven and with the 'corporeal function' revitalised were the remaining 50 miles so impossible? The question was still unresolved when we reached the van.

In the lee of the van the depleted pan of stew sat atop the gas stove, long blown out. The vehicle rocked gently in the breeze but a tiny glimmer of light gave evidence of occupation. We opened the door and before either Geoff or John could speak the question was resolved. 'I've had enough. I want to go home,' said a small voice. Poor man, unlike me, I'm sure he didn't know what he was letting himself in for – a winter Tan-Cat indeed! Driving home we were not surprised to learn that there had been record rainfall and floods in North and South Yorkshire.

PART 2 – *Exorcism*

Having taken 30 hours to cover merely half the total distance we could hardly claim a near miss. We were, however, quite determined to try again. Although none of us were inexperienced before this, we had learned a good deal more. I spent a long time planning a meticulous campaign. I think we all had our own ideas but I was so convinced of mine I managed to persuade the others to my way of thinking. Briefly, I felt that if we were to be out for 55-60 hours in true winter conditions we needed more than simple toughness to succeed. We needed strong support points where we could re-gather our strength. The sheer length of the winter night was appalling. If we could spend part of that time in a short sleep with the opportunity to eat well and have a complete gear change, we would benefit physically and mentally.

I don't think Brockbank ever commented on the ethics of sleeping during 'continuous' walks. In the absence of rules I proposed that if the walk felt continuous and occupied a similar time span to that of the summer version it would satisfy me. If others demanded a 'purer' approach they were welcome to achieve it first and formulate the ethic later. So far, no-one has. In any case winter conditions are so enormously variable there seems little point in either rules or comparative performances. There is fun in competition but the greatest fun comes from setting and striving towards standards which are as high, or a wee bit higher, than one might expect to attain.

I thought we might bite a couple of hours sleep out of each of our nights and still achieve a sub 60 hour completion. Much more than this would take us into a third night which was not desirable. I also had very firm ideas when and where I wanted those islands of support. John's own house lay very little off route and, by leaving Tan Hill at first light, we could reach it in the early hours of our first night and leave it towards daybreak. Another 24 hours would see us at Crowden in the Woodhead (Longdendale) valley. Support here had been arranged at the outdoor activities centre and would set us up for a strong attack on Bleaklow, Kinder and the last 30 miles. In addition, Alan would again meet us at Grassington, this time to organise a pub meal. John's wife, Sue, would feed us in Todmorden at 70 miles. A further fifteen miles and a descent into Marsden would set us up for the arduous leg over Black Hill to Crowden.

Given even the slightest chance with the weather I felt we now had the kind of back-up which would ensure success. As it happened, anything less would probably have resulted in failure.

Two days after Christmas we were again driven to Tan Hill by Alan. Eric's place had been taken by Ted D. who had been in the second party to complete the route – 25 years previously. Our start was a little delayed by ice on the steep hairpins near Keld. Comfortably ensconced in the rear seat, we shouted good advice to John who laboured bare-handed with a pile of grit. He shouted advice back but none of us cared to take it. Though Christmas had brought a repeat of last year's rains, yesterday had seen a change. We stepped out into a biting wind with ice forming on the puddles.

The weather continued raw but a whiff of sun kept spirits high and our pace brisk. Alan met us at road crossings and with cautious optimism I noted we were making time on our schedule. We picked up torches before Great Whernside but, chasing the light up the hill, got to the summit in the last glim. Suddenly a whirl of snow enveloped us and the light vanished. The reality of the walk was impressed upon us as, in full foul weather gear, we once more trailed John into Grassington.

At lower levels the snow turned to light drizzle and seemed innocuous enough. We turned our attention to bar meals in the Devonshire. Very tasty, but after 36 miles of hill and dale I could have eaten two. On emerging we found the world had changed. Snow had followed our downward trail. While waiting for us to finish our meal it had redecorated the landscape. A nice job it had made of it too. The wind had died and a uniform blanket of white had smothered the angular barrenness of winter. The world seemed silent and muffled. Our torches spread a brave light and though the night stretched long it was not quite so dark.

The snow made our ascent of Rylstone Fell an arduous slither. I was boiling up inside my cagoule and disturbed to find my legs felt far more fatigued than they should. Up on the moor there could be little argument that we were in true winter conditions. I think we all felt a muted excitement as we moved through the cold beauty of this winter night. The soft flakes brushed against our faces and spiralled through the torch beams. In the flowing pool of light at my feet I could see the deepening footsteps of the man ahead. All around one could sense the sweep and swell of the moor, empty of sound and devoid of life. And still the curtains of snow fell in soft drapes from the invisible sky.

At Watt Crag Obelisk we descended from the moor to make our way to Skipton via field paths and roads. Once we had lost a few hundred feet of height we moved back into an unfrozen, muddy world. The pure white snow covered the ground but concealed beneath was sucking, sliding mud and ooze. After a lengthy period of skidding along the soft ruts of a farm track we were relieved to reach the road. The relief did not last long. After the soft and variable going so far, several miles of hard tarmac made my legs as stiff as planks. I consulted Geoff, alarmed at what I thought might signal the end for me. His opinion was that it took time to 'get into' a big walk. He thought 50 miles was about right and that was what we were at now.

We trudged along the near deserted roads, slopping through the churned slush. At first we kept each other entertained with a stream of conversation; past walks, past epics, a spot of character assassination, etc. As the midnight hour came and went our thoughts were increasingly bent towards the warm comforts awaiting us. Silence spread among the party and almost imperceptibly the pace increased. I became aware that a rapid congealing was stiffening the slush and in an incredibly short time our progress was marked by the crunch of ice and squeak of snow, a cheerful, encouraging sound.

A little before 2am we crowded eagerly into John's kitchen. We were nearly three hours ahead of schedule, a fact which pleased Ted who was keen to convert this into sleeping time. I was less enthusiastic about this plan for a number of reasons. For a start I wanted to keep the feel of doing a continuous walk. Also I didn't want to lose too much momentum, the longer one stops, the more difficult it is to get going. On the other hand, it is desperately difficult to deny the temptations of the flesh when the flesh has just bought time and is yearning for a rest. We arranged, therefore, a mutually acceptable compromise.

We slept from 2:30 to 5:15 and should have been away for 6am. Bleary-eyed confusion delayed us until 6:30 at which time we emerged into a true winter landscape. While we were slumbering the snows came and were even now piling generously all around. At valley level there was enough to bury the foot and as we toiled upwards each hundred feet of ascent seemed to bring an additional inch. And toil it certainly was. Leading us up an interminable hill towards Ickornshaw Moor was the redoubtable Alan Heaton. In the history of fell walking and fell running there have been few to equal Alan. He is a former holder of the Pennine Way record, the Lake District 24 hour fell record and has won the 60 mile Fellsman Hike more times than I can remember. He was unable to join us at the start of our venture but was now obviously intent on making up for lost opportunities. We had intended leaving the road hill in favour of a tiny path which gave early access to the moor. We were not sure of its exact location and Alan was forging ahead so powerfully no-one could catch him to present the case.

With relief we eventually left the road and plunged into the white heather. I wondered how Alan would cope now he had to break trail across rough ground where obstructions and paths alike were completely obscured. To my amazement he hardly changed rhythm. It was like following a cruiser through a rough sea. Up and down he went, into holes and out of them, across boggy ditches and over heather hummocks. There were now five of us following him as Alan W. had been invited to stretch his legs as far as Todmorden, a sort of reward for his selfless support. With these numbers the best strategy was to jockey one's way to the back and take advantage of the beaten trail. It was also wise to be sensible to waving arms, desperate lunges and despairing groans from the vanguard, this generally indicated the necessity to take avoiding action. On the whole, however, the cold snap during the small hours had solidified the ground quite well. Thanks to this and Alan H's total disregard for the tough 60 miles already in our legs, we made surprisingly good progress.

In the circumstances our navigation was understandably rudimentary. To be plain, it consisted of staying within sight of Alan H's back. Whatever system he might have been using was never apparent. We were supposed to arrive at a small outcrop above Water Sheddles reservoir known as Wolf Stones. In thick mist and falling snow the only feature we could make out was Alan's trail. We seemed to be floundering steadily southwards downhill however, so there was no chance we could miss the Colne-Haworth road. Sure enough, we arrived just a little east of the reservoir and called a brief halt. Ahead of us once more lay the apparently innocuous Jackson's Ridge. This was a good time to re-fuel and fix compass bearings and map shapes in our minds. In fact, with the snow now limited to the odd flake and the mist dissipating rapidly we were faced with suspiciously good conditions. What, I wondered, was this untrustworthy piece of ground up to now? Perhaps I was becoming neurotic about this place. Still, forewarned is forearmed.

Well, four of us were forearmed. We really should have drawn Alan W's attention to Jackson's evil spirit. We didn't and it got him. Apart from the problem of keeping up with Alan H. our ascent of the moor had been uneventful. Alan yet again set such a fearsome pace all attention was directed towards keeping him in sight. Geoff could just see Alan, I could see Geoff and for what was happening behind me I had no concern to spare. Then on the edge of my perception came a faint cry. Looking back I saw two dark figures bending over a third, prostrate body. The demon had struck! Reluctantly, I plodded back over the hard-won ground.

The prostrate figure was that of Alan W. Face as white as the surrounding snow he lay on his back while John knelt beside him. He appeared to be forcing a frozen Mars bar between Alan's teeth. It was, without doubt, a most spectacular case of 'bonk', that is hypoglycaemia or low blood sugar. When the blood sugar level gets too low the brain goes on strike and leaves the body's vital mechanisms to their own devices. Basic equilibrium is lost and collapse may follow. As Alan graphically described it later, 'I lay on my back, focussing all my attention on attempting to raise an eyelid.' Alan had been engaged in an early, unaccustomed burst of fierce, energy burning activity and had not realised the importance of refuelling at our recent stop. The demon had, of course, seen his chance and selected his victim. It was fortunate Alan had not been 'off the back' when he collapsed.

Geoff had returned with me, but Alan H. had last been seen ploughing onwards and out of earshot. (He did later rejoin us). In view of Alan's shaky condition I suggested we take a less challenging line which would lead us to Todmorden by paths and tracks. Thus we missed Black Hameldon. Brock might not have approved and, in retrospect, Alan would probably have managed as he improved steadily, but never having suffered 'bonk' before, he had sustained a heavy psychological blow. For him the commitment of another snow-heavy moor might have been rather intimidating.

Our misadventure plus inevitable time delays in finding unfamiliar paths buried under snow carved away the time advantage we had started the day with. It was less than 20 miles from John's home to Todmorden but we lost two hours on this section taking nearly 8½ hours overall. Sue was understandably anxious waiting in the chill next to Todmorden railway station. We were all a little depressed, I think. It was nearly 3pm when we arrived. By the time we had eaten and changed dusk would again be falling. It seemed like no time since the morning, it just wasn't fair! We had come 70 miles, yet still another 50 miles remained, 50 miles of deep snow starting with sixteen hours of darkness. No-one spoke these thoughts aloud for fear of destroying morale already very low, but the looks on faces revealed them plainly enough.

As we packed sacks with gear for the night we realised Ted was missing. Suddenly he reappeared and in a calm voice announced, 'There's a train leaving for Manchester in ten minutes,' pause, 'and I've just bought a ticket for it.' An incredulous silence descended on us. There are moments in long, hard walks where the viability, validity or even stupidity of what you are doing should not be questioned if you wish to survive the walk. Ted had just asked those questions, for himself in theory, but the effects of his answer hit us all in the pit of the stomach. Why bother going on? This is a question which should be asked before the walk begins and after the walk is finished, never during it.

Had Ted been having a bad time, we would have been sad to see him go but relieved he was ending his suffering. At the time he appeared to be as strong, or as weak, as the rest of us, hence the blow to our morale. Later I remembered how he had been doctoring sore feet at John's and went down with influenza a few days after getting home. This rationale was not available at the time and we left Todmorden at 4:30pm in silence, the street lamps already glowing through the murk, the shops still bright with Christmas, our minds occupied only with thoughts of the next moorland passage.

Todmorden was our crisis point. We departed in a grim silence, determined perhaps, but uncharacteristically despondent. It was only when we had relinquished all thoughts of daylight and left the distracting bustle of the town below us, that our minds began once more to engage with the realities of our walk. The higher we climbed, the lighter became our spirits. It promised to be a fine night. Temperatures were creeping slowly below zero. There was a breeze, just sufficient to aid ventilation, and, above all, an early moon cast its cold light across the snowy wastes. We should not have that remorseless darkness which was becoming unendurable.

Gaining the tracks alongside the Warland reservoirs we made good progress for a time. Our next port of call was Marsden, still some ten miles and several hours away. It occurred to us that the White House Inn with a promise of fine ales lay at the next road crossing. Soon our imaginations were busy with thoughts of striding into a well dressed lounge like a gang of Yukon prospectors and demanding large quantities of foaming beer. Alas for dreams, when we did arrive the place was closed for business. Throats which had tickled in the anticipation of refreshment were suddenly on fire with the lust of unrequited thirst.

From the White House the route shares the same lines as the Pennine Way which, of course, it pre-dates. This was familiar country to all – or was it? Moving onto Blackstone Edge we began to realise we were in a new world. It was a world of awesome and desolate beauty. The moon continued to throw an eerie light across the landscape and, like hard, white gems, stars stabbed through the black void. But the landscape which was now revealed to us might have fallen from a lifeless planet and drifted across frozen aeons before settling here to astonish our gaze. The breeze carried dustings of powder and skimming veils of mist over the unbroken whiteness. Occasionally the mist would rise around us and when we emerged our sense of place and direction reeled.

It was probably the need to concentrate on our navigation plus the effort of exertion through the snow billows which prevented us from totally succumbing to 'raptures of the white desolation.' I don't think we were ever quite on line, but neither were we far astray, rather important, as at one point a narrow footbridge spanning the M62 must be located.

Our sense of time was quite lost on this surreal voyage across these moors of the moon. It was with some surprise that we reached the Nant Sarah's road (A640) and, slowly cranking our minds back into gear, realised we could be in Marsden in time for that delayed pint. I well remember the descent to the valley. The path is normally a fair one, though furrowed. I couldn't seem to stay on it. Wherever I walked I slid off into a hole or ditch. What was worse, this affliction appeared only to affect me. It was with great relief that I reached the *terra firma* of Marsden's streets.

At 10pm we turned sharp left into the first pub we reached. By this time our tastes had moderated, very wisely, to pints of orange. We slumped around a table in the 'snug', eyelids drooping in the sudden warmth. The place was full of locals who after an initial glance paid us no attention. Considering our total incongruity I was somewhat puzzled at this, perhaps there were a number of teams attempting a Tan-Cat that night. There again, folk in rural Yorkshire like to keep 'theirselves to theirselves'.

Marsden had one more bounty to bestow before we left its homely embraces. At the chip shop we each procured a 'Peel Street Special': fish, chips, peas and a muffin for 55p. Sitting in companionable if chilly silence in the bus shelter we munched our fill of sustaining stodge.

Although it still wanted an hour to midnight it felt as if we had been out all night as we tried to regain momentum up the Wessenden Valley track. The early moon had stooped lower in the sky but the snow magnified all available light. The track gained height less readily than the moors on either side. Their glistening white flanks swelled around us, while below us the stark, black waters of the reservoirs formed a striking contrast. Above us the blue-black canopy of the winter's night arched, cold and high. Indeed, the cold was so intense that I was none too pleased when John, who had been suffering an attack of the 'sleepies', suggested a brief halt for a kip. We found a ramshackle lean-to at the end of a farm track and clustered together while John enjoyed a five minute 'ziz'.

While I wasn't feeling sleepy, I wasn't going particularly well either. Along the track this was not so noticeable, but once we crossed the Isle of Skye road (A635) I began to have real problems. Black Hill is as rough a stretch of moor as any along the route. It appeared that it had rather greedily grabbed more than its fair share of snow. It would certainly be in character that it should seek to present its worst possible face, it usually does. As the others strode vigorously across the broad acres of snow-covered tussocks I became singled out for unfair treatment. Every hundred yards or so a broad ditch would cross our path. The other three would plough through without let or hindrance. I was at the back and, inevitably, when I attempted to cross I would flounder to the waist in an unseen hole. By way of variation, as temper increased momentum, my legs would plunge downwards and my upper body forwards. With a thrashing of arms and legs I would extricate myself, hurry after the others, just catch them and then fall into another ditch. Why it never happened to them I couldn't make out. But they never paused or even looked back in sympathy. I wished them all to perdition and gave up the unequal struggle.

As it transpired, Geoff and Alan were punished for their cruelty, but John, repenting, was ultimately saved. This is how it happened: I knew exactly where, in this white wilderness, I wanted to go. I was, furthermore, confident I could follow the most economical lines to the road by the Holme Moss television transmitter. I also had a strong suspicion that Geoff and Alan were enjoying a little test of strength. This would almost certainly blight their somewhat delicate navigational skills. Of course John was a superb navigator, but could he stand the pace? Geoff and Alan heads down, blinkers on, antlers locked – hmm, *trés formidable*! The answer came as a shadowy figure hailed me from below, it was John.

Finding the pace a little too extreme he had let the others go and had last seen them following the straightest of lines up the hill. All very well, but the notion of a straight line as the shortest distance between two points is an abstract one. It has little relevance to finding one's way over Black Hill at night.

John and I had the same idea, traverse into Issue Clough and ascend its steep northern edge to pick up groughless lines to Holme Moss. As we stepped round the corner into full view of the clough we were held spellbound. The opposite side which we proposed to climb was, in John's words, 'a thing of terrible and daunting beauty, immediately reminiscent of an Alpine winter face.' In something of a daze we launched ourselves at the shining slope towering above us. Unbelievably, in just a few minutes of heart-pumping, step-kicking effort we had scaled the face and stood once again on the familiar moorland plateau.

We now had a good line to our objective, the summit of the Holmfirth road. Following easy, flat-bottomed groughs winding a sinuous way between floury peat banks we were soon in view of the TV mast soaring to invisibility. As we passed under the massive securing cables I noticed thick manacles of ice which the cables had shrugged off to let thump heavily into the snow... we discovered a little extra spring to our step.

There would be no traffic on the road tonight. The day's slush had frozen iron hard and the alternately polished and ridged surface was dusted with spindrift. Our first action on reaching the road was to look for Alan's and Geoff's footprints. I thought I could detect them in the drift though the ice was telling no tales. We both agreed they would be well on the way to Crowden by now. Meantime we enjoyed easy walking downhill on a firm surface. Normally road walking is anathema to me, but with not even the tarmac in sight we could forget we were on a road and contemplate the vast white solitude, partly seen and keenly sensed, which wrapped so completely around us as we walked quietly together amid the utter peace of the winter night. We felt more strongly than ever the close affinity which binds those who share the joys and vicissitudes of long journeys; so it is that old friendships are renewed, deepened and given meaning.

It had occurred to me as a matter of some regret that Alan's strong lead which had helped us maintain schedule had also somewhat split the group. Each one of us was a strong and competitive walker, it was inevitable that whoever was strongest at any one time would attempt to follow Alan's lead. Consequently, we had become fragmented at times with everyone chasing the man in front and no-one quite making it because at the front was Alan, not only very fit, but 50 miles fresher than the rest. Of course we should simply have asked Alan to ease up a little, but we were all too proud I suppose.

From the number of times John and I commented how Geoff and Alan would already be at the Crowden Centre crawling into sleeping bags, eating all the stew etc., I knew we were sharing another, unvoiced, thought. At 3:30am we reached the haven of our second night's harbour, Crowden Outdoor Activities Centre. It was due to the generosity of the Principal and the diplomacy of John Beatty that we had been given the use of a sort of annexe/cum porch which was ideal for our needs. Geoff's wife had driven out from Glossop and stocked the place with all the heart could desire: sleeping bags, dry clothes, food for the remainder of the journey and a cauldron of juicy stew complete with stove.

Surprisingly, when we arrived the cauldron was still completely full, not a spoonful missing. On the other hand, Geoff and Alan had no brew ready for us... because they weren't there! I admit we were unfeeling enough to chortle quite inordinately. We remembered how they had been going full steam ahead for Black Hill summit, an unnecessary diversion, and we indulged in the most dreadful slanders concerning their navigational ability. Of course you would guess we made plans to search for them if they hadn't appeared after a certain time. In this you would be quite mistaken. After rapidly gorging some stew John entombed himself in his bag and was soon asleep. I decided to wait up and enjoy our errant comrades discomfiture 'live' as it were. (Though mutual suffering is the seal of friendship formed).

They arrived little more than 30 minutes after us. Remarkably, Geoff was beaming and warbling cheerfully about the merits of a 'little epic' on a big walk. Their little epic had been that they had indeed bee-lined Black Hill summit. They had then, presumably under a wee impetus of competition, hurtled straight into Heyden Clough. Nemesis followed at their heels. The clough was choked with deep powdery snow which hid a tumble of boulders and other delights. They had, Geoff proudly announced, maintained their level of work output if not their speed. Looking at their gaunt, sweating faces I could see what he meant. 'Well done chaps,' I murmured, 'best stick with the navigators next time, eh?' In fact, that little episode seemed to dissipate their head of steam nicely. From then on we formed a companionable and tight-knit group. We slept from 4:30 to 6:15 with plans to be away before first light at 7am. No chance! The rigours of the hard and sleepless hours were slowing mind and body. It was 7:45 when at last we stepped out into a quietly hostile world. The glory of the night sky had been replaced by a thick, creeping mist through which a drift of snow swirled ominously. We all knew that the traverse of Bleaklow would be the final crux. Already the snow was deep, if this was the start of a blizzard or even a heavy snowfall, could we force our way over the moor's rough contours?

Slowly, we plodded upwards following the steep ridge of Rollick Stones. Thankfully the flakes dwindled and soon died altogether. The mist, however, was thicker than ever, its impenetrability aided by full snow cover. We picked up the stream bed of Wildboar Clough and followed its dwindling intricacies deeper and deeper into the moor, a ghostly kingdom of faintly glimpsed, shifting shadows, drifting aimlessly between unseen sky and unfelt land. The hypnotic effect of this phantom world intensified slowly, a deep and timeless silence seized us. We maintained but a tenuous hold on reality. Yet somewhere within our blurred consciousness John and I were still vaguely aware of the need to navigate.

By instinct we both stopped at a point which felt like the watershed of Bleaklow's broad back. Swivelling our compasses we turned 90 degrees in what we hoped was the direction of Bleaklow Head. After a while John halted, convinced we had arrived. I was equally convinced we had not. A rather fierce argument ensued. In matters of doubt I nearly always bow to John's exceptional ability, but not this time. Stubborn as a mule even when I know I'm in the wrong, I don't know how John can detect my more honest obstinacy. He let me have my way and in a little while longer we arrived at Bleaklow Head. As we stood at this crux moment at the end of this last crucial section a remarkable event occurred: the cloying sea of mist suddenly fell away and in seconds had completely vanished.

We found ourselves immediately, almost unbelievably, transported to a new world. For 360 degrees all around us the searingly white waves rolled to the edge of sight. Directly in front of us, some four miles away, Kinder North Edge faced us with a shadowed frown. My heart leapt in delight to the place where, one day, my ashes will be scattered. Scowl as it might, it could not disguise the joy we had of each other. We all found cause for delight in the scene. Was it possible that the sky could be suddenly so blue? It must be, or how else could that blue be reflected in the shadows which lay at the foot of deep groughs and underneath little hanging cornices of ice-cream snow?

After the long, dark, suffering hours how glorious is sunlight and pure blue sky. How many times more blessed are the few precious hours which hold at bay the black and savage night? Never a winter sunbeam now but does not pierce my memories of darkness.

Although it is but eight miles from Crowden to the Snake Inn we needed nearly 4½ hours to cover the distance. An urgency seized me and I led a storming assault up the side of Kinder, our last big climb. It was amazing how slow had been our overall progress. A 'good' time for the Marsden-Edale walk would be six hours, an 'average' time about eight hours. Excluding our halt at Crowden, we took eleven hours. The temptation, therefore, to linger for mugs of tea at Cooper's Cafe in Edale was resisted. Already we could see ahead blue shadows curving down from Rushup Edge and creeping once again towards us.

There was now, however, a ringing confidence in our step. And above Rushup Edge we were truly delighted to be met by Ted bearing a huge flask of coffee and delicious bacon butties. We now had just one last obstacle, the short but rough moor of Combs Moss between Chapel-en-le-Frith and Buxton. Here, as our third night formed from the valley shadows, we found the powder piled high and totally unconsolidated. We tumbled through it, tripping, stumbling, falling, not caring. At 7pm we paused for a final brew at my Buxton home and, for once, left eagerly.

It was a fine, frosty night, again brilliant with stars. Our steaming breath was caught by the moonlight and the ice crunched to the rhythm of our steps. Yes, a grand night to be out. But we were walking just a little way now across Derbyshire Bridge into Cheshire. And there at the top of the moor a cluster of lights, England's second highest pub.

'Well now, what are you having?' A pint and a last quiet chat.

'Not many folk about!'

'Well done lads, and thanks, John, Geoff, Ted and Alan.'

'No, John, I know Brock may not approve of some aspects of what we did, but I feel satisfied in myself. I won't be doing it again. And look... Geoff's already asleep, what a nutter!'

P.S. It took us 61 hours, exactly.

chapter sixteen

HIGH WATERMARKS OF THE LAKE DISTRICT

Prologue

In an age when the Earth sought its genesis within the slow mystery of time there came an epoch of cataclysm. From subterranean depths fiery rocks issued in exultant chaos and the oceans boiled to the vigour of their birth. Impelled by the slow tectonic surge of wheeling continents they arched to airless heights. Roots of granite set their feet and they danced to the slow rhythms of the Earth's deep currents. But patient millennia eroded their giant splendour. Desert blasted and licked by hungry seas they tracked north. Once again fundamental forces pulsated beneath the prone giants. Slowly they awakened, stretched upwards on the swelling tide and, lifting their domed heads, gazed defiantly towards the horizons of time.

They observed the fall of stars and the journey of unknown comets. Long did they abide and suffered no stay or change. And yet, in time, they were assailed by the stealth of an ultimate and deadly enemy. In time, they slept, in time a bitter foe crept out of northern wastes and, in time, gossamer webs of snow wreathed and bound the sleeping giants. Thin, icy fingers grappled inwards. With slow, cruel malevolence they probed, ripped and then grew stronger. Hard was the rock and bitter the struggle. Shard by shard and fragment by fragment, yielding at last to inevitable forces, the proud rock crumbled. Then came a time when only the most defiant heads of the primeval giants were raised above the white savagery. And the creeping death gnawed beneath. Grim and taut they endured the rictus of their travail awaiting the expiring groan of entropy.

Then there came another force, one who's soft breath and gentle ways astonished the savage ice. Warm caresses destroyed white cliffs, dissolved glaciers and spread a gift of flowers around the feet of the ancient giants. And they wept, never having known such beauty. Their tears gathered and mingled with all the waters of change. Down weathered cheeks and scarred flanks the healing streams flowed into ice-scoured wounds and gashes. They lay as a balm on the land which became rare and beautiful under their influence. Time passed and man came. He marvelled at the tears of the ancient giants. Not knowing them for what they are he considered these pools and what he knew of beauty and called them 'the jewels of Lakeland'.

Top Twenty Tarns

And so the tears of the ancients lie to this day. A kaleidoscopic confusion of waters, meres and tarns they reflect the changing mood of sky and season. The ancient solace is still within them, too. Follow the dance of a mountain beck to its issue from the tarn which gives it life. As you go the magic of beck and tarn will seek the springs within your own heart. A journey which visits any order of tarns will find that touchstone of enchantment which forms the essence of any truly great walk. Remember, each pool is a unique gift and each water sprite guarding it will bestow a blessing on you, do you dare doubt it? Come only with the right heart.

When does a piece of water become a 'top twenty tarn'? Objective criteria were that it should have 'a name and be present on the ground and map'. Subjectively, when it is at least above 1,650ft and can be woven into a pleasing circuit. So two tarns (Scoat and Sprinkling) which were high enough were replaced by others producing a more pleasing route.

My 'High Watermarks' presented itself at about 60 miles and 20,000 feet. It would nicely fill a summer weekend, for which I was joined by six companions. Working on a fairly brisk Naismith formula (three miles per hour and 20 minutes per 1,000 feet) indicated a start at the civilised hour of noon. The route outline can best be described as a long narrow anti-clockwise horseshoe with the start end at Kirkstone pass, the finish end at Coniston and the northernmost apex being Blencathra.

Bashing straight up Red Screes from the Kirkstone Inn gives little time to ease into a rhythm. On the other hand, the inn already stands at 1,500 feet. The bleak little pool at the summit was not on my 'official' list; Scandale Tarn was, however. We rapidly lost most of the height we'd just won to visit its lushy, rushy, soft mossy bed. My companions wanted to know what ceremony was to be performed at our tarns. In my younger, no-nonsense days it would have been 'strip off and get in there'! Having become wiser and mellower (i.e. older and softer) I thought we might paddle the odd toe, sip a droplet or simply smile benignly at them (and the water sprite should he or she happen to be there).

A gentler climb saw us onto the broad undulating back of the Hart Crag-Fairfield ridge. By now the day was waxing warm as was the pace. Nobody seemed to be paying much attention to Naismith but that meant we would have more time to enjoy the tarns. We made an economical descent to Grisedale Tarn by a secret trod which avoids the bald scree down to Grisedale Hause. A rude wind was blowing from without the bowels of Patterdale making my non-commitment to swimming seem very sensible. We now deserted orthodox lines in pursuit of our next objective. Hard Tarn nestles snugly and invisibly below Nethermost Pike. It is pleasingly difficult of access. To gain it you may slog up Dollywaggon and plunge precipitously down either Ruthwaite or Nethermost Coves, or copy our line. We dropped down to Ruthwaite Lodge, smelling, as always, of smoked kippers (the Lodge, I mean), and then toiled through rich grasses up into the lonely coves.

The soft pathless rise of 1,000 feet guarantees the almost unique solitude of these deep green wells of shadowy peace. Above, the busy feet score their way ceaselessly to Helvellyn's high Mecca. A few hundred feet below we smiled for sheer joy at the beauty of Hard Tarn. A sapphire set in soft emerald mosses, white clouds gleaming across its surface and grey stones melting into its depths. With little urging we slipped into the waters and emerged invigorated. A slip-sliding traverse on scattered scree brought us to an easy, enjoyable scramble up Nethermost Pike's modest competitor to Helvellyn's Striding Edge. We did not linger on Helvellyn but dipped down to Swirral Edge which we followed in glorious slanting sunlight to Red Tarn, at 2,400 feet remarkably high for so extensive a tarn.

As the brassy afternoon mellowed into a golden evening we followed a sun-burnished traverse of the dales which flow eastward from the Dodds. First we crossed Glenridding, then on a perfect contouring path we looped Glencoyne. For a while we passed through the shadows before blinking into the sunlit acres of Dowthwaitehead. Here, even the lake-wise peered curiously about them at this little visited hamlet of farms and cottages, forgotten and remote.

Our next target lay still miles away but it held great promise. After ploughing through the rough heath below Clough Head we emerged from cool evening shadows cast by Scales Fell to walk over coppery grass towards the darker hollow scooped below Tarn Crags and Sharp Edge. Here lies Scales Tarn, a grey mirrow-mere, cold and stern after our sun-drenched miles. I had wanted to visit Scales Tarn for three reasons. Firstly, it is a true mountain tarn lying below steep craggy slopes - it occupies a depression carved in glacial ages long ago. As night shades the eastern slopes it breathes again the chill fastness of an ancient kingdom of ice. Secondly, the mountain which claims it is Blencathra, a massive whaleback, smooth along its crest and northern slopes, yet on its southern side throwing out rough rocky ridges to separate deep, unvisited recesses. But, perhaps best of all, approaching Blencathra from Scales Tarn invites a traverse of Sharp Edge. We ate by the tarn Andy striking off into the icy waters shattered the sombre quiet of the combe. He said it did him good to slough off the day's grime but I think he offended the water sprite. A grimmer, less playful spirit surely inhabits this place. At any rate, Andy took poorly before the end of the walk.

Through good planning dreams become reality. But I had no right to expect such perfection as attended our ascent of Blencathra by Sharp Edge. Just when I thought the sun had gone, we stepped once more into its generous light. The hard crest of rock shone like polished leather and our bare limbs became golden in the kindly glow of the westering sun. Like the ridge of Crib Goch in Snowdonia or Striding Edge on nearby Helvellyn, Sharp Edge in winter may ring to the battle clash of steel on ice, now we were just tickling the giant's ribs.

There was no anti-climax in attaining the smooth summit ridge. We were soaring above the stealthy shadows of Threlkeld and to our right the steepening grass rolled down and out across the rough solitude 'Back o'Skiddaw'. Then, mounting on the surging updraughts from the valley came the swifts to play. Wing curving glorious flight, riding the brave airs in joyful dance, their joy was a reflection of our own.

Ambling contentedly down the western slopes of Blencathra's Blease Fell we crossed the Glenderaterra valley and picked up the old track carved in the flanks of Lonscale Fell. It provided us with a relaxed and pleasant approach to Keswick. After a day in the peace of high places Keswick was, in part, an unwelcome intrusion. But also in part, if not in whole, man lives by bread and the Moot Hall chip shop has sustained many a hard walk. We ate largely and leisurely while our noble support member provided copious brews.

Leaving the Keswick revellers in welcome possession of the town we crept quietly out. With bellies full and feet pampered we swayed over the pedestrian suspension bridge spanning the River Derwent on its exodus to Bassenthwaite. The waters under our feet were drawn from the great peaks of Bowfell, Great End and Gable, even from one of our yet unvisited high watermarks - Angle Tarn. When would the cycle revolve full circle and these waters flowing from beck to tarn, and tarn to river, and river to sea be drawn purified into the atmosphere once more? And would these same waters come again and nourish the grasses on the Lakeland fells? Nature's cycles are slow and unhurried and we move through them like brief sparks from a spitting fire.

After Portinscale we passed into the deep, wooded shadows of Fawe

Park where the trees had trapped the warmth of the day. At the end of the woods Cat Bells rose in a steep cone, unseen but sensed. The air was almost unnaturally still. Our rhythmic ascent was silent save for the crunch and scrape of stone on stone. High Spy ridge is an agreeable place to be walking at night. It is a fine thing to be stepping out high above the sleeping valleys. Beyond Maiden Moor the path climbs gently to High Spy itself. Then, for a time it wanders nervously above the dark bounding crags which frown above the Newlands valley.

Our next target has the peculiar name of Launchy Tarn. However, I had decided to visit Dale Head Tarn first. This allowed us to establish our precise location and meant we could include a bonus tarn of considerable charm, nestling on the broad bosom of its parent mountain and peeping down the Newlands Beck and back towards High Spy. There are many tarns clustering between the 1,650 and 1,800 foot contours. The slight lack of agreement between various OS map series prompts a pleasant freedom and flexibility in planning. Unlike Dale Head Tarn only 500 yards away, Launchy Tarn is of the moors. A peaty hole among the red and brown grasses it is really a large puddle having neither inlet nor outlet. It is connected to a series of smaller bogholes by an ancient boundary fence of once brave iron now a line of rotting malevolent teeth.

The ground lay dark and sleeping but the eastern sky paled before the unseen approach of the hurrying sun. Below us, at the top of Honister Pass, we could view his coming from our final support point. From my privileged position in the leader's deck chair I observed that some of my companions were attentive only to material splendours like pots of tea and bowls of porridge. Yet others closed their eyes altogether in the face of the coming glory, pious reverence, I expect.

When dawn did arrive it was curiously unreadable. High above us there seemed to be a whispered debate among the minor gods of the weather. Would they grill us, chill us or pour forth their deluge? Like Odysseus I stopped up my ears to the sirens' seductive song ('More tea? Another slice of cake?') and rallied temporarily comatose companions. Ahead of us lay the tough guts of the walk. No anti-climax to this route, the majesty lay still before us and would not be won easily with tired legs: 34 miles covered, 26 to go, 9,250 feet climbed, 11,000 feet more left. But a new day spread long across the hills.

At 4am we followed the tramway path towards Fleetwith Pike. Dusk was still gathered in sleepy hollows. Our destination was Innominate Tarn; the tarn is tucked under Haystacks and is apt to its surroundings. It is rimmed by rocks, heather and bilberry. What enhanced its grave beauty at this moment was the glowing sunrise soaking into the eastern sky. It seemed fitting to visit this reflection of wilderness at a solitary time of day.

Our next prize would exact a hefty toll. Kirkfell Tarn was third highest on my list. It is almost a summit tarn, ensconced between Kirkfell's twin tops. It would entail a mainly pathless ascent of 1,500 feet. A silence descended on the party as we made our studied and systematic way up the steep grass. However, fatigue was soon forgotten as the views over to the Scafells began to rise before us. In a direct line some two and a half miles across Wasdale, the deep unmistakeable notch of Mickledore separated England's two highest peaks. I stood for a while, indulging the desire for wings which overcomes me now and then, before hurrying after the others already descending to our next tarn.

In this dry summer Beckhead Tarn was little more than a stony puddle. I have always privately thought that its sprite would do much better for himself if he moved his pool across to the other side of the col. Kirkfell seems unable to afford much water whereas the Gable side of the col has generous springs of icy elixir. Few in our party had heard of our next tarn and none had visited it. Dry Tarn occupies a small ledge some 650 feet above Sty Head and only a few feet away from the main path up Great Gable. I had verified its credentials a couple of weeks previously and had found a discreet and charming pool hiding shyly from prying eyes.

Although only an extra 550 feet of ascent are needed to approach Dry Tarn via the summit of Great Gable, we elected to follow the 'Climber's Traverse' towards Sty Head and re-ascend just before the Kern Knotts Crack area. Under the stimulus of this demanding and occasionally elusive path our vigour was necessarily renewed. Napes Needle was identified but looked disappointing from this perspective. What never disappoints however, given good visibility, are the views down Wasdale and across to Great End and the Scafells. Lakeland's superb contrast between rugged mountain and soft valley is perfectly epitomised in Wasdale. Across the Sty Head path the massive muscled flanks of Great End, Lingmell and Scafell heaved and bunched in the probing caresses of the day's early light. Titans, riven and crossed by gorge and ghyll, knotted and hard with crag and stone they are improbably traversed by the Corridor Route.

On the ascent to Dry Tarn from the Climber's Traverse we lost Pete S. He felt his climbing legs were deserting him and elected to make a leisurely search for them on his way back to the club hut. Another sad blow fell at Dry Tarn itself. I had foolishly attached little significance to its name, well it had looked very wet and permanent ten days ago! To be honest I suspect, more mischief from a water sprite. Startled by my earlier visitation, an almost unique event, he had divined my intentions. I guess he had hidden the tarn in a nearby hollow. Shyness should be respected, so we didn't pry about.

Sprinkling Tarn should have been next on our list. Including it however, would have produced an illogical route since we had to visit the Scafells to collect the two highest watermarks. It had also occurred to me that if we followed the logical line of the Corridor Route on the east side of the Scafells we could replace Sprinkling Tarn with a very high pool absolutely in character with the walk. Lambfoot Dub is beautifully situated, remote, wild and could be of unfathomable depth. Truly of the fells it casts a brooding gaze towards the spectacular bulk of Great Gable and Kirkfell. The Dub lies a little way above the path and can be tricky to find in mist. We spent a little time admiring the spot and enjoying the atmosphere of wild, inviolable tranquillity.

Rejoining the Corridor Route we passed over Lingmell Col and traversed below Pike's Crag. Across the notch of Mickledore, Scafell itself thrusts near impregnable ramparts north and east. On the hard, rocky bosom of Scafell the spirit of rock-climbing in this country was nursed and suckled. Stand and watch the interplay of light and shadow across the gnarled surface of the living rock, follow the soar and spread of buttress, tower and pinnacle, listen to the voice of the wind among these mistborne castles of dreams, and feel your heart leap with excitement and fear towards them, for the lode stone in your heart which draws you to this place is of the stuff of the mountains.

Even under the morning's brightness, Scafell's north buttress held the gravity of history. Closing my eyes I could almost hear the scratch of nailed boots and the scrape of hemp across rock. Perhaps the atmosphere reached Pete C. too, for at Mickledore he decided to rest and meditate on the glories of this place. Meanwhile, the rest of us found the only chink in Scafell's northern armour. 'Broad Stand' is a scramble on highly polished and, in places, rather exposed rock. However, we suffered no mishaps on Broad Stand's shortcut to Scafell and soon we were on England's second highest peak, poised above her second highest tarn. Foxes Tarn at 2,650ft is a tiny pool, little more than a well in the ground, but its delicacy is sustained by the summated drainage of a vast area of craggy hillside. An oasis of emerald green at the foot of the arid scree it conveys the promise of eternal refreshment as permanent and pure as truth itself.

We left the tarn by the rocky gully which carries away its waters to join those of the River Esk via Cam Spout. By now the sun was kindling inner memories within the ancient rocks, they resonated to the distant echo of their fiery birth. Already warm and unusually dry, soon they would be unpleasantly hot. I was not surprised to find a pair of climbers taking advantage of the conditions. The leader was on the start of a modern extreme, 'Midnight Express'. As we plodded up and across Mickledore's red scree he began a carefully focussed series of moves across the pale, apparently blank slab. There was an alert repose in his body which spoke of skill and concentrated strength. Without fuss or fumble he placed a protective runner, clipped in and climbed quietly on. Across on the Pike side of the amphitheatre we, for a time, neglected our own dialogue with the mountain in contemplation of his. Gazing through my thoughts I watched the small figure handling the rock with the 'solemnity of a sacrament'. He moved upwards, growing less distinct, dissolving finally within the living rock of an overhang, emerging transubstantiated, from vision of sight to vision of dream, a symbol of those before, those to come, those who seek, those who strive, and find...? Patiently we resumed our quest.

We had steadily worked our way towards the highest tarn on our walk. Broad Crag Tarn lies a little beyond a small pool draining from luxurious masses of voluptuous green sphagnum. Though small, the tarn was deep enough to cool our overheated bodies. It was an ideal spot for a high camp. Indeed, of our group, Inken had camped here during a mountain marathon event. Her account of spending the night next to the Lake District's highest tarn had lodged the germinating seed for the walk in my mind.

While our dawdling was understandable it didn't bring the finish any closer. Having toyed with Naismith at the start of the walk he was now tightening the screws on us. Of course there is no allowance for temperatures of 30 degrees centigrade in Naismith's formula. I made a mental note

Hard Tarn (Nethermost). Andy plunges, Joe, Inken and Pete look on.

not to succumb to the temptation of a picnic at every tarn. In fact, there was soon an additional reason to maintain pace. As we started to head for High House Tarn between Allen Crags and Glaramara, the sky became a nasty, sullen grey. Considering the grey heaviness that was creeping into the atmosphere, High House Tarn managed a sad but noble beauty. There was no bathe this time, just a bee-line for Angle Tarn. Under the threatening sky, the waters of Angle Tarn ran deep and dark down to the ancient ice-scoured floor. Only Inken was brave enough to tackle a full immersion. I thought we would soon be washed clean enough.

There were various alternatives now open to us in order to reach Three Tarns lying between Bowfell and the Crinkle Crags and we chose a little known 'direttissima' above Angle Tarn. The route follows scratches made by fellrunners pursuing the Bob Graham Round. Though tenuous it poses no real problem with the possible exception of the exit via a steep stony gully. My recommendation here is to elbow your way to the front or wear a helmet. I did neither and in order to minimise the velocity of falling stones had my head and hands stepped on by the clumsy oaf above me.

As we topped Bowfell summit large drops of rain smacked onto my thinning pate. With Crinkle Crags and the Coniston Fells still to go I began to feel a mite anxious. Pausing only long enough to record Three Tarns on film I hurried on, pondering briefly on the ethical problems posed by a name that was really a number, and a number of tarns that, for the purpose of this walk, should have been only one. Perhaps it was a mystery like the Trinity? By now our little party was scattered among the multitude of paths and trods which apparently lead to every outcrop pinnacle and sly by-pass along the jumbled ridges of Crinkle Crags. I observed most of my companions seemed to be employing that well tried navigational technique best described as 'follow your nose'. This is the hallmark of the long term fellrunner, which most of us were. It relies mainly on generating sufficient velocity to proceed in accord with that law of Newton's about a body continuing in a straight line until it realises it is lost. Joe K. was demonstrating the principle to great effect – as befits a mathematician. He was straight-lining every lump and bump before him. Imagine Ghengis Khan wearing blinkers driving a steam roller – that's Joe. Feeding off the bold but wasteful lines of those in front I sneaked an economical line under the inessential climbs and emerged ahead. I was accused of unfair knowledge and cheating, the ultimate accolade, which I modestly acknowledged.

Our speed over the Crinkles must have reached critical escape velocity. To everyone's surprise we had darted under the weather and enjoyed a dry descent to Red Tarn. Coming fresh from the rocky wastes of Bowfell and Crinkle Crags, Red Tarn is an anomaly. It is a rush-trimmed mere in which a hand clutching a long sword would not appear amiss.

Beyond enchanted Red Tarn we reached Wrynose Pass, our first road since leaving Honister Pass. At this point a major disintegration of the party occurred. Andy H. was suffering under the influence of too much sun and the threat of visiting relatives. He opted for the shortest way back and took Pete C. for company. John C. decided a more leisurely pace than the one I was currently pursuing would suit him better, I pressed on with Joe and Inken. Having paused for the swiftest of picnics, we discovered John ambling in front of us – you can't trust some people!

Together we followed the flowing ridge over Swirl How and onto the broad hump of Brim Fell. Here we halted for a brief consultation. From our present position Low Water was not so much inaptly, as ambiguously named. At 1,800 feet it certainly qualified as a high water mark. On the other hand it was exceedingly low in relation to our stance. As walk leader I decided to assume a brave nonchalance. After all, it was only 800 feet down to the tarn followed by, well err, 800 feet straight up again.

We found the descent a strain on tired knees but, with Low Water appearing almost directly below our feet like a pool in an inverted cone, it was unexpectedly fine. Calling on leader's guile I had rallied my troops by promising to scramble out of the corrie by a series of buttresses. As luck would have it, the rain began again as we reached the tarn. It was high density drizzle which fell like a gentle blanket. The promised rock looked repellent and felt greasy. While debating certain ethical and moral problems associated with 'a leader's responsibilities' some 30 feet above the ground, the team resolved them by making off up a disgusting vegetated gully. Slightly, but not too obviously, relieved I followed soggily.

Back on Brim Fell the 'gentle blanket' had been transformed to whiplash rain. While my cagoule was no doubt windproof, it revealed qualities more generally found in blotting paper. Shorts also felt a little inappropriate. None of us were over-dressed but we did not pause to discuss the situation. There were still two tarns left. We slid and skidded down to rocky Goats Water. Above the scree the bulging triple buttresses of Dow Crag thrust half invisible into the streaming air. Rain devils were dancing madly across the alarmed waters of the tarn. Half-remembered thoughts of 30 years ago came back to me: clambering with stiff hawser-laid nylon and a couple of slings on this mountain crag, seeing for the first time the corrie wind lift the skirts of Goats Water and set them dashing into the boulders. And that is how I have always remembered this place, elemental, raw, apparently tamed by hordes of trippers, yet always ready to bare gaunt and savage teeth.

As I bent in thirst and tribute to the tarn's powerful outflow a pair of bedraggled climbers hurried past looking a little shocked. Even modern gear is no protection on the rock in such weather. I hoped no-one else was up there, pinned to a buttress in lycra tights like butterflies on a pin-cushion. My own, lesser, worry was to find Blind Tarn quickly and efficiently. Blind Tarn! Appropriate enough now, but so called because it has no outlet. Angling up across the scree I went propelled by the imperative to find the mere scratch of a path and the certainty that I would. This confidence carried us blindly with unwavering determination along the paths of faith, they had no other reality. I had no intention of risking exposure by consulting the map for information that was (I hoped) better represented in my brain. Going beyond a steeper bulge in the slope I cut up and then back on myself. Oscillating between the cold clutch of despair and a primitive more certain exultation I raced to the rim of Blind Tarn.

Turning in what I hoped was modest triumph I got a real going-over from Inken who, being German and a 'proper' orienteer, places her trust in rather more orthodox navigational techniques. In high dudgeon despite rapidly decreasing body temperature I flew faultlessly along the well remembered exit lines to the Walna Scar path. This time I did not pause but with water spraying at every footstep ran shivering the whole way down to our destination on the shores of a very low, extremely large watermark – Lake Coniston.

There are a thousand ways to finish an epic walk. None of them are bad and some may be superb. Like the conclusion of a long novel or a great symphony, the end will resonate to the chime of those thoughts, emotions and dreams drifting like living ghosts across the mysterious interface between the conscious and subconscious mind. Is this a claim too exaggerated? Only by undertaking such journeys will you resolve this question, and then only for yourself.

(We spent 30 hours on the walk.)

chapter seventeen

THE SCOTTISH CARDINALS

The Venture

When the brain of an ultra man is not switched off for long periods, as inevitably it must be, it has a strong tendency to wrestle with projects of ever increasing difficulty. Emerging from one such bout I conceived the ambition to create a Scottish mountain round, not one of 24 hours but a proper 'ultra', seven days in fact. I did not repeat the mistake made by Ted on the North Wales Horseshoe. Not for me the confusing of the half inch with the one inch map series, no, I didn't use a map at all! I thought it would be grand to visit the four Munros at the cardinal points on the mainland and throw in a few other hill objectives on a fine cross-country journey.

When I finally got round to doing the sums, I realised I would actually need a fortnight. My 'creation' weighed in at around 525 miles and nearly 100,000 feet of ascent. Well, I did not have a fortnight to spare or, rather more importantly, my support team did not. After tough negotiations the line was drawn at ten days. I was pretty sure I could not complete the project in so short a time – but ten days playing out in the Highlands, yes please!

Reconnaissance

I concentrated on reconnoitring the connecting sections between hill groups. It was fascinating to go out with the map, wave the vehicle farewell and negotiate unknown country. In those pre-mobile-phone days there was always a frisson of doubt about whether we would actually meet up again. Some stalkers' paths were as shown, many were not and careless forestry had swallowed others. I really enjoyed my exploration. Hill tops always have visitors. I roamed straths, glens and moors where the only footprints were mine.

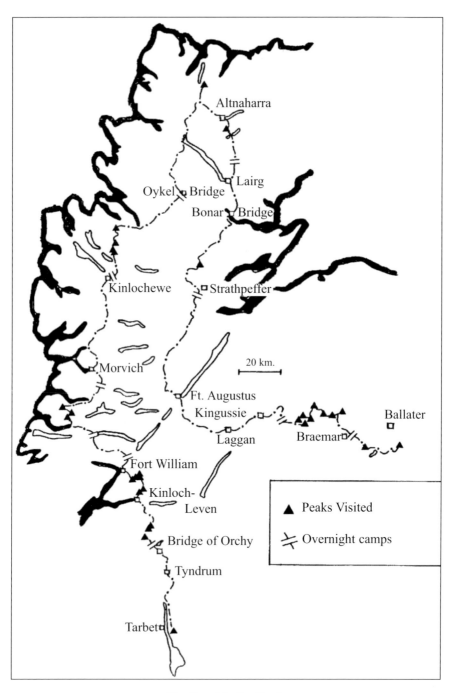

The Scottish Cardinals

The Account

It turned out that the support which enabled my venture to take place was extraordinarily demanding. Partly in tribute to this, but also because it helps give a much more accurate 'three-dimensional' picture, I have included some extracts from the log of my support supremo, IB. Perhaps more than anything, I hope that by so doing I am acknowledging and paying homage to all those who help others achieve their ambitions and dreams. When I turn and look back, as one occasionally should, along the travelled path, I see more than hills. I hear footsteps, I see smiles and I feel steadying hands. As Hugh Symonds agreed in his fine book *Running High*, the runner's tale is only half the story.

DAY 1: *Mike*

This was really 'Day ½' as I planned a midday start followed by nine full days and a midday finish on Mt. Keen. How ridiculous! As if I could plan with such nicety over 500 miles of mainly unknown terrain. Nevertheless, it was a strangely uncomfortable walk up Ben Lomond with Don. We must have been in a reflective mood as a vague metaphysical discussion accompanied our upward progress. At 11:59 Don and I shook hands solemnly and surveyed the unfathomable haze to the mighty North. I distinctly remember two strong, contrasting thoughts: 'what an empty gesture given almost certain failure' and 'for me, this is a momentous occasion.' Was there, I wondered, the dimmest possible chance of a handshake on Mt. Keen ten days from now? Soon, the ache aroused by that question was eased by movement. As we tussled with the rough ground north west of Ben Lomond I had an indefinable sense of a journey begun and of mysteries awaiting.

Beyond Ben Lomond I picked up the West Highland Way by Lomondside. It was my plan to follow this long distance footpath to my evening stop just beyond Bridge of Orchy some 38 miles away. Starting with a half day was designed to ease me into the trip which I felt would really begin tomorrow with a mainly mountain traverse. Even by the shores of the loch it was intensely hot and humid. I was well acclimatised, but Don was finding it unpleasant. At the end of Loch Lomond it was good to see IB, the first of many support points. Fruit, custard and plenty of liquid slid easily down. With the odd burp and slurp I jogged cautiously off, leaving Don to retire to a shady place.

****

IB: 'Decide on leisurely start after seeing Don and Mike off – Mark helps by reading and occasionally passing comments on his Dad's perception of some past events. I fiddle around. Sometime before midday I peer upwards through binoculars to possibly catch a glimpse of my man; too murky.

Depart after midday on lengthy, circuitous drive... Mark tries for fish and chips... long wait.

At Inverarnan walk out to support point. Try to avoid thinking about how many hours I have spent thus, anxiously waiting, but the joy of meeting usually compensates by far. Surprised when Don and Mike are more than quarter of an hour late. Don looks very hot... Retrace steps to van... concerned about getting to next support point on time, so bundle Don in and drive round. Fix everyone up with eats... Don noticeably silent. At the next support point M appears a little early wearing his standard mask of cheerfulness.

****

MIKE: The West Highland Way follows easy ground. I was trying to be a wheel, rolling along without expending energy, impossible but a useful strategy. Meeting with Mark near Crianlarich broke the monotony as for him the route was new and he is still young enough to enjoy running for its own sake. On the endless track parallel to the railway and the A82 I perceived that my 'roll like a wheel' strategy was not working so well. Perhaps I had developed a puncture? My legs felt like planks, furthermore, I was bored with the West Highland Way. I started to look forward to the hill day tomorrow, carefully ignoring the proposed 3am start. As I grind to a halt at Inveroran, near the foot of the Black Mount Munros, I become aware that it is obviously an evening on which it is a delight to be a midge.

****

IB: 'As we arrive at Inveroran the last of the breeze dies and... we all have to beat a major retreat... against clouds of midges. We seal ourselves in the van which becomes a sauna. M comes and suffers similarly. We prepare our gear for an early start. I have been subconsciously psyching myself up for tomorrow, one of my chosen big hill days. To my surprise I manage to persuade M to start at 3:30 rather than 3am (in the dark).'

****

DAY 1: *Ben Lomond-Inveroran*; 38 miles, 5,065 feet; 9 hours.

DAY 2, MIKE: After a midge infested night we awoke to a midge infested morning. Staggering about in the half light at 3:30 my usual sparkling morning spirits were a little muted. Even worse was the early realisation that I was not climbing well. As I intended to traverse the Black Mount, cross the Mamores ridge at its highest point and tootle over the Four-thousanders of the Ben Nevis group this was not reassuring.

It took 2½h of plodding effort to climb Stob Gabhar but above 2,500 feet

Mike on Aonach Mor, with Ben Nevis behind.

Knoydart traverse, Ladhar Bheinn.

there was a cold breeze and after making a route-finding error in mist (too much reliance on 'feel for the country') I began to revive nicely. There was a further boost for we rose above the mist on Clach Leathad and enjoyed that 'early morning mountains belong to me' feel. However, by Meall a'Bhuiridh it began to spot with rain. Above the White Corrie empty ski chairs came clanking down and we discussed the ethics of hitching a ride down to save my knees.

****

IB: 'We left the ridge in clear conditions but were soon enshrouded in mist. I held my peace, having in the past been told not to interfere with navigation unless absolutely certain (which I never am). However, eventually I started to grumble. We continued until it was obvious we were wrong. Nothing for it but to descend, then reascend... M started going better and better, while I sagged (characteristic responses for each of us to a route error). We could see our final peak... encircled by tremendous valleys with perfect, smooth, glaciated curves, some with large areas of polished rock slabs, magnificent... M cheered up noticeably.'

****

MIKE: At the van it was raining steadily but having picked up I felt quite cheerful. After a quick brew I trotted along past the Kingshouse Hotel to the bottom of the Devil's Staircase. The track from here to Kinlochleven is an old Military Road and part of the West Highland Way. Here I was joined by Don always keen to extend his knowledge of hills and paths. The weather stayed grey and low cloud bundles gave evidence of heavy local showers. From its highpoint at almost 2,000ft the track drops to sea level in about three miles of stony going, an ideal stimulant for knee pain. To the north lay one of the major objectives of the trip, the Nevis group of Fourthousanders. First, however, the barrier ridge of the Mamores must be crossed.

****

IB: 'Mark and I drove down Glencoe... It was not long before it started to rain with an almost monsoon-like quality. I took stock. While rather perturbed that M did not seem to be climbing well... I was secretly relieved since it meant I stood a good chance of surviving my chosen support sections without undue pain and suffering. Miscellaneous bitter thoughts about being condemned to traverse the highest hills on the route in poor conditions; attempts at feeling heroic. Park with great care close to where West Highland Way joins road. M and Don emerge elsewhere. Fortunately no reproaches... Pack two pieces of choc for me, three for M and one spare.'

****

MIKE: Some time ago IB had chosen to accompany me on the long hill sections of Day 2. She's quite a nifty navigator too, providing she can summon the courage to tell me when I'm wrong and providing I listen. My plan was to cross the Mamores ridge via Na Gruagaichean and Binnein Mor, the highest of the group at 3,700 feet. I hadn't reconnoitred the approach from Kinlochleven so was pleased when orienteer Blunk suggested a wee path through the vegetation. The path failed miserably in head high sopping bracken set around 90 degrees. Naturally, I cursed IB roundly.

Despite gradual upward progress the peaks looked grey, inhospitable and out of reach. Quite a way up we passed an expanse of brilliant white foxgloves looking beautiful but out of place. At last I glimpsed the north west ridge of Na Gruagaichean about 700 feet above the wandering path. Losing patience I headed straight for it, some bulls are best grasped firmly by the nettles. I kept forgetting that we had started from sea level; the ridge still rose another 750 feet to the summit. It was then less than a mile and 600 feet of ascent to Binnein Mor, but it was now misty and rather wet. After probing around in the cloud cap I decided we were where we should be and selected our downward ridge to Glen Nevis. IB, perhaps unnerved by her earlier failure, seemed a little unsure. Soon, however, we heard voices and an unlikely couple with a dog came clambering up towards us. As everyone knows, if you see someone else around, it means you are going the right way. Observing IB I must say I was faintly surprised to see how quickly the science of orienteering gave way to ancient folklore.

The descent was another bit I wished I'd reconnoitred. It was desperate and I eventually fell into a hole or something which caused astonishing pain to my bad knee. Still, we were down and, urged on by midges, addressed ourselves to the four Nevis Fourthousanders – soon be home now!

****

IB: 'Leave Kinlochleven on unreconnoitred line, soon in waist high dripping bracken. Dissatisfied noises from M. Trod does not seem to be path shown on map... bash through deep vegetation... M rumbling very loudly. I refuse to feel guilty, it was not my responsibility to recce the route. Proceed peacefully and amicably... into the heart of the gigantic Ba Choire. Scale emphasised by clouds swirling round Mamores ridge... locate path to col. M climbing slowly but with great determination. To my surprise he chooses a short-cut... a yet steeper gradient on grass, his pet hate. Obviously have no idea what is going on inside the man.

Pick our way over two peaks. Reflect how confusingly contorted the main ridge line seems when compared to the map representation. Cloud cap sitting on highest peak. Clamber past large cairn... then aréte ends surprisingly. Fiddle with map. I am dubious (as ever) but soon we hear voices...

a couple of casual walkers, damp but enthusiastic. They seem the type that, while strictly speaking foolish, I nevertheless prefer: apparently no navigational aids, no stout walking gear, just common sense, determination and a love for the hills to guide them. I feel a little foolish clutching map. As we descend the Aonachs and the Ben beckon. First the interminable descent... this is another section that needed a recce.'

****

MIKE: We approached Aonach Beag via a line I had descended one time and seemed to remember as being reasonable; I seemed to be mistaken. The vegetation was a good deal higher than my rate of climbing. There again, 3,000ft from glen to summit is not to be sneezed at. At last the final steep pull. Suddenly it felt good to be up high with the lofty traverse to Aonach Mor inviting a swift flight in the biting wind. Descending to the col below Carn Mòr Dearg we sheltered and took light refreshment – feelings of comfort and desires to linger. Such feelings are to be resisted, at least they are if the flesh is to be subdued and the spirit released.

Off and up once more then, the long dreaded pull up to Carn Mòr Dearg beckoned with stony fingers. Surprisingly, my climbing legs rejoined me somewhere here. The boulder hopping along the Carn Mòr Dearg Aréte was very stimulating and likely to be more so should one's hop skip a boulder. No mishaps, but time was slipping away and the Ben Nevis boulder field seemed interminable. IB appeared to be experiencing some fatigue now. I suspected the troublesome head wind and a slight food shortage. I can go well on very little sustenance but she insisted I should eat all my ration. However, after some tedious argument we made a compromise.

I was not too concerned that it was 21:15 by the summit. I now had one of my major sub-objectives in the bag and, after all, you can zip down a mountain in no time, can't you? Hmmm, a big mountain, the Ben. And I wasn't going the short way down either. Mark and Don were waiting at Victoria Bridge near the distillery. When reaching the lochan (Meall an t-Suidhe) it was very dim and we still had to descend 2000ft and cover around three miles. Of course we didn't have torches, no incentive to beat the dark if you have a torch. At some kind of track I made an inspirational mapless guess. Just as faith gave way to faint hope charity appeared in the form of walkers heading upwards, to the CIC hut I guess. They said we should cross the golf course. Here, apart from small, well spaced potholes the going underfoot was, naturally enough, good but we had little idea of our overall direction. Reaching a railway line we pottered along it with me reassuring IB that no trains would be using it at this time of night.

Eventually we reached a likely looking gate and had just got through it when something bearing a suspiciously close resemblance to an express train nearly removed my rucksack. We looked around curiously, large court-yards, large sheds, delightful smell. Of course! The distillery (sadly locked). Soon we were at Victoria Bridge but, panic – no van. We were two hours overdue but surely they wouldn't be off alerting the Mountain Rescue so soon? No need to worry, they'd parked over the road and were concerned but not as yet alarmed. By the time I'd eaten it was nearly midnight and there were still ten miles of path and road to go. I seemed to have made a miscalculation in my plans somewhere. However, I now felt as if I was get-ting into my stride and this decided me to plod on for a while. Mark and Don's cheery welcome had made me quite enthusiastic.

****

IB: 'I cling to M's memory of a descent down the line we are now to ascend [*up Aonach Beag*] as being 'not bad'. I am not really surprised when things continue as tortuous as ever. M's memories are usually as optimistic as the man... On the shorter turf of Aonach Beag I suddenly feel weak for the first time. Am determined not to eat till summit in order to stretch my chocolate ration. The whole ridge section leading to Carn Mòr Dearg looks very dif-ferent than on previous traverses from the Ben Nevis end. Consume the last of my chocolate below Carn Mòr Dearg and give M his third piece. Teeter upwards... manage to crest Carn Mòr Dearg in reasonable style and steel myself for the last climb to the Ben... realise I am not going to manage with-out more chocolate... after inward struggle ask M for some of his. Argument ensues as pride prevents me from accepting more than a small half...

The summit of the Ben is empty. A quick glance down the gullies... I begin to prepare for sore feet. Neither can believe how long it is before we glimpse Lochan Meall an t-Suidhe. We stick to the projected but unrecon-noitred line. It is now so gloomy that M cannot see the map clearly... After the golf course we halt at a railway line. Approximately 500m beyond is a road but the intervening land is buried in bracken, bushes and small trees. Plod along railway. Thoughts along the lines of ****ing disaster loom large together with fears of high speed trains. Slowly the yellow lights of Fort William approach... Thoughts about the organisation begin to crowd in. It is 23:30 and another ten miles to the scheduled overnight camp.'

****

MIKE: After a little pressure from IB I decided to continue for only five miles to the start of Glen Loy. At least I had reconnoitred the next section. Through the scrap yard and straight along the Caledonian Canal. For the first time I used a 'walkman' and strolling along listening to my beloved Bach was a delightful experience. It was critical however, if I was to avoid a swim across, to locate a small track which would lead me through an ancient, waterlogged tunnel underneath. Tootling along I was puzzled to see what looked like a 'Pete Bland' carrier bag and an old but familiar tea towel waving at me from a bush. Too soon for hallucinations, surely? Then I chuckled, signals left by my faithful support and, sure enough, here was the vital track. Bach having concluded I gave a fine rendition of *Fee–Fi–Fo–Fum* as I splashed through the echoing tunnel. My chortles were hastily subdued on meeting IB at the Glen Loy road – the lads had got their heads down along the glen. At 1:40am she looked tired and obviously needed to do the same. We grabbed a plateful of stew and bedded down in the van. Before gentle Morpheus took me to his bosom I reflected that I'd been going for 22 hours and still hadn't made my objective; the usual embarrassing discrepancy between ambition and ability. Still, I'd had a good day.

****

IB: 'Don and Mark are cheerful despite understandable anxiety... our descent was not fixed so they would not even have known where to start looking. I made another mental note never to let such a logistical slip happen again... Glen Loy, send Don and Mark through tunnel to leave markers on tow path. Tunnel is ankle deep in water, feel guilty. They come back pleased with their efforts.

I start cooking something. I am very displeased with bad scheduling. How can anyone hope to do four miles per hour plus twenty minutes per 1000 foot on a day comprising a traverse across the Mamores ridge at its highest point, the 4000ft peaks above Glen Nevis and three Munros above Loch Tulla besides? The whole day seems a shambles, finishing impossibly late, keeping support up waiting. When M arrives he seems slightly high... quite enjoying a dark, entrancing stroll along the canal. I suppress irritation. Unfortunately it is vented with force on the unlovingly slapped up meal that even I, despite great hunger, find tasteless. M complains of milk shortage which I resent. Don and Mark only bought two pints... another failure. Approve of M's decision to stick to the full four hour sleeping time.'

****

DAY 2: *Inveroran-Glen Loy* (via Black Mount, Mamores, Ben Nevis); 44 miles, 16,500 feet; 22 hours.

DAY 3 MIKE: The day started with a fateful decision. A late finish meant a late start (6:30am) and there were five miles of road before I could even get on the hill. IB knows I hate road and there was a calculating gleam in her eye when she suggested I use her bike. It was a hard decision. After all, there is a Bengali saying 'The sight of a horse makes a traveller lame.'

However, I had overplanned. I couldn't realistically hope to improve my overall mph much and I had an uncomfortably certain feeling that if I played out for another 22 hours I would face a mutiny. I eased stiffly onto the bike and entered a new world. Magic! The tarmac slid effortlessly beneath the wheels and the morning mists kissed my placid brow. Why hadn't I made this part of the plan? Imagine how much more I could have aimed for!

****

IB: 'I wake reasonably fresh, M rather bleary. M decides to cycle up road. I am overjoyed to encounter such an incredible amount of sense, particularly as it opens up prospects of shortening other tedious sections. At the road end M is cheerful and full of how enjoyable the cycle ride was. I am also glad but for more calculating reasons... it will be easier to persuade him to do more... we now seem to have arrived at a mutually agreeable mode of progress.'

****

MIKE: It was already 8am when I set off from the road end in intense heat and pursued by armies of horse flies. We took a dreadful toll on each other. They were heavily into the psychological and attritional effects of guerilla warfare, while I exercised an erratic but ultimate deterrent. The day's objective was Knoydart and its three Munros, the highest of which, Ladhar Bheinn, was my western Cardinal. First, however, I had to traverse about twelve to fourteen miles over two ridges to reach the junction of Loch Arkaig and Glen Dessarry where Mark and Don would join me. My traverse lay west then north over fine, wild and mainly pathless country. What with the heat, fulsome vegetation and accumulated fatigue, my progress was slow. It was lunchtime (1:30pm) by Glen Dessarry and there was now insufficient time to complete the 30 miles Knoydart traverse in daylight. Various messy options were considered. Eventually, I went for the simplest; stay here, rest and put in a long day tomorrow. With apprehensive thoughts about losing my grip already I enjoyed a lovely bathe and wash in the river, endured a points gaining exercise accompanying IB on a shopping trip and had a refreshing afternoon nap.

****

IB: 'Don describes another poor night (midge-ridden and stifling). He spends some time checking over the bicycle... Afterwards he settles down to a snooze in the van. Mark is up and stirring. Don sleeps until I pack rucksacks on top of him – make a mental note we must let him sleep as much as possible.

Glen Dessarry: Don and Mark start getting ready immediately, keen to go. No sign of M. I wander out with camera... M appears in an unexpected place... he reluctantly goes back onto bridge for photo. After deliberation he decides it is too late to traverse Knoydart. Don and Mark having psyched up decide to bag Corbetts. I ruefully embrace the prospect of driving out to Spean Bridge for supplies. M nobly offers to come with me.

On the way back the hills surrounding Loch Arkaig were backlit; staggered outlines of mountain spurs in subtly varying tones of grey plunged into the glistening lake. I knew when I got back supper would have to be cooked and hence on and on... no chance to relax before bedtime... Don and Mark were sitting by the river, full of a glorious afternoon's walking and a possible sighting of a golden eagle. They exuded a warm glow that cheered me for a good while... I finally decide to waken M and coerce him to eat. Rather selfishly I reflect I cannot go to bed till he has dined... I suppose these journeys are conceived so that everything is subjugated to the runner... Fortunately, M ate with much appreciation and, simple soul, I was happy again since everyone had praised the stew. Sleep at last, with a gentle breeze wafting through the tent.'

****

DAY 3: *Glen Loy-Glen Dessarry* (East end; via upper Glen Loy, Choire Reidh, Glen Camgharaidh, Strathan); eighteen miles (five miles by bike), 3000ft; seven hours.

DAY 4 MIKE: In retrospect this was a big 'test' day. After struggling against time on Day 2 and 'failing' on Day 3, today might decide the validity of the whole concept.

At 4am the still grey dawn was hushed and misty. We had a gentle nine mile stroll on stalker's paths to Sourlies bothy at the east end of Loch Nevis. Here it was gloomy and dank and at 6:45am no one was stirring, except, that is, for a cloud of patient midges. On the bridge across the River Carnach sat two stoical turbanned cyclists, eating one breakfast and providing another. We started heaving sweatily upwards, endless zig-zags on a perfectly graded stalker's path, sea level to nearly 2000ft in a straight mile. I detected a lag in conversation. And then it got steep and pathless, 1300ft in half a mile. We struggled grimly on the treadmill; a hot, sticky, impenetrable wall all round. I seemed to be getting lightheaded. A white glare spread across my eyes then, incredibly, we burst through the cloud into a different world.

The transition was so sudden it almost surpassed our belief. The blue sky burned our vision and the brown summit of Meall Buidhe appeared to be carved from mahogany. All those who toil on misty slopes know the sensation and few other rewards match it. I was glad because if I had been offered any gift to bestow on Mark and Don, it would have been this. Our spirits soared and we dashed to the summit as if we had wings on our heels.

Descending towards our next peak, Luinne Bheinn, we once more plunged into mist, but this was now merely a game to test our navigation. After much intricate weaving we again emerged to sunlit upper pastures and turned our gaze north and west. There stood my western Cardinal, Ladhar Bheinn, one of the most beautiful in shape and location of all Scotland's mountains. And hard won by any route, though surely our approach could not be bettered? The descent to Mam Barrisdale and subsequent climb to Ladhar Bheinn has the merit of requiring constant care and vigilance. Having prevented Don from trotting south west down an inviting ridge (probably in pursuit of a Corbett) we at last stood on the imposing summit crest. Around us lay the sea and we soared high as above a burnished shield. Some places fix power and below our feet was a focal point. Then out along the splendid north east ridge where, aptly, Mark found what we decided was an eagle's feather.

The ridge was too short and the descent into the burning depths of Coire Dhorrcail too long. After plunging into rock pools we crossed above the sands of Barrisdale Bay. We were well grilled on the tough six mile traverse above Loch Hourn. The wonderful day bore us along but, while Don and Mark were winding contentedly down, I was attempting to psyche up for a hard finish. Suddenly, I got the boost I needed. Perched on a rock was IB and beside her stood my old buddy John ('Navigator') Richardson. I had thought to see John and number two son, Sean, further north at the day's end. They had, however, chosen to brave the narrow 22 mile drive in by Loch Quoich and now I would have both John and IB with me for the eight hilly miles to the A87.

****

IB: 'Reveille at 3am... I try not to waken too much. Turn restlessly despite myself until final slam of van door and retreating voices... note time and doze off. Wake to sound of two motor vehicles, loud conversation and dog yapping. Reluctantly leave very comfortable bed... Decide to spring clean the van... pack up everything, swatting eighteen horse flies. More cars bump up the track disgorging fully equipped walkers waving binos.

The single track road to Kinlochhourn is amazingly long... Pleased to spot grey van complete with John and Sean. Leisurely lunch of left-overs. Sean whizzes round on bike, John reads newspaper. Walk out; too early, as usual. John joins me and we chat amiably. Finally spot figures... All cheerful and rather hot. Very relaxed support stop. M pleased to have bagged another key section and happy to see John.'

****

MIKE: The section over to the day's finish involved two stiff climbs. On the first of these we all enjoyed following the old stalker's path to the remote lochan on the bealach of Coire Sgoireadail, a quintessential Highland location. However, the second climb was up and over the Cluanie ridge. This time the ascent was compressed into less than a mile. I began to realise I'd made a mistake, my schedule gave 1,750ft of ascent for the whole section; it should have been for each climb! Then, at the col John strongly advised another 400ft up Sgurr Beag to attain a good spur down. What a way to test a friendship! In the last of the light I tottered through deep vegetation and dense midges to the refuge of the van. Across the road tomorrow's first ascent leered at me horribly.

****

IB: 'Conversation shortened the climb to the first col. Looking across to the last high col of the day finally clinched my growing suspicion that M had made a calculation error... 1750ft, not 750ft were yet to come. John forged ahead. M exuded such stoic determination I would have gladly carried him up. After a small eternity we reached the col. We had to climb again to Sgurr Beag. If I had been M, I would at this point have had a little weep. Another black mark for lack of reconnaissance. At A87 we were greeted by the usual swathed and hooded figures. In the hermetically sealed van with the stove on, the atmosphere dense with fly spray and mosquito coil smoke, we were in for another sweaty evening. M and John were yattering cheerfully while I was trying to work out how much cycling we could foist on M the next day.

****

DAY 4 : *Glen Dessarry-A87* (via Knoydart); 38 miles, 12,550 feet; eighteen hours and six minutes (03:44-21:50)

DAY 5, MIKE: Today was a 'journey' day. No summits but paths and tracks reaching north to ancient Torridonian sandstone and the fairy mountain An Teallach. But first I had to get into position at Kinlochewe over 40 miles away.

Off alone at 4am, still dim and the steepest climb so far; 1,800ft compressed into less than a mile. Slowly the systems awaken as the blood circulates. Mist slides in beneath my feet blotting out sleeping friends. At last the col on the Five Sisters ridge. How beautiful is this ridge in the pale morning sun, so still and quiet, I should be following it along its crest and, for once, I lose faith in my journey. But the die is cast and plans confirmed. Down now into a vast bowl, mind pleasantly occupied in picking a line through wild ground.

The plan is to pick up the bike at the Glenlicht Hut but there is no bike there. I expect I'll meet Mark with it very shortly. But no bike, no Mark. I stop and nearly go back several times. Four miles on at Morvich the mystery is revealed; wanting to ensure everyone's rest except her own, IB took the bike out. Unfortunately, she left it at the end of the track above the hut and not at the hut as arranged. There were harsh words. Tolerance is lowered by fatigue and few have ever accused me of tolerance at the best of times. Fortunately, humour soon replaces anger.

After a couple of miles on John's super bike I headed cross-country from Dorusduain to Glen Elchaig. It was lovely to go high again, to go once more into shining light and emptiness. Wading the Elchaig I met Sean with the bike and first bumped then skimmed the four miles to the next support point at Killilan. The day was waxing hot.

****

IB: 'More murky twilight. I calculate when to wake Mark to drive him round to take bike to Glenlicht House. Suddenly it occurs to me that if I set off early, I can do the job, thus ensuring all the others get as much rest as possible. Leave bike at track end, above bothy but clearly visible. Walk back rewarded by surreal glimpse of Five Sisters suddenly clearing; floating, illuminated orange in the rising sun on a bank of cloud; incredibly high; no need to travel to the Himalaya.

M arrives, having missed bike; get large earful, aggravated by Mark confirming he wouldn't have minded getting up. Feel cornered, but temper soon subsides. Sean rushes off to retrieve bike. He returns in record time having run all the way out and cycled all the way back without getting off. Don't know whether to be more amazed at his or bike's survival. At Killilan I relax a little and expand. Then suddenly decide M needs company on next leg to Achnaschellach.'

****

MIKE: Although the day contained no Munro summits it epitomized for me the essence of the whole journey. Series of paths, tracks and open ground linked together to swing ever northwards. The route therefore became uniquely my own, crafted to carry me over this complex north west landscape to my next objectives.

With IB swatting me (and occasionally a cleg) viciously from behind we jogged and walked in temperatures in the 80s. Our route lay across unfrequented country west of Mullardoch and Monar. At Bendronaig Lodge we paused and had a reading of the Victorian newspaper used as wallpaper lining; entertaining stuff with a selection of 'breach of promise' cases written in great style by an obvious admirer of Dickens.

At Bearnais bothy we rousted out its inmate who looked suitably embarrassed at my, 'What on earth are you doing inside on a day like this?' (He was an exhausted Munro bagger; over a year later he reminded me of the incident at a Karrimor Mountain Marathon.) On the broad ridge over-looking Achnashellach we spied a familiar figure and the 'lean, bronzed, keen-eyed' Richardson strode effortlessly towards us. All together we descended to the valley, making a deliciously cold fording of the River Carron on the way.

****

IB: 'We set off into flimmering heat. I swat myself and M who protests at my vehemence; agree to give notice of impending attack. At Bearnais I read the dedication tablet and instantly forget the text again, a tribute to my weary, slightly overheated brain... On the ridge something red unbends into a familiar shape, JR, pleased we press on. At the bottom we splash through the lovely cool river. The team have been practising water sports and exploring the wire bridge and are consequently much refreshed. I perk up when M suggests a slight route change enabling a much more rapid approach to Kinlochewe, our finish point for the day.'

****

MIKE: I set off alone through the shady forest above Lair, pleasant and relaxed. Beyond the Coulin Pass the stony track winds endlessly though easily. The Torridon giants Liathach and Ben Eighe dominate the view ahead, hazy with humidity. Already I am looking forward to meeting Mark with the bike at Coulin Lodge. No hitches, there he is and the weight is off my legs as I cruise to an 'early' finish at last at Kinlochewe. Even time to visit the convenience and clean my teeth. Pity about the lumpy tent pitch; JR's revenge for over a decade of my pinching the best side at the KIMM overnight camp!

****

IB: 'At camp a happy atmosphere, M talkative. I begin to imagine he is content to remain a day behind schedule. Major preparations by Don and Mark for tomorrow: An Teallach day. Retire without need for torches, for once. M grouses about lumpy pitch – thank goodness John is to blame.'

****

DAY 5: *A87-Kinlochewe*; 41 miles (thirteen miles by bike), 8,050ft; fifteen hours twenty minutes (04:05-19:25).

DAY 6, MIKE: For once the alarm failed. Thank heavens for IB who's reflex woke her up at 4am (our agreed leaving time) despite it being her 'rest' day. Good bustle got us off at 4:30am. A large party, too: John, Don and Mark. Alternate jogging and walking saw us along seven miles of track and deteriorating path below Loch Fada. A stiff two mile heather bash at last placed us in position to start our Munro traverse towards An Teallach. The rocky ridge of Sgurr Dubh lifted our spirits into the mountain realm and soon we crested the first of the day's five Munros, Mullach Coire Mhic Fhearchair. Here, Don left us to indulge in some outlandish form of 'top' bagging. We thanked him for his preparation yesterday of today's butties and wished him well, sentiments to be entirely reversed a few hours later!

Despite the profusion of quartz boulders we managed a good descent off our next peak, Sgurr Ban. To make up for this the descent off Beinn a'Chlaidheimh ranks as possibly my worst ever. We all took independent lines and, if a good one exists, none of us found it. In the valley an occluded sun oozed a humid heat and we had a little sag at Shenavall, perhaps Scotland's most famous bothy.

With sixteen miles and three Munros behind us and An Teallach before us it was a bad time to discover Don had been parsimonious with the butties. There was scarce enough for one, let alone three hungry mountaineers. Perhaps he'd thought he was doing food for me alone? If he did, I didn't get it!

Once we had thrutched our way up Sail Liath (3,150ft) our traverse of An Teallach was rewarding. What a superb mountain! Its soaring pinnacles, truly windborne castles of the air, have an unreal, fairytale quality. And when mist boils deep within its perfect corrie, as from a cauldron, it may be understood why it is An Teallach which means 'The Forge'.

Up the second of An Teallach's Munro summits was enacted a small pantomime. You'd think a youth at least 30 years my junior would have enough respect to follow discreetly behind, wouldn't you? But where is respect for venerable white hair these days? I tried a hint; a casual, even friendly, rearward glance, a firmer step. It was ignored, his pace even palpably increased. Furthermore, he was wearing a Goretex designer jacket of a kind I could never afford. I made a cautious assessment of the state of my stomach in respect of Don's wanton disregard of my well-being, curse him too. I threw caution into the Forge and quietly slipped on my mental nostril expanders and adjusted my rear view mirror. Let slip the dogs of war! He was game, give him that, despite his fancy jacket. But by the time he reached the summit cairn I was calmly slavering over my last half inch of choc and my pulse was already down to 200bpm. Not much sense though, for he now followed us down our non-regulation descent route: 1,500ft of quartz boulders. Revenge was complete, he was forever lost to sight some 500ft down. Serve him right, pride is a nasty vice, as is disrespect for senior mountaineers.

Pausing only to slough off the day's grime in a black pool of rather stygian aspect we trotted to meet IB at Dundonnell House. Another wonderful mountain day in the bag and now only 24 miles to go to our night stop!

****

IB: 'I wake up with a guilty start, alarm set for 3:15am, it is now 3:45, 'bother'! Rouse M who comes awake instantly, steel myself for a rebuke that doesn't materialise. Doze until they depart at 4:30am rather than 4am as planned, not too bad. Get up... painstakingly anchor washing in stream and treat myself to a gentle cycle rather than a drive to the shops... Toil back uphill with a sac full of tins and gallons of milk. Sean now up; tells me troops off OK, however, they forgot maps – except Don who is doing a different route! Another slip, try not to feel responsible.

Dundonnell: Settle down to domesticity; cooking stew; tidying up; draping washing. Sean tries mending tent pole; succeeds at cost of lacerated finger. Don arrives, very cheerful and full of beans. Pack camera and walk out along track... final look at map, suddenly spot M intends footpath further north. Panic! Fling everything in van and drive back towards footpath.

Mike running into Glen Shiel, Sgurr na Sgine behind.

Team arrive after 20 minutes very cheerful; little stories about incidents on An Teallach and major digs at Don for parsimony with the sandwiches. Since I alone have traversed the next section, I decide to accompany M. Try to keep him moving and am so successful he walks off before me.'

****

MIKE: We left Dundonnell at 16:25. I had completed the 24 mile 'mountain' section but there still remained another 24 miles of the day's traverse. I must say that if the Devil's temptations were resisted with the vigour with which my friends resisted the temptation to accompany me at the end of the mountain day the world would be a better place. Fortunately, IB was keen to take over the two-legged baton. We both enjoyed the tenuous path through rock and heather to Inverbroom, I basking in the after glow of a large, tasty meal and IB pleased to demonstrate canny memory for a tricky route. After Inverbroom I launched myself upwards into the desolate, lonely country west of Seana Bhraigh. I love the feeling of being on my own with evening coming on, vast tracts of truly open ground before me, a line to be crafted, fatigue, not to be resented but treasured as memory of a recent traverse and, waiting for me, good friends, good food and a comfortable mattress. Although I was alone I did not feel alone, I may have been tired but I felt strong, and the moors flowing around me like the sea spoke of home.

With guesswork inspired by previous reconnaissance I picked up paths and tracks leading to Strath Mulzie. Once the need for navigational acumen was removed, the way became gradually more monotonous. Settled into a jog/walk routine I was astonished when Sean suddenly appeared clattering round a corner three miles sooner than expected. He assured me the track was good from here on and then ran off cheerfully back towards Oykel Bridge. I soon proved him wrong and was left pushing the damn bike. Wondering why I hadn't passed him, Sean returned and received a (small) earful. Thereafter, until the track improved, he rode and I jogged. I still didn't outpace him when eventually mounted as darkness and rain swept in making me feel most insecure. At least we had not transgressed the pumpkin hour, it was 23:30 when we reached a slightly anxious IB at camp.

****

IB: 'The route to Inverbroom offers a stunning prospect back to the An Teallach massif. Many pinnacles can be distinguished and the white quartzite boulder cones gleam against the overcast sky. M still riding high on the An Teallach wave. Particularly pleased to tell me how he 'burnt off' another, not very perspicacious walker.

Inverbroom: M rather circuitously and clumsily explains details of bicycle support. 'Beginning to slow down a little' I register. Make doubly sure he has maps and compass. Am never very happy about letting him go out alone when a little vague... Settle down to another long drive. Troops opt for fish & chips at Ullapool instead of stew at Oykel Bridge – feel irritated. Find shop selling Calor Gas but can't buy because person required to unlock store has gone home; more irritation. Mooch around shop again, unable to form plan as to what to buy. Emerge still ill-humoured.

Oykel Bridge: John already pitching camp. Sean and John cycle off to meet M. Don turns in. John returns – punctured! Mark drops hints about the pub, but I click into worrying mode and (tactlessly) send John and Mark out to explore possible cyclable route to Benmore Lodge for the morrow. Want to retire but can't until M comes – resent waiting. Amble out to prevent route finding error. Soon two torches appear, Sean jogging alongside the bike... John returns – only limited success. I feel sorry to have cajoled him out at the end of a hard day. We all retire rather late.'

****

DAY 6: *Kinlochewe-Oykel Bridge (via Fisherfield)*; 48 miles (six miles by bike), 13,270 feet; nineteen hours (04:30-23:30).

DAY 7, MIKE: This day was to be both a literal and metaphorical turning point on the journey. Cardinal Ben Hope would today receive my obei-sance, after which only Cardinal Keen remained inviolate. However, five and a half days had gone with 227ml covered while there were only four and a half days left in which to cover 290 miles. That lazy day at Glen Dessarry had taken its toll. Clearly, in order to raise the daily average from 41 miles to 64 miles, velocipedic assistance would have to be recruited.

Almost the first thing the velocipede did was to crack me painfully be-hind the knee as I carried it through a section of double-plough separating tracks to Benmore Lodge. Any lingering intention to climb Ben More Assynt en route to Loch Shin was dispelled by low cloud and frequent showers. It was quite a relief to swap the boggy descent to Glen Cassley for the power station road up out of it. At the top I met Mark with the bike and fairly flew the six miles with their 1,000ft of descent to a second breakfast at Loch Shin. John had arrived with some nice fresh bread which he kindly shared with us. I noticed Don was looking rather *hors de combat*, draped horizontally across van seats and not registering my arrival (nor anything else). Another five miles on the bike then off on good running tracks feel-ing strong and determined as the sun at last broke through. However, after ten miles of track I was pleased to swap hoof for saddle on the two miles of road to Altnacaillich below Ben Hope.

With John and Sean for company I ascended Ben Hope with a growing sense of anticipation and urgency. At last we stood together on the north point. Vast, translucent skies curved over us, deep moorland grasses billowed in the wind, a sense of space and freedom lay all around. A feeling of fatigue I certainly had but above all I was aware of gratitude, joy and utter contentment. Turn for home then, still about 250 miles left and the hours dwindling.

****

IB: 'Grey start, M cycles off. I wake Don to help in bike shuttling routine. He is fairly quiet and grey as the dawn. I try to organise all the things I must remember into a plan for the day. They refuse to be ordered and keep popping up... rouse Mark. Drive to Lairg for supplies, then drop Mark to take bike out. John arrives with new gas bottle and Don asleep in back. M arrives and asks for things I do not have; annoyance. We pack up and John leads the way back driving inordinately fast. When we arrive I discover he wanted time for a snooze before going up Ben Hope since he intends to return home this evening. I am disappointed about this. Sean volunteers to stay but the fewer occupants in the (remaining) van the better. I feel guilty at being brutally honest.

M arrives. He is obviously hurrying, trying to regain his lost day. He resents me trying to nail him to giving estimated times of arrival. Worry about Don, still dead to the world; should he return with John as well? I depart in very ill humour towards Tongue, a 50 mile round trip, to complete the shopping. So far this journey has been brisk but relaxed, a style to my mind much preferable to the frenzied haste surrounding record-breaking attempts. I muse; it dawns on me that M will want to push on over Ben Klibreck. Mark had a big day yesterday and with Don ill, I will have to turn out for hill support. I am tired. Team arrives, tales of superb views on Ben Hope – I wish I could have come.'

****

MIKE: John's super bike came into its own on the twelve miles from the foot of Ben Hope to Altnaharra. With a tail wind I was topping 30mph in places. Intoxicated with speed I skidded to a stop in the village. Suddenly and too late I remembered the toe clips. Eschewing further displays of style I opted instead to demonstrate the law of gravity.

My hard pace now gave me the chance to claw Ben Klibreck into the day's total. There were four hours of daylight left and the van could get out to Dalnessie, seventeen miles away on my route. The way beyond Klibreck was rough but I had been over the ground and discovered old paths threaded most of it. As further incentive to hurry I decided not to take a torch. In retrospect, I should have gone alone. I enjoy the extra challenge of solo travel in committing circumstances but IB seemed set on accompanying me and I didn't realise how tired she had become.

Waving farewell and thanks to John and Sean we set off at 17:45 feeling determined and cheerful. What was intended as a helpful discussion on the role of support soon exposed my fatigue weakened tolerance. A blazing row was mercifully extinguished by a prolonged, bitterly cold and vicious shower. Having opted for thin cagoules this was worrying; if it continued we might not reach Dalnessie. Fortunately it did not and a stumbling descent at last restored circulation. The country south of Klibreck feels truly remote and the sense of journey again became strong as we threaded between Lochs Choire and a'Bhealaich to tread long forgotten stalking paths.

Worried to find that we had still nearly ten miles to go and less than two hours of daylight I walked hard and jogged bits of uphill. Still unaware of her overall fatigue I did not understand IB's resentment of my urgency. At last the boggy col, but over five miles to go and dusk hovering. Off I go, careless of energy. This provokes IB into another outburst and my comment that Mark will be keeping an eye open for us brings accusations of exploiting the support. I reflect that this is a perfect spot to commit undetected murder then clamp my lips shut; I'm exhausting valuable reserves.

Kind Providence who sent the vicious shower now sent a perfect peacebringer; not a dove but an otter. Suddenly IB called softly and pointed. There, on a boulder in a stream was a superb animal, the first otter I'd ever seen but unmistakeable. We regarded each other for a while, then with lithe agility it leapt from the stream, crossed an isthmus and vanished in a dark pool leaving no ripple but peace between us; bless the wild things.

And Mark fulfilled my faith in him. A welcoming light gleamed through the dark, guiding our weary footsteps over the last and most awkward ground. I said nothing. I hadn't asked him to do this and actions speak better than words. After the drama I felt suddenly drained. A short meal, then we staggered to the tent shaking with cold and feeling exhausted. Had I blown it?

****

IB: 'For some reason I do not want to do this leg over Ben Klibreck, I am having an anti-day. Ascent fades under criticism from M. I am aware of some truth in it. But how can I be at fault by trying too hard? Petty detail argued to pieces. Very wet, heavy rain starts. Did not expect sudden cold. Scramble towards loch, M follows slowly downhill... M is pushing on any flat or half reasonable going. Now slow jog even on uphill path. I am stubborn and unwilling. If we are not going to finish in daylight after all, why bother hurrying? Of course, root cause is my fatigued legs. Angry words. I launch strong attack on M for exploiting support. Break in communications. No idea how to retrieve situation. Contemplate but dismiss total strike. Then, something in the stream, an otter! Together we watch the nimble, lovable creature play in a rock pool, shoot out suddenly, skip briskly across shingle and dive under a deep bank. Gone with it is my antagonism.

Gloom is setting in rapidly. I am unprepared for the sheer interminable scale of the valley we are in. Even gloomier. Silence now full of concentration. A tin shack appears – a landmark for M, only three kilometres left but no improvement in path. Then I glimpse a figure and a light; Mark come out to guide us in. Conflicting feelings; relieved to see him but logistical mind protests he would have been better off sleeping.

We reach van; Mark puts on stew and retires, I sag. Pull myself together when M comments. He too is weary but has clawed back a section. I say something about making up more time tomorrow although I really could not care less. One hundred yards to the tent in inky blackness and a chill breeze seems a very long way.'

****

DAY 7 : *Oykel Bridge-Dalnessie (via Ben Hope, Ben Klibreck)*; 77 miles (34 miles by bike), 9,480 feet; eighteen hours and 35 minutes (04:20-22:55).

DAY 8, MIKE: Tomorrow's another day! I felt better than expected despite heavy showers being thumped down from impressively towering mountains of cumulus. What reconnaissance I had done paid off and nowhere more than on this section to the A839 east of Lairg. I patiently nosed my way through head high vegetation knowing it led to better things. A good second breakfast and a short ride saw me improving on the recce as well as discovering a series of unmapped stone circles on my way to Bonar Bridge. The four mile cycle along the A9 caused me more anxiety than any pathless moorland could ever have done. I was relieved to be trudging across a superbly featureless example of the genre in one piece having avoided wobbling 'neath a juggernaut. The route from Bonar Bridge to Loch Glass below Ben Wyvis had been reconnoitred in snow storms, and very exciting it had been. The old stalking paths had often lain invisible beneath snow and heather, but the feet could follow them well enough.

At Strath Rusdale the team were in place. Apparently small hitches had been taking place. I couldn't quite register the details but was quite clear about continuing Wyvis-wards and that Mark was coming with me.

****

IB: 'Red edges to grey clouds. Rise, still very weary. Troops appear. Don retells his valiant efforts of the previous night to obtain permission to camp from a surly farmer. It is amazing how his winning, amiable character far outweighs his present tramp-like outer appearance, even with strangers... more rain... I attempt a reversing manoeuvre, one back wheel drops alarmingly into a ditch – stuck! Don and Mark leap out. Instead of feeling a shove, the whole back end lifts up (rear engined van!) as if by magic. Don modestly admits to this feat. I secretly wonder whether he invests some of his leisure time in powerlifting... M appears, not squashed by a lorry, thank goodness. He seems a little vague, in automated mode... Drive through private gate in Strath Rusdale as per M's instructions, thank goodness Don is there if explanations are needed. We park up. A car approaches, stops and a lady gets out. Don goes to explain. I listen dumbfounded to the BBC accents of the woman. I bet we stand no chance. Don flaps a little, then somehow he has found the right turn of phrase. The accent softens into agreeable politeness.'

****

MIKE: Ben Wyvis – 'hill of terror', apparently; perhaps this huge green curling wave of a mountain is home to bogies and hobgoblins. Its scale is enormous, emphasized by unbroken slopes of sweeping grass. I'm glad Mark is with me to confirm that it really is taking us ages to get anywhere near the summit. Earlier, we had passed Wyvis Lodge, an impressive pile despite its flamingo pink. Situated in a commanding position at the head of Loch Glass it is obviously little used, perhaps only for huntin' and fishin'; make a good rest home for clapped out club members, starting with...

The eastern corrie, Coire na Feola is remarkable. It must be rare to see grass growing so high and lying so steeply. No wonder Martin Moran (M. Moran (1986): The Munros in Winter) managed to be avalanched here. The only wonder is that snow manages to lie at all. Our descent to the A835 had not been recce'd and it was neither clear nor correctly mapped. Don had done a terrific job in identifying the best approach from the road and 'guestimating' our descent line. He had brought the bike up the track and I swept down to meet IB and prepare for the last stage.

The route now linked pleasant tracks and bits of road for twelve miles, including a crucial crossing of a hydro dam. Leaving at 20:20 we all anticipated an 'early' (pre 22:00) finish. Unfortunately, doing a rare bit of 'pedal-dancing' up a hill I pulled the back wheel askew. Then I discovered the basic tool kit I had requested to be always attached to the bike was not there. After a short but impressive temper tantrum I found a shed and unearthed a lump of iron. With this and the creative use of a boulder I 'sort of' righted the wheel. I kept the iron bar, boulders were fairly abundant. Hopping on, hopping off, clanging, cursing, pushing, freewheeling I made smooth progress and then... the bloody dam was closed for repairs! Well, I certainly wasn't going back. Draping the bike round my neck I swarmed up and over the scaffolding like Tarzan up a tree (alright then, like Tarzan's granny). The support were on the other side looking anxious; whether this was because I hadn't arrived, or because I just had, remained unclear. Anyway, the last few miles were unexpectedly enjoyable, riding to the light of the van's main beam, feeling strong and sniffing the scent from a profusion of hedgerow honeysuckle.

****

IB: 'M appears... somewhat laboriously conveys that I am to study maps to calculate whether he can complete the trip within ten days by a continuous push over the Cairngorms and Lochnagar to Mt Keen; also whether there are any cycle short cuts to the foot of the Cairngorms. I quake inwardly at the thought of 48 hours on the go at the end of eight demanding days, reason revolts... I say little and promise to do my best. While waiting I study the maps. One option will take him to Dalwhinnie fairly readily by bike but proceeding on foot from there will probably engender the continuous finish I wish at all costs to avoid. The alternative is a long (40 mile) cycle to Glen Feshie. If he gets to Feshie rather than Dalwhinnie the Cairngorms can be tackled next day after a sleep. Now, how to sell that? I rehearse arguments... I begin to hope for an early finish; only twelve cycle miles to go. We drive to wait by dam. To my horror 'CLOSED' notices are posted around it due to extensive repairs... we wait, no cyclist appears... then a figure emerges from the dusk, pushing bike... brace myself but reproaches are relatively mild. Onward to the end.'

****

DAY 8: *Dalnessie farm-Aultgowrie Bridge (via Ben Wyvis)*; 60 miles (27 miles by bike), 6,920 feet; seventeen hours and 25 minutes (05:15-22:40).

DAY 9, MIKE: The first adventure was with a stroppy bull. It hadn't been there on the recce but it was there now and obviously feeling protective of its harem. 'You can't out-run it, you can't out-fight it but, with an effort, you might outwit it.' So, give it a quick flash over here; then, tippy-toe over there, head down, behind this wall. If all goes well, stick your head through that gap and blow a razzberry; if it doesn't, you've got about 50 yards start to the gate. Time for a double razzberry and a triple ole; an early goal to provide a bit of impetus for a 100 mile day. By hook or by bike I had to get to Glen Feshie sometime in the next 24 hours, preferably tonight. The Greater Cairngorm Traverse would need a complete day and 'twere best tackled after a sleep. Today was always going to be a 'connecting' day. The barrier of Loch Ness could be passed north or south. To avoid becoming embroiled in the environs of Inverness I had chosen the latter.

The route had a bleak austerity, consisting of stony tracks over low, sombre hills. The reconnaissance of this section had been memorable. After a lean winter snow made a belated appearance in March; wet and heavy, it had not helped at all. However, having faithfully transported 'skinny' skis I thought the chance had at last arrived to use them. Visions of gliding effortlessly to Fort Augustus were rudely dispelled. In mist and driving snow I was soon navigating by pylon, as it were. I suppose the skis were helpful as I was only sinking to the knees, at least on the good bits. My rather rudimentary technique was also unable to cope with a six inch 'ball-up' on the bottom of the skis. Later, on the steeper descent slopes, I was able to refine certain principles of ski manoeuvre. Suffice to say the onset of each directional change is punctuated by a hole in the snow.

Such reminiscences allowed the miles to pass by almost agreeably. It also meant I could manage without company. Working as hard as they were, it pleased me to feel that my support could enjoy rather than endure the miles we shared. These were the 'tracks of stony dreams' and as the dreamer I was content.

A good second breakfast was followed by a twelve mile 'breeze' on the bike to Tomich for brunch. Here, none other than Bach insisted on lighting the path to Fort Augustus and his energy I always find infectious. Entertaining my mind alongside the double violin concerto was the route choice beyond. I had originally planned a challenging but interesting line from the Corrieyairack Pass to Dalwhinnie. From here the tough moorland slog pioneered by John Richardson on the 1977 traverse of the Scottish Fourthousanders would take me to Glen Feshie ready for the Cairngorms. If I reached Dalwhinnie late I would have to travel on to Feshie during the night to stay on schedule for the Greater Traverse. This would be a serious decision to make as I would then be faced with the most committing mountain day in the most fatigued condition. Providing I travelled through the night alone, it should not inflict extra hardship on the support, but somehow I didn't think they would be happy with the idea. Don and Mark I could persuade but IB would undoubtedly prove difficult.

The route IB favoured was a long (35/40 mile) bike ride from the foot of the Corrieyairack to Glen Feshie bypassing Dalwhinnie. This would save the overnight traverse, but the ethic disturbed me; so far the bike had served my route, now I might be changing the route to serve the bike. I didn't want to be tempted into a choice I wouldn't have made when strong simply because I was tired. On arduous ventures fatigue is certainly one of the factors which may be allowed to influence decisions. However, fatigue is a many faced villain, bland and rational, cruel and despairing, he will always seek to subdue the will and exercise undue influence.

****

IB: 'Another 'badly designed' day where the first section on foot is only a bit longer than the drive round, not enough to have a lie in. While motoring it strikes me that we had set off never thinking to get so far. Suddenly, the desire to finish in style awakens and smoulders away. More showers. At Erchless Castle M embarks on the first cycle short cut of the day; Don retires to a sleeping position in the back. Try to set up Mark for a running leg. He's a little reluctant and settles for more 'bringing out bike' options, but Don willing to turn out for the major haul over the Corrieyairack. At Tomich M asks again about the route options for later. I repeat my conclusions, sensing resistance I retreat. Because the trudge from Dalwhinnie to Feshie forms part of the Rucksack Club traverse of the Fourthousanders it seems fixed in M's mind. I suppose I get the wrong line by saying that starting from Feshie tomorrow would almost certainly guarantee success, i.e. portraying it as a safe option, therefore to be eschewed. I despair, bite back bitter words. Don and Mark do their best on my side. Stubbornness sets in. We all shut up and get on with the job.

Mark cycles out from Glen Moriston; Don eats then dozes; I wash up and walk out a little; M arrives well on time. If we can keep a reasonable pace going all might yet be well. Must make an effort not to slow down too much at the stops. M departs cheerfully, we make post haste to Fort Augustus... I fulfil final obligation for a weather forecast. It is bad: rain a.m. followed by brief bright interlude in the east only, then heavy rain and hill fog. I don't want to be out in that sort of stuff at night. I pray M will somehow see sense. When he arrives I relate the news. There is a pause and to my relief he changes his mind; the overnight traverse from Dalwhinnie to Glen Feshie is off. I am so glad to be rid of that long approach trudge that even the prospect of a miserable outing over the Cairngorms seems almost palatable.

After a mile M flags us down, he's spotted a chip shop and is watering at the mouth. I sigh at the delay but M's enjoyment of a relaxed hour and appreciation of the food compensates. We leave Don and M at the start of the fifteen mile leg over the Corrieyairack Pass.'

****

MIKE: Above Fort Augustus I had a lovely run through the forest on, for once, velvet grass. The forecast for tomorrow's Cairngorms was rather alarming. It was this that tipped the balance in favour of the ride direct to Feshie. The cheerful response of the team helped me bury any lingering qualms from the ethics department. Anyway, 35-40 miles of cycling wasn't a wholly soft option.

Passing through Fort Augustus I was sorely tempted and fell – upon a double mound of chips. Getting enough food down was a continual problem. So I not only ate the chips but dipped each one in a tub of margarine. Deep within there arose a chorus of rejoicing from the assembled corporeal functions. Fortified against the steady rain Don and I set off up the Corrieyairack on an old Military Road connecting Glen Mor with Speyside. As an old campaigner, Don certainly knew how to pace himself, sleeping whenever possible, he was always terrific on his chosen support legs. Marching along I felt as if we had managed to create a sanctuary of warmth and humour around us which was impervious to the weather. So effective was he that he brought me to the bothy at Melgarve nearly an hour up on ETA. Sadly, this meant we 'copped' IB at the moment she laid her head down. How she still managed a cheerful face I don't know.

At 19:40 I steeled myself for the 'big ride'. Setting off too enthusiastically down the lumpy road I hit a pothole sequence at speed. Everything except my hands flew into the air. Fortunately all parts crashed back into roughly the right places, but was that rattling noise mudguards or bones? With dear old Bach on the headphones and a westerly wind on the nether quarter I was powered by two irresistible sources of energy. Once more dusk gathered and hedgerow scents stole abroad. At Kingussie I had more chips, then onto the south Speyside road, hillier but quiet. It was now dark and my weak night vision was worsened by fatigue. IB drove behind with full headlights but the undulations made it impossible to keep a steady distance and the stroboscopic effect was disturbingly hypnotic. Now the final five miles to Achlean, turning into the wind, steadily gaining height, and at last real fatigue, heaving on the pedals, commanding patience, staying in control; made it! Walk the final half mile to loosen up. Back on schedule at last! A big day for all of us.

****

IB: 'Mark bedded down in Melgarve bothy together with the 'walkman'. To speed my stew making I switched on radio and was condemned to *The Archers*! Unhappy about the stew, not enough gravy powder left. Just starting to make myself comfortable when two wet, merry walkers appear, I sag a touch though pleased to see them. They had entertained each other famously over the pass. Weather drying up but gloomy... After Kingussie we proceed in convoy along the twisty B970. I find it difficult to maintain the correct distance behind the bike. Eyes very strained, I am mesmerized by the cone of light and the figure on the bike. The road winds interminably. If M is feeling the strain as much as I am then I have pushed him into a wrong choice. I feel as if I have anyway. He is locked into automaton mode, very determined despite fatigue. Turn into Glen Feshie, pace slows uphill. I long to pack M and bike into van and have done, sod the ethics, this endless crawl through the dark is inhuman.

We leave the woods. M dismounts to walk in. We park and pitch tents, it is midnight. M is very clear and contained. Obviously worried about the morrow, he gives precise instructions. Earlier, with Don, he had worked out a (fail safe) strategy to escape from the tops should the need arise. Mark volunteers to do sandwiches, I am too weary to be bothered. M is itching for an early start but I put in a strong plea for the statutory four hours, I fear collapse otherwise. At 1:15am we retreat to flapping tents.'

****

DAY 9: *Aultgowrie-Glen Feshie*; 97 miles (52 miles by bike), 6,825 feet; eighteen hours and 45 minutes (05:15-24:00).

DAY 10, MIKE: Despite my desire for an early start to this big day IB had insisted (wisely, I think) that I should have the full four hours scheduled sleep. This meant a rather late start, 6am, but what was infinitely worse was that for the first time I slept badly; that damn weather forecast. I was worried that over-committment might lead me to take my two less experienced companions, Mark and IB, into rash situations. In retrospect this was unjustified. I should have had absolute confidence in their judgement and resourcefulness. Be that as it may, my nerves were like piano wires and my hands were trembling; this was a new experience.

On the long, high approach to Cairn Toul the clag moved in and soon we were being lashed by heavy rain driven on a penetrating wind. My body fat must have been very low by now as I felt unusually cold. Peculiar mental gymnastics led me to conclude that if this rain ended it would mean that it was only a shower and I stood a chance. If it didn't? Well, a hard decision must be made. It didn't feel like a shower, but slowly it eased, then stopped. The clag thickened with height however, and in order to motivate and occupy myself I started doing some complex navigation. It was a success, my mind became absorbed and anxiety vanished. The techniques worked too, and confidence and self-belief restored sagging morale.

With Cairn Toul at last 'in the bag' we started groping our way towards Braeriach. Somewhere beyond Angel's Peak the mist assumed a brighter radiance. Still braced for the next shower, I was incredulous when, on Braeriach, the mist receded and the sun fingered through. I can hardly describe the overwhelming change of spirits this event triggered. The clearance in Knoydart had seemed a minor miracle, but here, because it was so desperately wanted, it seemed unbelievable. Down in the Làirig Ghru we all sat in hot sunshine munching away by the infant Dee.

Even the long ascent of Macdui assumed a pleasurable aspect, especially after Mark relieved me of my sac! By 3pm we sat on Cairngorm making plans. My fail safe strategy was that Don would be waiting at the Linn of Dee ready to receive an enforced retreat from any of the 'Big Four'. If no one came by 6pm he would know the Greater Traverse was under way and drive to Invercauld further down Deeside. Mark had been complaining of a headache so it suited him to jog the fourteen miles or so down to the Linn and carry definite news to Don.

Now the four High Tops had been completed some of the earlier urgency left me and was replaced by fatigue. My food consumption was giving cause for alarm. I was scoffing bars of chocolate which seemed to be dropping into a bottomless pit with about as much effect. Leaving poor Cairngorm's desecrated summit we dropped slowly into a hallowed place; Glen Avon was suffused with golden light and a mighty peace seemed to bestow a benediction of utter tranquility on our souls.

I was now very weary indeed and had we been anywhere other than this

Near the end of the Greater Cairngorm traverse, looking back from B. Avon across the Sneck to B. à Bhùird.

most remote, wild and beautiful of places fatigue might have assumed his face of despair and counselled short options. Overcome by elemental beauty he kept quiet. We passed on, firstly over Beinn a'Chaorainn, then across the rough moor leading to Beinn a'Bhùird. As we travelled showers chased out of the west, annoying perhaps, but no; they were only part of a most magnificent setting which was now in preparation. As we rose high on Beinn a'Bhùird lower sank the sun, lower and more golden. Its radiance ignited a carpet of jewelled raindrops across the summit mosses. By the lingering of its last rays the great crags which buttress the eastern corries were thrown into sculpted relief. Impossibly high, an issue of crystal water chuckled between green banks, in symbol and reality an emblem of purity. Lulled by fatigue and enthralled almost beyond recall it took an effort to realise the journey must not end here.

Never have I been so willing to ascend a slope and never so weary as on the flanks of Ben Avon. But it submits to time and after another 'Tarzan's granny' on the rocky summit tor we turn at last; turn for the long, dark path home. Twilight flowed in like a slow wave and familiar landmarks sailed quietly up to greet me, then faded silently into darkness. Poor IB too, troubled with sore feet as ever on this stony road home. Still supporting as I well knew, for I could feel an aura that would not be extinguished. Now, ahead, a solitary torch – Don guiding us in like a homely star. Gradually looser became the bands of tension and I knew I was, at times, literally asleep on my feet. I tried riding the bike on the track but my balance had gone. Less than a mile now. Better arrive on foot than on a stretcher.

The big day was over and accomplished. But not only had the bolt been shot, I'd almost certainly snapped the string. Midnight now and still not eaten, changed or prepared for the morrow. Tomorrow only Lochnagar and Mt Keen remained but the latter still lay twenty rough miles away. My dream was to stand on it before midday. What did this mean in terms of hours of sleep and probable mph? My head whirled and refused to take any further part in calculations. I made some sort of compromise with IB and fell asleep on top of the stew. Tired, happy and... almost satisfied.

****

IB: 'M and Mark seem to get into gear smoothly. I am disorganised, mind bogged down, what to pack and have I got everything? M has insisted on carrying a rucksack and his share. I cannot help thinking that if he had been going with two male companions he would have trusted them to carry all. Feel slightly hurt... Rain starts as we cross towards the base of Cairn Toul. Things are hostile but not dire; M still apprehensive and talks of decision points. Rain stops; M insists on some super-duper navigation, step counting and all. It actually works quite well, never does when I try for real. For some reason I am unduly optimistic. The mist is still thick but the wind is less strong. No real reason to cut plans yet; we potter on... Mark progresses smoothly and evenly; at the start he had been apprehensive of feeling ill. M more relaxed after Angel's Peak. He talks steadily about past Cairngorm experiences...

On the climb to Macdui I am heartened to find my legs doing well. I have had such struggles with the Cairngorms that I cling to every confidence boosting shred. M climbs slowly. Mark volunteers to take his rucksack and, to my surprise, he relinquishes it. So I was right, he shouldn't be carrying anything. On Cairngorm Mark decides to opt out, he is not weary but has a strong headache, probably lack of sleep we agree. M explains the way out to him with exaggerated care, first sign of tiredness so far. Heading towards the Fords of Avon there is more sitting down. The rot is starting, creeping up on us. Gazing south and east we identify Ben Avon and Lochnagar, shower-capped. Away in the distance is a shapely cone I am convinced is Mt Keen – the journey's end. M seems rather disinterested, maybe to him it looks a long way... Near the shore of Loch Avon we meet some reindeer, friendly beasts. One of them chews wistfully on an empty gas cylinder. M signs the book in the Fords bothy – no problem crossing the ford, a source of anxiety yesterday in view of the forecast.

On the approach to Beinn a'Bhùird showers begin to interfere – cags on, cags off. Last time we had been here was at night and my memory was of a short approach, now we seemed hardly to be advancing. Just before the plateau rim a prolonged shower set in but at North Top we had a vision: before us, brightly lit, lay the tors of Ben Avon spanned by a rainbow, in the foreground the grass glowed green, magic beyond words.

One last steep climb to Ben Avon. The air is clear and fresh and views in all directions astonishing. Conscious of time escaping I bully M into relinquishing his sac. One hour round trip to the summit and back. If we jog a little we can get well down before dark. M did not jog much and, truthfully, I was not displeased. My feet were beginning their usual complaints. Soon it became very dingy. At last discover Don with bicycle. After his restful day I have lined him up to go with M over Lochnagar first thing tomorrow, he seems keen.

The track is endless. I swear a complicated oath never to come this way again. At last the van. I am engulfed by hunger and fatigue. M practically asleep the moment he sits down. He tries to peer at the map. Our eyes are so weary even the torchlight seems dim. Despite the late hour (1am) M insists on minimal sleep, anxious to arrive on Mt Keen by midday. He seems so drugged I remonstrate, I cannot bear the thought of a zombie-like finish to such a magnificent journey. Better to finish in style and human if a little late. We compromise; the alarm is set for 3:45am, if he awakes feeling poor he will sleep on. I know he has won.'

****

DAY 10: *Glen Feshie-Invercauld (via the Cairngorm Six Tops)*; 40 miles, 10,150 feet; seventeen hours and 40 minutes (6:00-23:40).

DAY 11, MIKE: I awoke instantly as the alarm sounded. There were no doubts whatsoever. It felt almost as if the journey were freshly beginning so keen was anticipation. Our route lay through Balmoral's Ballochbuie Forest, a fine remnant of old Caledonia. Above it I knew there was a faint trod through desperate heather which would lead to better things. Like a questing hound Don settled on it. After a relatively short if painfully enforced silence we gained the height of Cnapan Nathraichean, an old friend. From here we delighted in picking a route over untamed ground to the foot of mighty Lochnagar. A fierce pull through granite boulders and we were up.

At 7am there was a quiet, shy morning light and an indefinable sense of autumn in the air. The whole gave rise to a pervading atmosphere of peace, solitude, tranquility and a sweet nostalgia. The traverse across Lochnagar lives in the memory. Don had been with me (so long ago!) on Ben Lomond. Now we shared that wonderful feeling of anticipation, electric yet calm. Time to savour the moment and the mountain, time to savour our gifts.

Running across Glen Muick in soft sunlight I could almost feel the weight of previous miles but somewhere stirred the faded memory of once having been an athlete. Not much flag waving from IB though as I'd managed to race her here. She doesn't seem to realise it doesn't matter. Nothing will stop me reaching Mt Keen in time.

****

IB: 'Cold, grey, still morning. M alert at first call, Don too. Discover M has left rucksack behind on track last night. Bang goes my chance of a little extra sleep. When I return Mark is stirring, a good sign, he must have had a reasonable night. Do not hurry. Get to Glen Muick on schedule. Visit WC; as I emerge M and Don appear, early. I am somewhat flustered, annoyed. So, despite protestations we are going to have a fast finish; would have preferred another hour in bed. Emphasize that I am unlikely to manage to both drive round and walk out to Mt Keen before midday. M estimates 11:30. I try to be enthusiastic. Don and Mark are going with him, slight pangs of jealousy. I never share the glory of the finishing leg unless it is a full 30 miles of Pennine Way over the Cheviots. Drive out of Glen Muick against the incoming tourist tide as fast as possible.'

****

MIKE: Last winter I had discovered the most superb route to bog encircled Mt Keen from Glen Muick. It goes up the 'Fairy Glen' then follows the grass flats and slowly swelling upper Waters of Mark. With Mark and Don for company an ambling approach is adopted, partly to give IB time to walk out to Mt Keen. Don ambles so well he has to be prevented from leading us on a disastrous detour. Leaving the river behind we at last strike across the moor, Mt Keen's summit an unimpressive whaleback before us. The heather steepens for the last climb of all. Mark and Don appear to be drawing off a little to one side allowing me moments of final contemplation. I stoop to a piece of white heather, an offer to Inken. On the path now, sandy granite crunching. Ahead the rocks gather themselves to mark the summit. As soon as I see them I am drawn irresistibly into a run, curiously aware that gravity still holds sway despite euphoria. Clamber clumsily to the trig point and gaze west through tears back to the Cairngorms; into wind, into sun, into the Blue Mountains; 'autumn mists and silver sun and wind upon my hair'.

After shaking hands with Don and Mark I make an effort to grasp the reality that I have actually got here, finished, made it! Mark produces a small leather bound flask of whisky, a present from Sean – bless him! We huddle out of the cold wind enjoying a nip and waiting for IB. But cold forces us down eventually. Then, a little lower, I spot her toiling up as ever, bringing a sac of clothes, food, everything except the requested camera! I pick her up and hope my hug says what is in my heart.

****

IB: 'Screech to a halt outside shop in Dinnet – shut, but man prepared to sell some milk. I explain about friends walking from Glen Muick to Mt Keen. He opens out, says he has been longing to do that but can't persuade his wife to drive round (hmm)... Arrive at Glen Lee (Invermark) after two hour drive feeling very rushed. Chain bike to fence; pack frantically; bivvi bag in case I have to wait, warm coats for all, camera in poly bag. Early walkers study my antics curiously. Set off on foot, re-think after 200 yards, dump sac, run back for bike. Spectators now very bemused. I have one hour to make Mt Keen. If the cycling is good... it isn't! I oscillate between resentment at being rushed and a desire to live up to expectations. Negative thoughts become more vehement on the approach slopes. If I meet the team halfway down I shall feel very vitriolic. On the other hand, there is obviously a fair breeze up there.

I toil up a steep section, dismayed to find another one beyond, and then the team appear. I struggle to dig out camera as M comes jogging ahead.

Have obviously forgotten camera. This strikes me as so ludicrous, the main reason for hurrying was a 'victory picture', that I burst out laughing. This wipes away all belligerent thoughts. M seems unperturbed that I have failed him at the last which promotes my carefree attitude. Mark produces Sean's hip-flask. It is a fine finish, squatting on the flanks of Mt Keen on a bright blustery day.

Elation carries us a long way back then my feet begin to burn. Mark cycles ahead to get a brew on. M tries to draw Don into a conversation about another major undertaking. Don seems a little reticent, maybe tired again. We finally arrive.

****

DAY 11 *Invercauld-Mt Keen (via Lochnagar)*; 20 miles, 6,871 feet; six hours and 55 minutes (04:15-11:10)

JOURNEY SUMMARY
521 miles (384 miles on foot + 137 miles by bike); 99,040 feet ascent; 239 hours 50 minutes (170 hours 11minutes travelling + 69 hours 50 minutes rest)
Daily average: 38.4 miles on foot + 13.7 by bike; 9,904ft ascent; seventeen hours in motion (three to four hours sleep per night).

"It   is   not   the   beginning   but   the   continuing   of   the same until it be thoroughly finished that yieldeth true glory."

chapter eighteen

CHARIOT OF DREAMS

Oh for a chariot of fire to pursue the fleeting dreams of youth! As the 'sword outwears the sheath' so the taste for adventure outlasts our capacity to indulge in it. But maybe a solo winter traverse of all Scotland's Fourthousanders done continuously and linked east to west by bicycle... Approaching 60 and rattling with arthritis I was aware that inspiration should be tempered by realism, but infirmity cannot stop your dreaming, neither should it prevent your striving.

Success would be determined by weather, fitness, skill and good fortune. The latter is often the outcome of the other three, so I concentrated on build-ing winter strength and winter skills while waiting on the weather. Snow was scarce until February, when ferocious storms deposited moderate amounts. Here perhaps was adventure, but little prospect of success. March came in like the proverbial lion – and stayed roaring. Then, with one day of official winter left, came a forecast which gave some hope, providing I could survive initially foul conditions: 'strong north-west winds, frequent hail and snow showers dying out; freezing level 3,000 feet, lowering to 1,000 feet; cloud base 2,500 feet then rising.'

Next morning in Braemar I stood despondently watching clouds like storm tossed galleons driven off the Cairngorms. Conditions on the plateaux would be horrendous. Retiring to the van I sent IB out to confirm this prog-nosis. We would have a pleasant day at lower levels instead. She returned with an enigmatic little smile, "I think you should go." I was gobsmacked, she's normally so caring. She explained, "it's already quite bright here and with an improving forecast it could be fine by the time you get high. At least you'll have tried." Not only am I getting old, I thought, I'm getting soft. "Just what I hoped you'd say," I lied.

My start point was Derry Lodge, a time hallowed entrance to the Cairn-gorm wilderness. IB strolled out with me in sunshine and snow to Corrour bothy. As we stuck our noses into the Làirig Ghru, a boisterous shower bounded down the glen obscuring the gleaming Devil's Point. The pattern was clear, a swirl of dark cloud, a lather of snow and then a short but sunny respite. What lay on the plateau, inspiration or desperation? 'If it's really bad I'll make Braeriach than come through the Chalamain Gap to the Cairngorm car park I hope!'

I left Corrour at midday and headed for Cairn Toul in sunshine reflected fiercely by new snow. Higher up old *névé* facilitated fast progress. Inevitably, a vigorous shower set in and, obviously enjoying the higher reaches, wouldn't go away. Previous showers had also been playing round the summit boulders leaving a treacherous obscuring blanket. Tottering around in the summit wind I was glad of my stick. Drop through these boulders, I thought, and you could snap your leg like a carrot.

I made the descent to the plateau both carrots intact. Views opened to the west. The humpbacks of Beinn Bhrotain and Monadh Mòr lay steel grey and white against the oblique rays of the sun. After Angel's Peak mist again cleared to reveal the awesome, heart-stopping sight of the cornices and cliffs of the magnificent An Garbh Choire. Here, in a single statement, was everything I understood and loved about Scotland in winter, everything that underlay my desire for this journey. But a brief glimpse had to suffice as spicules of ice lashed out of the north and I found myself in white-out conditions. I laid bearings to keep me well away from those yawning cliffs and beautiful, treacherous cornices. So absorbed was I with the intricacies of navigation that only belatedly did I realise I was shivering. With the temperature about –4 degrees centigrade the 40mph wind was producing an

Mike starting traverse, Devil's Point behind.

equivalent chill of around –26 degrees. I snuggled into more clothes.

The summit of Braeriach is poised atop the cliffs of Coire Brochain. I approached with caution to find black boulders looming through the whiteness and safely restoring depth perception. Visibility deteriorated on the descent, a squall tore in, dashing at me from all angles, spindrift scoured my face. The damn forecast was wrong and I'd seen nothing since Angel's Peak. I decided to quit and slid and scuttered down old snow to stand stiff-kneed back in the Làirig Ghru. To the north all was black, but head down into it and a couple of hours would see me at the van. I cast a last glance upwards. The broad flanks of Macdui soared into mist. As I looked a strange radiance appeared. If not a chariot of fire, at least a patch of sunlight. A favourite quote of Tilman's came to mind:

'Harder should be the spirit, the heart the bolder,
Courage the greater as the strength grows less.'

Munching a lump of marzipan and slugging a bottle of stream water I lurched off inspired by Beowulf's stern exhortation. In less than an hour I was just below the summit. The massive shoulder of the mountain was unrobed by the wind and shone in the light like the limb of a mighty giant. In excitement and delight I hurried to the summit where I crammed on all clothes. Then, with a relish that surprised me, I faced the beat of winter's wing. This was the quintessential moment. An uncompromising wind, innocent, elemental, savage. No margin there for fudge or fumble. Underfoot hard polished *névé*, night coming on, miles to cover, a journey to follow.

Eventually lee slopes brought soft snow, white-out and a loss of momentum. After one undershoot I located ice-bound Lochan Buidhe. From there I took a bearing for the edge of Coire an t-Sneachda. As I approached in the dark I was nervous about plunging over the edge. I need not have worried. The wind was booming over the head-wall, a ferocious cacophony of almost palpable sound. I navigated with care round the edges, using the torch only when the mist wouldn't reflect the light. A final climb on shifting snow placed me on Cairngorm summit. The first part of my trip was complete. As I swung north to descend, my shadow sprang before me. Right above the summit a nearly full moon blazed momentarily through a hole in the cloud wrack.

Within an hour, at 9pm, I was stepping into the van. 'Old Arthur' in the form of burning hips and popping knee caps caused me to consider the wisdom of continuing. After a meal and a change I thought a gentle spin on the bike would be therapeutic. The sky had cleared, the moon was radiant and in the north-west quadrant rode my chariot – the Hale-Bopp comet, if you wish; for me, that night, my chariot of dreams.

I negotiated the ice glistening ski road to Aviemore with caution. Turning onto the B9152 I rode beneath moon and comet through Kingussie, Newtonmore, then Laggan. Occasionally a pub door opened discharging a whiff of beer and an unsteady figure. Time passed, the road slid past the wheels and a quiet, cold night held thrall. After Laggan not one vehicle until the A82 at Spean Bridge. High cloud crept out of the west, but Loch Laggan lay silver yet under the moon.

At 4:30am I rejoined the van below Aonach Mòr. Now was the test of resolve, the hour at which intimations of mortality nudge, wink and leer. At 5:30 I lowered myself out and creaked stiffly upwards. *'Tho' we are not now that strength which in the old days moved earth and heaven, that which we are, we are... made weak by time and fate.'* The van, with what I thought unseemly haste, departed for the final rendezvous in Glen Nevis.

It is almost four miles and 4,000 feet to the cairn on Aonach Mòr. It was not until the better defined snowy ridge at 3,000 feet that my spirits lifted. And if they lifted then, they soared at 4,000 feet for here I came level with the summit plateau and an enchanting view filled sight, heart and mind.

It seemed as if half the Scottish Highlands lay before me. Not just the nearby Grey Corries and Mamores, but Ben More, Stobinian, the Lawers group, Beinn a'Ghlo, the Tilt hills and, far away to the north-east, the Cairngorms shone majestically. But most remarkable of all, for it rose improbably like a slender volcanic cone in striking isolation, stood Schiehallion bathed in the benediction of a golden light on this first morning of spring. It might have been the first morning of the first spring of the world. Schiehallion, the 'fairy hill of the Caledonians'...

Warm sun on my face strolling across the Aonach's mini-plateau was another benediction. Aonach Beag's slopes were glazed and a few snicks with the axe aided security. From the top I could see journey's end. The ridge of snow leading north to Carn Mòr Dearg was an unbroken curve of elegance picked out in sunshine and shadow. Beyond, the north-east buttresses of the Ben raised black ramparts in confident assertion of superiority.

Below the curving ridge I encountered more glazed *névé* and donned crampons, a mistake. Step cutting would have been quicker as the *névé* slopes were short and the snow on the ridge soft and deep. It was, however, alpine in its symmetry and impossibly beautiful. But the real mistake lay in keeping the crampons on. I had difficulties on the Carn Mòr Dearg arête in mind, but many boulders lay exposed. As I exchanged my first greetings of the trip on the summit concentration lapsed. I stumbled over a rock and described an inelegant but energetic tango downhill. This rather alarmed my fellow summiteer, who maybe thought he was about to witness an attempt on the fastest traverse of the CMD arête. Worse than this was a jarring sensation in one ankle and worst of all was a definite dent to the 'street cred'. Anyhow, I hastily removed the crampons and you may be sure my focus along the arête was pin sharp.

At half past noon I topped out on Ben Nevis. My aim of sub 24 hours for the whole trip was unrealised, but I'd gone first to last summit in just under 23 hours. Time was largely but never entirely irrelevant. The schedule generated a certain urgency which propelled the chariot towards its goal. But now a wheel fell off. A nasty twinge gave notice of my ankle's displeasure at the crampon tango. It was on my (relatively) good side too, so effectively both wheels were off. The hobble down took three hours and that retrospection of achievement, the savouring of the dream, had to wait.

Later, I sat, strapped to a bag of frozen peas, celebratory glass in hand, staring into a fire of memories, musings and still returning hopes. I recalled something I'd written years ago: 'Life is short and our fleeting dreams run fast before us.' I feel it more than ever and so it is good if even for a short space we are able to run as swiftly and catch hold of our chariot of dreams.

'How dull it is to pause, to make an end,
To rust unburnished, not to shine in use!' (Tennyson: Ulysses)

APPROXIMATE 'STATISTICS'
Cairngorm 4s Traverse - 22 miles, 7,500 feet
Lochaber 4s Traverse - 12 miles, 6,500 feet
Cycle ride - 65 miles

chapter nineteen

CLASSIC ROCK

"However, I shall not climb if it's wet."

She shook her head emphatically, "No, of course not."

"Furthermore, I may be a little lacking in energy after the Mountain Trial, so I propose nothing too desperate."

More emphatic head-shaking, a pause, then, "Where were you thinking of?"

"Gimmer," I replied nonchalantly. It made no impression.

"Where's that?"

"Upper Langdale. We're staying at RLH after the Trial, so we might as well climb from there." I pushed *Classic Rock* across. "There, look!"

"Hmm, it looks steep."

Trust her to put her finger on it. Why did she have to say that?

"Yes, it is rather steep, but, err, it's very good, rough rock."

"Those routes look wonderful."

I began to get nervous. "They are; I well remember doing 'Ash Tree Bracket' and 'Kipling Slab', must be 20 years ago. But don't build yourself up. Could well be Upper Scout Crag."

"What are the routes there like?"

'Not worth doing' I nearly replied. "Oh, quite interesting really; you could lead a bit perhaps." The more I looked at the shots of Gimmer and stirred about in the debris of ancient memories, the more attractive became Upper Scout.

"Can I read the route descriptions?"

"No, don't bother. They might make you as nervous as... They might make you nervous." It's quite true. You read a description in *Classic Rock* and as your palms start to sweat you think you've picked up 'Extreme Rock' by mistake. Then you look at the grade and realise that you have been conned. "They're all a piece of duff in there. But they can't say that; got to soup it up so people will feel challenged. Mind you, with Ken Wilson's insistence that everyone has to be seen climbing in hairy tweeds, huge bendy boots and loaded rucksacks, it probably is a challenge."

"But we'll be using EBs, won't we?"

"Sure will," I said reassuringly. "But if it's raining, forget it."

"Of course, yes," she said wistfully.

The Mountain Trial was a stinker. I was out for over seven hours. At least it had been a fine day. Unfortunately, it was still a fine evening. "Looks like we're on for Gimmer tomorrow," she said, "I'm really looking forward to it." I lurched stiffly to the window. "I'm not sure my knees will stand it. There's over 1,000 feet of climbing to reach the crag. Anyway, I think that's a cloud over the Crinkles, might be wet tomorrow." Another cloud of disappointment crossed her face and smote my tender heart. "Don't worry," I said, "it might not rain and anyway, there's always Upper Scout."

Ten minutes after turning in the patter began. In another ten minutes the patter became drumming. After an hour the voice of the little beck, long mute in this torrid summer, warbled once more through its dry stone throat. If there was conflict within my breast, it was very slight. 'No chance of Gimmer' I thought. 'Probably too wet even for Upper Scout. Eggs and bacon for breakfast, several cups of tea, then a leisurely drive home.'

"I think it's beginning to clear."

Damn! I knew I shouldn't have lingered over that third pot. And how is it that such a devout pessimist can turn so bloody optimistic just when it suits her? "Nonsense. Here, let me have a look. What! That microscopic patch of blue over Bowfell, pah! Anyway, Gimmer will be streaming and I told you, I'm not climbing in..."

Again that cloud of disappointment cast a shadow where no shadow has a right to be. "Well look, I've got an idea."

"We'll go to Scout?"

"No, it's still wet here, but the wind is from the north, that's where the good weather is coming from. There's a climb in Borrowdale that's a real classic. It's called 'Corvus' and it'll go in any weather. I took a group of students up it fifteen years ago in the wet."

"Fifteen years ago? Can you remember it?"

"Well, it's around Seathwaite. There's a prominent hand traverse on it somewhere. The first pitch was very greasy and I remember I fell off the path showing the students how to tie a bowline."

"Isn't Seathwaite supposed to be the wettest spot in England?"

"Look, 'Corvus' is 450 feet of classic rock. By the time we drive round, the sun will be brillig and the slithy toves will be gimballing. It's only Hard Diff and a bit of damp rock won't stop me. Unless you'd rather go home?"

"Oh no, it sounds great and look, the sun's shining."

The weather was coming from the north all right. Floppy clouds squelching across the sky. On their way to Langdale perhaps, Borrowdale certainly had plenty to spare. Now, where to park? I was sure we'd parked at Seatoller all those years ago. I distinctly remembered hiding the minibus key under some vegetation, then we'd returned to find that the council strimmer had been round... But someone in the Mountain Trial had recommended trying Gillercombe, hmmm, Gillercombe is miles from Seatoller. We'll try Seathwaite. We parked just below the farm. I gave the hillside the studied frown of the seasoned mountaineer and looked for a likely lump of rock. The map didn't seem to be much use; it hadn't been in the Mountain Trial either. Sour Milk Ghyll in good form. I was sure we hadn't walked past that. "Eh, what did you say?"

"I said we could ask that National Park ranger at the farm. He seems to be on a recruiting drive." A spasm of anxiety clenched my wallet. This could be a delicate business. I packed the gear making sure I left the wallet behind.

"Are you going to ask him where the climb is?"

"Just follow me and keep quiet. I'll do the talking."

A National Trust Land Rover was drawn up sporting racks of pamphlets. You know the sort of thing: smiling families tripping through verdant scenery and stately homes. A message was being preached and the NT archdeacon was trawling round the yard looking like a Jehovah's Witness in shark's clothing. I paused as if arrested by one of his fly-blown posters. I waited for him to make polite enquiries about our plans as a necessary prelude to his sales pitch.

"Ever thought of joining the Trust, sir?" The swine, the opening gambit direct. A ruthless counterstroke was needed.

"No, we're on our way to Gillercombe to climb Corvus. It's up there, isn't it?" (Waving arm in a general northerly direction.)

"Yes, it's on Raven Crag. You can just see the top of it when the mist lifts." He pointed to a very distant black smudge beyond Sour Milk Ghyll. "But perhaps you'd like to hear about the work of the Trust. Our footpath main-..."

Desperately, I parried with the cross-buttock interruption. "Splendid route. Climbed it, oh, fifteen or twenty years ago."

"...-tenance scheme. Do you know, people complement our path workers but never put..."

"...though I'm sure I didn't walk up past Sour..."

"...their hands in their pockets."

"Not everyone likes constructed paths." (Ha! Switch to southpaw, that'll wrong foot him.)

"It's really about putting something back in for all we've taken out."

So! A knee in the conscience. I can fight dirty too. "What about fox hunting on Trust land?" (Gotcha!) But I hadn't. He'd obviously fielded shots like this before. He had a good chin and a scientific defence. Time to shift ground and bring up reinforcements. "I live in Scotland now and avoid the Lakes like the plague," and, turning to my ally, "you're in the err...'

"Ramblers' Association, John Muir Trust."

"Greenpeace," I chimed in eagerly. She ignored me and went on to give a thoroughly articulate and logical account of why it was better to support the John Muir Trust than the NT. I hugged myself gleefully, but too soon.

"Well, that's the young lady. Now, what about you? Why don't you join the National Trust?"

Something snapped. "It's my bloody money she's joined with! And one other thing."

"What's that sir?"

"She's not a young lady, she's my wife!" Fancy him falling for that. With a parting smirk I spun on my heel and headed for Sour Milk Ghyll. "We'll put something in his tin on the way back," she said. I contemplated a sheep turd and said nothing.

From the top of the Ghyll we gazed across the combe. At this distance Raven Crag looked uninviting and unfamiliar. After more steady plodding particular details of rock architecture became clearer. I revised my first impression; it might be unfamiliar, but it was more repelling than uninviting. It was a black dripping mass of slimy rock. The only clean bit was right in the middle. The middle bit was the longest and steepest part of the crag. I could just see an old fence post at the top, an obvious final belay point should we ever get there.

"Do you recognise anything yet?"

Well, I think I recognise this bit of path."

"Where you fell off, you mean?"

"I mean where I gave instruction. Your selective memory betrays an unfortunate tendency for spite."

"Well, are we going to get started? It's nearly three o'clock."

"Certainly we are. I believe the weather's picking up just like I said. A bit of wet rock isn't going to stop me. Just wait till I get swarming across that hand traverse, 'it's a beaut." I paused, "You fell off the hand traverse on 'Cornflake', didn't you?" (Touché!)

Before setting off I made sure I was in the right place. A few minutes sufficed to establish there were no easier lines around: to the right perpendicular walls sprouting small waterfalls and to the left a near vertical gully choked with jungle vegetation and dripping blocks. (Still, might escape into that if the worst comes to the worst.) I was prepared for the first pitch of awkward slimy moves and, seeing only a puddle to sit in, ran out the second pitch too, also slimy. Having brought up my second, I looked round in confident expectation of the hand traverse. To the right, the perpendicular walls continued in series; to the left, the gully had become a cleft flanked by more nasty looking walls. As an old friend used to remark (before handing me the pointed end), 'no place to go but up, no place to fall but off.' So up it was on even more greasy rock. Perhaps I was demonstrating how the route would go in any conditions, but it felt more like the route was about to demonstrate that it wouldn't. At the next belay I began to have a smidgeon of doubt about if this was indeed 'Corvus', or Raven Crag, perhaps it wasn't even Gillercombe? And where was that bloody classic hand traverse? I remembered it crossing a left wall, but the only left wall lay on the far side of that horrible cleft, which was virgin territory for the usual reasons why certain territories remain virgin. However, there now seemed two upward choices. What looked like a bold line swung up steeply to the left of the stance. Just the kind of place I would have loved to tackle in dry conditions - with a competent leader keeping a tight rope from a bomb-proof stance above; so that was out. Slightly right a sloping ledge gave access to what seemed easier ground. I could just see a rectangular block above the ledge and it had a comforting gap behind it which was obviously tailor-made for a nut and all my fingers. Like they say, these classic routes go in any conditions. Just as well, the rain had started again and the clag was descending.

I perched on the end of my sloping ledge and started to move across it. There seemed to be things missing: handholds, footholds and protection to mention just three. Decent friction I'd given up on some time ago. There was, however, a handsome drop below the ledge. I did a few wibbly-wobblies back and forth. Time to rationalise. This being classic rock it would go in the wet, therefore, despite appearances to the contrary, I could tippy-toe across the ledge to where the holds proper began. Off I went, fingers slithering in the slime. I reached the point of complete commitment and just as I realised I could neither return nor reach the proper holds my fingers lit on an unseen wrinkle. It was enough to steady myself and make a successful lunge for a decent hold. I heaved up and found myself in possession of another ledge, flatter, but much narrower. However, across to my left was that block with the lovely gap behind it. At this closer range I had to revise my opinion of the size of nut it might accept. Thank goodness I'd doubled up my wires, by chance I had some smaller ones. I shuffled across and made a grab for my block. It wasn't that my hands didn't disappear into the gap, more that the gap hardly accepted my fingernails. Nearly time to have a panic. First hang on by one set of fingernails and get something into the crack. The smallest wire wouldn't go in but at least it sat there on the edge of the block giving the semblance of security.

OK, time to panic! Bloody classic rock, this isn't classic rock, this is something mean and nasty. I am in a fix. No chance of reversing those last moves and no chance of moving up, especially on this pro'. Abseil? The answer to a coward's prayer! Hmm, that would mean abandoning gear and anyway, would I ab' off that nut? Time to get a grip, look around. The result of looking around was conclusive: no place to go but up... etc. But there's the rub, tiny holds, all slimy, until about six feet above a square nose of rock sticks out. I feel like Tantalus, so near and yet so far: but not too far for me to be able to lasso that nose and do something unethical. After a few left-handed casts my belay sling nestles squarely over the flat neb of rock. I give a few sturdy tugs, the neb is unmoved. I prepare for lift off - rope manoeuvres: real classic stuff. If she was up here, I could step on her head. Mind you, if this sling slips I probably will. Should I add an extension and step up carefully first? Bugger it! Take a hefty handful and heave into space. With a mighty bound Jack was free - in fact standing triumphant on the neb, feeling like Jack the Lad.

By the time she was up, my elation had been a little dampened by the effects of the rain. In the interest of the classic rule, 'The leader must never fall' (with key sub-clause 'especially when the leader is me'), I had left the matter of conveying spare gear to my second. "Err, got my windproof in there by any chance?" knowing full well I had tipped out all my gear except trainers.

"Better than that, I've got your cag."

"My cag? I chucked all my gear out."

"I chucked it back in again."

I suppose pessimists have their uses. "Well done, Blunk, you can come again. Pity you only brought your windproof."

She pouted, "I'm fed up of this rain, I'm wet and I want to get off this crag."

"Tut, tut; this should be looked on as a pioneer's day, quintessential experience, redolent with historic authenticity, etc."

"You can **** your historical **** up your **** and enjoy another quintessential experience. Just get me off this crag."

Her English vocabulary is more extensive than I thought, or was that High German? "I'll have a last look for that hand traverse." After a little soft-shoe shuffle leftwards I reappeared, still sans hand traverse. I looked up. *Mein Gott!* I'm not going up there. Time to test that eye of a not-so-bold wishing-to-grow-old climber.

I trundled off right through bunches of soaking heather and sturdy little junipers. After about 100 feet the ledge ended, but above me the crag was split by a gruesome cleft. It was beginning to fulfil the function of a drainpipe, but it sported a fine array of determined looking plants and even the odd nobble of rock. "Come on across," I shouted, "I've found an alternative, I think." She peered up at the drainpipe without enthusiasm. "Does it go to the top?"

"No idea, hope so. It's getting wetter."

"Are you going to climb the outside?"

"Not likely, I'm going to get well wedged inside. I've had enough excitement for one day."

The climbing was 'mixed' and a short axe might have given a good placement in the occasional mud bank. The water, now gurgling merrily, was making a playful entrance at my sleeve and a belated exit out of my trousers and into my EBs. I ran out a full pitch and brought her up. The craven swine was avoiding the traditional backing, footing and thrutching. Instead she was high-stepping up the outer edges with a disdainful elegance, like a cat in deep snow.

"Hey, that's cheating. Get into that bloody chimney!"

"Sod off." She arrived, hardly more than very damp and not a speck of mud in sight. "How much farther?" she wanted to know. I glanced down at the receding ground and up into the swirling mist. I assumed my deeply experienced mountaineer's frown, as remembered from pictures of Messner. "No bloody idea," I said. However, after another 100 feet I was able to shout. "You know that fence post you spotted?"

"Which fence post?"

"The one right at the top of the crag."

"Well?"

"I'm just tying on to it." I needn't have climbed up to tie on to it. Just that it seemed symbolic: solid iron sunk into solid rock. I sat solidly belayed to it. Only when I stood up again did I realise I'd been sitting in a pool of water; only a fairly shallow one, of course.

It was failing light when we strolled back through Seathwaite Farm. To be honest, it was pitch black. The man from the National Trust had gone. "No need to put pennies in his box," I said with satisfaction.

"Thank goodness he didn't send for the Mountain Rescue," she said.

"Nah, he'd know these old classics go in any weather."

"They might do if you can find them," she said.

P.S. We were of course on Gillercombe Buttress. 'Corvus' is on Raven Crag, a mere three miles away.

chapter twenty

MOUNTAIN KALEIDOSCOPE

In 1994 I completed a fastest 'all on foot' traverse of all the Munros (then 277) in 66 days. This is an account of three episodes.

> *And should I seek by mountain height*
> *A pale horizon's dawning light?*
> *And shall I catch your slow song when*
> *I trail the secret random glen?*
> *Seek shining burns that restless rise*
> *In silver loch and northern skies?*
> *Windborne castles of the air*
> *And rocky summits might I dare*
> *Your solitude, quiet wilderness,*
> *With silent mind in day's dim west?*

As a child I was given a kaleidoscope. It was a fascinating toy. Every turn or shake would produce a different pattern from the same shards of colour. I find it is similar with images formed from long hill journeys. Every turn of memory rearranges scraps of the journey into new patterns and perspectives. Of course, the kaleidoscope of memory glitters with more than visual images. It is also lively with fragments of sound, touch, smell and, importantly, feelings and emotions. Finally, the patterns of my kaleidoscope are shaped by the dimension of time.

To create a coherent pattern from the elements of a journey to which I have been committed physically, emotionally and spiritually I find difficult. To do so immediately on completion of such a journey I find impossible. The memories then are clear, but stark. They are newcomers to an inner world of familiar and treasured experiences. In this respect it is like making a new friend; one needs time to integrate and adjust. New friendships and new experiences need the nurture of time. The hidden dimensions are sometimes the most imperative.

I have long been fascinated by the shifts in significance which occur as time works its magic on a journey, sometimes for years afterwards. Perhaps I may liken it to the weaving of cloth from threads of many colours. The quick shuttle of thought moves patiently back and forth. The warp and weft of the journey take shape on memory's loom. Given the time to reflect and incident to reflect upon, then, with luck, a rich tapestry will emerge, a cloak with which to drape the shoulders of advancing years. For once the journey has been completed, where lies its value? Why, there in the glowing fire, or there in the sweep of that remembered hill and always in the laughter of good friends.

The longest and most committing of all the journeys I have made is my traverse of the Munros. It is a kaleidoscope of images which flicker in and out of my consciousness at all times. These images have a charming quality of spontaneity and freedom. They flip effortlessly from one mountain to another, taking me from sunlight to storm, from despair to delight. Apart from trying to review the whole journey for my club journal, I have been unwilling to impose any coherent structure on this kaleidoscopic jumble of images. However, were I to build them into a structure, there must inevitably emerge episodes which would serve the same purpose as the keystones which lock the span of bridges. As stones can be raised and held in arch above turbulent waters, so our memories, dreams and dances can be lifted and locked

*Mike above
Loch Avon,
Cairngorms*

by key defining moments. Whether it be illusion or not, we can stand awhile above the river of time which busily hastens us towards oblivion.

Of all the many stones which build my bridge of memories, there spring to mind three key episodes. I shake the kaleidoscope once, hold the pattern motionless and gaze at the vaulting architecture of the Skye Ridge. Another shake, another pattern – the immense landform of the Cairngorms rolls into view. A third and final shake and out of the mists and vapours of a Tolkienian Middle Earth the wilderness of Fisherfield forms slowly, irresolutely, and a small wet figure hunches in a small stone howff chewing a thoughtful butty.

Cairngorm Traverse (Days 32 & 33)

This particular keystone was made up of two linked blocks. The Cairngorm Munros comprise seventeen summits.[1] Even a linear traverse yields over 60 miles with nearly 18,000 feet of ascent. A good day out when fresh, but instant death on a continuous Munro round. Indeed, IB held the lure of a three day traverse before me, a temptingly logical and enticingly moderate plan. She thought my two planned loops most immoderate and I agreed, except I'd heard the weather forecast for the next three days! We compromised on a route which allowed me home early if necessary. Even so, I'd had to exercise my *droit de seigneur* – the right of the guy at the front to violate his own or anyone else's common sense.

One of my most striking memories of the Cairngorms traverse is what happened the day before. My complete awareness of the commitment and effort which would be needed produced a fit of the 'wobblies'. All those attempting their Bob Graham Rounds, first 'extreme' rock climbs, etc. will know what I mean. After completing a relaxed traverse of three Lochnagar Munros I marched out from Invercauld on Deeside like a man going to the scaffold.

My destination was a secret howff about six miles up the glen, a launch pad for the morrow. I felt incredibly weary, almost asleep on my feet as I walked at what seemed tortoise pace. IB said I was moving briskly, but I couldn't believe her. I was either into terminal galloping decrepitude, or the 'mind-body' was trying to close all functions in order to store energy. I've experienced the latter frequently, but this was like being sand-bagged.

Day 32 – Eastern Ranges.

After a comfortable but tense night in the blessed little howff, we rose at 4:15, and at 5am Don and I stepped into a grey silence. At 2,000 feet the silence

---

[1] Eighteen now.

became white and our steps pressed into the soft June snow. After exchanging views on this unexpected fact conversation lapsed into companionable silence. We were heading for a high col known as the Sneck. On one side rises Ben Avon with its pepper-potting of summit tors, on the other Beinn a'Bhùird with its two mile whaleback of high tundra. The Sneck is embattled with granite shapes. It is a weird place in mist. The solid rock swells, shrinks, soars in endless misty metamorphoses. An ancient stone man materialises with prehistoric fury and is restrained and hidden only by the white sheets of vapour flapping like sails amid the masts of a doomed galleon.

It was here that I left Don. He would share company with the guardian of the Sneck. I must add it was his choice, not mine. I could collect Ben Avon while he awaited my return. By repeating this trick at various points Don would save himself both climbing and distance. In his immortal phrase he would *'mosey along quietly'* (usually with my sac), while I *'mosied'* along a bit quicker. Thus did he verify the motto of the illustrious de Talbot's *'With age, wisdom'*. Nice motto, pity about the wardrobe. At nearly 3,000 feet the Sneck in snow is no place for the threadbare cast-offs so beloved of ancient fell runners in general and de Talbots in particular. Still, the blue nose and white cheeks went well with the natty road menders' pantaloons. Better get him moving, I thought. He revived on the ascent of Beinn a'Bhùird, no doubt warmed by my tale of epic struggle up the snow/hoar encrusted north face of Ben Avon's summit tor.

He was also gratifyingly impressed by my impeccable line to the pimple on the elephant's bum which is the summit cairn on Beinn a'Bhùird. I do love the 'left hand down a bit, feel for the country' style of navigation. I think it's because one experiences real joy and amazement when it works, but is never too surprised when it doesn't. In the latter event I am pleased to employ, even extend, my very necessary navigational skill of 'getting unlost'. The 'art of getting unlost' proved a beguiling topic for us as we ambled amiably over the generous miles. And thus we walked out of the clag and onto the rarely frequented moor of the Mòine Bhealaidh. This extends from Glen Avon in the north to the young Dee in the south and is bordered to the west by the deep trench of the Làirig an Laoigh. When Gerard Manley Hopkins wrote:

> *What would the world be, once bereft*
> *of wet and of wilderness? Let them be left,*
> *O let them be left...'*

He might have had this place in mind.

Here I made a diversion south to Beinn Bhreac, rejoining Don on Beinn a'Chaorainn. Soon we were faced with the crossing of the Fords of Avon.

This was a year of late (and heavy) spring snow, which was why the stepping stones were well under water. I gave Don the camera so he could snap the intrepid Munroist skipping across the raging torrent. 'Especially if I fall in,' I added with a hearty, dismissive chuckle. At my first leap onto a submerged rock the unexpected force of the water violently displaced my foot downstream. Only my incredible reactions and consummate agility saved me (he said; Don thought: 'amazing in one so old and decrepit'). We paused briefly at the Fords of Avon refuge, a dingy, claustrophobic den that nevertheless has given me a peaceful shelter and is set as close to paradise as I am likely to get. Again we parted company, Don easing into the Saddle (above Loch Avon) and me doing a barn dance (those near the summit of Bynack More).

I was beginning to feel quite strong by now and with Don's approval decided to go for the day's 'full monty'. I could have struck south over Beinn Mheadhoin and Derry Cairngorm to our camp at Luibelt above Derry Lodge. By heading for Cairngorm and leaving Beinn Mheadhoin lurking untouched behind my back I was committing myself. Failure to complete the day would leave a horribly uneconomical mess for tomorrow. This sense of commitment is the ingredient usually missing from hill walking. It can sometimes be found on night walks, more frequently in severe weather, and is heightened in proportion to the distance one has to cover before support or safe haven. However, unfortunately or otherwise, there is little to compare with the trepidation of making irreversible moves on rock well above an insecure belay as is the joy of the climber.

Nevertheless, the prospect of night or bad weather catching us now or on an enforced third day was enough to put a spring in our step. Thus we cantered gently across the high plateau, shielding eyes against intense dazzle as the sun-come-lately flashed off the newly coated snowfields. What a palette of colours here! Red granite, white snow, greens of lichen and spring moss, reflected blues in crystal water, small pink flowers whose delicacy provided a perfect counterpoint to the immense landscape. Seen occasionally through the heaving clouds the curves and sweeps of Braeriach, Cairn Toul and Angel's Peak beckoned a future promise. Devil's Point sat in gloom like an anorexic Buachaille, contemplating mischief and rude thoughts.

In what seemed no time we had cleared Macdui and descended to Loch Etchachan. Just above, on the path, a sad sight greeted us: an evenly spaced line of dead ptarmigan chicks. They lay like golden flowers on the cold rocks, utterly pathetic and stirring within us an aching sense of loss. Perhaps the snow had caught them. But I feared their parents had met with some hard fate and never returned. We now had unfinished business. Fortunately for me, Beinn Mheadhoin was on Don's tick list. We talked our way up the loose stony slopes keeping each to the other's rhythm. Despite years of fell racing Don is one of the least competitive people I know. I shall always remember his quiet companionship at this crucial stage in my walk. At 7pm we stood happy on the summit, then in cheery vagueness disappeared off the wrong way into the mist. Soon 'unlost' however and back at Etchachan, we wolfed the last of our food in anticipatory triumph.

Only Derry Cairngorm to go, but I celebrated too soon. My spring had sprung, so sprang I not over the interminable boulders. The sky lowered, the wind rose and shortly I discovered my pertex top had not the waterproof coating I fondly imagined. Somewhat chastened and decidedly wet I took a careful bearing off the summit. I was anxious to get a good line on this 2,000 foot plunge into Glen Luibeg. The 1:50,000 map promised a line but failed to show the vigorous heather which lower down assumed the proportions of young rhododendron bushes. Even my imperturbable mate was heard to mutter!

At 9:30pm we emerged from mist and dripping heather to find the support tents beautifully pitched near Luibeg ford. In one of the tents was a mountain gremlin – a disgruntled and bad tempered gremlin. It began a stern lecture on planning over-long mountain days and proceeded to elaborate on the perils facing old gentlemen who over-tax their strength and play out late in the hills. Finally, it turned quite savage and spoke of ruined dinners going cold, etc., etc. But I knew its lack of gruntle was due to its not having played out for two days. Tomorrow would restore its humour.

Day 33 – West of the Làirig Ghru

Planning for my Munros trip had been akin to planning several dozen Karrimor Elite courses. I had, as Whymper remarked in a different context, 'from the beginning to think what the end might be.' Each day's end had to merge into another beginning. Keeping to the right balance of miles and slotting home the pieces of this huge jigsaw was an absorbing task which had consumed many a winter's night. Viewing with pride the growing edifice of mountains and miles, all held in place with Naismith's bomb-proof corsets, I cocked a snook at von Moltke's gloomy prediction 'no plan withstands contact with the enemy.' The problem of how best to traverse Derry Cairngorm and Carn a'Mhaim approaching from Cairngorm/Macdui is a classic mountain marathon poser. After some head banging I applied a bit of lateral thinking – camp after Derry Cairngorm and treat Carn a'Mhaim as if it lay west of the Làirig Ghru. This not only balanced the two days but, interestingly, gave the most economical line.

Thus, at 7am on a cold, misty morning, IB and I stood atop Carn a'Mhaim. Though modest in other respects it possesses one of the

Cairngorms' few ridges. It can be a pretentious little number in winter when taken with a little ice, snow and the usual 60mph wind. After a short, rough descent we fetched up at the Allt Clach nan Taillear, the 'burn of the Stone of the Tailors' – a memorial stone as it happens, for these merry fellows perished some way short of fulfilling their boast of dancing reels on Speyside and Deeside in the same night. Since then the hollow, hungry gut of this lonely pass has digested many another unwary traveller. (Who said walking wasn't particularly committing? Oh, 'twas me!)

We began the day's longest climb. The slopes of Braeriach are where I believe the young Sisyphus carried out his early training. Well, he certainly left an untidy mess of boulders behind. To enliven the ascent I took to a bit of boulder hopping. This was followed by boulder staggering and, before you could say 'snap your leg like a carrot', boulder stumbling. Fortunately, at this point we came upon boulders which had defeated even Sisyphus. We were able to bring arms into play and now with Simian stability we polished off the remainder of Sisyphus' left-overs. The plateau stretching to Cairn Toul was a fine airy place in clearing mist. Here lie the Wells of Dee, an area of green mossy magic and such pure, clear water. It is a life enhancing, life affirming place and each time I pass this way I experience a bubbling sense of excitement, wonder and delight.

After further developments in the art of boulder hopping over shapely Cairn Toul we approached the Devil's Point with some apprehension. Well, I did. Old sinners should be wary in such places. A dark, hairy figure leaping from behind a rock brandishing a sharp, pointy object – woof! Instant cardiac arrest. Perhaps Auld Reekie was off propositioning the Angel's Peak for the summit was quiet and peaceful. Sticking out into the south end of the Làirig it provides an excellent viewpoint. I first came here nearly 30 years ago. Armed with an ice axe and the old red Cairngorms climbing guide I'd climbed Geusachan Gully with a mate. For the first time I'd discovered that Scottish turf is generally sounder than Scottish ice.

Now we were off on ground that didn't sprout memories. New ground, new mountains – the 'swelling eminences' of Monadh Mòr and Beinn Bhrotain. In a perfect world these twins would be traversed on ski – deep powder, blue skies. I'd missed my chance. The massive falls of this late winter were still in evidence though. They enhanced the wild aspect of these unfrequented slopes above Geusachan and bountifully fed the steep torrents of the riven hillside. After a safe, though wet, negotiation we climbed to lonely Loch nan Stuirteag situated on a pleasant shelf. At 2,840 feet it would make a truly remote high camp. Quite often on this journey it was the discovery of these wild, untrodden places that provided the delight of travel. Summits were won, but somehow these places were gifts. On the traverse of Monadh Mòr and Bhrotain there was a sense of height and solitude. The vegetation struggles to maintain a foothold here and does so by stealth and tenacity. Here is not fertile abundance. Here is the realm of wind, air, rock, space, uncompromising freedom.

Paradoxically, the mist which had now re-formed enhanced the feeling of space. Vision was reduced and imagination released. Retracing our steps after Bhrotain to avoid boulder fields, we side-slipped down and round to a shallow col below Monadh Mòr. In steady rain we followed deer trods through increasingly rough heather country. I only realised how dark was the soggy heather when a fox in day-glo orange trotted across our path, grinning. Before the crossing of the River Eidart we ate our last butty. I must admit that, stood under the glowering clouds with the rain plopping steadily, I felt a trifle less than joyful. However, the Eidart proved a positive sort of Rubicon. I was soon engrossed in careful navigation which would set us up for the trip's third and final plateau. I was aiming for the end of a track hidden somewhere in the clag above. My complete return to good spirits came when I walked straight onto this terminus. My companion, erstwhile gremlin Blunk, who is a fully paid up orienteer, complimented me on hitting a linear feature head on. What I'd done was walk uphill in a straight line for one and a half miles. I reckoned I could hardly miss the plateau and, with luck, would hit the track. Paint with a wide brush and fill the details in later.

On the traverse of the Mòine Mhòr above Glen Feshie we were pleased to be able to swing along with the weather on our backs. At the track below the demoted Carn Bàn Mòr IB hung a left to descend to Feshie. I won't say she deemed it likely she would have to wake the Great Preston Kipper in order to prepare for my arrival, but it wasn't impossible. The final few miles over to Sgòr Gaoith and back were quite surreal. If there had been snow I would have experienced a perfect white-out. The atmosphere was saturated and the wind was rising with the passing minutes. The forecast storm was gathering force. Inside my hood my brain was sinking into a cosy armchair. Without, I stared into the miasma, sensing the groundfall, feeling the distance. It was most unlikely I could walk over the precipice above Loch Einich, but I could imagine doing so. Nervously hanging onto the summit rocks I was consciously leaning away from the drop which seemed to be dragging at my feet. 'Nonsense!' I said, but I put some safe ground between me and the tremendous void above Loch Einich which I felt to be exerting an unnatural force on me.

It was now 8:30pm and home lay less than five miles away and 2,500 feet down. Gradually on the long stony path the tension gave way. Fatigue made a premature attempt to interpose, but I needed still to concentrate on secure, efficient foot placement. I also needed to be patient and not long too soon for that first cup of tea. Eventually, I settled into a state of weary contentment. The Cairngorms lay behind me. I had traversed them successfully in a journey of love and affection, mighty mountains, fragile wilderness, the keepers of hopes and dreams, the source of life and renewal of spirit.

Day 47 – The Cuillin Ridge – Skye

'No part that I have seen is plain; you are always climbing or descending, and every step is upon rock or mire. A walk upon ploughed ground in England is a dance upon carpets compared to the toilsome drudgery of wandering in Skye...' (Dr. Johnson)

Two days previously I had descended from Beinn Sgritheall in a storm and jogged across Skye to Broadford. That evening I made a pact with Jed S. to meet him the day after tomorrow at the Thearlaich Dubh gap. We would then traverse the eleven Munros of the main Black Cuillin ridge. Just like that – ha!

Next day I continued what was surely a pointless exercise. I was jogging and walking eight miles of road to Bla Bheinn. The rain had eased, but it was dark with cloud and clag down to 1,000 feet. Skye is the only place where I've set off up one mountain and arrived at the top of another. (And I was with ace navigator JR, too!) With the weather I'd been 'enjoying' it could be weeks before I completed the ridge. I don't like travelling by road. My hip was hurting. The scenery was draped in mist. I was depressed, it felt like mission impossible. In this cheerful state I arrived below Blà Bheinn. At least, I was reliably informed Blà Bheinn was up there, somewhere. Sons Gerard and Liam were waiting with IB. We made complicated, probably futile plans. I plodded off solo into the unknown.

Fetching up in a corrie I met a youth group. This was embarrassing as I'd just decided to wander around until I found some kind of trail. Now I had to give the map an authoritative glare and stride upwards into the murk. Never mind, once hidden I could creep around until I found something, a path hopefully. My embarrassment deepened as the mist rose with me and I was aware of the idle gaze of the curious watching my progress. Where was that bloody path? Suddenly I popped out on a shoulder and with equal suddenness the clag dispersed and I got views, spectacular views too, over the gnarly bones of Clach Glas and, beyond the buxom contours of the Red Cuillin. By the summit the sun was shining and in the west the curtains of mist were rising on the coming drama. I had traversed 190 Munros on this journey so far, but the eleven now stretched across my gaze in a dragon's back of sharp spikes were something else. I remembered what the professional mountain guide had said when asked for advice, 'I recommend that you don't attempt the ridge in a single traverse.' I could see what he meant.

I met the others at Camasunary. All were toting impressive loads. IB, in what I thought a vain attempt not to be outclassed by youth, strength and masculinity, seemed to have packed out a marquee. At the Bad Step, fearing for her safety, I exercised my shaky authority and tethered her to a rock while Gerard returned, plucked up her pack and floated easily across. Much teutonic shouting and stamping ensued to which I turned a Nelson's ear. After this I relapsed into a weary plod. Extreme lassitude once more gripped me and with the poet I felt,

> *My heart aches, and a drowsy numbness pains*
> *My sense, as though of hemlock I had drunk,*
> *Or emptied some dull opiate to the drains...*
> *And Lethe-wards had sunk...* [2]

– or, in my case, Coruisk-wards.

We had intended to camp across the outflow from Loch Coruisk but this would obviously entail quite a paddle. We decided to keep our powder dry for tonight since I thought that on the morrow wet feet would be the least of my worries. Gerard had no such problems. Just as it went dark he swam across the loch to investigate a small island. Ah! Carefree youth. During my last supper I was interested to note that the usual feelings of doom and foreboding had been replaced by a patient resignation. Heaven forbid that anything so frivolous as cautious optimism should raise its head, but I was aware that Jed and his son, Andy, had promised to be waiting at the Thearlaich Dubh gap at 8am tomorrow. I thought I could get as far as that.

At 4:15am I poked my head out and experienced one of the unforgettable moments of the trip. We were enclosed in deep, dark shadow, all was silent and sombre. Away above us there gleamed another world. Beyond stony flanks still clothed in night shone a ridge of gold; and behind the ridge, a pure translucent blue. It could have been a glimpse into heaven, a mountaineer's heaven. The only thing in the world I wanted, as I gazed spellbound, was to be up there. Even at this distance it remains an incredible vision and an incredible fact. Day after day I'd endured storms and gales. The Munros of Skye seemed likely to involve a war of attrition. The complete ridge traverse had become a hopeless dream. Now, here it was, spread before me. No wonder the ancients had such strong faith in their gods, those capricious, jealous wretches with too much time on their hands –

> *...As flies to wanton boys are we to the gods. They kill us for their sport.* [3]

But when they relent, don't ever scorn their gift, just keep checking the rear view mirror.

---

[2] John Keats, *Ode to a Nightingale.*

[3] Shakespeare, *King Lear,* IV, I, 36.

Such was the beauty of the morning that IB postponed her plan to carry out with Gerard and accompanied Liam and me onto the ridge. We scrambled up through the Garbh Choire. The Gaelic 'garbh' means 'rough'. I wonder if there's any Gaelic for 'boy, this is humungous.' It's on record that even Sisyphus invoked his get-out clause here and allowed the giants to indulge their rock-tossing penchant. Someone should have made them tidy up. At the col we turned to gaze at the red and liquid dawn pouring over the hills and down the glens. The colours were volcanic, the silence held us like a vice, stones belled like the ringing of unsheathed swords. Our journey was begun.

The first Munro of the ridge, Sgùrr nan Eag, gave us a rocky but straightforward walk. The second consumed much more time. Not only did it lie off the main ridge, but it was guarded by a castle (Caisteal a'Garbh Choire). We first snuk under the castle's defences, then Liam and I scrambled up Sgùrr Dubh Mòr. IB, still reluctant to abandon upper sunlit rockeries, scrambled ahead to check whether Jed and Andy had materialised, apologise for us being late and try, if possible, to gauge their calibre. Being, to my shame, a Skye novitiate, I was heavily, if not completely, dependent on Jed and Andy for expert guidance. During our 'phone conversation I had been rather disconcerted, even alarmed, to hear a certainly bronchial, possibly tubercal Jed explaining that he knew the ridge pretty well. Unfortunately, the ravages of anno domini, illness, lack of fitness, etc. ...On the other hand, his lad didn't know the ridge at all but could climb anything. God, I thought, an invalid, a rock-jock and a geriatric novice all on the Skye Ridge together. It is true that Horace adjures us to 'mingle some brief folly with your wisdom', but this seemed to be reversing the recommended order. Heaven help us, I thought, which is when I seemed to hear a chuckle; probably just an odd rumble of thunder. Anyway, Jed had come 'Rucksack Club Recommended' (by Eiger ace Cec R). His solid, if muffled, Lancashire tones conveyed a sense of no-nonsense dependability and, to clinch matters , a bona fide professional guide, if one had been available, would have clocked in at three arms and two legs (about £250).

When IB returned from the T-D gap she was wearing her Mona Lisa smile. 'Jed and Andy are there,' she said, 'and I don't think you've got anything to worry about. I think you're going to be in good hands. Bye-bye.' As we moved towards the gap I looked around for a lycra-clad dandy mincing about in too tight rock boots. Instead, there was a very solid looking character wearing a broad grin and hefty mountain boots. This was Andy and, after supervising our abseil into the gap, he treated Liam and me to a muttered commentary concerning the antics of a pair of climbers shinning up the other side. They looked like hard alpinists to me and after much precarious slithering the leader reached the top and called down, 'OK, it's only VDiff.'

Andy gave an audible snort and with enviable Anglo-Saxon elegance cast doubts not only on the alpinist's immediate parentage, but also the doubtful versimilitude of his recent verbal assessment. Well, here was the first test. There were a few grunts and heaves, an extra grunt at the previous sticking point then, from the top, the fair-minded Andy conceded, 'Yeah! It is only VDiff.' Maybe the climb is, but who is it who goes round applying the Mansion polish? I skidded to a halt to behold a rock-like figure, white-bearded like myself, but about three times as wide. Undoubtedly this was Jed, still spluttering a bit from a recent cold, but apparently unlikely to fade away just yet. I don't know how it was with them, but I felt instinctively that all would be well. My earlier tensions slipped away and I suddenly started to relish the whole experience. My only doubt concerned the weight of climbing gear carried by Jed and Andy. Perhaps they were only coming as far as the 'In Pin'? My doubts were soon dispelled. Andy was keen to do the whole ridge and Jed, using Don's ploy of only doing what was necessary, intended to make sure we didn't stray.

I had often wondered why I knew Skye so little. In some ways I had 'saved it up.' Faced on this journey with the necessity to complete the ridge I regretted earlier missed opportunities. But now, in a wonderful way, it all seemed to fit perfectly; not only that, but Liam had the opportunity of his young life. My only regret was that Gerard and IB would even now be humping heavy packs back out past Camasunary. Never did I want more to share a journey through this exotic fairyland of fantastic rock. From Sgùrr Alasdair, the highest of the Cuillin, we had a wonderful view of what was to come. Below us, looking enticingly impossible, ran Collie's Ledge, our route to Sgùrr Mhic Choinnich. Sweeping over the curtain of scree racing down to Coire Lagan, the strong line of the crenellated ridge swooped first down, then up and up until the eye was arrested by the thrusting spearhead of the Inaccessible Pinnacle piercing the crest of Sgùrr Dearg.

Sgùrr Dearg was where we had arrived in error a few years ago. We knew we were somewhat astray, at least Chief Navigator JR and I did. Geoff forging ahead in his innocence knew he was on a mountain and even that the mountain was on the Cuillin Ridge. Greater precision was not to be expected. Unusually though, he supplied it. There was a gurgling wail, 'Oooh! There's something horrible up here.'

I must admit, the black cliff of the Inaccessible Pinnacle looming through the streaming mist like the towering prow of a colliding ship had struck awe into all our hearts. Today, it presented a dry and beaming face. Its fine ridgeback was an invitation to dance. Below the 'In Pin', at the foot of the hump backed An Stac, we again met the two alpinists. Their game was the traverse of the main ridge crest. They were examining the ethics of avoiding or climbing An Stac. They looked pretty weary and I guess the ethical discussion was not entirely objective. I felt only sympathy. This was tough country. We were going well, if steadily. The heat was not yet a problem, but it was becoming one. Andy guided us expertly up the 'In Pin' – an imperative moment in any Munroist's career. We had a pleasant, airy wait on top while another party abseiled off. Last was a lassie sporting an arm in plaster and showing no fear whatever.

All had gone well so far, but now the heat began to build. I had woefully underestimated the amount of water we would need. Worse, I'd neglected to instruct Liam in matters aquatic. One is unused to water shortages in Scotland's hills. In addition, the heavy sacks were exacting their toll. Jed, not in full health, was suffering attacks of cramp. Dehydration was a probable factor in this. I felt guilty as Jed and Andy had shared their water with us – not even a hint of a justifiable complaint about our lack of provision. Barely half way, no water, the rocks radiating the sun's bounty. But as that arch Munroist Hamlet observed: 'There's a divinity that shapes our ends, rough-hew them how we will.' There, lying on a rock was a two litre bottle containing clear, transparent liquid. I expected like Alice, to find a label attached – 'DRINK ME'. But no, maybe the gods wished to observe a play of human ethics.

'Could have been left for a party comung along later,' said Andy. 'Litter!' said Jed, 'I don't agree with litter on the ridge.' 'Quite right!' we chorused. So we drank it and married pragmatism to ethics.

A couple of hours, later with the rock recalling its volcanic origins, our tongues were cleaving to our palates and cramp was stabbing the legs. The necessity of baling out to the glen's restorative waters was looming large. But once those deities embark upon a project, they like to see it through. After nudging that bottle in our direction, they now went gallons better. This time a complete snow bank was provided. It was tucked under the shady side of a rock wall and dripped succulently like an over-ripe melon. Jed slit the plastic bottle and the drips pattered along its length. We stretched at our ease and felt our desiccated tissues swell and plump. I think it was at this point that I definitely accepted that not only would the venture succeed, but it would not be allowed to fail.

Somewhere in the wastes of Druim nan Ramh Jed for once was undecided about a tricky descent. He disappeared down a stony slope to reconnoitre. After a time there was prolonged ominous rumbling and clattering; then silence. We exchanged glances. I tried to estimate how much noise a falling Jed would make. There came the thankful sounds of returning rumbles. A red and perspiring face emerged from a gully's stony bowels. 'Well, it's not this way.' Thus, having like Holmes dismissed the impossible, we embraced the improbable and reached safe ground. Just three summits remained. At the first and easiest of these, Bruach na Frithe, Jed consulted his watch and announced a north by east bearing would deposit him at the Sligachan Hotel in time for a pint, or possibly two. Losing no opportunity to display filial affection Andy encircled him with ropes, helmets and sundry climbing gear. A lesser man would have crumpled to the floor. Jed merely grunted and stumped off – *Sorrow and silence are strong, and patient endurance godlike.*[4]

Despite my reverence for Naismith we made no attempt to solo his route to Am Basteir which, from this angle, would have taken a Geoff B to describe in full horror. Down, reluctantly, and round we went, then up to find an awkward step, an obstacle to at least my progress. At last, the last! Sgùrr nan Gillean, the 'Peak of the Young Men' – nearly correct. Andy picked out a likely looking chimney, which in my stiffened state presented a bit of a thrutch. It would, however, have taken more than rigor mortis to stop me now. At 9pm we stood on our final summit and allowed the warm blood of success to flow through our tired bodies. The gods, too, kept to their script. The rocks on which we stood were glowing in the sun and we seemed at the centre point of a wheeling rim of red fire. I can't recall ever seeing a sunset spreading 360 degrees around the world. But I'd never completed the Cuillin Ridge before, never stood atop Gillean after a journey that was already beginning to feel like a fairy tale.

> *After the kingfisher's wing*
> *Has answered light to light, and is silent, the light is still*
> *At the still point of the turning world.*[5]

With Liam and Andy shouldering most of the gear we began our long descent to evening shadows and reality. It would have been appropriate had Andy's boots struck sparks from the rocks, such was his determined progress. I kept thinking he must slow, show some vestige of fatigue, but he never slackened – what a rock-jock!

When we opened the van door we were greeted by two very red faces. One belonged to Jed, the other to Ged, the latter had run up to the top of Gillean in 80 minutes. He had reached the top at 10pm and run back down in the gloaming in less than an hour. I was disappointed to have missed him. It was the only miscue of a perfect day. We all sat in the van beaming at each other in what in my case was an increasingly vague way. Maybe the dream-like quality of this journey came over me then, or maybe it was present from

---

[4] Longfellow, *Evangeline.*

[5] T. S. Eliot, *Burnt Norton.*

that first glimpse of the Ridge soaring like heaven itself in the flame of the risen sun. Whatever, dream or journey, it is locked away and never can or will be undreamt; 'at the still point of the turning world' it dances yet. Once again, and always, thank you Jed, Andy, Gerard, Liam, Inken.

Day 61 – Fisherfield

The common thread running through my account of these keystone days is the commitment they invoked and inspired. For several reasons this is especially true of the Fisherfield trek. As I mentioned earlier, the walker is rarely forced to display the commitment which is the common lot of the climber on a classic route, i.e. a climb from which escape is either impossible or leads to more difficult ground. Even on my 'big' days I could have backed off to remain safe; that, at least, was the objective reality. I was, however, living my journey at such an intense level day by day and week by week that objective assessment became overwhelmed by the subjective. From Day 1 I had been deeply committed and now, on Day 61, my commitment was absolute. Bill Shankley is famously credited with disagreeing with those who think football is a matter of life or death. He assured them it was much more serious than that. Exactly. *In extremis* I could in theory abandon my hills – it was more likely I'd leave my bones to bleach first.

Now, with 249 Munros completed, just one last 'big' day threatened my hopes. It didn't matter that I'd put other such days behind me. Perhaps, if anything, they'd shown me the faint line between success and failure; I felt they had exposed my weakness rather than my strengths. They had taught lessons of humility and confirmed the merits of quiet perseverance, as in the proverb: 'Be not afraid of going slowly, be only afraid of standing still.' This had become a mantra, one I would need for this last 'big' day. Only let me have good weather, I thought, and I will finish the job. Of course, it was not to be expected that the gods would heed my pleas again; or rather, they would heed, but where man proposes, god disposes – capriciously.

Before I could even begin my attempt on the six Munros of the Fisherfield group, I had to overcome a mighty spear that barred the way – Slioch. Rising in splendour from beautiful Loch Maree, Slioch has wonderful individuality and presence. It is a jewel in the treasure chest of the north west. Unlike more secretive wonders it radiates its full majesty to common view across the loch. It seems to revel in its own beauty – and well it night.

What cannot easily be realised is that this spear guards one of the great wilderness areas. This is because roads have outflanked its defences and most choose to win the prizes locked in its interior by low level approaches from north or west. Perhaps the greatest virtue of undertaking a complete Munro traverse on foot is the opportunity, even necessity, of journeying through hills by unusual and unfrequented ways.

I approached Slioch in the orthodox way, from the village of Kinloch-ewe. At 6am IB and I stole forth into a grey, quiet morning. The path led us through beautiful mixed woodland with the river running on our left. This sylvan start was made poignant by the knowledge that soon I would be exploring the wild, tree-less interior of Fisherfield. It was with some reluctance that we crossed the Abhainn Fhasaigh and started the long climb towards Slioch's sandstone battlements. Gradually, the loch and woodlands shrank beneath our heels. We turned the corner and they were gone. Coire na Sleaghaich, the 'Corrie of the Spear', was a huge amphitheatre, desolate and lonely as mist swept down from the heights. We had difficulty keeping to the faint path and, striking off on our own bearing, attained the south east ridge by a small, sad looking lochan.

Conversation was muted and confined to mutterings about the correct line. My mind was largely occupied with the uncertainties ahead. One uncertainty at least was being resolved. My plea for fair weather looked like being rebuffed. There was a wet edge to the mist which promised later misery. IB

After Skye Ridge, Sgurr Nan Gillean behind.

was probably performing logistical somersaults in her mind. She should really not have been here given that she had yet to drive round to Dundonnell and then carry out tonight's camp five miles to Shenavall bothy. She would be loaded with about 50lbs and I wondered if she realised the path became rough and rose to 1,500 feet. At last the twin summits arrived. I was surprised to see three hours had elapsed and consulted Naismith. He said we must have been hurrying and I'd pay later. Based on the considerable experience I'd accumulated during this trip I told IB I thought fourteen hours for the day would be the best I'd manage. Once again we parted on the top of a mountain, each vanishing into a portion of mist. Better than catching the 8:10 to the office, I thought.

I now nervously remembered the statement in the SMC guide that three quarters of Slioch's perimeter is defended by towering sandstone buttresses and steep crags. Apparently, the only breach in these defences lay in the south east, the way I'd just ascended. I had to depart by the north east slopes which I thought I might manage if I could just see enough to pick a line. Not a chance! I started down anyway, experiencing that tingling in the toes you get when you think an abyss may suddenly open or a cornice break. After 500 feet I was committed (that word again). There was no way I was going to re-ascend, this line must go, it was a not a case of touching, but of embracing the void.

When it was too late to be of help the veils were withdrawn and the forward wilderness revealed. An unanticipated bonus of this trip was the increasing facility by which I was able to pick a line by 't'rack o' th'ee' (reckon of the eye). The lines I spotted usually went quite well and I came to both trust in and rely on this ability. However, the prospect ahead looked a formidable test. From my vantage point I selected a line and went for it. For a time everything was cross-grained, then I popped out above Lochan Fada and dropped easily down to the shore. Although only just over three miles long, this loch is around 250 feet deep. It lies like a sword thrust into some of the wildest and most remote mountain country in Scotland. Behind me lay the bulk of Slioch and the high wedge of rough ground known as the Letterewe Forest, ahead lay the great barrier of the Fisherfield mountains. Suddenly, despite the steel grey day, the haunting mist and my own inner tensions, I sensed a great peace. The anxiety dissolved. The day, the journey, affirmed its true values and an imperative sense of place overwhelmed transient and merely mortal concerns.

No footprints along the shore of Lochan Fada. But near the west end I passed the decayed hulk of a boat and the ground felt as if feet had passed this way. Crossing the loch's inflow I was faced with what looked like a grassy cliff. Missing contour lines on the map confirmed the eye's diagnosis, very steep! The cliff led to a Tarsuinn, which is the common Gaelic name for a ridge lying across the grain of the country. The climb went well but carried me into thick mist. I was now approaching the 'most remote' Munro, A'Mhaighdean, prized for itself and its wonderful prospect, which latter would obviously be denied me today. It was a curious anti-climax to be stood on the summit enclosed in a ten foot murky bubble. This trip had produced many such bubbles and I promised myself a leisurely return to all such summits in perfect conditions.

I'd read of a stone howff on the col between A'Mhaighdean and Ruadh Stac Mòr and, with the rain now coming in earnest, hoped to find it. Keeping to the ridge line on stony, indeterminate ground was difficult, but Providence smiled and I found myself peering at a black hole which proved to be the howff entrance. I crawled inside, extracted a slightly soggy butty and evaluated my position. Thoughtfully adjusting my rose-tinted specs, I decided I'd got it cracked. When I realise I'm going to go for something whatever the problems, I employ a useful strategy. I note a point on the map some distance ahead and make a mental note saying, in effect, 'when I'm there, I'll be almost home.' This has the useful effect of removing however large a piece of ground you decide on from the equation. In this case I chose the summit of Mullach Coire Mhic Fhearchair. Once heading north from here I would be on familiar ground. Familiar ground has the added bonus of being shorter than unfamiliar ground. It is essential to maintain a fairly detached mind on the 'missing' ground. Unfortunately, the boulder fields of Torridonian Sandstone on Ruadh Stac Mòr caused a very conscionable temper tantrum. Later, on Beinn Tarsuinn (another Tarsuinn), heavy rain, swirling mists and high winds produced a dip in confidence. I sheltered behind a dripping black crag and bolted some food. This boosted me up the long ascent of quartzy Mhic Fhearchair, the point which I'd decided was 'nearly as good as home'.

At 3,344 feet this mountain is the highest of the group, so I really could convince myself it was all downhill now. It was therefore unfortunate that the next downhill was a real 'downer'. Sgùrr Ban throws out two ridges to the north. The one I needed, running north east, is poorly defined and difficult to locate in mist. On my first visit to these hills I had run from Kinlochewe to Dundonnell. I well recalled trotting blithely down unbroken sheets of firm névé , on my feet a pair of studded trainers. It had taken about ten minutes to descend over 1,000 feet from Sgùrr Ban summit to the tiny lochans on the broad col. The névé that day had hidden the extensive boulder field which was now revealed. In today's pea-souper accuracy was essential and speed desirable. But with the wobbliness that comes over one with time, gliding swiftly over greasy boulders with compass poised

Slioch across Loch Maree.

belonged to the realm of dreams. Between wobbly legs and wobbly compass it took an hour to descend the single mile to the col. 'Be not afraid of going slowly, be only afraid of standing still' – but I was forced to do both!

Perhaps I had acquired some mental strength on this trip, for I reached the lonely lochans and was able to put the slow torture behind me. I began to enjoy the easy slopes of Beinn a'Chlaidheimh. The sense of isolation was immense. It was late enough and wet enough to assume I would meet no one. Since leaving IB I had not seen a soul. The isolation, the abiding mist, the new ground I had traversed, all contributed to a wonderful sense of journey. It also sharpened my anticipation of soon being restored to human contact with its piquant contrast of warmth and intimacy. The final steepening to the summit cone reminded me that the day's climbing was not much below 10,000 feet. The old legs had stood the test well and had just one more stern task today. This was my third descent from Beinn a'Chlaidheimh, my third attempt to find a decent line – and my third failure. Judging by the lack of boot marks, I probably pioneered a virgin line but arrived *intactata* so to speak.

Now, the final question to be answered, would the Abhainn Strath na Sealga be in spate? I am rather nervous of water, apart from a drop in a glass of malt, but I reckoned if Moses could get the tribe of Israel across the Red Sea I would get to Shenavall. Fortunately, neither heroics nor miracles were called for. I waded across with the waters refreshing those parts not usually reached. Glancing at my watch, I saw that, despite the Sgùrr Ban hiatus, I was half an hour inside my predicted fourteen hours. Bosom just slightly aglow, I squared up to Shenaval. Outside I thought I espied the tent, but on approach I was proven mistaken. Never mind, she would be inside preparing the life giving elixir, strong, sweet tea.

I pushed open the door, restraining the impulse to shout 'Honey, I'm home!' Lucky I did. There was just one resident, a young man. We greeted each other civilly, but at that moment my heart dropped into a black void. In the instant I realised IB was not there I knew beyond doubt that she was lying beside the wrecked van 'out there somewhere.' The dream was over at the very moment I had finally reached out to grasp it. This was our 61st day of the trip. Not once before, on mountain, glen or road, had IB failed to make a rendezvous. I sat down, suddenly very tired under the weight of my journey. The force of that relentless commitment to it became nothing but a mockery. It vaporised leaving nothing but exhaustion and emptiness. The only refuge was rational thought and I began a review of my situation to construct new realities. Today, a big one, had been a 'four butty' day. I'd saved one 'just in case'. It was a two hour walk out to Dundonnell where I must start making enquiries.

The trip was over but other things were more important. For the first and only time I confided what I was doing to the young hill walker. He was duly impressed and kindly offered me a brew and a biscuit as hoped for and gratefully received. The clock showed that there remained a bare two hours of daylight. I scraped myself to a standing position and started for the door. There came a footfall outside and a familiar face pushed against the window. Two such startling reversals of fortune when one is in extremis, as it were, was too much. Without thinking I automatically resorted to humour. 'Where the bloody hell have you been?' I said.

For one of Teutonic persuasion, IB's reply showed a remarkable and stylish grasp of basic Anglo-Saxon. The young man looked aghast and shrank against the wall. It occurred to me that my attempt at humour had not quite succeeded. I suppose when it comes down to it, Johnny Foreigner's sense of humour is not to be relied upon – your average German being, as regards this attribute, particularly suspect. Following Chamberlain, I tried a bit of appeasement, not one of my most practised virtues, admittedly. However, it brought forth the explanation – the blankety trek in had been a blankety sight longer and blankety harder than imagined. (Graphic account of staggering in under a heavy load.) Why start walk in so late? 'I blankety well did a seven mile round trip to that blankety bothy on Loch a'blankety Bhraoin to leave you some blankety butties for tomorrow.' (In my generosity I refrained from pointing out that this had not formed part of the agreed game plan.)

Soon the tent was up and the hot sweet tea being enjoyed. Warmth and humour combined with blessed relief were restoring functions both corporeal and spiritual. It seems to me that our relationships both with nature and our loved ones must, at times be tested in the crucible of fire if they are to continue to grow, strengthen, become purer, more delightful. Risk and hazard there may be, weariness and disappointment too, but to deny the venture is to lose without playing.

So I have crystallised these patterns from my kaleidoscope. I wonder, will they re-form in years to come? If I have lost something in holding fast their dance, I also feel I have gained from having once more danced along with them.

> *Let us probe the silent places, let us see what luck betide us;*
> *Let us journey to a lonely land I know.*
> *There's a whisper on the night-wind,*
> *There's a star agleam to guide us*
> *And the wild is calling, calling... let us go.*
> Robert W. Service, *Call of the Wild.*

chapter twenty-one

LOSS AND SALVATION IN HIGH PLACES

Loss

It is easy to imagine the Cairngorms before the Ice Age: a massive batholith of swelling granite bursting like an over-ripe pumpkin through the skin of north east Scotland. Featureless, so it largely remained until that great sculptor, ice, deftly carved it into three huge blocks. Today, these blocks form high plateaux sporting higher bumps or, to use a technical term, Munros. The central plateau is the loftiest but least interesting. It is merely terrific. The ones which lie to the east and west are not only terrific but more complex, richer in their bio-diversity, far less frequented and altogether wilder and more remote. The western plateau gathers itself above Glen Feshie, sweeps some six to eight miles to the summits of Braeriach and Cairn Toul, then crashes 2,000 feet into the ice gouged trough of the Làirig Ghru. It is known as the Mòine Mòr.

This tilted wilderness of granite and tundra-like vegetation, ravaged by ice, eroded by the constant attrition of snow, water and wind, vast and lonely, spreads over 40,000 acres. And I had left my ice axe in the middle of it. Nearly five months later I went to get it back. I'll tell you how it came to be left behind, not because it is all that interesting, but the story gives me an opportunity to do a bit of bragging while disguising (hopefully) my absent-mindedness.

The Mòine Mòr sprouts eight Munros around its edges. Two of these, Beinn Bhrotain and Monadh Mòr, are pretty remote whichever way you approach them. While doing my second round of Munros I'd climbed Bhrotain from the Braemar side on a winter's day. Running short of daylight I'd left its neighbour, Monadh Mòr, for another time. Opportunity presented itself on Peter's meet in Glen Feshie, also in winter. IB and I set off for the fifteen mile round trip confident that with firm névé smoothing the way seven hours should see us back in the last glim, ready for Pete's Big Eats.

Hard névé is one thing, breakable crust and powder another. Furthermore, as we gained height, we vanished into thick mist, white-out conditions in fact. If there is one thing your skilful navigator enjoys it's a white-out. (This is the bragging bit.) Thrusting compass to the fore and IB to the rear I marched resolutely forward.

Now, you probably know as well as I that distance estimate uphill, in snow is an inexact science. Seven hundred and fifty three steps later we were still going uphill. With a nod in the direction of logic, cunning replaced science. Monadh Mòr being an honest sort of creature (no false tops, simple contours, etc.) I reckoned if I followed the same bearing uphill until the 'up' just became 'down' then the top would be 'just' behind us. Plod, plod, plod... is that level? Plod, plod, plod... well, this is definitely down. Ergo, we must have passed the summit, but on which side of the cairn? Instead of going directly back I checked the mappy thing I often carry. It showed we had walked along a gentle ridge with the summit in the middle. Now I added 90 degrees to the bearing to take us at a right angle across the ridge. Depending on which side of the summit we were on this would take us either up or down. We sensed up, then level. As soon as I sensed down I about turned to get back on the level. This navigational strategy is known as the 'Grand Old Duke of York'. (I should add that during all these amazing peregrinations IB, to her eternal credit and sense of self-preservation, kept her gob firmly shut.)

Now for the *coup de main*! I reversed the original summit bearing. After a mere twenty double paces the trig loomed up at a visibility of only five to ten metres. And there, just ten metres away on the west side were our footprints from our first effort. We had drifted just ten metres off course in over a kilometre of white-out. Nonchalance failed me.

It was now nearly 2pm on a January day and the vast and awful majesty of the Mòine Mòr suddenly reasserted itself on my consciousness. Heady with success and not a little hubris I plotted an economical route back. This used a shallow re-entrant as a gathering feature thus dispensing with the need for pin sharp bearings and step counting.

Wouldn't you know! As soon as we ducked out of the miasma 'her at the back' began bleating about food. Less than five hours out and she wants to eat. Here's me with gammy joints and dodgy eyesight, winter's spectral hand drawing night's cloak over the cold shoulders of the Mòine Mòr. and all she can think of is 'what's in the nosebag?'

With some reluctance I indicated a group of boulders ahead, the only possible place to park my bum with any semblance of comfort. What a pity there was only enough space for me. With the 'ease born of long practice' I swung off my sac with one hand and with the other speared my axe into the snow. After several minutes of what the behavioural psychologists, in their quest to reduce us to machines, call 'eating behaviour' progress was resumed.

There was now some urgency in our plouter through the snow. Swirling both walking poles like a demented drum-major I hoppitty-skipped in the direction of Feshie, the anticipated smell of Pete's Peak District Goulash triggering gastronomic orgasms in those parts of the brain the behaviourists can't reach. Soon we came to the sharp break in slope below Carn Bàn Mòr. As my heel skidded on the first patch of hard névé I reached for my trusty ice axe. Discumnofferations! No ice axe. Where could it be? Rapid play-back of recent activity... realisation dawned. I turned on her. You... you... you (not quite sure of the word for women who make you forget your ice axe) JEZEBEL! (Don't think that's it either).

Sixty quids worth of Mountain Technology stranded in the wilderness, terrible. But what was worse was the shame. I would be a laughing stock. No I wouldn't. I should use a little discretion. Recount (with due modesty) the magnificent feat of navigation but regarding lost equipment, all orifices as tight as... well, never mind, but tight: Fool that I am, I once again left a certain something out of the equation. I failed to allow for the degrees of freedom consequent on the interaction between Pete's Côte du Rhône and the female brain, a particular female brain that is. Of course, in deference to my advanced age (and supposed senility) they were all very kind. Hardly laughed at all, in fact, but from that moment I knew that honour could only be redeemed by reclaiming my axe from the wilderness.

Salvation
'Whosoever delights in solitude is either a wild beast or a god.'

Francis Bacon.[1]

If you have scanned the map you will have seen that Monadh Mòr is remote, certainly not a quick tick in winter. However, even the remoter hills are ant heaps these days. My line leading to the re-entrant and the dropped axe might appeal to others. I resolved to reclaim it within a couple of weeks. Perhaps I would combine the salvage mission with my on-going quest to dis-cover a Corbett nearly half as fine as the Munros in the locale. (I'm still look-ing.) Then the big blizzards intervened. To the mind's eye my axe disap-peared under a depth of snow. A slow spring began to reduce the snow but now the foot and mouth epidemic caused the dithering policy makers to advise against access to most of our hills. Time, not unnaturally, passed. But 'time should be used as a tool not as a couch.' The foot and mouth curtain

---

[1] Bacon merely reports this statement and regards only one half of it as true.

was raised in time for the Easter Meet. IB did a splendid traverse of the Scottish Fourthousanders, skiing quite close to my still buried axe. In early May an excursion to Fisherfield revealed some excellent Corbetts, alas, sadly, eclipsed by even finer Munros. Then IB left me for Heidelberg. (A fair swap, I hear you mutter.) I remained behind, plotting.

In three weeks we were due to meet up with JR, Geoff and Wade for a bike trip over numerous Alpine passes. Last year I had been foolish enough to go on my mountain bike and had been badly mauled by these ultra competitive rascals. Once bitten is better than twice in the bush as they say. This year I intended a counter ploy. I would graft a pannier rack to my very light racing bike. The practicability of this engineering feat was uncertain. Test trials must be conducted and a cunning plan worthy of the great Baldrick had occurred to me. I would kill two stones with one bush... or should that be: a stone in the hand is worth two in the kidneys? Whatever, I could load the rack with bivvy gear, ride the 40 moderately hilly miles from home to Glen Feshie in the morning, walk out to hunt the axe, sleep in the fastness of the Mòine Mhòr and return, spiritually refreshed and hopefully financially relieved, next day.

Cyril (my road bike) stamped and snorted a bit under the unaccustomed burden of the panniers then settled to his new role. Apart from the odd buck and sideways prance as I did some pedal dancing on the steep bits he behaved impeccably. With the fearsome Tour de France passes of the Galibier, Iseran, Bonnette, etc. in mind I had fitted a triple chain ring and the hills were no problem. As I powered steeply past the Bridge of Brown tea shop the inevitable tourist made a witty thrust at the stunningly obvious, 'Eee: You must be fit.' 'Nay, Oscar,' I retorted, 'just low gears and clean living.' 'Not bad at a heart rate of 180bpm,' I thought.

Within three and a half hours I had hidden the bike in the woods at Glen Feshie, packed a small sac and set off. My route followed a marked path which ended on a steep heathery hillside. The day was fine and the May colours fresh and bright. After the slog up the heathery hill I found myself on a faint but definite trod. Unmarked on the map it led me beautifully to a high col south of Carn Bàn Mòr.

I now became a part of the Mòine Mhòr, holy ground indeed. To my left lay the ice-carved scoop of Glen Einich. If I'd turned and climbed just 300 feet to the rocky top of Sgòr Gaoith I could have looked 2,000 feet straight down into the glacial trough holding Loch Einich. I contented myself in gazing over to the eastern cliffs, still reamed with old snow. As I crested Carn Bàn Mòr I was impressed by the extent of the snow fields. All the higher re-entrants were packed as well as some lower stream channels. It was 23 May but I wondered if I had arrived too soon.

Gradually, I was drawn into that area of the Mòine Mhòr I consider to be its heart, the tumbled ground round Loch nan Cnapan. Here, for me, is a temple without an altar, a church without pews and a cathedral whose vault is the sky itself and whose music is the wind over the ground. A church stands as a monument to man's best intentions. The heart of the Mòine Mhòr simply is. It compels no act of worship for me at least. It is its own benediction and all may share it.

I climbed a little onto the flanks of Tom Dubh and at last could see my re-entrant. It now held a lively stream but the slopes were clear of snow. Just after I realised I'd left the axe I had guestimated a grid reference – 928952. This point lay less than a straight kilometre away but I could discern no group of boulders.

Originally, I had intended to leave the search for the morrow but now I was seized with a curious impatience, anxiety even. Strange, the axe had been not much more than an excuse for a little expedition. I hurried down to the Allt Luineag. This burn stretches its tributaries to almost the 4,000 foot contour, draining the entire west flank of Cairn Toul. Soon it becomes the river Eidart which joins the Feshie high on the Geldie moors. Geldie burn itself flows east to swell the Dee, but the Feshie sweeps west then north to the majestic Spey, a striking example of river capture. The Luineag, fed from extensive snow fields, was in fine form, rushing and gurgling along at a grand pace. In winter it had lain in frozen hibernation. Now it swirled between me and my objective.

First things first and don't count your chickens until you can see the whites of their eggs. Since leaving home at 9am I had cycled three and a half hours and walked four, all this on just one butty: I erected my one man bivvy (incidentally, it wasn't a one person bivvy as there was only me going in it) and performed the sacred ritual of brewing tea. Refreshed and emboldened I removed socks from feet, insoles from shoes, inserted feet into shoes and shoes into the torrent. Was it cold? Are Corbetts inferior to Munros? It was cold.

But now for the moment of truth. Was this the right brae? Is this the actual re-entrant? Could that be the windbreak of boulders? Does your chewing gum lose its flavour on the bedpost overnight? (Lost my younger readers there.) As I stood precisely where I had speared my axe into the snow five months before, I had that topsy-turvy sense of *déja vu*.

I gazed down at my axe which seemed to have just gently keeled over trailing its orange tape across the ground. Five months or five minutes? But no, its little head was red with rust. I felt as if I was reclaiming a lost child. I swear it gave a muffled sob as I gathered it to my bosom. (Amazing what a few hours of solitary walking can do to you.) I must be more tight-fisted than I thought for I plodded cheerfully back to and through the Luineag heeding not its Styx-like qualities.

For an encore I gathered handfuls of old dry grass which I stuffed into a poly' bag to make a passable pillow. With brewing materials and water within easy reach I snuggled into my goretex chrysalis. Sticking my head out I observed Cairn Toul snuggling into a duvet of lumpy, grey mist. The Luineag chattered its stony teeth and the rising wind gathered the sound and carried it over the brae. Tomorrow I would likely be flying by instrument across a mist shrouded wilderness.

At six o'clock next morning I peered blearily out. Overhead was a vast canopy of blue. Shortly, the sun would sail above the swell of Braeriach and Cairn Toul and bathe my bivvy spot. While this was happening I attended to the morning tea ritual. For once I came quickly awake, eager to be up and off over the Mòine Mhòr. On mornings such as this, no matter how early I've risen, I always wish it had been earlier. I've even walked through the night in order to be high on the hill at the moment of sunrise. It is like being present at and part of a birth; perhaps, a re-birth of the world made new, with hopes and aspirations refreshed and a bright chance to begin life again.

With the axe safely stowed and no reason for hurry I meandered over the wee eminence of Tom Dubh seeking drier patches of ground. There was a sudden flutter and a small bird pinged out from almost beneath my feet. Craning forward I soon spotted the nest, beautifully sited under a protecting veil of vegetation. There were four eggs, speckled and polished like dark marble, a tiny miracle, perhaps one of many taking place over this vast and beating wilderness. Having observed them on the High Tops I thought perhaps the bird was a snow bunting.

I walked on reflecting on the exquisite balance between fragility and strength, structure and chaos which is the essence of these high plateaux. Plants, insects and animals knit together in a symbiotic, precarious and, to my human perception, brave existence. This is a searching environment with extinction just a step away. The encircling mountain architecture speaks of immense cosmic forces. But the minute fecundity at my feet was equally the product of this energy. Rarely is the counterpoint between macrocosm and microcosm so poignantly evident as it is on the Mòine Mhòr. What does it mean? I do not think it has to mean anything, it just is. However, it certainly turned my thoughts to the meaning of the funicular railway under construction on the flanks of Cairngorm. I know what that means. It means commercialism, greed, culpable ignorance and an over-whelming crassness of mind and spirit. I despise it and all those who con-trived it.

Which did not include the poor frog who sat, quite immobile, near the middle of a large snow field. It was not there yesterday when I passed this way. In fact, it sat in one of my footprints. Poor thing! It had obviously set off full of hope but too late in the day to cross this polar waste (an 'Awful Warning'). I imagined the sun sinking as froggy battled the sastrugi. By the middle of the ice-cap the cold would be intense. Hypothermia begins to paralyse the autonomic centres. A final croak of 'For God's sake look after our tadpoles.' Then what? Suspended animation, perhaps. I picked him (or her) up; deathly cold but a flicker of movement. I carried him east as this seemed to be the direction he had been keen to head for. Soon he was perched on a nice high tussock away from the snow and in direct sunlight. I would have stayed to watch him revive but it could have been a long process. So brave, yet so foolish. I wonder what had driven him. It couldn't have been a lost ice axe.

By now the sun was slanting obliquely across the eastern ramparts of Glen Einich. Misty vapours gathering in the snow filled gullies rose and were bathed in a diffuse ethereal light. Beneath these elven clouds lurked the gaunt black bones of the mountain. But where I stood the pale, golden grass rippled and swayed to the blessing of the spring time wind. The poet Yeats longed to lay beneath his love's feet,

> ... *heavens' embroidered cloths,*
> *Enwrought with golden and silver light,*
> *The blue and the dim and the dark cloths*
> *Of night and light and the half-light,'*

now here they were, laid beneath mine.

At the start of my discovered path back to Glen Feshie I paused and enjoyed a 'Wilson of the Wizard' episode. Opening my box of raw oats and raisins I mixed them with a draught of pure spring water. Then, donning a black one-piece swimming costume I hefted a 100lb boulder and ran lightly to the summit of Sgòr Gaoith. (Well, the bit about the oats is true.) Reluctantly, I picked my way down. Back through the sweet scented Caledonian pines, beneath new sprung birches, beside the vigorous burn. In the plantation Cyril waited, refreshed and eager to be off, certain now of his selection for the Alpine tour.

chapter twenty-two

THE ART OF STREAM CROSSING

WARNING **The following contains explicit examples of political incorrectness and may cause offense.**

'Discord', says Tilman's favourite Chinese sage, 'is not sent down from heaven, it is brought about by women.' Nonsense, of course; it certainly wasn't her fault that I had just stepped on an icy boulder and fallen in the Dee. The infant Dee, I should add, a mere foot or so of somewhat chilly water. If I hadn't been carrying a heavy rucksack I could have leapt up again in an instant. And if my arm hadn't been soaked, the water would not have drain-piped into my mitt, my unfortunately waterproof mitt; still, it took my mind off my leg.

Have you noticed when you're out with mates and you have, let's say, a misfortune, the hoots of laughter at your expense stimulate your own cheerfulness. You proceed onwards chuckling and, in a way, a bit of a lad, almost a hero. Why is it that in similar situations women can always manage sympathy? Real sympathy, too. And isn't it just bloody infuriating? You stand there dripping/trembling/bleeding and you don't even get your richly deserved credit for entertainment value. More like: 'Oh dear! Are you alright? You must be awfully wet/bruised/blistered/maimed etc. Do be careful... especially at your age.' They never seem to realise it's all part of the game. Having dragged yourself out of the river/bog/crevasse/volcano you're given no time to strike the nonchalant pose or even utter the manly oath before they are making you feel the incompetent bumbler you undoubtedly are.

A less charitable person might have construed the original fault, like Eve's, to have been hers anyway. I wouldn't normally fall into a piddling little stream like this. I might get swept away making a perilous crossing of the Spey in spiteful spate. But not this babbling brook. It was the dingy light; and the light was dingy because she wouldn't get a move-on; had been irresponsibly slow; had, in fact, taken advantage of my tolerant ways. I should never have let her walk the three miles of stony track to Derry Lodge in trainers. Then she wouldn't have had to unpack her boots and climb a deer fence (both ways) to find a hiding place for the said trainers. The fuss she made, you'd think it was treasure trove. She just wouldn't hurry to catch me up either, sheer obstinacy. I could see that in order to get over Càrn a'Mhaim and Ben Macdui in good order I would have to take a very stern line, not only with her but also with Naismith and his formula.

She would undoubtedly plead for a food stop if the wind and spindrift eased a little. They did and she did. I will admit the snowy boulder fields wantonly strewn around Ben Macdui were a bit steep, awkward and went on a great deal. However, her rate of climbing was abysmal; I'm sure she was resting when I was out of sight. I knew I shouldn't have let her carry most of the gear, she's just not trustworthy. Still, I must have impressed her with the seriousness of the situation when I strode ahead into the summit mist; particularly as I had the compass, and the map.

Perhaps I overdid it. She flew past me downhill. Just no consideration for the dilapidated state of my leg hinges. Proper mountaineers don't race downhill like that. But she didn't attempt to be first across the Dee. Too cunning for that; knew there was ice about; hasn't got a very good record with river crossings.

I sometimes imagine I must be a born leader. I always seem to be in front over insecure ground like bog, snow bridges, slippery planks, and... icy boulders. (Perhaps 'born leader' is not quite the phrase I'm looking for.) Yes, of course I probed the boulders for ice, I'm not a fool. It would take a crafty boulder to catch me out. And it was. This boulder was wearing ice like a monk wears a tonsure. Treacherous swine! (The boulder, I mean.) Naturally, had it not been so dingy I would have spotted the tonsure, I mean the ice. And it would not have been dingy if she, standing there patronisingly sympathetic, had got a bloody move-on!

But I'm not a born whatever for nothing, besides I remembered what happened to the trapper in that Jack London tale who fell into a river in Arctic Canada and had his fire doused by a branchful of snow (he froze to death). It's the double whammy you've got to watch. Staggered by the straight left you switch your attention and catch the *coup de grace* amidships. Still a good mile to the refuge in An Garbh Choire and getting darker by the stumble. The map seemed fairly useless, I've not much faith in mappy things in daylight and I can't see them at all when it's dark.

Fortunately, I have a mountaineer's memory. Once I've been to a place, I can always find it again. Well I can, sometimes. Wouldn't you know, some

---

[1] Naismith's rule for estimating walking time is three mph + 25 minutes per 1000 feet of climbing.

damn fool had moved the refuge to the other side of the stream since I was last here, only 20 years ago? For 'other' side of stream read 'far' side, i.e. the side opposite to the one on which we stood. The 'true right bank' as they say, we being on the true left bank as it were.

Fortunately, as an old campaigner I can spot a double whammy a mile off, literally in this case. After that mile we could make out the tantalising hump that denoted the refuge, still, alas, on the true right bank of yet another infant Dee. This one was the issue of the Wells of Dee, high above on the Braeriach-Cairn Toul plateau. More of a juvenile delinquent Dee, I should say. Deeper, wider, faster and a good deal icier; darker, too. (Her fault again.) 'You go first, your eyesight is better than mine,' says I (I can be crafty, too). Did me no good though. A certain amount of timorous probing and she was back looking for leadership. On my mettle I spied a mercifully narrow channel with a neatly placed boulder half way. The crucial question was whether it glistened with water or ice. The shrewd glance of experience proclaimed the former. With one mighty bound I hurtled across. As my foot hit the boulder it skidded violently – black ice. Before I had a chance to shout 'double whammy' my velocity had carried me to safety, apart from some minor splashing.

Triumph was shortlived. I realised I was now in possession of a small island. Peering through the gloom I could see little beyond the impossibility of going further. For some moments I shared the indecision suffered by the ranks of Tuscany where those at the back cried 'Forward' and those at the front cried 'Back'. The honest certainty of getting very wet going forward contrasted with the horrible uncertainty of returning via the icy boulder. Flinging caution to the winds and myself over the icy boulder I sprawled in an ungainly heap back on the 'home' bank. I don't suppose I would have fallen if I hadn't been expecting to. My serious loss of dignity was quite overshadowed by my severe loss of temper. Her words of sympathy were withered on the bough. 'Go,' I said (or words to that effect), 'go ye and seek a safe way across. Thou art a woman and hast craft and guile, go forth and use it. And be bloody quick about it.'

It may be suspected that I was losing faith in my mountaineer's instinct for choosing a line through bad ground. I was, until pride intervened. Born leaders don't send women out to do men's work, do they? By the time she returned, having failed in her mission, muttering some defeatist nonsense about paddling across, I had it cracked! Quite astonishingly, the stream converged into a narrows a mere five or six feet across. True, one had to jump onto a higher, sloping bank. True, the take-off boulder was at a funny angle and had a bit of ice. Admittedly, if you should miss the jump you would either fall into the deep pool below or fall into the narrows and be swept forthwith into the pool, but all that was negative thinking. I could see that my leadership qualities would be needed to the full here as she was already eyeing the proposed leap like a nervous filly at Beecher's.

Waving my axe for emphasis I explained how I would leap across *sans* sac, and she would join me after flinging the ruckers over for me to catch. As I said this I belatedly recalled that, last time she had attempted to fling a heavy sac across a stretch of water, she had omitted to let go. I hoped she had forgotten though the look on her face suggested she hadn't. Leaving her opening and shutting her mouth (she may have been saying something), I psyched myself up for the leap. Whirling my axe high I went for it... and cleared the narrows easily, whacking the pick into the sloping turf to arrest any tendency to roll backwards. I was exultant. 'No problem, dead easy, it must only be a couple of feet wide.' (I seem to recall the same sentiments expressed on the crag as the leader reaches the top of a particularly scary pitch and is anxious his second should share the same fun.)

'I can't do that,' she said very firmly. 'Yes you blankety well can!'

'No I can't.'

This 'conversation' was repeated several times with the rapid addition of more blankety's. I adjusted my tactics. 'You've got to try. Get on that boulder.' I swear I'd scraped off all the ice but she skidded about like a demented banana at a disco. 'I can't even stand up.'

'Nonsense, I just jumped off it.' 'But you've got such wonderful balance.' A difficult one to counter so I ignored it. 'You've got to get across, I can't jump back down onto that boulder, and the blankety sacs are on your side.' 'But you said the boulder was safe.' Deadlock...

...Broken by temper; with sanctuary 50 yards behind me and an obstinate mule in front I know what I should have done, if only I had my sac. But I hadn't. With a mighty oath I flung myself across the by now very black gap, landing plumb on the boulder and arresting my flight in an adjacent boulder field. It was perhaps as well I'd forgotten to bring the axe but I made partial amends with a speech of amazing violence whose general tenor was the unreliability and pusillanimity of the female species, in particular... etc. Right, it was every man for himself or herself. To hell with responsible leadership. As I turned to storm the very Wells of Dee if necessary I noticed she was removing boots and socks. Treachery added to cowardice! After all I'd been through she was now going to desert me. There are only three things I cannot tolerate: cold water, walking around in bare feet and carrying a rucksack through cold water in bare feet. She knows this very well. So be it.

After twenty yards I saw where her boot prints had gone to the stream edge earlier. Knocking the brittle shell of ice off a couple of boulders with my ski stick I crossed with embarrassing ease. I met her coming to look for me, still in bare feet. 'Imbecile,' I remarked, 'and how are your feet?'

'Just drying off in the snow. It's good for your circulation, you know.' I shuddered.

In the bright morning light I insisted on returning to 'Beecher's Brook' so she could see the feeble little gap at which her craven nature had baulked. It was appalling. Surely I hadn't leaped from icy rock to frozen bank across that savage slit through which swirled a powerful torrent on its way to a black pool many feet below; and back again? I felt her gaze upon me. 'Well?' she said. I reflected. 'Thank God for my awful night vision.'

PS: After an enjoyable traverse of the Braeriach plateau we came once again to the Dee. This time a little further down, near Corrour Bothy. I stood musing on the bank. Was this the spot where I'd fallen in twenty years ago? Well, no point messing about, time to exercise those famous qualities of intrepid leadership again, and this time... 'Hey!'

'Hey, what?'

'Why are you staring at that boulder, aren't you going to use the footbridge? It says it's been here since 1959.'

Footbridge, *mon dieu*, what is the world coming to?

'Of course I am. What do you take me for, some kind of fool?' No reply was the diplomatic answer.

chapter twenty-three

A STILL POINT IN THE CAIRNGORMS

The idea was born one time when I stood on Ben Avon, gazing west into the rolling Cairngorm sprawl of mountain and heathland. Sharp, soaring peaks, as may be found in the west of Scotland, invite conquest. They challenge the gladiatorial instinct. But the traverse of remote wilderness areas is more likely to constitute an enriching journey of exploration.

Just eight weeks after taking possession of a shiny new hip I again stood atop a Munro. Fitness gradually returned as did plans and dreams. Once more I gazed west across the Cairngorms. I was confident now of my ability to undertake the traverse of the high uplands. I solved the logistical problems by inviting Inken to do my traverse in reverse. She would cycle eight miles of estate road up Glen Avon; after leaving our van at Coire Cas below Cairngorm, I would traverse east to the bike and we would all be reunited at Tomintoul (hopefully!).

At 7am on a breathless summer morning I waved a hasty farewell to wife and bike. It was the kind of morning that prompts impatience to be off. A temperature inversion filled the glens with mist. Cobwebs held up prisms of dew to the seeking sun. High above, the hills were sharp and beckoning. I started from Coire Cas in cold shadow, my back to the desolation of concrete and steel that marks the ski 'development' and that monument to crass commercialism, the Cairngorm Funicular. Mountains in general and the Cairngorms in particular for me represent temples of the spirit. Here, at the portal of a great cathedral, traders had erected a market stall.

Closing my mind to the ugliness I lifted my gaze to the splendours of the new day. The path carried me easily towards Lurchers. To my left the winter playgrounds of Corries an't Sneachda and an Lochain waited in shadow; to all things their season. Last time I'd been here the whiplash of spindrift had scourged the skin. Now, approaching the Cairngorm plateau, I was unlayering like an onion as the sun burnt down. In shorts and vest I picked my way towards Ben Macdui. The granite underfoot clunked and rang through the still air. The visibility was outstanding. Behind me the Monadhliath rolled their peaty waves into northern distance, ahead, Beinn a'Ghlo bulked on the horizon and, almost within touching distance it seemed, Braeriach and Cairn Toul stood sharp against a sky of rarest blue. Just one tiny shield of snow remained high in the Garbh Coire, a link between the seasons.

So far the plateau had been deserted. On the summit of Macdui I met just one walker. I had not left Coire Cas until after 8am it was now after 10am, but where were the crowds celebrating this incredible morning? Weather forecasts and maps may be used as keys to unlock those proverbial windows of opportunity. I had tracked weather patterns for the past few days to help me stalk and pounce on this rare day. But I was not about to complain of the solitude and meeting the odd person is never a problem. Rarely is friendly contact made more naturally and easily than on a hill top. This rugged individual was a South African in Scotland for the first time and exploring the high plateau alone. I persuaded him to deviate a little from the high ground. By coming with me to Loch Etchachan he would be able to descend north to discover the hidden gem of Loch Avon, peer up in awe at the mighty Shelter Stone Crag and visit its eponymous and historic howff.

We parted cheerfully at Etchachan from where I dropped steeply down to the Hutchison Hut. It seemed Braemar had produced some early birds as I greeted folk toiling upwards in various states of repair, all looking warmish. Around the hut itself was a merry group of more 'senior' walkers. They seemed impressed I was already descending Macdui. A smiling lady enquired if I sometimes indulged in a little running. 'Only when I trip up,' I replied modestly and almost truthfully.

After the Hutchison my route headed for the wilderness. I cut across a rough shoulder of ground that linked bog, tussock and heather in a devilish combination. Soon I stood in the Làirig an Laoigh (Pass of the Calf), one of the old droving routes which the tough Highlanders of old used to get their great horned beasts to the cattle fairs of Crieff and Callander. At the mercy of weather and midges they would sleep out here wrapped in their plaids. A different breed of man; but they would have their 'crack' and drams of *uisge beatha* to sustain their spirits.

My own spirit could have benefited from an infusion of theirs as I selected a poor line up the steep side of the pass. By the top I was ready for an early lunch. Perched on a boulder I gazed back west to the mountain panorama across which I had picked my way. Soaring above the drovers' pass was Beinn Mheadhoin ('Vane') or 'middle' mountain lying in the deep, beating heart of the whole massif. Like Ben Avon its top is sprinkled with huge granite tors. This east facing aspect told its tale of former glacial savagery and the ripping power of melt water. Crags encircled the Hutchison refuge and formed a brooding backdrop to Loch Etchachan. Humped above all was Macdui, probably by now as busy as a hive at a bees' wedding.

Fortified, I turned to face one of the great wilderness areas of the Cairngorms, the Mòine Bhealaidh. On an east to west traverse, there is a distinctive route choice. The low road involves a fair amount of bog hopping over the cross-grained terrain. So, for me it's the high road, over the remote Munro summit of Beinn a'Chaoruinn. This hill lies directly across from Beinn Mheadhoin with the Làirig an Laoigh recessed 350 metres below them. With a linear separation of only two kilometres Beinn a'Chaoruinn is quite different in character, for its summit boulder fields are matched only by those of Derry Cairngorm.

Another reason for choosing the high line was that I knew Inken would be taking this route. Sure enough, I met her, jinking an intricate line through the round, pink granite. We spent a few moments swapping and sharing the joy of what was turning out to be one of the great days. From here on I saw no other person, nor did I expect to. The Mòine Bhealaidh is a domain where solitude reigns.

In the col between Beinn a'Chaoruinn (the Hill of the Rowan) and its lower twin, the 'Wee Hill of the Rowan', nestle a group of tiny lochans. Reflecting the light of the sky, bordered by brightly lichened rocks, they lay like jewels on the dark ground. The nearest trees were miles away, but it was not hard to imagine a scattering of rowans fulfilling the ancient role of sanctifying this holy ground. When the deer were encouraged to multiply and munch their way over the hills a precious measure of fragile beauty was lost to the Highlands. Yet even without trees the scene was utterly beautiful; water, rock, lichens, arctic mosses and rough grasses. A place of enchantment seldom gazed upon. It would bestow peace through quiet contemplation in days yet unborn. A little later I thought how my journey had contrived to bring me here at this moment in time. Equidistant from my start and finish I stood at the pivotal point, this place held poised and still.

> *After the kingfisher's wing has answered light to light and is silent the world is still at the still point of the turning world.* [1]

Stillness, peace and beauty and the wisdom to understand the fundamental and imperative nature of these qualities to the human spirit; this is what the wilderness will teach us if we but pause and reflect.

My journey over the remainder of the Mòine seemed to be a celebration of mosses. They lay like sponges in streams and carpeted acres of bog, all colours from black to lurid green. The arctic-alpine plants of the Highlands and Cairngorms in particular occupy a precarious niche. Arctic-alpine

---

[1] T. S. Eliot, *Burnt Norton.*

implies that they are normally found at much higher altitudes or in more northern latitudes. In this regard they are a gift left behind by the last ice-age, 10,000 years ago. As I picked my way across this rare tapestry which had established a tenuous hold in a harsh environment a half-remembered line of verse whispered in my mind,

Tread carefully, for you may be treading on hallowed ground.

The Mòine began to heave itself upwards. A final weaving around vigorous head waters and deep sphagnum mosses started a climb towards the great wave crest of Beinn a'Bhùird. The map belies the detail on the ground. Gaunt outcrops of rock break the contours, energetic streams leap over mossy boulders. This immense flank of the mountain is a stratified eco-system. Varied and vigorous vegetation clothes its lower slopes. This diminishes as one climbs. By the summit, only 1,000 feet higher, the plants are sparse and tundra-like, clutching the gravelly ground. And at the top a few more strides brought greater changes. The hill is a whale back ridge, nearly two miles in length, nudging the 4,000 foot contour. But an icy shark has taken huge bites out of the whale's east flank. Dropping abruptly below my feet the ground tumbled down to some of the grandest corrie scenery in the Highlands. This is the winter preserve of the ice-climber. However, nearly ten miles from the nearest road only the dedicated hard man, howff dweller or anchorite will endure the rigours.

The Linn of Avon.

Not far beyond the summit I sat and ate at a favourite place. Almost impossibly high on these wild uplands streams with an imperative sense of purpose rise, swell and hurtle down. Joining waters from the Mòine Bhealaidh in Glen Quoich they bolster the flood of the noble Dee. This is another blessed place of life and light. Green mosses, alpine plants, pink shelves of granite, dancing waters; here was a refuge for the spirit indeed. And so down steeply to the Sneck with a quick glance to the crags on my left. Here the classic rock of Mitre Ridge sweeps up from the desolate bowl of the Slochd Mòr. The Sneck is the tenuous col between Beinn a'Bhùird and Ben Avon. It has a guardian. A granite 'man' hides in the scoured boulders. Cross here when the mist banners are flying and you will encounter him looming and shrinking. I doubt you will be inclined to argue territorial rights.

The climb from the Sneck was the last of the day. It carried me to the tor-littered uplands of Ben Avon. The mountain is perhaps the most complex in the Cairngorms, if not the whole of Scotland. It is a swirl and roll of broad-backed ridges, sweeping grasslands, deep cut glens and brooding corries. The distinctive tors can be seen from distant Deeside and Donside while the actual summit, Leabaidh an Daimh Bhuidhe (Bed of the Yellow Stag) is a massive granite bastion. Today, it was a simple scramble, armoured in ice it might prove a test.

The final glen beckoned yet still there was time and space for a gentle leave taking. The peace of the high places, the imprint of this pilgrimage across hallowed ground slowly suffused mind and spirit. The threads of my plans for just another journey had been woven into a magical tapestry, a thing of beauty to shine through the years ahead.

In time, I stood on the final slopes looking down to the dancing waters in the Linn of Avon. Beyond it was the river's birch scattered glen. Here, two weeks earlier, we had watched an osprey poaching fish. Soon I was ambling along the glen on the bike. The life force of the River Avon rising from the living heart of the Cairngorms was ever alongside; leaping, foaming, dancing, flowing, a celebration of life itself.

In my mind, moments before the turning world turned again, I stood once more at the still point of the lonely lochan. I re-lived that same sense of wonder. Einstein said that a sense of wonder is the mysterious emotion which stands at the cradle of true art and science. I believe it also signifies a gleam of gold among the dross for it reveals the spiritual aspect of our nature, an aspect which finds its counterpoint in the beauty, innocence and joy of wild places. In the innocence and beauty of wilderness there is yet hope.

Final Munro,
B Hope.
Record 66 days
7 hours

chapter twenty-four

ROUND AND ROUND AND ROUND

By Mike Hartley, abridged by Mike Cudahy

Preamble

This ultimate account is just that. It was written by my friend Mike Hartley. It is his story of the ultimate ultra. What Mike achieved has, to my mind, never had the recognition it most assuredly merits. Perhaps it is so extraordinary it defeats the imagination, is almost literally incredible in fact. But this is far more than a tale of amazing statistics. His account will transport you to realms far beyond the quotidian of hard endeavour. Earlier in the book I wrote that our frailty is not what matters but how we embrace that frailty. When we are at our most frail our spirit may shine most brightly. This is the story of a journey which moves through that arch of frailty, shedding one kind of strength but gaining another and greater. It is inevitable that on such a journey, when the dark shades create shadows of doubt the flame to which our eyes are drawn is held aloft by our friends and those we love.

I hope you find inspiration in what follows and what has gone before.

Recovery from the Pennine Way[1] left me feeling I had achieved what I considered the ultimate record but not necessarily the ultimate run. I knew I could have gone farther, certainly into another night, not very quickly and maybe not without sleep, but I could have carried on. I still needed to experience the ultimate effort. I had to know just how far I could really go, to see what was round the corner of the third night.

Once the enjoyment of breaking the record had subsided I mulled over a few possibilities for 1990. Eventually I hit upon an idea that suited me ideally - the Three British Rounds.[2]

This consecutively would surely provide the ultimate test, at 183 miles and 83,000 feet of ascent I would be in no doubt as to just where my limits lay. It seemed such an obvious challenge it was surprising it hadn't been

---

[1] This refers to Mike's as yet unbeaten Pennine Way record run of two days seventeen hours and twenty minutes.

[2] Details at end of this chapter.

tried before. After all, the Three British Peaks are often done, running, cycling, sailing, etc., so I would look upon it as an extended version of that: Ben Nevis, Scafell Pike and Snowdon – plus 110 tops.

As the day drew near the run took on an ominous feeling, the 83,000 feet seemed to be getting bigger by the day. Gill told me to keep it in perspective. 'Lots of people have done this sort of thing before,' she said. Not that I knew any. Well, it was too late to change my mind now, everything was ready, pacers clued up. I'd opened my big mouth so many times I had to do it. I searched in vain for some physical reason why I couldn't start. I had to admit I was fully fit. At last I convinced myself it wouldn't be any harder than the Pennine Way, the 83,000 feet of ascent would be offset by the fact that it was 90 miles shorter. If only I'd known how wrong I was.

Ramsay Round

At 1am on Friday, 13 July, the moment arrived. On Thursday I'd enjoyed the company of my support team but I'd only been able to pick at my meal and had not been able to sleep at all. As I jogged alone along the lane and up through the mist shrouded forest I had time to weigh up my chances. On the minus side I had been suffering increasingly bruised feet through the summer. On the plus side I had found a solo Bob Graham[3] – in 20 hours and five minutes fairly easy so I knew I had the stamina and, probably, the right mental attitude. It felt exciting to take on something that had not been tried before. I also knew there were some who thought it could not be done.

I was running solo for the first seven hours and the Mamores were dark, misty and lonely. If the weather forecast was correct the mist would clear by lunchtime. Descending Stob Ban the mist parted just long enough to reveal Fort William far below. 'Fort William,' I shouted to the mist, 'it can't be.' With relief I realised it was, of course, Kinlochleven. I ran with caution downhill through the mist, compass in one hand, torch in the other. I wasn't looking at a map but using detailed notes and bearings that I'd established on training runs, this worked very well. Soon I passed the place where I'd lost part of my torch while helping Pete Simpson on his round in June; following him down the steep rocky descent of Stob Ban at night without a torch was frightening. I've never been so glad to see the dawn in my life.

Alex (Macrae) had all my food and drink laid out when I reached An Gearanach, he had been there some time and must have been frozen. It was nice to take a five minute breather on this rocky perch. After making the awkward contour of Stob Choire a'Chairn I was soon climbing Na

---

[1] The Lake District 24 hour round.

Gruagaichean, almost treading on a family of ptarmigan as they scuttled round my feet. On Binnein Mor I faced what is probably the most important route choice on this leg. The north ridge looked longer but also easier than the one to the north east, so with my compass at north I set off down. Soon the small path disappeared into boulders and rough ground. It was too late to change my mind. Suddenly I was out of the mist and, as if by magic, onto short grass all the way to the lochan. Passing this on its west side was also good going. The gamble had paid off. I was on Binnein Beag in 35 minutes against a schedule time of 40. The isolated aspect of Binnein Beag makes it look quite intimidating. But in what seemed no time at all I was up and down and running along the superb descending path towards Sgùrr Eilde Mor, the last hill of the Mamores.

John and Clive were waiting at Loch Eilde Mor with welcome food and hot tea. Having just run over the eleven Munros of the Mamores ridge solo, partly in darkness and mist, I was feeling pleased. I was seventeen minutes up on schedule and, with so much potential for mishap, relieved to get this ultra off to a good start.

I was apprehensive about the punishment 83,000 feet of descent would inflict on my already bruised feet. So clean socks, vaseline and soft road shoes seemed sensible preparation for the next eight stony miles to the foot of Beinn na Lap. As I set off with John, I first noticed a slight but ominous twinge behind my right knee. While Clive returned to Kinlochleven to set up a 24 hour telephone check with Gerald Woolley, John and I gained steadily on the schedule over Beinn na Lap and the next two Munros. After the complex top of Stob Coire Sgriodain we dropped off steeply to the railway alongside Loch Treig.

Loch Treig dam is the only support point near a road head on the Ramsay round. At 37 miles, fourteen Munros and twelve hours into the circuit it is well over half way. However, the second part of the round has most of the longest climbs and on very rough going. This, combined with the lack of road support probably make the Ramsay two hours harder than the Bob Graham. Clive had all my gear ready and after ten minutes I was off, in shorts at last.

I enjoyed feeling the wind and sun on my legs as I set off up Stob a'Choire Mheadhoin accompanied by Brian Dodson and Nigel Rose. I'd not met them before but their friendliness and obvious expertise made me feel at ease. They took me up a cunning route on small trods and tracks, jogging and walking we arrived on this majestic top another eight minutes up on schedule. We were due to meet Pete Simpson and Ian Leighton in the Làirig Leacach but we could not see them and I began to feel anxious. Then, with impeccable timing, we all coincided after crossing the burn.

The long climb up Stob Ban took its toll. But sixteen Munros and 44 miles were bound to have an effect. I told myself not to worry. It was nothing I hadn't experienced before and wouldn't experience again. With 97 tops and 139 miles still to go I must be patient and, as Dennis Beresford so often said to me during the Pennine Way, 'just keep putting it away'. The weather was now perfect and the switch-back ridge of the Grey Corries stretching before us under a crystal clear sky made for a truly memorable traverse. The Ben looked quite close, but the rough going over the nine and a half miles and 6,500 feet of ascent to reach it would take five hours.

I glanced south to the Mamores which looked impressive. I felt a good deal of satisfaction in having traversed them in the dark solitude of the night, taking full responsibility for my decisions. As we climbed Sgùrr Chòinnich Mòr I remembered my last visit here, caught in a white-out without axe or crampons. I'd crept down snow slopes fearing at any moment to start an uncontrollable slide. Now the boulders were white but dry and the wind just refreshing to working muscles and a concentrating mind. Soon we were meeting Alex with more food before the major ascent to Aonach Beag. The climb up to the Aonachs was gigantic. The 1,650 feet seemed to take forever. But in due course we made it to Carn Mòr Dearg and the traverse of its famous arête; airy, spectacular and very enjoyable. It was such a great place to be at the end of a great day that our slow progress seemed not to matter. After a photograph on the summit of the Ben I changed into soft shoes for the long, stony descent to the Nevis Youth Hostel. As I followed Pete I reflected how odd it was that, instead of relaxing and sleeping, I would be climbing Skiddaw with Graham Eccles and Geoff Fletcher in a few hours.

Soon we crossed the footbridge to finish this first and toughest round in 21 hours and 14 minutes. It was such a shame that my wife Gill wasn't here, it was the first time I'd completed a major run without her. I knew it was going to get harder, she would be there when I really needed her. Within six minutes I'd changed, said a hurried thanks to Pete and Alex. Ian ran up to the car just in time to pass my feeder bottle through the window as we drove off.

The plan was to eat then sleep. I started gulping down pasta and soup. It had been quite cool on the Ben but now I was boiling over, my thermostat could not cope. The pasta was on its way back up the expansion pipe. Luckily there was a plastic bag at hand, unluckily it contained spare gear. Perhaps I should have used the food flask and recycled it later. I eventually managed to eat, but only some tinned oranges. The plan didn't seem to be working too well. I wrapped a blanket around me and tried to sleep. It was a four and a half hour drive and I slept for perhaps two hours or less.

The Bob Graham Round

At Keswick Moot Hall (2:45am) Geoff and Graham were surprised to see me jump out of the car ready to go. My legs felt stiff on the climb to Skiddaw, but a steady walk put us on top in one hour and 30 minutes, fourteen minutes up on schedule. After Great Calva and a pleasant foot cooling splash through the river Caldew I enjoyed weaving down the rocky ridge of Halls Fell, always an exciting run.

At Threlkeld I spent time urgently attending to a lump of hard skin on my foot. Then, with Andy Brear and Howard Sawyer, I was off over the Dodds on what was now a beautiful morning. Compared to Scotland the going seemed like a run in the park. However, I was definitely tiring and I knew things were going to become much harder.

Descending Seat Sandal I was astonished to see six cars and Pete's motorbike waiting for me. Gill was by the stile, expectant, wondering how I was. From now on I would have her strength and optimism to help me. I left for Steel Fell on schedule and in good spirits. With Clive and John I was up in 25 minutes and continued to pick up time over the Pikes to Rossett Pike, where Frank Yates appeared with a succulent lump of melon. Rejuvenated, we took the diagonal line to Bowfell and soon met up with Andy and Howard on Scafell Pike. Beyond Mickledore we all headed for Broad Stand, the quickest way to Scafell and a route I'd enjoyed climbing many times.

After some foot aid at Wasdale I set off up Yewbarrow with Colin Brooke. I had gained one hour and sixteen minutes on my original schedule of 25 hours and 18 minutes so a sub-24 hour round was just possible. It was the day of the Wasdale Fell Race and some of the long distance specialists had waited to see me come in. Martin Stone accompanied us part of the way, while Colin made light work of the heavy sac. He always had what I wanted at the top. Although it was now 6:45pm the heat was intense, burning the backs of my legs and radiating off the boulders. It was one of those occasions in ultra running when the atmosphere and the environment are so perfect, so unforgettable and, for me, indescribable. Perhaps the mind is more receptive to these times when the body is tired, or maybe it just wants a distraction and clings to it when it finds one.

On Great Gable the sun was setting and the wind was cold. Graham and Geoff met us there and I was glad of their help to put on extra clothes as my balance didn't feel too good on steep ground. By Green Gable it was dark and with the darkness came a wave of fatigue. My system wanted to shut down, I couldn't seem to coordinate properly. Every stone I stepped on was a loose one and every tussock turned my ankle. Stumbling down to John's van at Honister my enthusiasm was evaporating. I wanted to stop but knew that with a big effort a sub-24 hour Bob Graham was just possible. That would be a real thrill, something to be proud of. I could almost justify stopping at the Moot Hall. Almost! The problem was that I'd set out to complete all Three Rounds, I'd said I was going to do it. I knew deep inside, when I got to Keswick I would get in the car and go down to Wales. If the Paddy Buckley Round was going to hurt, then so be it.

Dale Head, Hindscarth and Robinson went quite easily. We made the road at Newlands Church with one hour left. At the end of a Bob Graham these last undulating four miles usually take about 46 minutes. For me, today, I knew it would be a close run thing. I channelled every last bit of energy and determination into it, pushing hard all the way. Never once did I allow myself to ease off. My mind kept turning to the Moot Hall. A part of me didn't want to go any further, a part of me didn't think I could. A last and more insistent part knew I would carry on.

We arrived at the Moot Hall in 23 hours and 48 minutes. I was soaked in sweat and totally exhausted. Gill and I didn't even discuss stopping the attempt, we both knew I would get to Wales, start the Paddy Buckley Round and see what happened. After all, that was one of the reasons I started this escapade, to go that bit farther than last time, to find the ultimate experience, to do the ultimate run.

Richard Ezard drove me down to Plas-y-Brenin with Gill navigating. I had too many aches and pains to sleep properly. Every time I slipped into a fitful doze some physical discomfort would wake me up, either a painful muscle or joint, but usually it was my feet pressing against the side of the car as we went round a corner. As we sped along the coast road towards Conwy the rising sun was a huge red ball sat on the horizon behind us. A new day, a new experience to live through. Next time the sun rose I would be up on the Glyders somewhere.

The Paddy Buckley Round

My feet were so sore and battered they would need some extra protection if they were to survive the next 30-odd hours. I left Plas-y-Brenin wearing a pair of lightweight boots, one and a half sizes too big with two pairs of insoles. Although a bit on the heavy side they worked quite well. The insoles gave underfoot cushioning, the large size prevented my toes from being hurt on the descents. The rubber and general strength made the stubbing of toes not as painful as it might have been.

My walk up Moel Siabod can only be described as slow, taking one hour exactly. As we jogged slowly along the ridge towards Clogwyn Bwlch-y-Main I felt I had to apologise to Geoff Pettengell and Mike Laurence for going so slowly. As we picked off these minor tops it became tempting to stop, just for a few seconds or a minute, at each summit cairn. Eventually I conceded on Allt Fawr and took a five-minute break, stupid really as it was downhill all the way to the next support point at Bwlch Cwmorthin. I was glad to see Gill and Richard had walked up with food and drink. A pain-killer here helped to relieve devastated feet and an increasingly painful knee.

John Amies joined us as we set off for the Moelwyns, all three of my companions were carrying water bottles. I was drinking every few minutes in an attempt to combat the heat of the day. The potentially awkward con-tour to Cnicht was easy today in good visibility, but not so the final pull to its top. I felt I was now running low on reserves, reserves that couldn't be replenished by food or rest. When I finished this epic, if I finished it, I would have nothing left. We soon jogged into Aberglaslyn, still ahead of a three and a half day schedule.

John and Frank Thomas talked me up Moel Hebog, a long and desper-ately hard climb at this stage. We discussed the wisdom of including a cou-ple of minor tops but did them anyway. A front of bad weather had moved in almost unnoticed, suddenly it was raining and I felt cold. Such was my tiredness I needed John's assistance with zips and fastening of my water-proofs. The normally enjoyable, airy and technical ridge to Y Garn was today wet, slippery and hateful. My spirits were raised enormously when at one point on the descent John slipped onto his back. The combination of wet waterproofs and wet grass caused him to accelerate at an alarming rate. It was the funniest thing I'd seen for three days.

At Rhyd Ddu I took a 26 minute break, the longest during the actual rounds so far. It was the lull before the storm. The storm was not to be a bat-tle against wind and rain or hill and bog but a battle with physical and men-tal trauma at a level I'd never experienced before. In the comfort of John's van Gill and I went through the ritual of her trying to find something I want-ed to eat and me finding everything unappetising. The simple task of chang-ing my clothes was difficult, painful and tiresome. At least the anti-prona-tion pad on my heel was working well. We packed food, drink, warm cloth-ing and plenty of torch power for the coming night.

With Anne Stentiford and Pete Simpson I left Rhyd Ddu at 7:37pm in improving weather. My schedule times now looked ominous, although I was one hour and 40 minutes up on my three and a half day schedule, I was also one hour and nineteen minutes down on my 29 hours and ten minutes allowance for this round. I was slowly but surely losing time. The vague idea that I might speed up was always in my mind, maybe I could do the Buckley Round in 27 hours and therefore average 24 hours per round. Ever the optimist!

As we set off up the track I felt quite reasonable, all things considered.

Certainly, I was tired, this would be my fourth night without any real sleep. It would require a massive effort, my breaking point would be tested. But my spirits were good, in an odd sort of way I was looking forward to this challenge. Despite my quiet confidence I was not prepared for the sheer physical effort required to walk uphill, to put one foot in front of the other, I was not prepared for the mental application required just to keep going, to stay awake, to survive. My pace slowed all the time.

By Craig Wen we were in mist, which thickened as we approached Snowdon, my senses also became dulled and confused. I was sinking into depths of tiredness I didn't know existed. There was no fear (yet), for the moment I was happy to be in the company of Anne and Pete on the brink of what promised to be the ultimate experience, the ultimate run. Suddenly we stepped out of the mist, we stood only a few feet above the clouds, a raging, silent sea lapping at our feet. Anne said it was as though we could jump off to float and swim on the clouds. It was the most incredible thing I've ever seen.

Night fell as we left Crib-y-Ddysgl. We descended into the boiling sea of cloud, into a swirling darkness that made my head swim. I was having difficulty focussing, I was falling asleep, grinding to a standstill. Anne turned round, she must have sensed something was wrong. I was on the point of collapse. Pete felt that a ten minute rest would either make or break me. Not having much choice I pulled my cag hood up and, thankfully, lay down on the side of the track, it was sheer bliss, an indescribable relief from pain and effort. My two companions sat by me and patiently waited, it was only afterwards I realised the responsibility I had placed upon them. High on the mountains in the middle of the night, responsible for someone suffering extreme exhaustion, yet they were always calm and reassuring. I would have been petrified in similar circumstances. Pete woke me after fifteen minutes, apparently I'd been coughing, retching, but also singing. The mind boggles, I can't sing normally, heaven knows what it sounded like.

As we climbed Moel Cynghorion Pete was about 100 yards in front, leading the way. I could sometimes see his shape outlined against the night sky, or the light from his torch when he turned round. Anne stayed close by, talking to me, encouraging me, a tangible link with reality in an increasingly frightening world. A black dreamlike world of wind, grass and stones. A world of never ending effort, seemingly with no light at the end of the tunnel. Time and distance no longer had any meaning, I had to keep going, I had to get to the top of this hill, I had to get to Gill at Llanberis. I had to complete my ultimate run.

Stumbling down Moel Eilio, I knew proper sleep at Llanberis would be essential, indeed unavoidable. For the first time the thought of stopping the attempt occurred to me. I didn't need to go through this torture, what was I trying to prove? The thought of quitting was worse than the thought of climbing Elidir Fawch. I hadn't simply invested a lot of time in this venture, it wasn't just that I had all my friends out helping me. It was so much more than that. I had invested every last bit of mental application and every last bit of physical strength from each muscle and each joint. The disappointment of stopping would far outweigh the relief.

I must have been a dreadful person to have been with that night. 'Forty-five minutes sleep and I'll be away within the hour,' I snapped at Gill as we arrived at Llanberis. I don't know how she found the strength to wake me, but wake me she did, and encourage me to get ready, to carry on. She could see I was dead on my feet, but she would never ask me to stop. There were tears in our eyes, it was a very difficult time.

Clive Lane and Clive Russell accompanied me on the penultimate leg over to Ogwen. The climb up the incline was long but easy underfoot. As daylight came I mused on my physical condition. The only things that could stop me now were either the inability to stay awake or the refusal of my body to take another uphill step. The realisation that I was so committed I could not stop came as a slight shock. It dawned on me that my inner self, my very soul would never admit defeat. If I came to a standstill I could imagine myself saying, 'well, I want to carry on, but this thing I'm inside won't go any farther, I must get a better one.' By Mynydd Perfedd I wasn't doing much running, Y Garn signalled another bout of tiredness; if I concentrated on the ground my vision would clear, the stones and grass would come back into focus.

The nightmare of last night was being replaced by a morning of stunning beauty, the incredible cloud formations and Brocken spectres seeming in sharp contrast to my tortured body. Being anxious, Gill and John met me at Llyn-y-Cwn with a spaghetti breakfast, feeling much revived the next steep pull didn't seem too bad. After painful and laborious scrambles up the Glyders and Tryfan, we at last started the descent to the A5. Every step hurt my bruised feet, I tried to tread carefully, but my patience was wearing thin.

My arrival at Ogwen felt something of an anti-climax, we all knew I was going to finish. Anne and Pete walked me up Pen-yr-ole-wen, my mood was one of quiet satisfaction, albeit somewhat travel-stained and tattered, I would just keep walking along, putting one foot in front of the other. Gradually we worked our way along the Carnedds, the uphills slow, the downhills painful, Anne and Pete passing me sweets and water. My mood of quiet satisfaction was being replaced by impatience, I just wanted to get to Plas-y-Brenin, the end. Every muscle, every fibre was asking to stop, my eyes felt sunken, the skin on my face stretched tight. The spare end of my bumbag strap was a lot longer than when I'd started, I really didn't think I had any weight to lose.

Congratulations on Pen Llithrig-y-Wrach, the last hill. Pete said it was an historic moment. I didn't feel any emotion, I'd used all that up along with everything else, I was just glad it was almost over because I was almost finished. We found a good route down through the heather on small trods and tracks. My earlier thoughts of a sprint finish down the road had been abandoned, slowly the three of us walked down to Plas-y-Brenin, to the two Clives and my long-suffering wife. Stopped! Finished, after three days, fourteen hours and twenty minutes.

Appendix – Schedules
Charlie Ramsay Round – 59 miles, 28,000 feet, 24 tops; Total time – 21 hours 14 minutes, including 33 minutes rest.
Transit Glen Nevis-Keswick – 4 hours 15 minutes.
Bob Graham Round – 63 miles, 27,000 feet, 42 tops; Total Time – 23 hours 48 minutes, including 50 minutes rest.
Transit Keswick-Capel Curig – 3 hours 25 minutes.
Paddy Buckley (Welsh Classic) Round – 61 miles, 27,000 feet, 47 tops; Total time – 33 hours 30 minutes, including 2 hours 44 minutes rest.

MOORLAND SOLILOQUY

I was born of the high moor,
A child to dream dawning.
I slept by the dark stones,
Ancient shapes boding.
I followed the faint pipes,
Called by the morning.
Windborne on wild moor,
I awoke to grass stirring.
I dance with the white hare,
In startled strength bounding.
I slant along mist-light,
Formless and fading.
I rejoice as the curlew
Returns with his singing.
Windborne on wild moor
He flies beyond caring.
I sing to the wind's song,
Cry my heart's longing.
I race with the bright stream,
Renewed and restoring.
I gaze from the North Edge,
Sight to soul piercing.
Windborne on wild moor
I hear the grass singing.

I have passed through the year's change,
Observed the moor sleeping.
I have laughed as the cold earth
Bursts green into morning.
I am gone beyond day's end
And never returning.
Windborne on wild moor,
Joined your heart beating.
My roots are in gritstone,
Deep and sweet lying.
I draw from your moss springs
Crystal life founting.
In peace follow night stars
Cold, kindly and guiding.
Nightfall wraps wild moor,
Wind shadows swaying.

Mike and Badger.

epilogue

And now my story is told. Like my journeys, it has not always followed the directions I thought it might, and sometimes the outcomes have remained obscure until the very end. It has been a voyage of discovery for me, as all journeys should be. It has also become an act of love and trust. I have tried to be guided by the truth and have discovered that, as in my running, honesty, courage and a determination to succeed bring rewards and joys quite unlooked for. I have searched for the words which resonate with what is in my heart. There is omission . . . of course, but there are some things which belong to me only, and I will not share them. I hope that what I have shared reflects some of the beauty and joy in your own life, yes, and perhaps the sorrow, too. The human condition is an amalgam of all these things, and human frailty itself is not so important as how, in the short pulse of our life, that frailty is embraced.

> I sit beside the fire and think
> of all that I have seen,
> of meadow-flowers and butterflies
> in summers that have been;
>
> Of yellow leaves and gossamer
> in autumns that there were,
> with morning mist and silver sun
> and wind upon my hair.
>
> I sit beside the fire and think
> of how the world will be
> when winter comes without a spring
> that I shall ever see.
>
> For still there are so many things
> that I have never seen!
> in every wood in every spring
> there is a different green.
>
> I sit beside the fire and think
> of people long ago,
> and people who will see a world
> that I shall never know.
>
> But all the while I sit and think
> of times there were before,
> I listen for returning feet
> and voices at the door.

J. R. R. TOLKIEN
The Lord of the Rings

Outside my window, in view of my heart, October is once again bestowing its soft enchantment on the hills. I feel its gentle call stirring within me. In the corner over there, do I detect one disreputable and still muddy running shoe nudging its mate knowingly? My older dog appears asleep, but I am not deceived. I shall lay aside this pen, call the dogs and go where I truly belong. Once more I shall run gently through the soft October sunshine into the soft October mists over the moors I love so well. And as I run, I shall wonder: is this the beginning of the end or is it just the end of the beginning?

appendix one

ERRATUM

We apologise for a technical error which left the final eight pages of the original edition missing from this revised edition.

These pages have been added here to make this revised edition complete.

Support stop at Kidhow Gate on the 1988 Pennine Way attempt. Left to right: Mike, Chris, Mark, John Richardson, Geoff.

And now began the physically most difficult part of the entire journey. I would never waste time trying to identify my 'worst ever miles', but there are some which will undoubtedly live on in black memory. The worst are those which involve despair of the spirit. No matter how horrendous the purely physical experiences, they fade into old friends, almost, with the passage of time. The following 20 miles (32 km) were unable to assail my spirit except for the briefest of moments. They must constitute, however, some of the most physically exacting conditions I have ever encountered on a long run. First, I was worn down on that endless track leading to Horton. The mist became almost palpable and precipitated a premature twilight. In this dank miasma I began to lose all sense of time and place. We were moving, but seemed to be arriving nowhere. Landmarks appeared which I was sure we must already have passed, and no effort I made produced the feeling that we were covering the ground in anything other than slow motion. Even John seemed affected by our dismal and sombre surroundings, and there were long periods of silence between us.

After only an hour, at least as indicated on the watch, the day began its surrender to night. My pace, too, succumbed to the dark and became even slower. By 10.00 p.m. darkness was total and, only yards in front, John was swallowed up. I was alone. My frustration got the better of me and I started to curse my predicament. Hearing my complaints, John turned back and unexpectedly produced a torch, he had obviously forgotten about my poor night vision.

WILD TRAILS TO FAR HORIZONS

I should have departed from Horton in the early evening, but it was not far short of midnight when I set forth to ascend Penyghent. I was now in full waterproofs as the rain was cascading in solid, unbroken sheets, which killed the wind and flooded the ground. I had covered 180 miles (288 km) and was starting my third night without sleep, it promised to be a testing one. In the shelter of the van I was being tended with a care and concern which I am as inept to describe as I am to express my thanks. There are not the words, or, if there are, I have not the power to conjure them. In truth, I can remember little detail of what happened when I came into support and stopped running, my conscious mind was locked into the journey, and only that. But the inarticulate knowledge and emotion is strong within my memory, and I shall never forget the role played by Mark. He appeared to be able to anticipate my every need. Whatever particular necessity of food and drink I required, I put out my hand and it was there.

And now my other son, Gerard, was adamant that he wished to accompany me over Penyghent. I would have been surprised had it been otherwise. With Chris taking over from John, I knew I was in good hands, but with Gerard to look after me, I knew I would come to no harm. I had watched him grow, I had guided his early footsteps along the wild paths, his strength was my strength. The rain was of such intensity that it deprived my senses of clues about time, location, balance and orientation. Naturally, the problems were greatly aggravated in my case, but I think not even Chris remained unaffected. At the end of the track out of Horton we were confronted by a locked gate. We puzzled vainly for some moments, at least Chris and Gerard did, I just stood gazing blankly at it. 'Bloody hell!', said Chris. 'They've locked up the mountain for the night!' Invisible in the deluge, the stile was eventually revealed a few yards away.

At first, our ascent of Penyghent proceeded more easily than expected. Extensive path renovation was being carried out and the result was a gravelled way, possibly necessary, certainly bizarre and incongruous. At some stage incongruity was replaced by nightmare. The path ended abruptly and I stepped into a vertical Somme. The normal route up the hill had been ripped apart by a mechanical digger. Old layers of fence lay like decaying rotten teeth in oozing mud. In the absence of any vegetation cover the floods of water were causing mud, bog and clay to creep and slide like legless vermin down the hillside, over my feet, round my legs. I staggered, slithered, lost balance, stumbled, fought a rising irrational fear. Suddenly, a mountain I had known since my youth was a malevolent heap of sliding mud. I could not relate to where I thought I was and where I appeared to be. With my fellrunner's and mountaineer's instincts I drove upwards, seeking comfort and safety in height. Ahead, just visible through the murk, was the glow of Chris's torch. I strove to catch him, to ask what was happening. Inexorably, the light drew away, it blinked and disappeared, reappeared, blinked again and vanished. I was not alone, by my side Gerard was tense and watchful. I tried to move sideways, to seek for a way off this dreadful battlefield, but it seemed to have no perimeter. At last, above us, the light appeared again and Chris shouted down words of encouragement. Although I had felt deserted by my trusted navigator, he was, of course, doing his best to

*Gerard
running over
the local moors
at Buxton.*

first locate and then guide us to better ground. We joined him at the accursed digger itself. He explained that it seemed best to stick with the track which he thought did not go far beyond the machine in this state. He was right. At last we stood on a piece of ground I could actually identify once more. It was the path which inclines diagonally up the steepest part of the hill, a little way from the flat summit.

What was beyond my grasp, however, was a 'valid' sense of the passage of time. It was barely half a mile from where we stood to the finish of the steep slope and the ascent a mere 300-400 ft (91-122 m), the equivalent of fifteen minutes' effort, at most. It felt as if I were fighting a treadmill which, despite all I could do, was holding me suspended in one location. A corner of my mind refused to accept this unreality, and when I examined my perception of the time it had taken me to cover the couple of hundred yards across the flat summit, I knew something was trying to confuse my mind. I put an extra guard on my faculties and allowed myself to rejoice in the summit attained.

If the ascent had assumed the characteristics of a horrible nightmare, the descent constituted a solid and all too dangerous reality. Leaving the summit we were all having difficulty maintaining balance on the running gutter which had replaced the path. Chris and I conferred and elected to move to and follow the wall which, though not taking the best line, would in these conditions provide a definite handrail in the right direction. After losing around 150 ft (47 m) of height gently, the route suddenly plunges 300 ft (91 m) in a series of rocky steps, first of gritstone, then of limestone. It was here I discovered I had lost all sense of balance. Whether it was a lack of sleep, the dark misty night, conflicting shadows, cumulative disorientation, I do not know, probably all of these. Whenever I stepped down and placed my weight on one leg, I lost balance.

Some of the rock ledges were high, they were all steep and slippery. Had I pitched forward, that would have been the end of perhaps more than this journey. I decided special tactics would have to be employed. With Gerard keeping watch over me, I tackled each step with as much reliance on hands and arms as feet. When I landed on a ledge, I deliberately leaned backwards so that I always lost balance into the hill. Suddenly, if there was anything sudden about my progress other than slips, I was peering with Chris over what looked like a precipice. The real hazard certainly concentrated my mind. I figured out what I was going to do next in very quick time, and it did not involve stepping over that black edge. Fortunately, Chris had reached the same conclusions and we continued our erratic progress off to one side.

At last we left the hazardous ground behind, but were not yet free of the difficulties. Had I been alone, I would have later imagined that my problems in orienting myself with respect to the lie of the land all originated in a lack of sleep. But I observed that Chris was having to use all his skill to take us over what is normally not difficult ground. He managed superbly and brought us safely to the small haven of the support vehicle at Dale Head. The six miles (10 km) across Penyghent had occupied almost two hours, slow progress as measured by the clock, a short eternity in my life.

I have no recollection whatsoever of the support stop at Dale Head. My record sheet shows that I stopped for 13 minutes, but what transpired, I cannot recall. I have a vague memory of keeling gently sideways with a drink in my hand and being pushed upright again, but whether this was here or at Stanggill, later, I do not know.

We were now deep into a black night. I left for Fountains Fell with Chris and John, conscious that their combined skill would be needed if we were ever going to locate the elusive path from the summit. I have no memory of whether or not the rain had stopped, it had become such a natural part of my world I no longer noticed it. We ascended to the top of Fountains Fell with relative ease, I could even orientate myself by small landmarks along the path. Within yards of leaving the summit, however, we had lost the path. In retrospect, having probably the most recent knowledge of the topography, I should perhaps have made an attempt to take over the navigation. It would, however, have been a purely intuitive navigation, as I was alert enough to realise. The path, in an attempt to circumvent bogs (unsuccessful), winds from the summit in a series of curves. Having descended below the bogs, it then runs almost parallel to the line of the hill, losing height slowly. John and Chris took the foolproof option of setting a bearing from the summit which would lead us diagonally down and bisect the path as it ran along the hill, somewhere below us.

The theory was impeccable, its execution excruciatingly difficult. The ground we found ourselves negotiating seemed to consist of great hummocks of vegetation lying at a steep angle and strewn with ankle and leg deep pits. The tendons around my feet and ankles were already terribly sore from the constant tugging and flexing, which is unavoidable over rough ground and had been enormously amplified by the effects of heavy rain. Even normally firm and level ground had become unstable. Rolling around now on this vegetation was, in effect, putting some final touches to a process which had begun on the Cheviots over two days ago. To add to these problems, Chris and John seemed to be having difficulties in judging the line, or, maybe, I could not follow. Their torches were ever probing ahead and, occasionally, they would vanish. When that happened, what followed with a frustrating inevitability was that, having lost my point of orientation, I would curve down to my left, my brain would blank into sleep, and then I usually fell over. I began to feel stupidly embarrassed about this and tried to get up before John or Chris realised what had happened. The sequence repeated itself dozens of times and I became, once more, locked into that distorted, evil time warp.

Throughout the whole process, however, my little spark would not be extinguished. I fully realised my plight, but it was a physical, not a spiritual weakness. If only I could get my legs onto some decent ground, I would stand a chance of picking up a rhythm once more instead of lurching around in this humiliating fashion. With infinite patience, my two friends coached me on, but even they, I think, did not fully understand that when I asked 'How much longer?', I was not so much hoping for this to finish as wanting to get to grips with the route again.

As a very thick grey dawn at last served to guide my stumbling steps, we once more reached the support vehicle. My final day was dawning, my last chance to salvage my dream. I may have approached the van in a daze, I may have sagged into unconsciousness as I sipped a drink, but I knew what had to follow that slow and terrible night. After 10 minutes I got out of the van and started to run across the fields.

It was artificial and forced, there was no natural rhythm to this running. But there would be, I could not feel it, but I believed it. Running at 4.00 in the morning with over 190 miles (304 km) in the legs is never going to be easy, and in this case I had another stinging blow to bear. Shortly after Malham Tarn we went wrong. No one to blame, unless myself, Chris swiftly located us and, together with John, alleviated the effects of the mistake. However, with every minute precious, I could ill afford such errors. Even now I can remember running into Malham, my head and legs telling me it was useless to continue this struggle against forces which had already beaten me, and my heart refusing to listen. On the Southern Uplands Way my obstinacy had been pointless, but here I was doing what I knew was right.

After another 10 minute re-fuelling stop, I left Malham with Mark. I was still not moving fluently, but it was only 5.30 a.m. and Mark cheered me enormously when he remarked how quickly I was going. My brain, alive and the servant of my spirit once again, was busy with, for me, difficult arithmetic. Since they gave me problems, I decided to shelve the calculations until Gargrave, which, being conveniently situated at 200 miles (320 km), would simplify the sums. Concentrating on effort alone for a time, we covered the seven miles (12 km) to Gargrave in 1 hour 20 minutes, 15 minutes faster than scheduled. A mere 15 minutes to set against the eight hours lost, but the first time I had beaten the schedule. It was a start.

The simplified sum I now rolled around in my mind was 70 miles (112 km) remaining and 17 hours in which to cover them to give a three-day completion. The 'answer' was 4 mph (6.4 kph). After years of ultra-running, particularly over the Pennine Way, I have a fairly precise knowledge of what kind of pace is entailed over a range of 'average speeds' from about 3 to 6 mph (5 to 10 kph). It was a very tantalising answer. It had taken me 16 hours 40 minutes to cover the first 70 miles (112 km), of which only 34 minutes were food stops. I had not even approached this speed since. There should be no way I could achieve this final target, but there was that within me, which hinted of strengths I had never before explored. If the moors, which lay waiting in long succession, were at their heaviest, I would probably have to accept defeat. If they were to give me the least chance, I could sense that I might be on the point of achieving the most incredible record. My little spark had carried me through conditions which would hitherto have stopped me. Already I was running at 5 mph (8 kph) on the good ground, and would get faster. I could drop speed on the rough and still maintain an average of 4 mph (6.4 kph). Could I? I honestly did not know. I knew where my heart and my dream lay, however. I was beginning to realise afresh what a strong spirit might make possible. Win or lose, I was not afraid of this challenge, I welcomed it. For even in losing I should win, my striving would contain all that I could ever give in strength and spirit.

After 200 miles (320 km) I left for Thornton with Mark. It was a beautiful, sunfresh summer morning. My body was weary, but my heart was strong. With a pace that was slowly becoming looser and freer we swung over the small green hills and fields. About a mile from Thornton, at the top of an incline, I started once more to stretch into a run, and as I did so, my dream ended.

I sometimes replay the scene in my mind, wondering if the ending will change, knowing it will not. The memory is still painful and will ever remain so. To set down this story I find difficult. But I must tell my tale to the end. When this book gathers dust on some forgotten shelf, there may be those close to me now, who will even then have memories of me, and if only for them and the love I bear them, I will tell my story to its conclusion.

Tennyson's line runs 'To strive, to seek, to find, and not to yield'. I had run over 200miles (320 km) in circumstances which, if they were unable to compel me to yield, would force me to realise some final truth about what I was doing. I think I had uncovered that truth, and it was very simple; it was to have no fear, to run with a calm and happy spirit, and to trust that spirit to guide and guard. There was nothing heroic in what I was doing. I was happy to be where I was, I would have been nowhere else. The harsh physical circumstances were of Nature, they assailed the body, never the spirit. Their very difficulty had enabled me to discover that perhaps the spirit has access to resources hardly mortal. But, 'the sword outwears its sheath'. As I embraced that final struggle with joyful anticipation, knowing I could not now lose, weakness of the flesh cancelled my dream; just one over-worked tendon yielded at last. My spirit was forced to return to the pain of physical reality. Clay is clay, but, for a short time, I had lived somewhere else, now that time had ended and another time had just begun.

I went on, just a few more miles, the sun still shining. I allowed my body to explore its pain. It told me I must surrender; those rough, insistent miles had conquered flesh as they could not conquer spirit. Together, Mark and I walked to the village of Lothersdale, leaving in Thornton the kindly figure of Geoff, cheerful as the summer morning he had been. In Lothersdale, with the last question answered beyond dispute, we sat on stones, leaning against stones. So many times have my journeys carried me through this quiet, happy place. The sun was warm. Mark offered me extra clothes, but they were not necessary. I sat on the stone flags with a sorrow too deep for tears. One day, perhaps, my spirit will undertake ethereal journeys across unimagined hills and horizons. But as yet, I am of the Earth, bound to it, and I love it. I must accept my part in it. Bound by my love of places and friends, I am not yet ready to escape on those mysterious journeys beyond dreams. But the sorrow was almost more than I could bear.

> Though here at journey's end I lie
> in darkness buried deep,
> beyond all towers strong and high,
> beyond all mountains steep,
> above all shadows rides the Sun
> and Stars forever dwell:
> I will not say the Day is done,
> nor bid the Stars farewell.

J.R.R. TOLKIEN
The Lord of the Rings